2nd Edition

Board of Registry Study Guide

For Clinical
Laboratory
Certification
Examinations

2nd Edition

Board of Registry Study Guide

For Clinical
Laboratory
Certification
Examinations

Edited by ASCP Board of Registry Staff

Barbara Castleberry, PhD, MT(ASCP)

Mary E. Lunz, PhD

Patricia A. Tanabe, MPA, MT(ASCP)

ASCP Press
American Society of Clinical Pathologists
Chicago

Library of Congress Cataloging in Publication Data

Board of Registry study guide for clinical laboratory certification
 examinations / edited by Barbara M. Castleberry, Mary E. Lunz,
 Patricia A. Tanabe. — 2nd ed.

 Includes bibliographical references.
 ISBN 0-89189-325-3
  1. Medical laboratory technology—Examinations, questions, etc.
I. Castleberry, Barabara M. II. Lunz, Mary E. III. Tanabe, Patricia A.
IV. American Society of Clinical Pathologists. Board of Registry.
  [DNLM: 1. Allied Health Personnel—examination questions.
2. Certification. 3. Pathology, Clinical—examination questions.
4. Specialty Boards. QY 18 B662]
RB37.B6 1991
616.07'5—dc20
DLC
for Library of Congress   91-4572
                                                               CIP

Printed in the United States of America.

95 94 93 92 91 5 4 3 2 1

Contents

To the Examinee

You have taken an important first step in your professional career by deciding to become certified. I wish you success as you prepare for these examinations.

Paul J. Cherney, M.D.

Chairman, Board of Registry

Introduction

Examination applicants have often expressed a need for a guide to help them prepare for the certification examinations. To respond to this need, the American Society of Clinical Pathologists (ASCP) Press and the Board of Registry of the American Society of Clinical Pathologists have produced this study guide for aspiring medical laboratory technicians and medical technologists. This guide contains background on the Board of Registry; guidelines for preparing for and taking the test; information on the development, content, structure, and scoring of the examinations; practice questions and answers in the content areas covered by the examinations; and a computer disk which can be used for self-assessment or practice testing.

The practice questions are constructed in a format and style comparable to those on the Board of Registry certification examinations; however, none of these questions has ever appeared on a Board of Registry examination, and none of the questions will ever appear in future Board of Registry examinations. The practice questions were developed from previously published materials including Continuing Education Update Examinations, Professional Self-Assessment Examinations Series III, Update/Educate, Audio-Visual Seminar Series in Immunology, and Tech Sample--which were prepared by the committees of the ASCP Commission on Continuing Education and the ASCP Commission on Associated Member Activities.

For applicants reading this book, taking the written practice examination or the computer administered examinations and answering the practice questions should help you prepare for the actual examinations. Use of this book, however, does not assure a passing score on the examinations. The Board of Registry's evaluation and credentialing process are entirely independent of this study guide.

For faculty, officials of clinical laboratory education programs, and examinees, this book provides information on how Board of Registry certification examinations are structured and scored. The technical summaries on these topics are designed to briefly explain the pertinent evaluation topics. Further information concerning evaluation techniques can be obtained from the books and articles noted in the education section of the reading list.

Question Reviewers

Our thanks to the following individuals who reviewed and/or contributed questions contained in this book.

Blood Bank

John A. Alfano, MS, MT(ASCP)SBB
American Society of Clinical Pathologists
Chicago, Illinois

Laurine T. Charles, MHS, MT(ASCP)SBB
Medical University of South Carolina
Charleston, South Carolina

Margaret Giddens, MA, MT(ASCP)SBB, Associate Professor
University of Alabama
Birmingham, Alabama

John F. LoRusso, MA, MT(ASCP)
Bergen Community College
Paramus, New Jersey

Graciela F. Taylor, MT(ASCP)SBB
University of Texas Southwestern Medical Center
Dallas, Texas

Body Fluids

Reginaldo B. Lauzon, MT(ASCP)
SUNY Health Science Center at Syracuse
Syracuse, New York

Kim O'Connell, MT(ASCP)
American Society of Clinical Pathologists
Chicago, Illinois

Tamela Turner, MA, MT(ASCP)
University of Alabama
Birmingham, Alabama

Chemistry

Gary Ballmann, PhD, MT(ASCP)
Northern Virginia Community College
Annandale, Virginia

Pamela Crider, MBA, MT(ASCP)
Baptist Medical Centers
Birmingham, Alabama

Cheryl M. Haskins, MS, MT(ASCP)SC
SUNY Health Science Center at Syracuse
Syracuse, New York

Angela Jones, MT(ASCP)SC
Baptist Medical Centers
Birmingham, Alabama

Tamela Turner, MA, MT(ASCP)
University of Alabama
Birmingham, Alabama

Hematology

Jeanne-Paule Hitlan, EdS, MT(ASCP)SH
George Washington University Medical Center
Washington, DC

Lynn Maedel, MS, MT(ASCP)SH
University of Colorado Health Sciences Center
Denver, Colorado

Ann Snyder, MT(ASCP)SH
Cleveland Clinic Foundation
Cleveland, Ohio

Nadine Sojka, MT(ASCP)SH
St. Luke's Hospital
Cedar Rapids, Iowa

Thomas B. Wiggers, MS,CLSpH(NCA),H(ASCP)
University of Mississippi Medical Center
Jackson, Mississippi

Immunology

Rasa Bertuzis, MT(ASCP)I,SI
Rush Presbyterian St. Lukes Medical Center
Chicago, Illinois

Catherine L. Bishop, MT(ASCP)SI
Rush Presbyterian St. Lukes Medical Center
Chicago, Illinois

Cynthia Booker, MT(ASCP)
University of Virginia
Charlottesville, Virginia

Candace Enockson, MT(ASCP)
Parkland Memorial Hospital
Dallas, Texas

Cynthia K. Karr, PhD, MT(ASCP)
Medical University of South Carolina
Charleston, South Carolina

Gloria Thompson, MT(ASCP)
North Carolina Memorial Hospital
Chapel Hill, North Carolina

Management

Marian J. Cavagnaro, MS, MT(ASCP)DLM
Memorial Hospital
Hollywood, Florida

Michael W. Morris, MS, SH(ASCP)DLM
SUNY Health Science Center at Syracuse
Syracuse, New York

Microbiology

Fran Fisher, MEd, MT(ASCP), CLS(NCA)
University of Florida
Gainesville, Florida

Patsy Greenup, MT(ASCP)SM
University of Alabama
Birmingham, Alabama

Anne L. Loving, M(ASCP)
Felician College
Lodi, New Jersey

Edward A. Sass, MS, MT(ASCP)SM
University of Texas Southwestern Medical Center
Dallas, Texas

Susan Wiseman, MT(ASCP)
American Society of Clinical Pathologists
Chicago, Illinois

MT/MLT Practice Examinations

Margaret Daniels, MA, MT(ASCP)SC
Veterans Administration Medical Center
SUNY Health Science Center
Syracuse, New York

Annette R. Heath, MLT(ASCP)
Kaiser Permanente
Denver, Colorado

CHAPTER 1

Certification

The Importance of Certification

The practice of modern medicine would be impossible without the tests performed in the clinical laboratory. A medical team of pathologists, specialists, technologists, and technicians works together to determine the presence, extent, or absence of disease and provides data needed to evaluate the effectiveness of treatment.

Laboratory procedures require an array of complex precision instruments and a variety of automated and electronic equipment. However, men and women interested in helping others are the foundation of a successful laboratory. They must be accurate, reliable, have an interest in science, and be able to recognize their responsibility for human lives.

Critical to high-quality health care is the assurance that individuals performing laboratory tests are able to carry out their responsibilities in a proficient manner. Therefore, laboratory personnel of demonstrated competence are of prime importance.

Certification is the process by which a nongovernmental agency or association grants recognition of competency to an individual who has met certain predetermined qualifications, as specified by that agency or association. Certification affirms that an individual has demonstrated that he or she possesses the knowledge and skills to perform essential tasks in the medical laboratory.

Role of the ASCP Board of Registry

Founded in 1928 by the American Society of Clinical Pathologists (ASCP), the Board of Registry's mission is to develop and establish standards and procedures for individuals to enter, continue, or advance in a career in medical laboratory science, and to certify and register those individuals who meet the required criteria. This mission is accomplished through four major ongoing activities: (1) receiving and evaluating applications for examination and certification; (2) developing, administering, and scoring examinations; (3) conducting examination-related research to monitor and improve the quality of tests and testing methodologies; and (4) maintaining official records of all individuals certified by the Board.

The keystone of the Board of Registry is the team of approximately 100 volunteer technologists and technicians, laboratory scientists, physicians, and professional researchers in education, evaluation, and psychometrics who make up the Board of Governors, the Research and Development Committee, and the examination committees. These individuals contribute their time and expertise to achievement of the goal of excellence in the certification process for medical laboratory personnel.

The Board of Governors is the policy-making body for the Board of Registry and is composed of twenty members. These twenty members include technologists, technicians, and pathologists nominated by the ASCP and representatives from the general public and the following societies: American Academy of Microbiology, American Association of Blood Banks, American Society of Cytology, American Society of Hematology, National Registry in Clinical Chemistry, and National Society for Histotechnology.

The Research and Development Committee's activities include the review of current methods and research related to competency definition, test development, validity and reliability assessment, examination performance, and standard setting.

The examination committees include technologists, technicians, laboratory scientists, and physicians. These committees are responsible for planning, development, and review of the examinations; determining the accuracy and relevancy of the examinations; and confirming the standard for each examination.

After Certification

Certification affirms that an individual has demonstrated that he or she possesses the knowledge and skills to perform essential tasks in the medical laboratory. The Board of Registry certifies individuals upon completion of academic prerequisites, clinical laboratory education or experience, and successful performance on a competency-based examination.

Registration is the process by which names of individuals certified by the Board of Registry are identified on an annual basis as being currently registered. Annual re-registration benefits include an identification card, registration seal, one-year subscription to <u>Laboratory Medicine</u>, eligibility for insurance programs, and upon request, written verification of certification.

Certification in a given category means that an individual has met all criteria for career entry in that category. As they continue on in their careers, many individuals who are certified at one professional level may work to obtain certification at a higher level to reflect their continued growth and development. Thus, a technician may move to the technologist level and even to the specialist level in a specific discipline.

The clinical laboratory sciences are among the fastest changing segments of the health care field. Therefore, each certificant should embrace a philosophy of life-long learning to remain current in a chosen discipline. This may be accomplished through formal course work, professional continuing education offerings, as well as individual regimens of journal reading and subscription to professional self-assessment examinations.

CHAPTER 2

Technician and Technologist Certification

The professional levels of practice (<u>Laboratory Medicine</u>, 13:312-313, 1982) for which Board of Registry certification may be attained include technician and technologist. These professional levels define in a general sense the skills and abilities that an individual is expected to have at career entry. The professional levels are considered hierarchical; that is, each level encompasses the knowledge and skill of the preceding level.

There are several aspects of these definitions that should be noted. First, the roles are defined in a general sense. For example, Technologist describes the role of technologists in all categories, ie, general medical technology, chemistry, hematology, blood banking, immunology, microbiology, cytotechnology, and histotechnology. Second, the roles refer to skills and abilities that the individual is expected to have at career entry, not those that may be acquired with subsequent experience. Career entry is defined as the point in time when the individual meets all educational and/or experience requirements and is therefore eligible for Board certification. Thus, while supervision, management, and teaching are skills that technicians may possess and apply in the laboratory, they are not skills that the technician is expected to have learned prior to a career-entry examination.

Technician

<u>Knowledge</u>. The technician has a working comprehension of the technical and procedural aspects of laboratory tests.

<u>Technical Skills</u>. The technician is able to read and follow directions and to perform those tests in a clinical laboratory that are considered to be of a straightforward nature. The technician has a practical understanding of quality control that is sufficient to enable him or her to determine whether or not tests are within control limits and to make the requisite adjustments according to specified procedures. The technician is capable of performing simple instrument maintenance.

<u>Judgment and Decision Making</u>. The technician is able to recognize the existence of common procedural and technical problems and to take corrective action according to predetermined criteria.

<u>Communication</u>. The technician communicates straightforward information, eg, reports test results and quotes normal ranges and specimen requirements.

<u>Teaching and Training Responsibilities</u>. The technician is capable of demonstrating learned technical skills.

Technologist

<u>Knowledge</u>. The technologist has an understanding of the underlying scientific principles, as well as of the technical and procedural aspects of laboratory testing. The technologist has a general comprehension of the physiologic, biochemical, immunologic, microbiologic, and genetic factors that affect health and disease; laboratory tests; and the importance of laboratory tests to medical care. The technologist is familiar with the various services available in the hospital and has an appreciation of the roles and interrelationships of paramedical and other health-related fields.

<u>Technical Skills</u>. The technologist is capable of performing technically demanding tests. The technologist has a theoretical understanding of quality assurance sufficient to enable him or her to monitor and to implement quality control programs. The technologist is able to participate in the introduction and implementation of new procedures and in the evaluation of new instruments. The technologist has a basic knowledge of accuracy, precision, normal ranges, and the ability to correlate this information with existing methods.

<u>Judgement and Decision Making</u>. The technologist has the ability to exercise initiative and independent judgment in dealing with the broad scope of procedural and technical problems. The technologist is able to participate in, and may be delegated, the responsibility for decisions involving quality control programs, instrument selection, preventative maintenance, safety test procedures, and reagent purchases.

<u>Communication</u>. The technologist communicates technical or general information to medical, paramedical, or lay persons. Information may include problems or matters of a scientific, technical, or administrative nature.

<u>Supervision and Management</u>. The technologist has a basic understanding of management theory and functions. The technologist is able to participate in and develop responsibility for establishment of technical and administrative procedures. The technologist can supervise technicians, aides, and clerical personnel as directed.

<u>Teaching and Training Responsibilities</u>. The technologist is able to provide instruction in the basic theory, technical skills, and application of laboratory test procedures. The technologist may participate in the evaluation of the effectiveness of educational programs.

CHAPTER 3

Applying for the Certification Examination

The Board of Registry administers examinations on the third Friday of February and August of each year.

Approximately one year before the date you wish to take the examination, you should contact the Board of Registry to obtain a current application packet. In addition to the application form, the application packet includes the <u>Procedures for Examination and Certification</u>. This booklet contains the application deadlines and examination dates, the examination eligibility requirements and a list of test centers. Since the examination requirements, as well as other information included in the application packet, are periodically revised, be sure you have the most recent application packet available from the Board of Registry office. Once you have obtained these materials, it is important to review them to make sure that you have adequate time to obtain any required documents prior to the application deadline. Please contact the Board of Registry office at P.O. Box 12270, Chicago, Illinois 60612, for application forms and general information.

Application Deadlines

Your application and fee must be in the Board of Registry office by the first working day of October for the February administration and the first working day of April for the August administration.

Examination Eligibility

To be eligible to take the examination, you must (1) meet the <u>current</u> stated minimum requirements for a particular category or level of certification, and (2) submit a formal application form and pay the appropriate application fee. The minimum requirements for each examination are listed in TABLE 1. Specific requirements vary. For specific information, refer to the current Board of Registry Eligibility Requirements.

TABLE 1: Certification Requirements for BOR Examinations

Certification	Requirements
Medical Technologist (MT)	Baccalaureate degree and either 1) CAHEA accredited MT Program OR 2) MLT(ASCP) certification and 3 years experience or 5 years experience
Medical Laboratory Technician (MLT)	One of the following: 1) Associate degree or equivalent including CAHEA accredited MLT program or military Medical Laboratory Specialist program OR 2) 30 semester hours of college credit plus CAHEA accredited MLT program or military Medical Laboratory Specialist program OR 3) Associate degree or equivalent and 5 years experience OR 4) CAHEA accredited MLT program or military Medical Laboratory Specialist program and 1 year experience
Histologic Technician (HT)	High school diploma and one of the following: 1) CAHEA accredited HT program OR 2) 2 years experience or Associate degree or equivalent and one year experience
Histotechnologist (HTL)	Baccalaureate degree and one of the following: 1) CAHEA accredited HTL program OR 2) 5 years experience
Categorical Certification (BB,C,H,I,M)	Baccalaureate degree and one to two years experience
Cytotechnologist (CT)	Baccalaureate degree and one of the following: 1) CAHEA accredited CT program OR 2) 5 years experience
Specialist in Cytotechnology (SCT)	One of the following: 1) Baccalaureate degree, CT(ASCP) certification and 5 years experience OR 2) Masters degree, CT(ASCP) certification and 4 years experience OR 3) Doctorate degree, CT(ASCP) certification and 3 years experience
Specialist Certification (SBB,SC,SH,SI,SM)	One of the following: 1) Baccalaureate degree, Technologist certification, and 5 years experience OR 2) Masters degree and 4 years experience OR 3) Doctorate degree and 2 years experience
Diplomat in Laboratory Management (DLM)	Baccalaureate degree, Masters degree or Doctorate and appropriate laboratory management education and experience
Phlebotomist Technician (PBT)	High school graduation (or equivalent) and one of the following: 1) completion of NAACLS approved phlebotomy program OR 2) completion of acceptable phlebotomy program at a regionally accredited college/university or accredited laboratory OR 3) 1 year of full-time experience in an accredited laboratory

CHAPTER 4

Preparing to Take the Examination

Begin early to prepare for the Certification Examination. Because of the broad range of knowledge and skills tested by the examination, even applicants with a great deal of college training and professional experience will probably find that some review is necessary, although the amount will vary from applicant to applicant. Generally, last-minute cramming is the least effective method for preparing for the examination. The earlier that you begin, the more time you will have to prepare; and the more you prepare, the better your chance of doing well on the examination.

The following are some guidelines for studying for the examination.

Diagnose Your Strengths and Weaknesses

There are two ways to diagnose your strengths and weakness which are explained in Chapters 9 and 10 of this study guide. In Chapter 9, two written practice examinations are presented for the technician (MLT) and technologist (MT) levels. The written practice tests have the same distribution of questions across content and skill areas as the Board of Registry examinations; however, none of the questions will appear on a Board of Registry examination.

Try to take the written practice tests under conditions similar to actual testing conditions. Find a quiet place and time yourself. Allow one hour to take the 50-question practice examination. Most Board of Registry examinations have slightly over 200 questions and four hours are allowed. Do not look up any answers while you are taking a practice examination and answer all the questions as best you can. After you have taken the written practice test, use the directions provided to score it.

Because this practice examination is shorter than the actual Board of Registry examination and therefore provides a smaller sample of the information, you should supplement the written practice test scores with other information that you have about your strengths and weaknesses. For example, if you currently work in the laboratory and do hematology tests, you may want to study the other laboratory areas more thoroughly. If you are a student and your lowest grades were in clinical chemistry, you may want to spend more time on that subject than the others. After you have diagnosed your weaknesses from several sources, such as the practice test, course grades, class tests, and laboratory experience, you are ready to begin studying.

Chapter 10 provides instructions for using the IBM compatible computer disk which constructs tailored tests. The computer disk may be very useful for continuous self-assessment as you prepare for the examination.

Follow the directions presented in Chapter 10 to operationalize the disk. The computer will administer practice tests of 50-100 questions. The distribution of questions across content areas will be comparable to BOR written examinations. Upon completion of a computer administered test, all of the questions you missed will be displayed on the screen along with the correct answer. As your knowledge increases the difficulty of the questions presented will also increase.

You will be able to take computer constructed practice tests as often as you wish. Different questions will be presented until all questions in the bank have been presented. At that time you will be notified and questions will be reused for additional tests.

When you take a computer constructed test, try to take it under conditions similar to actual testing conditions. Use a computer that is located in a quiet place, allow approximately one and one-half hours, and do not use reference materials.

Study for the Test

Plan a course of study that allows more time for your weaker areas. Although it is important to study your areas of weakness, be sure to allow enough time to review all areas.

It is better to spend a short time studying every day than to spend several hours every week or two. A regular time and special place to study will help because then study will become part of your daily routine.

Several resources can be used to help you to study. The reading lists at the end of this book identify many useful books by subject area. The practice questions in this book provide an extensive overview of the content of medical technology. They can be used to test your knowledge in each subject area or they may be used to acquire experience in answering multiple-choice questions. You may also wish to consider the following.

Standard Textbooks. Textbooks tend to cover a broad range of knowledge in a given field and thus help you survey an entire field. An added benefit is that textbooks frequently have questions at the end of the chapters that you can use to test yourself.

Competency Statements, Content Outlines, and Item Descriptors. The Board of Registry has developed the competency statements and content outlines to delineate the content and tasks included in the test. Content Guidelines for the MLT and MT appear in Chapter 7, "Examination Content Guidelines." The Board of Registry provides, as a part of score reporting, a list of item descriptors for each examination. An item descriptor is a shorthand method of describing the content and skill tested in a specific test question. The list of item descriptors shows the distribution of questions across content and skill areas by providing a description of each question (item). Item descriptors are explained in Chapter 8, "Examination Scoring." The lists of item descriptors for recent Board of Registry Examinations appear in Appendix A, "Item Descriptor Lists for Medical Laboratory Technician Examinations," and Appendix B, "Item Descriptor Lists for Medical Technologist Examinations."

Current Publications. It will be helpful to scan major journals from the past few years to keep up with the innovations in the field. Textbooks may be updated only every few years whereas new questions are added to the examinations every examination cycle. Therefore, it is possible that questions will be asked on content that is not yet in textbooks but has been added to the literature via journals and other periodicals.

Get Enough Rest Before the Examination

Ease up on your studying before the examination. Try to get plenty of rest and eat a good breakfast before going to take the examination. Most examinations are scheduled for a four-hour period.

Locate the Test Center

The authorization slip will have the room location of the examination test center, address, and proctor's name. Plan to arrive early at the test site to familiarize yourself with the area and locate the room in which the examination will be administered.

CHAPTER 5

Taking the examination

Test Center Procedures

1. When you take the examination, you should bring with you at least two No. 2 soft lead pencils with good erasers.
2. Scratch paper will be provided for you. No books, dictionaries, or paper may be taken into the examination room.
3. Though they are not necessary, the Board of Registry does allow the use of slide rules and calculators during the test. They must be brought in without carrying cases.
4. You must present photo identification to the proctor along with your authorization slip (sent to you after your examination eligibility has been determined).
5. You will be required to sign the following statement: "I have read the Examination Instructions. I understand that if an applicant is caught cheating on a certifying examination, his/her results will be held until such time as the applicant appeals to the Board of Registry, at which time the Board will decide each individual case. I certify that I am the candidate whose signature appears below. I also certify that, because of the confidential nature of these copyright materials, I will not retain or copy any examination materials and I will not otherwise reveal the content of these materials."

Irregularities

If an examinee is suspected of cheating on a certifying examination, the results will be held until such time as the examinee appeals to the Board of Registry. If such an incident occurs, the examinee will be notified and informed of the appeals protocol. The Board will review each individual case and determine the appropriate consequences.

Suggestions for Taking the Test

1. Read the instructions carefully before beginning.
2. Read the questions carefully looking for words such as best, most likely, least likely, and not.
3. Read all the answer choices before answering. Sometimes what appears initially to be a correct answer may not be the best answer.
4. Budget your time so you can answer each question. Do not spend an inordinate amount of time on any one question.

5. Record your answers directly on the machine-scorable answer sheet to avoid transcription errors and conserve examination time.
6. Try to stay relaxed so that you can think through clearly and logically the problems presented on the examination.

Should You Guess?

There is no built-in penalty for guessing on Board of Registry examinations. In other words, if you have some knowledge about the content of the question, it is advisable to select a response. If you can narrow the options to two answer choices, it is a good strategy to guess. However, an incorrect answer or no answer always results in the loss of the point value assigned to the question.

CHAPTER 6

Examination Development

Examination Committee

The Joint Generalist Examination Committee, which prepares the Medical Technologist and Medical Laboratory Technician examinations, is composed of medical technologists, medical laboratory technicians, and pathologists. The committee represents both diverse geographical areas and diverse types of practice. The responsibility of item writing, evaluation, and selection rests with the examination committee members. Question writing requires mastery of the subject as well as an understanding of the examination population and mastery of written communication skills. Question review by the entire committee ensures that the item adheres to appropriate technical and/or scientific principles. The committee is also responsible for maintaining the currency of the content of the examinations and writing item descriptors. It is supported by the Board of Registry staff which provides expertise in psychometrics and production.

Criterion-Referenced Testing

The Board of Registry's process of examination construction and analysis is based on the concept of criterion-referenced testing. Generally, a criterion-referenced examination is designed to ascertain an individual's knowledge as measured with respect to a set of previously defined competencies that summarize the domain of knowledge and skill represented on the examination. Each examination question is designed to test some aspect of the competencies that have been developed as criteria against which examinees are measured. Thus every question on an examination becomes a "criterion" against which the examinee is measured. If an examinee answers an item correctly, he or she has met the criterion; if an examinee answers incorrectly, he or she has not met the criterion. Since it is unlikely that one question would be the absolute measure of a competency, the Board of Registry examinations are carefully planned so that several items measure each competency.

In criterion-referenced testing, the domain of practice of the Medical Technologist or Medical Laboratory Technician is delineated in the competency statements and content outlines (see Chapter 7, "Examination Content Guidelines"). These competency statements are the basis for writing examination questions.

Purpose of the Examination

The Board of Registry certification examinations measure an examinee's level of skill and knowledge (competency) at a particular point in time. Each examination question because it is tied to a competency statement, contributes to the pass/fail decision. Because questions must accurately distinguish between qualified and unqualified candidates, each question is carefully written, reviewed, and evaluated. A very comprehensive process is used to assure that each question measures that which it is intended to measure.

Components of Competency

Examination items are written from competency statements. The Board of Registry competency statements were developed based on selected components of competence.

The three components are (1) knowledge, (2) technical skill, and (3) cognitive skill. The components expand into competency statements in which knowledge is represented in the content areas and technical skill is represented by task and task definitions (see Chapter 7).

Knowledge. This is the first dimension of competency and a criterion against which examinees are measured. Knowledge is the content base upon which the field of practice in Medical Technology is built. Content areas of Medical Technology typically include Blood Banking, Body Fluids including Urinalysis, Chemistry, Hematology, Immunology, and Microbiology.

Technical Skill. The second component of competency and a criterion against which the examinee is measured may be defined as the ability to complete an assigned activity or apply knowledge to a procedure. The implication is that laboratory tasks can be defined and that one's ability to perform them can be measured on a test. While these are not the only tasks completed by laboratory staff, they are the areas that are considered essential to test on the examinations.

Cognitive Skill. The third component of competence is the ability to deal with data at various cognitive skill levels. Cognitive skill refers to the cognitive or mental processes required to answer the question. Questions are classified into three cognitive skill levels, based on the structure of the question. The three cognitive skill levels used by the Board of Registry are defined as follows:

- Recall (level 1), the ability to recall or recognize previously learned (memorized) knowledge ranging from specific facts to complete theories;
- Interpretive skills (level 2), the ability to use recalled knowledge to interpret or apply verbal, numeric, or visual data;

- Problem solving (level 3), the ability to use recalled knowledge and the interpretation/application of distinct criteria to resolve a problem or situation and/or make an appropriate decision.

The cognitive skill level of a question is influenced by the construction of the stem in concert with the responses. Thus, a concept such as coagulation provides the content for the development of questions on all three cognitive skill levels. The sample questions in Figure 1 demonstrate this point.

All items appearing on a Board of Registry examination were written to test one of the competency statements listed in Chapter 7. Each question (item) in the examination is described by an item descriptor, which describes the content (knowledge), tasks (technical skills), and cognitive levels (also called taxonomy) covered in each question. The details about item descriptors appear in Chapter 8, "Examination Scoring."

Question Development

The Board of Registry examinations consist of multiple-choice questions. A multiple-choice question may be defined as a measuring device that contains a STEM and four RESPONSES, one of which is the best answer. The form is flexible so that an item may ask a specific question, describe a situation, report laboratory results, etc.

The stem of a multiple-choice question (1) asks a question, (2) gives an incomplete statement, (3) states an issue, or (4) describes a situation. The content of the stem focuses on a central theme or problem, using clear and precise language, without excessive length that can confuse or distract examinees. The stem may describe clinical data and laboratory results that require interpretation or problem solving. The question or issue presented in the stem is relevant to the knowledge and task delineated in a competency statement.

The responses present the "best" answer and the "distractors." Each multiple-choice question has four independent responses. The best answer is the one agreed upon by the experts; however, the other three distractors may seem plausible to the examinee who has partial, incomplete, or inappropriate knowledge. The distractors may therefore be considered logical misconceptions of the best answer. The responses are written to be parallel in content, length, and category of information.

As you review the questions included in this book, it may be useful to note the construction of the question carefully reviewing both the stem and responses as you practice selecting the best answer.

Cognitive Skill Level 1:   Recall

The prothrombin time test requires that the patient's citrated plasma be combined with:

    a. platelet lipids
    b. thromboplastin
    c. Ca^{++} and platelet lipids
  *d. Ca^{++} and thromboplastin

Cognitive Skill Level 2:   Interpretation

A patient develops unexpected bleeding following three transfusions. The following test results were obtained:

        Prolonged PT and APTT
        Decreased fibrinogen
        Increased fibrin split products
        Decreased platelets

What is the most probable cause of these results?

    a. familial afibrinogenemia
    b. primary fibrinolysis
  *c. DIC
    d. liver disease

Cognitive Skill Level 3:   Problem Solving

A patient develops severe unexpected bleeding following four transfusions. The following test results were obtained:

        Prolonged PT and APTT
        Decreased fibrinogen
        Increased fibrin split products
        Decreased platelets

Given these results, which of the following blood products should be recommended to the physician for this patient?

    a. platelets
    b. factor VIII
  *c. cryoprecipitate
    d. fresh frozen plasma

Figure 1:   Sample questions that illustrate cognitive skill levels.

* Correct answer

Color Plates and Other Visual Materials

Some of the questions on the examination will refer to color plates that contain photographs of clinical materials and other visual materials such as graphs or charts. Subject areas that may have color plates include Hematology, Urinalysis, and Microbiology (including Parasitology and Mycology). Although color plates are not provided in this book, you should study books containing color plates (often called atlases) as you prepare for this part of the examination. Some of these books are listed in the reading lists at the end of this book. In addition, many journals frequently contain photographs and graphs. One example is Laboratory Medicine, a monthly journal of the American Society of Clinical Pathologists. This and other journals are available in the laboratory or a medical library as well as by subscription.

To sharpen your ability to understand and analyze visual materials, a good exercise might be to look at an illustration and attempt to evaluate it without referring to the legend. Once you have analyzed the photograph, compare your analysis with the legend. Practice this exercise in your reading whenever the article or book contains photographic material.

An example of a question that contains visual material appears in Figure 2.

Preparation of Examinations

The Board of Registry maintains databases containing more than 10,000 examination questions. This computerized database system has extensive identification and sorting capabilities. The number of multiple-choice questions in each Medical Laboratory Technician or Medical Technologist examination varies between 200 and 230. The average length of the examinations is 200 items.

Board of Registry examinations are carefully constructed according to the specific predetermined criteria summarized in the competency statements and content outlines. Each examination is constructed according to a "multidimensional examination blueprint." The blueprint delineates the number of questions that will be used to measure each competency statement and each content area. In this way the examination committee keeps the examination balanced with regard to knowledge, technical skills, and cognitive skills. The distribution of items across content areas, tasks, and cognitive skills on each examination is reflected in the item descriptor list that accompanies the Examinee Performance Report.

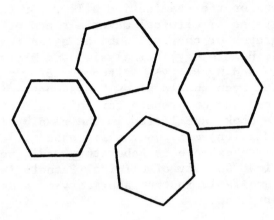

The crystals depicted above were seen in a urine specimen. This patient is most likely to have which of the following clinical conditions?

    a. gout
    b. renal damage
    c. bilirubinuria
*d. cystinosis

Figure 2: Sample question containing an illustration

* Correct answer

CHAPTER 7

Examination Content Guidelines

The content of each examination is determined based on the competency statements and content outlines developed and published by the Board of Registry. These competency statements and content outlines are provided to show you the topics and tasks that will be covered on the examinations.

COMPETENCY STATEMENTS
MEDICAL LABORATORY TECHNICIAN

In regard to laboratory operations and the performance of laboratory tests involving Microbiology, Hematology, Chemistry, Body Fluids, Immunology, and Blood Bank at career entry the Medical Laboratory Technician:

APPLIES (32-34% OF TOTAL EXAMINATION)
- principles of basic laboratory procedures in order to perform tests
- principles of special procedures related to testing
- knowledge to identify sources of error in laboratory testing
- knowledge of fundamental biological characteristics as they pertain to laboratory testing
- principles of theory and practice related to laboratory operations (safety)
- knowledge of standard operating procedures

SELECTS (18-20% OF TOTAL EXAMINATION)
- procedural course of action appropriate for the type of sample and test requested
- methods/reagents/media/blood products according to established procedures
- instruments to perform test appropriate to test methodology according to established procedures
- appropriate controls for test performed
- routine laboratory procedures to verify test results according to established protocol
- special laboratory procedures to verify test results

PREPARES (10-12% OF TOTAL EXAMINATION)
- reagents/media/blood products according to established procedures
- instruments to perform tests
- controls appropriate for testing procedures

CALCULATES (2-4% OF TOTAL EXAMINATION)
- results from test data obtained from laboratory procedures

CORRELATES LABORATORY DATA (8-10% OF TOTAL EXAMINATION)
- and clinical data to assess test results
- and quality control data to assess test results
- with other laboratory data to assess test results
- with physiologic processes to assess/validate test results

EVALUATES LABORATORY DATA (26-28% OF TOTAL EXAMINATION)
- and clinical data to specify additional tests
- to verify test results
- to check for possible source of errors
- to determine possible inconsistent results
- to recognize health and disease states
- to assess validity/accuracy of procedures for a given test
- to determine appropriate instrument adjustments
- to recognize common procedural/technical problems
- to take corrective action according to predetermined criteria
- to recognize and report the need for additional testing
- to make identifications

CONTENT OUTLINE
MEDICAL LABORATORY TECHNICIAN

NOTE: Laboratory Operations is part of all content areas.
LABORATORY OPERATIONS
1. Quality assurance
2. Safety
3. Instruments
4. Laboratory mathematics

All percentages are approximate ranges to be included on the examination.

I. **BLOOD BANK (20% OF TOTAL EXAMINATION)**

  1. **Red Blood Cells 60% of subtest**
       12% of total exam
    A. Immunologic genetic theory and principles
    B. Specimen and component selection, collection, transport, storage and processing
    C. Laboratory examinations
      1. basic tests
      2. special tests
    D. Donor requirements
    E. Laboratory operations

  2. **Platelets 5% of subtest**
       1% of total exam
    A. Immunologic genetic theory and principles
    B. Specimen and component selection, collection, transport, storage and processing
    C. Laboratory examinations
      1. basic tests
      2. special tests
    D. Donor requirements
    E. Laboratory operations

  3. **Other Components 10% of subtest**
       2% of total exam
    A. Immunologic and genetic theory and principles
    B. Specimen and component selection, collection, transport, storage and processing
    C. Laboratory examinations
      1. basic tests
      2. special tests
    D. Donor requirements
    E. Laboratory operations

  4. **Hemotherapy 25% of subtest**
       5% of total exam
    A. Transfusions
    B. Phlebotomy
    C. Apheresis
    D. Adverse reactions
    E. Clinical applications
    F. Laboratory operations

II. **BODY FLUIDS (10% OF TOTAL EXAMINATION)**

  1. **Urine 80% of subtest**
       8% of total exam
    A. Anatomy and physiology
    B. Specimen selection, collection, transport, storage and processing
    C. Laboratory examinations
      1. basic tests
      2. special tests
      3. principles of microscopy
    D. Related conditions and disorders
    E. Laboratory operations

  2. **Other Body Fluids (CSF, feces, others) 20% of subtest**
       2% of total exam
    A. Anatomy and physiology
    B. Specimen selection, collection, transport, storage and processing
    C. Laboratory examinations
      1. basic tests
      2. special tests
      3. principles of microscopy
    D. Related conditions and disorders
    E. Laboratory operations

III. CHEMISTRY (20% OF TOTAL EXAMINATION)

1. **Carbohydrates 10% of subtest**
   2% of total exam
   A. Biochemical theory and physiology
   B. Specimen selection, collection, transport, storage and processing
   C. Laboratory examinations
      1. basic tests
      2. special tests
   D. Biochemical manifestation of disease
   E. Laboratory operations

2. **Lipids and Lipoproteins 5% of subtest**
   1% of total exam
   A. Biochemical theory and physiology
   B. Specimen selection, collection, transport, storage and processing
   C. Laboratory examinations
      1. basic tests
      2. special tests
   D. Biochemical manifestation of disease
   E. Laboratory operations

3. **Heme Derivatives 5% of subtest**
   1% of total exam
   A. Biochemical theory and physiology
   B. Specimen selection, collection, transport, storage and processing
   C. Laboratory examinations
      1. basic tests
      2. special tests
   D. Biochemical manifestation of disease
   E. Laboratory operations

4. **Proteins and Enzymes 25% of subtest**
   5% of total exam
   A. Biochemical theory and physiology
   B. Specimen selection, collection, transport, storage and processing
   C. Laboratory examinations
      1. basic tests
      2. special tests
   D. Biochemical manifestation of disease
   E. Laboratory operations

5. **Acid Base-Electrolytes 25% of subtest**
   5% of total exam
   A. Biochemical theory and physiology
   B. Specimen selection, collection, transport, storage and processing
   C. Laboratory examinations
      1. basic tests
      2. special tests
   D. Biochemical manifestation of disease
   E. Laboratory operations

6. **Special Chemistry (Endocrinology, TDM and others) 10% of subtest**
   2% of total exam
   A. Biochemical theory and physiology
   B. Specimen selection, collection, transport, storage and processing
   C. Laboratory examinations
   D. Biochemical manifestation of disease
   E. Laboratory operations

7. **Instrumentation 20% of subtest**
   4% of total exam
   A. Principles of operation
   B. Essential components
   C. Laboratory operations

IV. HEMATOLOGY (20% OF TOTAL EXAMINATION)

1. **Erythrocytes 35% of subtest**
   7% of total exam
   A. Anatomy and physiology of hematopoiesis
   B. Specimen selection, collection, transport, storage and processing
   C. Laboratory examinations
      1. basic tests
      2. special tests
   D. Hematopoietic diseases
   E. Laboratory operations

2. **Leukocytes 35% of subtest**
   7% of total exam
   A. Anatomy and physiology of hematopoiesis
   B. Specimen selection, collection, transport, storage and processing
   C. Laboratory examinations
      1. basic tests
      2. special tests
   D. Hematopoietic diseases
   E. Laboratory operations

3. **Thrombocytes 10% of subtest**
   2% of total exam
   A. Anatomy and physiology of hematopoiesis
   B. Specimen selection, collection, transport, storage and processing
   C. Laboratory examinations
      1. basic tests
      2. special tests
   D. Hematopoietic disorders
   E. Laboratory operations

4. **Hemostasis 20% of subtest**
   4% of total exam
   A. Physiology of hemostasis
   B. Specimen selection, collection, transport, storage and processing
   C. Laboratory examinations
      1. basic tests
      2. special tests
   D. Hemostatic diseases
   E. Laboratory operations

V. **IMMUNOLOGY (10% OF TOTAL EXAMINATION)**

1. **Humoral Immunity 65% of subtest**
   6.5% of total exam
   A. Anatomy and physiology
   B. Specimen selection, collection, transport, storage and processing
   C. Laboratory examinations
      1. basic tests
      2. special tests
   D. Immunologic manifestation of disease
   E. Laboratory operations

2. **Cellular Immunity 10% of subtest**
   1% of total exam
   A. Anatomy and physiology
   B. Specimen selection, collection, transport, storage and processing
   C. Laboratory examinations
      1. basic tests
      2. special tests
   D. Immunologic manifestation of disease
   E. Laboratory operations

3. **Autoimmunity 20% of subtest**
   2% of total exam
   A. Anatomy and physiology
   B. Specimen selection, collection, transport, storage and processing
   C. Laboratory examinations
      1. basic tests
      2. special tests
   D. Immunologic manifestation of disease
   E. Laboratory operations

4. **Allergy and Immediate Hypersensitivity 5% of subtest**
   0.5% of total exam
   A. Anatomy and physiology
   B. Specimen selection, collection, transport, storage and processing
   C. Laboratory examinations
      1. basic tests
      2. special tests
   D. Immunologic manifestation of disease
   E. Laboratory operations

VI. **MICROBIOLOGY (20% OF TOTAL EXAMINATION)**

1. **Bacteria 75% of subtest**
   15% of total exam
   A. Morphology, cultural and growth characteristics
   B. Specimen and/or media selection, collection, transport, storage and processing
   C. Laboratory examinations
      1. basic tests
      2. special tests
   D. Infectious diseases
   E. Laboratory operations

2. **Fungi 5% of subtest**
   1% of total exam
   A. Morphology, cultural and growth characteristics
   B. Specimen and/or media selection, collection, transport, storage and processing
   C. Laboratory examinations
      1. basic tests
      2. special tests
   D. Infectious diseases
   E. Laboratory operations

3. **Mycobacteria 5% of subtest**
   1% of total exam
   A. Morphology, cultural and growth characteristics
   B. Specimen and/or media selection, collection, transport, storage and processing
   C. Laboratory examinations
      1. basic tests
      2. special tests
   D. Infectious diseases
   E. Laboratory operations

4. **Parasites 10% of subtest**
   2% of total exam
   A. Morphology, cultural and growth characteristics
   B. Specimen and/or media selection, collection, transport, storage and processing
   C. Laboratory examinations
      1. basic tests
      2. special tests
   D. Infectious diseases
   E. Laboratory operations

5. **Viruses, Rickettsiae and Other Microorganisms 5% of subtest**
   1% of total exam
   A. Morphology, cultural and growth characteristics
   B. Specimen and/or media selection, collection, transport, storage and processing
   C. Laboratory examinations
      1. basic tests
      2. special tests
   D. Infectious diseases
   E. Laboratory operations

COMPETENCY STATEMENTS
MEDICAL TECHNOLOGIST

In regard to laboratory operations and the performance of laboratory tests involving Microbiology, Hematology, Chemistry, Body Fluids, Immunology, and Blood Bank at career entry, the Medical Technologist:

APPLIES (24-26% OF TOTAL EXAMINATION)
- principles of basic laboratory procedures in order to perform tests
- principles of special procedures related to testing
- knowledge to identify sources of error in laboratory testing
- knowledge of fundamental biological characteristics as they pertain to laboratory testing
- principles of theory and practice related to laboratory operations (management/safety/education/research and development)
- knowledge of standard operating procedures

SELECTS (17-19% OF TOTAL EXAMINATION)
- procedural course of action appropriate for the type of sample and test requested
- methods/reagents/media/blood products according to established procedures
- instruments to perform test appropriate to test methodology according to established procedures
- appropriate controls for test performed
- routine laboratory procedures to verify test results according to established protocol
- special laboratory procedures to verify test results
- instruments for new laboratory procedures

PREPARES (8-10% OF TOTAL EXAMINATION)
- reagents/media/blood products according to established procedures
- instruments to perform tests
- controls appropriate for testing procedures

CALCULATES (2-4% OF TOTAL EXAMINATION)
- results from test data obtained from laboratory procedures

CORRELATES LABORATORY DATA (10-12% OF TOTAL EXAMINATION)
- and clinical data to assess test results
- and quality control data to assess test results
- with other laboratory data to assess test results
- with physiologic processes to assess/validate test results and procedures

EVALUATES (32-34% OF TOTAL EXAMINATION)
- laboratory and clinical data to specify additional tests
- laboratory data to recognize common procedural/technical problems
- laboratory data to verify test results
- laboratory data to check for possible source of errors
- laboratory data to determine possible inconsistent results
- laboratory data to recognize health and disease states
- laboratory data to assess validity/accuracy of procedures for a given test
- laboratory data to determine appropriate instrument adjustments
- laboratory data to take corrective action according to predetermined criteria
- laboratory data to recognize and report the need for additional testing
- laboratory data to determine alternate methods for a given test
- various methods to establish new testing procedures
- laboratory and clinical data to assure personnel safety
- laboratory operational procedures
- test results obtained by alternate methodologies
- laboratory data to establish reference range criteria for existing or new tests
- laboratory data to make identifications/recommendations

TAXONOMY
MEDICAL TECHNOLOGIST

TAXONOMY 1 - *Recall:* Ability to recall or recognize previously learned (memorized) knowledge ranging from specific facts to complete theories.

TAXONOMY 2 - *Interpretive Skills:* Ability to utilize recalled knowledge to interpret or apply verbal, numeric or visual data.

TAXONOMY 3 - *Problem Solving:* Ability to utilize recalled knowledge and the interpretation/application of distinct criteria to resolve a problem or situation and/or make an appropriate decision.

CONTENT OUTLINE
MEDICAL TECHNOLOGIST

NOTE: Laboratory Operations is part of all content areas.

LABORATORY OPERATIONS
1. Quality assurance
2. Safety
3. Management
4. Research and development
5. Instruments
6. Education
7. Laboratory mathematics

All percentages are approximate ranges to be included on the examination.

I. **BLOOD BANK (20% OF TOTAL EXAMINATION)**

1. **Red Blood Cells 60% of subtest**
   12% of total exam
   A. Immunologic genetic theory and principles
   B. Specimen and component selection, collection, transport, storage and processing
   C. Laboratory examinations
      1. basic tests
      2. special tests
   D. Donor requirements
   E. Laboratory operations

2. **Platelets 5% of subtest**
   1% of total exam
   A. Immunologic genetic theory and principles
   B. Specimen and component selection, collection, transport, storage and processing
   C. Laboratory examinations
      1. basic tests
      2. special tests
   D. Donor requirements
   E. Laboratory operations

3. **Other Components 10% of subtest**
   2% of total exam
   A. Immunologic genetic theory and principles
   B. Specimen and component selection, collection, transport, storage and processing
   C. Laboratory examinations
      1. basic tests
      2. special tests
   D. Donor requirements
   E. Laboratory operations

4. **Hemotherapy 25% of subtest**
   5% of total exam
   A. Transfusions
   B. Phlebotomy
   C. Aphersis
   D. Adverse reactions
   E. Clinical applications
   F. Laboratory operations

II. **BODY FLUIDS (10% OF TOTAL EXAMINATION)**

1. **Urine 80% of subtest**
   8% of total exam
   A. Anatomy and physiology
   B. Specimen selection, collection, transport, storage and processing
   C. Laboratory examinations
      1. basic tests
      2. special tests
      3. principles of microscopy
   D. Related conditions and disorders
   E. Laboratory operations

2. **Other Body Fluids (CSF, feces, others) 20% of subtest 2% of total exam**
   A. Anatomy and physiology
   B. Specimen selection, collection, transport, storage and processing
   C. Laboratory examinations
      1. basic tests
      2. special tests
      3. principles of microscopy
   D. Related conditions and disorders
   E. Laboratory operations

III. CHEMISTRY (20% OF TOTAL EXAMINATION)

1. **Carbohydrates 10% of subtest 2% of total exam**
   A. Biochemical theory and physiology
   B. Specimen selection, collection, transport, storage and processing
   C. Laboratory examinations
      1. basic tests
      2. special tests
   D. Biochemical manifestation of disease
   E. Laboratory operations

2. **Lipids and Lipoproteins 5% of subtest 1% of total exam**
   A. Biochemical theory and physiology
   B. Specimen selection, collection, transport, storage and processing
   C. Laboratory examinations
      1. basic tests
      2. special tests
   D. Biochemical manifestation of disease
   E. Laboratory operations

3. **Heme Derivatives 5% of subtest 1% of total exam**
   A. Biochemical theory and physiology
   B. Specimen selection, collection, transport, storage and processing
   C. Laboratory examinations
      1. basic tests
      2. special tests
   D. Biochemical manifestation of disease
   E. Laboratory operations

4. **Proteins and Enzymes 25% of subtest 5% of total exam**
   A. Biochemical theory and physiology
   B. Specimen selection, collection, transport, storage and processing
   C. Laboratory examinations
      1. basic tests
      2. special tests
   D. Biochemical manifestation of disease
   E. Laboratory operations

5. **Acid Base-Electrolytes 25% of subtest 5% of total exam**
   A. Biochemical theory and physiology
   B. Specimen selection, collection, transport, storage and processing
   C. Laboratory examinations
      1. basic tests
      2. special tests
   D. Biochemical manifestation of disease
   E. Laboratory operations

6. **Special Chemistry (Endocrinology, TDM and others) 10% of subtest 2% of total exam**
   A. Biochemical theory and physiology
   B. Specimen selection, collection, transport, storage and processing
   C. Laboratory examinations
   D. Biochemical manifestation of disease
   E. Laboratory operations

7. **Instrumentation 20% of subtest 4% of total exam**
   A. Principles of operation
   B. Essential components
   C. Laboratory operations

IV. HEMATOLOGY (20% OF TOTAL EXAMINATION)

1. **Erythrocytes 35% of subtest 7% of total exam**
   A. Anatomy and physiology of hematopoiesis
   B. Specimen selection, collection, transport, storage and processing
   C. Laboratory examinations
      1. basic tests
      2. special tests
   D. Hematopoietic diseases
   E. Laboratory operations

2. **Leukocytes 35% of subtest 7% of total exam**
   A. Anatomy and physiology of hematopoiesis
   B. Specimen selection, collection, transport, storage and processing
   C. Laboratory examinations
      1. basic tests
      2. special tests
   D. Hematopoietic diseases
   E. Laboratory operations

3. **Thrombocytes 10% of subtest**
    2% of total exam
    A. Anatomy and physiology of hemato-poiesis
    B. Specimen selection, collection, transport, storage and processing
    C. Laboratory examinations
        1. basic tests
        2. special tests
    D. Hematopoietic disorders
    E. Laboratory operations

4. **Hemostasis 20% of subtest**
    4% of total exam
    A. Physiology of hemostasis
    B. Specimen selection, collection, transport, storage and processing
    C. Laboratory examinations
        1. basic tests
        2. special tests
    D. Hemostatic diseases
    E. Laboratory operations

V. IMMUNOLOGY (10% OF TOTAL EXAMINATION)

1. **Humoral Immunity 65% of subtest**
    6.5% of total exam
    A. Anatomy and physiology
    B. Specimen selection, collection, transport, storage and processing
    C. Laboratory examinations
        1. basic tests
        2. special tests
    D. Immunologic manifestation of disease
    E. Laboratory operations

2. **Cellular Immunity 10% of subtest**
    1% of total exam
    A. Anatomy and physiology
    B. Specimen selection, collection, transport, storage and processing
    C. Laboratory examinations
        1. basic tests
        2. special tests
    D. Immunologic manifestation of disease
    E. Laboratory operations

3. **Autoimmunity 20% of subtest**
    2% of total exam
    A. Anatomy and physiology
    B. Specimen selection, collection, transport, storage and processing
    C. Laboratory examinations
        1. basic tests
        2. special tests
    D. Immunologic manifestation of disease
    E. Laboratory operations

4. **Allergy and Immediate Hypersensitivity**
    5% of subtest
    0.5% of total exam
    A. Anatomy and physiology
    B. Specimen selection, collection, transport, storage and processing
    C. Laboratory examinations
        1. basic tests
        2. special tests
    D. Immunologic manifestation of disease
    E. Laboratory operations

VI. MICROBIOLOGY (20% OF TOTAL EXAMINATION)

1. **Bacteria 60% of subtest**
    12% of total exam
    A. Morphology, cultural and growth characteristics
    B. Specimen and/or media selection, collection, transport, storage and processing
    C. Laboratory examinations
        1. basic tests
        2. special tests
    D. Infectious diseases
    E. Laboratory operations

2. **Fungi 10% of subtest**
    2% of total exam
    A. Morphology, cultural and growth characteristics
    B. Specimen and/or media selection, collection, transport, storage and processing
    C. Laboratory examinations
        1. basic tests
        2. special tests
    D. Infectious diseases
    E. Laboratory operations

3. **Mycobacteria 10% of subtest**
    2% of total exam
    A. Morphology, cultural and growth characteristics
    B. Specimen and/or media selection, collection, transport, storage and processing
    C. Laboratory examinations
        1. basic tests
        2. special tests
    D. Infectious diseases
    E. Laboratory operations

4. **Parasites 10% of subtest**
   2% of total exam
   A. Morphology, cultural and growth characteristics
   B. Specimen and/or media selection, collection, transport, storage and processing
   C. Laboratory examinations
      1. basic tests
      2. special tests
   D. Infectious diseases
   E. Laboratory operations

5. **Viruses, Rickettsiae and Other Microorganisms 10% of subtest**
   2% of total exam
   A. Morphology, cultural and growth characteristics
   B. Specimen and/or media selection, collection, transport, storage and processing
   C. Laboratory examinations
      1. basic tests
      2. special tests
   D. Infectious diseases
   E. Laboratory operations

CHAPTER 8

Examination Scoring

Setting the Absolute Standard

Criterion-referenced testing is a form of measurement designed to measure an examinee's performance compared to an established standard or criterion. For the Board of Registry examinations, the criterion is called the minimum pass score (MPS). Any individual who achieves the level of performance represented by the minimum pass score passes the examination. Those who do not meet this standard fail the examination.

In 1980, the Board of Registry adopted a policy of criterion-referenced testing. Absolute standards are established by the Examination Committee through a systematic evaluation of the content and skill represented in the questions. The standard is established as a scaled score of 400. Subsequent examinations are equated to this standard. This ensures that all candidates meet the same standard regardless of the difficulty of the particular questions or the abilities of the particular candidates tested at the administration.

Why Questions Are Deleted from Scoring

The Board of Registry uses standard procedures for psychometric analysis to ensure that each examinee receives a fairly prepared and scored examination.

After a question is given on an examination it is subjected to rigorous statistical evaluation. Questions are evaluated through item analysis statistics, and tests are evaluated based on summary statistics. Item statistics are used to identify items that should be deleted from scoring. To ensure the continued quality of the examination, questions that prove unsatisfactory are excluded (by deletion) from the calculation of examination summary statistics and examinee scores.

Item (question) statistics include measures of difficulty and discrimination. Difficulty is defined as the proportion or percentage of examinees selecting each response (p-value). The correct response or best answer should draw the highest proportion of the population while the distractors may draw a smaller percentage of the population. This provides an index of how easy or difficult the question was for a particular population.

Item discrimination provides an indication of how well the question differentiates between those examinees who did well on the total examination and those who did not. The computation compares or correlates the performance of candidates who selected the best answer on the question with the performance of those candidates who did well on the total examination. A positive correlation is anticipated for the correct response (best answer), and negative correlations are anticipated for the distractors. This is based on the assumption that those who did well on the question should do well on the test.

The difficulty (percentage selecting the response) and discrimination (point biserial correlation) are considered simultaneously to meaningfully evaluate a question. Together, they indicate whether a question is measuring appropriately. Item analysis data do not reflect the value of the knowledge, task, or cognitive skill being tested, but rather suggest the potential contribution of the question toward making the decision to pass or fail an examinee.

After each item in the test has been carefully reviewed, the total test is analyzed. The summary statistics for the examination are critically reviewed. Typically, summary statistics include the number and percentage of passing and failing examinees; the number of questions scored on the test; and the mean, standard deviation, mode, range, and internal consistency values.

The examination mean, the sum of the scores on a test divided by the number of scores, is the most important measure of central tendency. The examination standard deviation is the measure of the variance of the scores around the mean. A large standard deviation indicates a lot of variance among the examination scores. The examination mode is the most frequent score on the test. The examination range is the number of points between the highest and lowest scores on the examination.

The internal consistency or internal reliability estimate assesses the consistency of measurement among items on an examination. A perfect reliability among questions would be a one-to-one relationship or 1.0. The difference between perfect reliability and calculated internal reliability indicates the potential amount of measurement error on the test.

Score Reporting

After the examination has been statistically evaluated, Examinee Performance Reports are generated and distributed to the examinees approximately six weeks following the date of test administration. (Test results are not released by telephone to anyone.) The purpose of the report is to provide examinees with specific information about their performance on the examination.

The following explanation refers to the sample Examinee Performance Report in Figure 3. The first paragraph provides an explanation of how to interpret the profile. Key information is presented under "YOUR PERFORMANCE SUMMARY". A scaled minimum pass score (MPS) of 400 is the standard against which all examinees are measured. Individuals who achieve or exceed the MPS pass the examination; others fail. The decision to pass or fail is based on the candidate ability measure for the total test. Pass or fail status is noted under STATUS. The LIST OF ITEMS WITH INCORRECT RESPONSES provides the sequence number of the items answered incorrectly on the examination.

The following subtests appear on the Medical Technologist and Medical Laboratory Technician examinations: Microbiology (MICR), Blood Banking (BBNK), Chemistry (CHEM), Hematology (HEMA), Immunology (IMMU), and Body Fluids including Urinalysis.

The item descriptor list details the subtest, task, and cognitive skill levels of all questions scored on the examination. Passing examinees can assess their level of knowledge in each area, and failing examinees can determine weaker areas by comparing the list of items with incorrect responses to the Item Descriptor list. This can provide specific information regarding areas of strength and weakness. For example, if an examinee found in reviewing the item descriptors for incorrectly answered questions that many of the missed questions related to "specimen processing", it would then be possible to outline a course of study with this emphasis across all content areas.

```
                    B O A R D   O F   R E G I S T R Y


                    EXAMINEE PERFORMANCE REPORT


            MEDICAL TECHNOLOGIST EXAMINATION - AUGUST, 1990


    999999999
    JONES, JULIE L                              MT(ASCP) ****909999****
    600 W MAIN STREET
    SOMEPLACE, USA


    THIS REPORT PROVIDES INFORMATION CONCERNING YOUR EXAMINATION PERFOR-
    MANCE. A SCALED SCORE OF 400 WAS REQUIRED TO PASS THE TEST (MPS).
    A REPORT OF YOUR SCORE ON THE TOTAL TEST IS SHOWN IN THE TABLE.
    FOLLOWING THE TABLE IS A LIST OF EXAMINATION ITEMS THAT YOU ANSWERED
    INCORRECTLY.   INFORMATION CONCERNING THESE ITEMS IS SUMMARIZED IN
    AN ITEM DESCRIPTOR LIST ENCLOSED WITH THIS REPORT.   THESE ITEM
    DESCRIPTORS IDENTIFY SUBJECT AREA, CONTENT AND TAXONOMY LEVEL OF EACH
    EXAMINATION ITEM AND SHOULD BE USEFUL TO YOU IN EVALUATING YOUR
    PERFORMANCE MORE SPECIFICALLY.



                        YOUR PERFORMANCE SUMMARY

        MPS = 400           YOUR SCORE 550           STATUS PASS




                 LIST OF ITEMS WITH INCORRECT RESPONSES

     19  20  22  25  34  43  47  62  71  84  85  86  92 108 118 121 128
    135 144 156 157 177 180 182
```

Figure 3: Sample of Board of Registry Examinee Performance Report.

Item Descriptors

An item descriptor is a shorthand method of describing the content and skill tested in a specific test question. Item descriptors specify the content, competency (task), and cognitive skill (taxonomy) necessary to answer a given question. Through this feedback, examinees should be able to identify the content and task areas tested as well as ascertain their strengths and weaknesses as measured by the examination.

The form of the item descriptors requires some explanation. Item descriptors are developed using the following sentence structure:

In regard to _____ the examinee will
                         1. Subtest Category

          be able to _____
                              2. Task/Competence

             concerning_____
                              3. Subject Content

             for/of _____
                                 4. Specifics

          using the cognitive skill process of _____.
                                           5. Taxonomy

The first unit of the item descriptor indicates the SUBTEST or major content area in which the question is classified.

The TASK area is the second unit and relates directly to the competency statements found in Chapter 7, "Examination Content Guidelines." The third and fourth units refer to CONTENT SPECIFICS. In many instances, these words can be traced to the content outlines found in Chapter 7. However, in an effort to be as specific as possible, the item descriptors are often more specific than the outlines and specify the specific tests, types of organisms, or quality control procedures covered in a question.

The fifth unit indicates the cognitive skill required to answer the question, typically called the TAXONOMY level (see description and examples of cognitive skill levels in Chapter 6, "Examination Development").

The following are examples of printed item descriptors:

	SUBTEST	TASK	CONTENT SPECIFICS	CONTENT SPECIFICS	TAXONOMY
1.	BF	CCLD	URINE	SPECIFIC GRAVITY	3
2.	HEMA	EDVR	QC	PROTHROMBIN TIME	2

When translated from abbreviations, the item descriptors would read as follows:

1. In regard to <u>body fluids</u>, the examinee will be able to <u>correlate clinical and laboratory data</u> related to <u>urine</u> specimen, <u>specific gravity</u> test, at the <u>taxonomy level 3</u> (problem-solving cognitive skill level).
2. In regard to <u>hematology</u>, the examinee will be able to <u>evaluate laboratory data to verify test results</u> related to performing <u>quality control</u> procedures on a <u>prothrombin time</u> test at the <u>taxonomy level 2</u> (interpretative cognitive skill level).

Lists of item descriptors for the 1990 Medical Laboratory Technician examinations and for the 1990 Medical Technologist examinations are provided in Appendix A and Appendix B respectively.

Use the item descriptor lists to further structure your review for the certification examination. Each list represents the distribution of items on a particular examination and verifies the content, task, and cognitive skill distribution for each examination cycle.

CHAPTER 9

Written Practice Examinations

Directions

There are 50 questions on the MLT and 50 questions on the MT written practice tests. Not only will these tests give you the opportunity to simulate the test conditions, but they will also enable you to diagnose your strengths and weaknesses. In addition, you will have the opportunity to indicate your answers on an answer sheet like the one used on examination day. Since some people find it useful to repeat a test at several points during their course of study, extra copies of the answer sheets are provided at the back of this chapter.

Find a quiet place and allow yourself one hour of uninterrupted continuous time to complete the examination.

Choose the one <u>best</u> answer for each question and mark the appropriate response on the replica of the machine-scorable answer sheet by completely blackening the circle that corresponds to the response of your choice. Note that the questions are numbered consecutively DOWN (not across) the answer sheet. Be sure that the circle you mark on the answer sheet corresponds to the question on the test. DO NOT MAKE ANY MARKS ON YOUR ANSWER SHEET OTHER THAN YOUR IDENTIFICATION INFORMATION AND YOUR ANSWERS.

READ EACH QUESTION CAREFULLY. Pace yourself. Do not spend too much time on any one question. YOUR SCORE IS BASED UPON THE TOTAL NUMBER OF QUESTIONS YOU ANSWER CORRECTLY; therefore, it is to your advantage to record your best judgment for EVERY question, even if you are not completely sure of the answer.

On page 37 is a reproduction of the instructions for filling out examination answer sheets. It is not necessary to complete all of these instructions during the study process. After you have completed the examination, score it using the scoring instructions below and the answer key at the end of the test.

Scoring Your Practice Examination

1. Compare your answer choices to the correct answers indicated in the practice test answer key. Circle the INCORRECT answers on the answer sheet.
2. Review the items you answered incorrectly to identify areas that you need to study. Develop a systematic plan for studying these content areas and attempting the review questions in this guide.

INSTRUCTIONS FOR FILLING OUT
EXAMINATION ANSWER SHEET

CHECKING AND RECORDING IDENTIFICATION INFORMATION

ALL IDENTIFICATION INFORMATION AND ANSWERS MUST BE COMPLETED USING A NO. 2 SOFT LEAD PENCIL. Answers marked with a hard pencil, ink or felt-tip pen will not be scored. If you did not bring a No. 2 lead pencil, please ask your proctor for one.

It is imperative that all responses be enhanced with black heavy circles, so that all of your responses are counted.

Read these instructions carefully and fill out your answer sheet while you are waiting for the examination to begin. The answer sheet has two sides. Please turn to Side One.

YOU WILL NOTE THAT ON SIDE ONE IN THE GRID TO THE LEFT OF THE ANSWER SHEET YOUR EXAMINATION CODE HAS BEEN PRE-CODED AND PRE-PRINTED. Check to make certain that this code is for the examination for which you have applied and been determined eligible. EXAMPLE: MEDICAL TECHNOLOGIST – 01 (SEE LIST BELOW). You must complete this information if it has not been pre-printed and pre-coded. Answer sheets that do not contain this information cannot be scored.

INSTRUCTIONS FOR PRINTING AND CODING

Carefully print and code your Social Security Number (Personal Identification Number) in the designated area on Side One of the answer sheet. From left to right in the top row, print one number per space, and then code by filling in the corresponding circle in each column. Refer to your Authorization Slip for your personal Identification Number.

Check that both your Personal Identification Number and Exam Code have been entered correctly.

Record the test booklet number in the space provided below your Personal Identification Number on your answer sheet. Please be certain to include the letter that precedes this test booklet number (See example below).

The example given illustrates how the Identification Number and Exam Code should be printed and coded.

EXAMPLE: Identification Number 123456789 and Exam Code 01 – (Medical Technologist) are recorded in the example to the right. Note that the two digit Exam Code has been taken from the list below. USE your Personal Identification Number DO NOT use the number that appears in this example.

EXAM TYPE	EXAM CODE		EXAM TYPE	EXAM CODE
Medical Technologist ....MT 01			Cytotechnologist ....CT 12	
Medical Laboratory Technician ....MLT 02			Specialist in Cytotechnology ....SCT 13	
Histologic Technician ....HT 04			Specialist in Blood Banking ....SBB 14	
Technologist in Chemistry ....C 05			Histotechnologist ....HTL 15	
Specialist in Chemistry ....SC 06			Technologist in Immunology ....I 16	
Technologist in Hematology.............H 07			Specialist in Immunology...............SI 17	
Specialist in Hematology ....SH 08			Technologist in Blood Banking ....BB 18	
Technologist in Microbiology ....M 09			Diplomate in Laboratory Management ..DLM 19	
Specialist in Microbiology ....SM 10			Phlebotomy Technician ....PBT 20	

INDICATE YOUR NAME, EXAM TYPE AND EXAMINATION DATE IN THE SPACE PROVIDED ON SIDE ONE OF YOUR ANSWER SHEET.

WAIT FOR VERBAL INSTRUCTIONS FROM YOUR PROCTOR

NAME/ADDRESS CHANGES: Any change of name and/or address will not be made from the sign-in list or your answer sheet. Please indicate the change on the reverse side of your Authorization Slip supplied with your scheduling information.

MLT Written Practice Examination

FOR EACH QUESTION, CHOOSE THE ONE ANSWER THAT IS MOST CORRECT.
MARK YOUR ANSWER ON YOUR ANSWER SHEET IN THE APPROPRIATE SPACE.
ANSWERS WRITTEN IN THIS EXAMINATION BOOKLET WILL NOT BE SCORED.

1. A temperature rise of 1°C or more occurring in association with
   a transfusion is usually indicative of which of the following
   transfusion reactions?

   a. febrile
   b. circulatory overload
   c. allergic
   d. anaphylactic

2. For which of the following transfusion candidates would CMV
   seronegative blood be MOST likely indicated?

   a. renal dialysis patients
   b. pregnant women
   c. transplant candidates
   d. CMV seropositive patients

3. In the process of identifying an antibody, the technologist
   observed 2+ reactions with three of the ten cells in a panel
   after the immediate spin phase. These reactions disappeared
   following incubation at 37°C and after the antihuman globulin
   phase of testing. The antibody most likely responsible is:

   a. anti-P_1
   b. anti-Le^a
   c. anti-C
   d. anti-Fy^a

4. The blood sample of choice for the pretransfusion testing of
   neonates with HDN is:

   a. maternal serum
   b. maternal eluate
   c. cord blood serum
   d. cord blood eluate

5. One of the most effective methods for the elution of warm autoantibodies from RBCs utilizes:

   a. 10% sucrose
   b. LISS
   c. an organic solvent
   d. distilled water
   e. a freezer

6. Mixed-field reactions with anti-A and anti-A,B and negative reactions with anti-B and anti-A_1 lectin (*Dolichos biflorus*) are observed. Without further testing, the most likely conclusion is that the patient is group:

   a. A_1
   b. A_2
   c. A_3
   d. A_{el}

7. The antibodies of the Kidd Blood Group System:

   a. react best by the indirect antiglobulin test
   b. are predominantly IgM
   c. often cause allergic transfusion reactions
   d. do not generally react with antigen-positive, enzyme treated RBCs

8. A patient's red cells are typed as follows:

Anti-D	Anti-C	Anti-E
4+	0	0

   Which genotype would correspond to these results?

   a. R_0R_0
   b. R_1r
   c R_1R_2
   d. R_zr

9. A 10% red cell suspension in saline is used in a compatibility test. Which of the following would most likely occur?

   a. a false-positive result due to antigen excess
   b. a false-positive result due to the prozone phenomenon
   c. a false-negative result due to the prozone phenomenon
   d. a false-negative result due to antigen excess

10. During the preparation of Platelets from Whole Blood, the blood should be:

    a. chilled to 4°C
    b. kept at room temperature
    c. warmed to 37°C
    d. heated to 56°C

11. The part of the kidney in which there is selective retention and excretion of various substances and in which the concentration of urine occurs is the:

    a. glomerulus
    b. papilla
    c. tubule
    d. ureter

12. Which of the following crystals appear as finely scattered needles?

    a. cholesterol
    b. leucine
    c. starch
    d. tyrosine

13. A 21-year-old woman had glucose in her urine with a normal blood sugar. These findings are most consistent with:

    a. renal glycosuria
    b. diabetes insipidus
    c. diabetes mellitus
    d. alkaline tide

14. Which of the following would be affected by allowing a urine specimen to remain at room temperature for three hours before analysis?

    a. occult blood
    b. specific gravity
    c. Ph
    d. protein

15. Which of the following determinations is useful in prenatal diagnosis of open neural tube defects?

    a. amniotic fluid alpha-fetoprotein
    b. amniotic fluid estriol
    c. maternal serum estradiol
    d. maternal serum estrone

16. Which two conditions can "physiologically" elevate serum alkaline phosphatase?

    a. rickets, hyperparathyroidism
    b. obstructive jaundice, biliary cirrhosis
    c. growth, third trimester of pregnancy
    d. viral hepatitis, infectious mononucleosis

17. Lithium therapy is widely used in the treatment of:

    a. schizophrenia
    b. hyperactivity
    c. aggression
    d. manic-depression

18. Amniotic fluid scans are generally made to evaluate impending fetal distress from:

    a. maternal diabetes
    b. urinary tract infections
    c. respiratory distress syndrome
    d. hemolytic disease of the newborn

19. A physician suspects his patient has pancreatitis. Which test(s) would be most indicative of this disease:

    a. creatinine
    b. LD isoenzymes
    c. ß-hydroxybutyrate
    d. amylase

20. Which of the following serum constituents are unstable if a blood specimen is left standing at room temperature for eight hours before processing?

    a. cholesterol
    b. triglyceride
    c. creatinine
    d. glucose

21. Sixty to seventy-five percent of the plasma cholesterol is transported by:

    a. chylomicrons
    b. very low density lipoprotein
    c. low density lipoprotein
    d. high density lipoprotein

22. In the Total Bilirubin assay, bilirubin reacts with diazotized sulfanilic acid to form:

    a. diazo bilirubin
    b. biliverdin
    c. azobilirubin
    d. bilirubin glucuronide

23. The creatinine clearance (ml/min) is equal to:

    a. $$\frac{\text{urinary creatinine (mg/L)}}{\text{volume of urine (mL/min) x plasma creatinine (mg/L)}}$$

    b. $$\frac{\text{urinary creatinine (mg/L) x volume (mL/min)}}{\text{plasma creatinine (mg/L)}}$$

    c. $$\frac{\text{urinary creatinine (mg/L)}}{\text{volume of urine (mL/hour) x plasma creatinine (mg/L)}}$$

    d. $$\frac{\text{urinary creatinine (mg/L) x volume (mL/hour)}}{\text{plasma creatinine (mg/L)}}$$

24. An adult diabetic with renal complications has the following results:

    Sodium: 133 mEq/L   BUN: 84 mg/dL
    Glucose: 487 mg/dL   Creatinine: 5 mg/dL

    On the basis of these results, the calculated serum osmolality is:

    a. 266 mOsm/kg
    b. 290 mOsm/kg
    c. 304 mOsm/kg
    d. 709 mOsm/kg

25. In a spectrophotometer, light of a specific wavelength can be isolated from white light with a(n):

    a. double beam
    b. diffraction grating
    c. aperture
    d. slit

26. Which of the following is most closely associated with chronic granulocytic leukemia?

    a. ringed sideroblasts
    b. disseminated intravascular coagulation
    c. micromegakaryocytes
    d. Philadelphia chromosome

27. The following results were obtained:

WBC $1.8 \times 10^3/\mu L$ ($1.8 \times 10^9/L$)
Hgb 8.9 g/dL
Hct 27.4%
PLT $2,300 \times 10^3/\mu L$ ($2,300 \times 10^6/L$)
Differential:
    70% segmented neutrophils
    10% bands
    18% lymphocytes
     2% monocytes
Giant, bizarre platelets, rare megakaryocyte,
4+ poikilocytosis, 3+ anisocytosis, 4+ echinocytosis,
2+ schizocytosis

LAP 90

This is consistent with:

    a. neutrophilic leukemoid reaction
    b. polycythemia vera
    c. leukoerythroblastosis in myelofibrosis
    d. idiopathic thrombocythemia

28. The characteristic morphologic feature in lead poisoning is:

    a. macrocytosis
    b. target cells
    c. basophilic stippling
    d. rouleaux formation

29. Multiple myeloma is generally characterized by:

    a. plasmacytic satellitosis in the bone marrow
    b. many plasma cells in the peripheral blood
    c. many Mott cells in the peripheral blood
    d. rouleaux formation

30. A differential was performed on an asymptomatic patient. The differential included 60% neutrophils: 55 of which had 2 lobes and 5 had 3 lobes. There were no other abnormalities. This is consistent with which of the following anomalies?

    a. Pelger-Huët
    b. May-Hegglin
    c. Alder-Reilly
    d. Chediak-Higashi

31. The values below were obtained on an automated blood count system performed on a blood sample from a twenty-five-year-old man:

	Patient	Normal
WBC	$5.1 \times 10^3/\mu L$ $(5.1 \times 10^9/L)$	$5.0 - 10.0 \times 10^3/\mu L$ $(5.0 - 10.0 \times 10^9/L)$
RBC	$2.94 \times 10^6/\mu L$ $(2.94 \times 10^{12}/L)$	$4.6 - 6.2 \times 10^6/\mu L$ $(4.6 - 6.2 \times 10^{12}/L)$
Hgb	13.8 g/dL	14 - 18 g/dL
HCT	35.4% (0.354)	40 - 54% (0.40 - 0.54)
MCV	128 fL	82 - 90 fL
MCH	46.7 pg	27 - 31 pg
MCHC	40 g/dL	32 - 36 g/dL

These results are most consistent with which of the following?

    a. megaloblastic anemia
    b. hereditary spherocytosis
    c. a high titer of cold agglutinins
    d. an elevated reticulocyte count

32. Which of the following is typical of polycythemia vera?

    a. increased serum iron concentration
    b. decreased thrombocyte count
    c. increased erythropoietin
    d. increased leukocyte alkaline phosphatase activity

33. The most common form of childhood leukemia is:

    a. acute lymphocytic
    b. acute granulocytic
    c. acute monocytic
    d. chronic granulocytic

34. Which one of the following factors typically shows on increase in liver disease?

    a. factor VII
    b. factor VIII
    c. factor IX
    d. factor X

35. Thrombocytosis would be indicated by a platelet count of:

    a. $100 \times 10^3/\mu L$ ($100 \times 10^9/L$)
    b. $200 \times 10^3/\mu L$ ($200 \times 10^9/L$)
    c. $300 \times 10^3/\mu L$ ($300 \times 10^9/L$)
    d. $600 \times 10^3/\mu L$ ($600 \times 10^9/L$)

36. Which of the following chemical classes of antigens is most likely to activate the alternative pathway of complement?

    a. proteins
    b. lipids
    c. polysaccharides
    d. haptens

37. Antibodies to which of the following immunoglobulins are known to have produced anaphylactic reactions following blood transfusion?

    a. IgA
    b. IgD
    c. IgE
    d. IgG

38. Which laboratory technique is most frequently used to diagnose and follow the course of therapy of a patient with secondary syphilis?

    a. flocculation
    b. precipitation
    c. complement fixation
    d. indirect immunofluorescence

39. Rheumatoid factor is:

    a. an antigen found in the serum of patients with rheumatoid
       arthritis
    b. identical to the rheumatoid arthritis precipitin
    c. IgG or IgM autoantibody
    d. capable of forming circulating immune complexes only when
       IgM-type autoantibody is present

40. The following pattern of agglutination was observed in doing an
    antibody titer:

Tube	1	2	3	4	5	6	7	8	9	10	11
	0	1+	2+	4+	4+	3+	3+	2+	1+	1+	0

    This set of reactions most likely resulted from:

    a. faulty pipetting technique
    b. an inactive antigen
    c. prozoning
    d. a presence of a high-titer, low-avidity antibody

41. A liquid stool specimen is collected at 10:00 p.m. and brought
    to the laboratory for culture, ova and parasites. It is
    refrigerated until 10:10 a.m. the next day when the physician
    requests that the technician look for amoebic trophozoites.
    The best course of action would be to:

    a. request a fresh specimen
    b. perform a concentration on the original specimen
    c. perform a trichrome stain on the original specimen
    d. perform a saline wet mount on the original specimen

42. A Gram stain of a cervical exudate showed gram-negative
    diplococci, gram-positive cocci and gram-negative bacilli. A
    media for selective isolation of the gram-negative diplococci
    is:

    a. chocolate
    b. Columbia CNA
    c. Thayer-Martin
    d. CTA

43. *Legionella pneumophila* characteristically is:

   a. oxidase positive
   b. gelatin negative
   c. nonmotile
   d. gram-positive

44. The function of N-acetyl-L-cysteine required in the NALC-NaOH reagent for acid-fast digestion-decontamination procedures is to:

   a. inhibit growth of normal respiratory flora
   b. inhibit growth of fungi
   c. neutralize the sodium hydroxide
   d. liquefy the mucus

45. An organism which is frequently isolated from burn wounds and is often associated with nosocomial infections has the following biochemical reactions:

   Oxidase: positive
   OF glucose: oxidizer
   Pyocyanin: positive

   The organism is most likely:

   a. *Enterobacter sakazakii*
   b. *Pseudomonas aeruginosa*
   c. *Serratia marcescens*
   d. *Chromobacterium violaceum*

46. Which of the following would best differentiate *Streptococcus agalactiae* (Group B) from *Streptococcus pyogenes* (Group A)?

   a. ability to grow in sodium azide broth
   b. a positive bile-esculin reaction
   c. hydrolysis of sodium hippurate
   d. beta-hemolysis on sheep blood agar

47. Which disinfectant inactivates HIV and HBV?

   a. alcohol
   b. iodine
   c. phenol
   d. sodium hypochlorite

48. Which of the following organisms is considered universally susceptible to penicillin?

    a. *Haemophilus influenzae*
    b. *Neisseria gonorrhoeae*
    c. *Streptococcus pyogenes*
    d. *Corynebacterium diphtheriae*

49. Which of the following is most often used to prepare a slide from a plate culture for microscopic observation of a dermatophyte?

    a. lactophenol cotton blue
    b. potassium hydroxide
    c. iodine solution
    d. Gram stain

50. A TSI tube inoculated with an organism gave the following reactions:

Alkaline slant
Acid butt
No H_2S
No gas produced

This organism is most likely:

    a. *Yersinia enterocolitica*
    b. *Salmonella typhi*
    c. *Salmonella typhimurium*
    d. *Shigella dysenteriae*

END OF MLT PRACTICE EXAMINATION

MLT Practice Examination Answer Key

1.	A	14.	C	27.	D	40.	C
2.	C	15.	A	28.	C	41.	A
3.	B	16.	C	29.	D	42.	C
4.	A	17.	D	30.	A	43.	A
5.	C	18.	D	31.	C	44.	D
6.	C	19.	D	32.	D	45.	B
7.	A	20.	D	33.	A	46.	C
8.	A	21.	C	34.	B	47.	D
9.	A	22.	C	35.	D	48.	C
10.	B	23.	B	36.	C	49.	A
11.	C	24.	C	37.	A	50.	D
12.	D	25.	B	38.	A		
13.	A	26.	D	39.	C		

BOARD OF REGISTRY

NAME:

DATE:

EXAM TYPE:

SIDE ONE

IDENTIFICATION NUMBER

EXAM TYPE

TEST BOOKLET NUMBER

IMPORTANT DIRECTIONS FOR MARKING ANSWERS

- Use black lead pencil only (No. 2½ or softer).
- Do NOT use ink, felt tip or ballpoint pens.
- Erase cleanly any answer you wish to change.
- Make no stray marks on the answer sheet.
- Make heavy black marks that fill the circle completely.

EXAMPLES

1 WRONG: Fill in the circle completely.

2

3

4 WRONG: Make heavy black marks.

5 RIGHT: Make heavy black marks that fill in the circle completely.

BOARD OF REGISTRY

founded in 1928 by the
American Society of Clinical Pathologists

Representatives from:

American Society of Clinical Pathologists
Medical Technologists/Technicians
Pathologists
American Academy of Microbiology
American Association of Blood Banks
American Society of Cytology
National Registry in Clinical Chemistry
American Society of Hematology
National Society for Histotechnology

IMPORTANT DIRECTIONS
FOR MARKING ANSWERS

- Use black lead pencil only (No. 2½ or softer).
- Do NOT use ink, felt tip or ballpoint pens.
- Erase cleanly any answer you wish to change.
- Make no stray marks on the answer sheet.
- Make heavy black marks that fill the circle completely.

EXAMPLES

1 ⊗ Ⓑ Ⓒ Ⓓ Ⓔ   WRONG: Fill in the circle completely.
2 Ⓐ ⊘ Ⓒ Ⓓ Ⓔ
3 Ⓐ Ⓑ ⬤ Ⓓ Ⓔ
4 Ⓐ Ⓑ Ⓒ Ⓓ Ⓔ   WRONG: Make heavy black marks.
5 Ⓐ Ⓑ Ⓒ Ⓓ ⬤   RIGHT: Make heavy black marks that fill in the circle completely.

BOARD OF REGISTRY

NAME: ______________________

EXAM TYPE: ______________ DATE: ______________

IDENTIFICATION NUMBER									EXAM TYPE	
0	0	0	0	0	0	0	0	0	0	0
1	1	1	1	1	1	1	1	1	1	1
2	2	2	2	2	2	2	2	2	2	2
3	3	3	3	3	3	3	3	3	3	3
4	4	4	4	4	4	4	4	4	4	4
5	5	5	5	5	5	5	5	5	5	5
6	6	6	6	6	6	6	6	6	6	6
7	7	7	7	7	7	7	7	7	7	7
8	8	8	8	8	8	8	8	8	8	8
9	9	9	9	9	9	9	9	9	9	9

TEST BOOKLET NUMBER

IMPORTANT DIRECTIONS FOR MARKING ANSWERS

- Use black lead pencil only (No. 2½ or softer).
- Do NOT use ink, felt tip or ballpoint pens.
- Erase cleanly any answer you wish to change.
- Make no stray marks on the answer sheet.
- Make heavy black marks that fill the circle completely.

EXAMPLES

WRONG: Fill in the circle completely.

1 Ⓐ Ⓑ Ⓒ Ⓓ Ⓔ

2 Ⓐ Ⓑ Ⓒ Ⓓ Ⓔ

3 Ⓐ Ⓑ Ⓒ Ⓓ Ⓔ

WRONG: Make heavy black marks.

4 Ⓐ Ⓑ Ⓒ Ⓓ Ⓔ

RIGHT: Make heavy black marks that fill in the circle completely.

5 Ⓐ Ⓑ Ⓒ Ⓓ ●

1 Ⓐ Ⓑ Ⓒ Ⓓ Ⓔ	21 Ⓐ Ⓑ Ⓒ Ⓓ Ⓔ	41 Ⓐ Ⓑ Ⓒ Ⓓ Ⓔ	61 Ⓐ Ⓑ Ⓒ Ⓓ Ⓔ	81 Ⓐ Ⓑ Ⓒ Ⓓ Ⓔ	101 Ⓐ Ⓑ Ⓒ Ⓓ Ⓔ
2 Ⓐ Ⓑ Ⓒ Ⓓ Ⓔ	22 Ⓐ Ⓑ Ⓒ Ⓓ Ⓔ	42 Ⓐ Ⓑ Ⓒ Ⓓ Ⓔ	62 Ⓐ Ⓑ Ⓒ Ⓓ Ⓔ	82 Ⓐ Ⓑ Ⓒ Ⓓ Ⓔ	102 Ⓐ Ⓑ Ⓒ Ⓓ Ⓔ
3 Ⓐ Ⓑ Ⓒ Ⓓ Ⓔ	23 Ⓐ Ⓑ Ⓒ Ⓓ Ⓔ	43 Ⓐ Ⓑ Ⓒ Ⓓ Ⓔ	63 Ⓐ Ⓑ Ⓒ Ⓓ Ⓔ	83 Ⓐ Ⓑ Ⓒ Ⓓ Ⓔ	103 Ⓐ Ⓑ Ⓒ Ⓓ Ⓔ
4 Ⓐ Ⓑ Ⓒ Ⓓ Ⓔ	24 Ⓐ Ⓑ Ⓒ Ⓓ Ⓔ	44 Ⓐ Ⓑ Ⓒ Ⓓ Ⓔ	64 Ⓐ Ⓑ Ⓒ Ⓓ Ⓔ	84 Ⓐ Ⓑ Ⓒ Ⓓ Ⓔ	104 Ⓐ Ⓑ Ⓒ Ⓓ Ⓔ
5 Ⓐ Ⓑ Ⓒ Ⓓ Ⓔ	25 Ⓐ Ⓑ Ⓒ Ⓓ Ⓔ	45 Ⓐ Ⓑ Ⓒ Ⓓ Ⓔ	65 Ⓐ Ⓑ Ⓒ Ⓓ Ⓔ	85 Ⓐ Ⓑ Ⓒ Ⓓ Ⓔ	105 Ⓐ Ⓑ Ⓒ Ⓓ Ⓔ
6 Ⓐ Ⓑ Ⓒ Ⓓ Ⓔ	26 Ⓐ Ⓑ Ⓒ Ⓓ Ⓔ	46 Ⓐ Ⓑ Ⓒ Ⓓ Ⓔ	66 Ⓐ Ⓑ Ⓒ Ⓓ Ⓔ	86 Ⓐ Ⓑ Ⓒ Ⓓ Ⓔ	106 Ⓐ Ⓑ Ⓒ Ⓓ Ⓔ
7 Ⓐ Ⓑ Ⓒ Ⓓ Ⓔ	27 Ⓐ Ⓑ Ⓒ Ⓓ Ⓔ	47 Ⓐ Ⓑ Ⓒ Ⓓ Ⓔ	67 Ⓐ Ⓑ Ⓒ Ⓓ Ⓔ	87 Ⓐ Ⓑ Ⓒ Ⓓ Ⓔ	107 Ⓐ Ⓑ Ⓒ Ⓓ Ⓔ
8 Ⓐ Ⓑ Ⓒ Ⓓ Ⓔ	28 Ⓐ Ⓑ Ⓒ Ⓓ Ⓔ	48 Ⓐ Ⓑ Ⓒ Ⓓ Ⓔ	68 Ⓐ Ⓑ Ⓒ Ⓓ Ⓔ	88 Ⓐ Ⓑ Ⓒ Ⓓ Ⓔ	108 Ⓐ Ⓑ Ⓒ Ⓓ Ⓔ
9 Ⓐ Ⓑ Ⓒ Ⓓ Ⓔ	29 Ⓐ Ⓑ Ⓒ Ⓓ Ⓔ	49 Ⓐ Ⓑ Ⓒ Ⓓ Ⓔ	69 Ⓐ Ⓑ Ⓒ Ⓓ Ⓔ	89 Ⓐ Ⓑ Ⓒ Ⓓ Ⓔ	109 Ⓐ Ⓑ Ⓒ Ⓓ Ⓔ
10 Ⓐ Ⓑ Ⓒ Ⓓ Ⓔ	30 Ⓐ Ⓑ Ⓒ Ⓓ Ⓔ	50 Ⓐ Ⓑ Ⓒ Ⓓ Ⓔ	70 Ⓐ Ⓑ Ⓒ Ⓓ Ⓔ	90 Ⓐ Ⓑ Ⓒ Ⓓ Ⓔ	110 Ⓐ Ⓑ Ⓒ Ⓓ Ⓔ
11 Ⓐ Ⓑ Ⓒ Ⓓ Ⓔ	31 Ⓐ Ⓑ Ⓒ Ⓓ Ⓔ	51 Ⓐ Ⓑ Ⓒ Ⓓ Ⓔ	71 Ⓐ Ⓑ Ⓒ Ⓓ Ⓔ	91 Ⓐ Ⓑ Ⓒ Ⓓ Ⓔ	111 Ⓐ Ⓑ Ⓒ Ⓓ Ⓔ
12 Ⓐ Ⓑ Ⓒ Ⓓ Ⓔ	32 Ⓐ Ⓑ Ⓒ Ⓓ Ⓔ	52 Ⓐ Ⓑ Ⓒ Ⓓ Ⓔ	72 Ⓐ Ⓑ Ⓒ Ⓓ Ⓔ	92 Ⓐ Ⓑ Ⓒ Ⓓ Ⓔ	112 Ⓐ Ⓑ Ⓒ Ⓓ Ⓔ
13 Ⓐ Ⓑ Ⓒ Ⓓ Ⓔ	33 Ⓐ Ⓑ Ⓒ Ⓓ Ⓔ	53 Ⓐ Ⓑ Ⓒ Ⓓ Ⓔ	73 Ⓐ Ⓑ Ⓒ Ⓓ Ⓔ	93 Ⓐ Ⓑ Ⓒ Ⓓ Ⓔ	113 Ⓐ Ⓑ Ⓒ Ⓓ Ⓔ
14 Ⓐ Ⓑ Ⓒ Ⓓ Ⓔ	34 Ⓐ Ⓑ Ⓒ Ⓓ Ⓔ	54 Ⓐ Ⓑ Ⓒ Ⓓ Ⓔ	74 Ⓐ Ⓑ Ⓒ Ⓓ Ⓔ	94 Ⓐ Ⓑ Ⓒ Ⓓ Ⓔ	114 Ⓐ Ⓑ Ⓒ Ⓓ Ⓔ
15 Ⓐ Ⓑ Ⓒ Ⓓ Ⓔ	35 Ⓐ Ⓑ Ⓒ Ⓓ Ⓔ	55 Ⓐ Ⓑ Ⓒ Ⓓ Ⓔ	75 Ⓐ Ⓑ Ⓒ Ⓓ Ⓔ	95 Ⓐ Ⓑ Ⓒ Ⓓ Ⓔ	115 Ⓐ Ⓑ Ⓒ Ⓓ Ⓔ
16 Ⓐ Ⓑ Ⓒ Ⓓ Ⓔ	36 Ⓐ Ⓑ Ⓒ Ⓓ Ⓔ	56 Ⓐ Ⓑ Ⓒ Ⓓ Ⓔ	76 Ⓐ Ⓑ Ⓒ Ⓓ Ⓔ	96 Ⓐ Ⓑ Ⓒ Ⓓ Ⓔ	116 Ⓐ Ⓑ Ⓒ Ⓓ Ⓔ
17 Ⓐ Ⓑ Ⓒ Ⓓ Ⓔ	37 Ⓐ Ⓑ Ⓒ Ⓓ Ⓔ	57 Ⓐ Ⓑ Ⓒ Ⓓ Ⓔ	77 Ⓐ Ⓑ Ⓒ Ⓓ Ⓔ	97 Ⓐ Ⓑ Ⓒ Ⓓ Ⓔ	117 Ⓐ Ⓑ Ⓒ Ⓓ Ⓔ
18 Ⓐ Ⓑ Ⓒ Ⓓ Ⓔ	38 Ⓐ Ⓑ Ⓒ Ⓓ Ⓔ	58 Ⓐ Ⓑ Ⓒ Ⓓ Ⓔ	78 Ⓐ Ⓑ Ⓒ Ⓓ Ⓔ	98 Ⓐ Ⓑ Ⓒ Ⓓ Ⓔ	118 Ⓐ Ⓑ Ⓒ Ⓓ Ⓔ
19 Ⓐ Ⓑ Ⓒ Ⓓ Ⓔ	39 Ⓐ Ⓑ Ⓒ Ⓓ Ⓔ	59 Ⓐ Ⓑ Ⓒ Ⓓ Ⓔ	79 Ⓐ Ⓑ Ⓒ Ⓓ Ⓔ	99 Ⓐ Ⓑ Ⓒ Ⓓ Ⓔ	119 Ⓐ Ⓑ Ⓒ Ⓓ Ⓔ
20 Ⓐ Ⓑ Ⓒ Ⓓ Ⓔ	40 Ⓐ Ⓑ Ⓒ Ⓓ Ⓔ	60 Ⓐ Ⓑ Ⓒ Ⓓ Ⓔ	80 Ⓐ Ⓑ Ⓒ Ⓓ Ⓔ	100 Ⓐ Ⓑ Ⓒ Ⓓ Ⓔ	120 Ⓐ Ⓑ Ⓒ Ⓓ Ⓔ

NCS Trans Optic 10 9196 321

BOARD OF REGISTRY
founded in 1928 by the
American Society of Clinical Pathologists

Representatives from:

American Society of Clinical Pathologists
Medical Technologists/Technicians
Pathologists
American Academy of Microbiology
American Association of Blood Banks
American Society of Cytology
National Registry in Clinical Chemistry
American Society of Hematology
National Society for Histotechnology

IMPORTANT DIRECTIONS
FOR MARKING ANSWERS

- Use black lead pencil only (No. 2½ or softer).
- Do NOT use ink, felt tip or ballpoint pens.
- Erase cleanly any answer you wish to change.
- Make no stray marks on the answer sheet.
- Make heavy black marks that fill the circle completely.

EXAMPLES

1 Ⓧ Ⓑ Ⓒ Ⓓ Ⓔ   WRONG: Fill in the circle completely.

2 Ⓐ Ⓕ Ⓒ Ⓓ Ⓔ

3 Ⓐ Ⓑ Ⓓ Ⓔ

4 Ⓐ Ⓑ Ⓒ Ⓔ   WRONG: Make heavy black marks.

5 Ⓐ Ⓑ Ⓒ ● Ⓔ   RIGHT: Make heavy black marks that fill in the circle completely.

121 Ⓐ Ⓑ Ⓒ Ⓓ Ⓔ	141 Ⓐ Ⓑ Ⓒ Ⓓ Ⓔ	161 Ⓐ Ⓑ Ⓒ Ⓓ Ⓔ
122 Ⓐ Ⓑ Ⓒ Ⓓ Ⓔ	142 Ⓐ Ⓑ Ⓒ Ⓓ Ⓔ	162 Ⓐ Ⓑ Ⓒ Ⓓ Ⓔ
123 Ⓐ Ⓑ Ⓒ Ⓓ Ⓔ	143 Ⓐ Ⓑ Ⓒ Ⓓ Ⓔ	163 Ⓐ Ⓑ Ⓒ Ⓓ Ⓔ
124 Ⓐ Ⓑ Ⓒ Ⓓ Ⓔ	144 Ⓐ Ⓑ Ⓒ Ⓓ Ⓔ	164 Ⓐ Ⓑ Ⓒ Ⓓ Ⓔ
125 Ⓐ Ⓑ Ⓒ Ⓓ Ⓔ	145 Ⓐ Ⓑ Ⓒ Ⓓ Ⓔ	165 Ⓐ Ⓑ Ⓒ Ⓓ Ⓔ
126 Ⓐ Ⓑ Ⓒ Ⓓ Ⓔ	146 Ⓐ Ⓑ Ⓒ Ⓓ Ⓔ	166 Ⓐ Ⓑ Ⓒ Ⓓ Ⓔ
127 Ⓐ Ⓑ Ⓒ Ⓓ Ⓔ	147 Ⓐ Ⓑ Ⓒ Ⓓ Ⓔ	167 Ⓐ Ⓑ Ⓒ Ⓓ Ⓔ
128 Ⓐ Ⓑ Ⓒ Ⓓ Ⓔ	148 Ⓐ Ⓑ Ⓒ Ⓓ Ⓔ	168 Ⓐ Ⓑ Ⓒ Ⓓ Ⓔ
129 Ⓐ Ⓑ Ⓒ Ⓓ Ⓔ	149 Ⓐ Ⓑ Ⓒ Ⓓ Ⓔ	169 Ⓐ Ⓑ Ⓒ Ⓓ Ⓔ
130 Ⓐ Ⓑ Ⓒ Ⓓ Ⓔ	150 Ⓐ Ⓑ Ⓒ Ⓓ Ⓔ	170 Ⓐ Ⓑ Ⓒ Ⓓ Ⓔ
131 Ⓐ Ⓑ Ⓒ Ⓓ Ⓔ	151 Ⓐ Ⓑ Ⓒ Ⓓ Ⓔ	171 Ⓐ Ⓑ Ⓒ Ⓓ Ⓔ
132 Ⓐ Ⓑ Ⓒ Ⓓ Ⓔ	152 Ⓐ Ⓑ Ⓒ Ⓓ Ⓔ	172 Ⓐ Ⓑ Ⓒ Ⓓ Ⓔ
133 Ⓐ Ⓑ Ⓒ Ⓓ Ⓔ	153 Ⓐ Ⓑ Ⓒ Ⓓ Ⓔ	173 Ⓐ Ⓑ Ⓒ Ⓓ Ⓔ
134 Ⓐ Ⓑ Ⓒ Ⓓ Ⓔ	154 Ⓐ Ⓑ Ⓒ Ⓓ Ⓔ	174 Ⓐ Ⓑ Ⓒ Ⓓ Ⓔ
135 Ⓐ Ⓑ Ⓒ Ⓓ Ⓔ	155 Ⓐ Ⓑ Ⓒ Ⓓ Ⓔ	175 Ⓐ Ⓑ Ⓒ Ⓓ Ⓔ
136 Ⓐ Ⓑ Ⓒ Ⓓ Ⓔ	156 Ⓐ Ⓑ Ⓒ Ⓓ Ⓔ	176 Ⓐ Ⓑ Ⓒ Ⓓ Ⓔ
137 Ⓐ Ⓑ Ⓒ Ⓓ Ⓔ	157 Ⓐ Ⓑ Ⓒ Ⓓ Ⓔ	177 Ⓐ Ⓑ Ⓒ Ⓓ Ⓔ
138 Ⓐ Ⓑ Ⓒ Ⓓ Ⓔ	158 Ⓐ Ⓑ Ⓒ Ⓓ Ⓔ	178 Ⓐ Ⓑ Ⓒ Ⓓ Ⓔ
139 Ⓐ Ⓑ Ⓒ Ⓓ Ⓔ	159 Ⓐ Ⓑ Ⓒ Ⓓ Ⓔ	179 Ⓐ Ⓑ Ⓒ Ⓓ Ⓔ
140 Ⓐ Ⓑ Ⓒ Ⓓ Ⓔ	160 Ⓐ Ⓑ Ⓒ Ⓓ Ⓔ	180 Ⓐ Ⓑ Ⓒ Ⓓ Ⓔ
181 Ⓐ Ⓑ Ⓒ Ⓓ Ⓔ	201 Ⓐ Ⓑ Ⓒ Ⓓ Ⓔ	221 Ⓐ Ⓑ Ⓒ Ⓓ Ⓔ
182 Ⓐ Ⓑ Ⓒ Ⓓ Ⓔ	202 Ⓐ Ⓑ Ⓒ Ⓓ Ⓔ	222 Ⓐ Ⓑ Ⓒ Ⓓ Ⓔ
183 Ⓐ Ⓑ Ⓒ Ⓓ Ⓔ	203 Ⓐ Ⓑ Ⓒ Ⓓ Ⓔ	223 Ⓐ Ⓑ Ⓒ Ⓓ Ⓔ
184 Ⓐ Ⓑ Ⓒ Ⓓ Ⓔ	204 Ⓐ Ⓑ Ⓒ Ⓓ Ⓔ	224 Ⓐ Ⓑ Ⓒ Ⓓ Ⓔ
185 Ⓐ Ⓑ Ⓒ Ⓓ Ⓔ	205 Ⓐ Ⓑ Ⓒ Ⓓ Ⓔ	225 Ⓐ Ⓑ Ⓒ Ⓓ Ⓔ
186 Ⓐ Ⓑ Ⓒ Ⓓ Ⓔ	206 Ⓐ Ⓑ Ⓒ Ⓓ Ⓔ	226 Ⓐ Ⓑ Ⓒ Ⓓ Ⓔ
187 Ⓐ Ⓑ Ⓒ Ⓓ Ⓔ	207 Ⓐ Ⓑ Ⓒ Ⓓ Ⓔ	227 Ⓐ Ⓑ Ⓒ Ⓓ Ⓔ
188 Ⓐ Ⓑ Ⓒ Ⓓ Ⓔ	208 Ⓐ Ⓑ Ⓒ Ⓓ Ⓔ	228 Ⓐ Ⓑ Ⓒ Ⓓ Ⓔ
189 Ⓐ Ⓑ Ⓒ Ⓓ Ⓔ	209 Ⓐ Ⓑ Ⓒ Ⓓ Ⓔ	229 Ⓐ Ⓑ Ⓒ Ⓓ Ⓔ
190 Ⓐ Ⓑ Ⓒ Ⓓ Ⓔ	210 Ⓐ Ⓑ Ⓒ Ⓓ Ⓔ	230 Ⓐ Ⓑ Ⓒ Ⓓ Ⓔ
191 Ⓐ Ⓑ Ⓒ Ⓓ Ⓔ	211 Ⓐ Ⓑ Ⓒ Ⓓ Ⓔ	231 Ⓐ Ⓑ Ⓒ Ⓓ Ⓔ
192 Ⓐ Ⓑ Ⓒ Ⓓ Ⓔ	212 Ⓐ Ⓑ Ⓒ Ⓓ Ⓔ	232 Ⓐ Ⓑ Ⓒ Ⓓ Ⓔ
193 Ⓐ Ⓑ Ⓒ Ⓓ Ⓔ	213 Ⓐ Ⓑ Ⓒ Ⓓ Ⓔ	233 Ⓐ Ⓑ Ⓒ Ⓓ Ⓔ
194 Ⓐ Ⓑ Ⓒ Ⓓ Ⓔ	214 Ⓐ Ⓑ Ⓒ Ⓓ Ⓔ	234 Ⓐ Ⓑ Ⓒ Ⓓ Ⓔ
195 Ⓐ Ⓑ Ⓒ Ⓓ Ⓔ	215 Ⓐ Ⓑ Ⓒ Ⓓ Ⓔ	235 Ⓐ Ⓑ Ⓒ Ⓓ Ⓔ
196 Ⓐ Ⓑ Ⓒ Ⓓ Ⓔ	216 Ⓐ Ⓑ Ⓒ Ⓓ Ⓔ	236 Ⓐ Ⓑ Ⓒ Ⓓ Ⓔ
197 Ⓐ Ⓑ Ⓒ Ⓓ Ⓔ	217 Ⓐ Ⓑ Ⓒ Ⓓ Ⓔ	237 Ⓐ Ⓑ Ⓒ Ⓓ Ⓔ
198 Ⓐ Ⓑ Ⓒ Ⓓ Ⓔ	218 Ⓐ Ⓑ Ⓒ Ⓓ Ⓔ	238 Ⓐ Ⓑ Ⓒ Ⓓ Ⓔ
199 Ⓐ Ⓑ Ⓒ Ⓓ Ⓔ	219 Ⓐ Ⓑ Ⓒ Ⓓ Ⓔ	239 Ⓐ Ⓑ Ⓒ Ⓓ Ⓔ
200 Ⓐ Ⓑ Ⓒ Ⓓ Ⓔ	220 Ⓐ Ⓑ Ⓒ Ⓓ Ⓔ	240 Ⓐ Ⓑ Ⓒ Ⓓ Ⓔ

MT Written Practice Examination

FOR EACH QUESTION, CHOOSE THE ONE ANSWER THAT IS MOST CORRECT. MARK YOUR ANSWER ON YOUR ANSWER SHEET IN THE APPROPRIATE SPACE. ANSWERS WRITTEN IN THE EXAMINATION BOOKLET WILL NOT BE SCORED.

1. Which of the following red cell typings would most commonly be found in the Black donor population?

    a. Lu(a-b-)
    b. Jk(a-b-)
    c. Fy(a-b-)
    d. K-k-

2. Which of the following procedure(s) must be performed prior to the transfusion of Granulocytes?

    a. direct antiglobulin test on patient's RBCs
    b. HLA matching of donor and recipient
    c. a complete red cell phenotype on the recipient
    d. major crossmatch if product contains more than 5 mL of RBCs

3. The following results were obtained when testing a sample from a 20-year-old, first-time blood donor. What is the most likely cause of this ABO discrepancy?

Forward Group		Reverse Group	
Anti-A	Anti-B	A_1 Cells	B Cells
neg	neg	neg	3+

    a. loss of antigen due to disease
    b. acquired B
    c. phenotype O_h "Bombay"
    d. weak subgroup of A

4. Individuals at risk of developing graft-versus-host disease include patients:

    a. with congenital immune deficiency disease
    b. having a history of febrile transfusion reactions
    c. with a positive direct Coombs test due to drugs
    d. receiving blood products from immediate family members

5. Refer to the following panel:

Cell	D	C	E	c	e	M	N	S	s	Le^a	Le^b	P_1	K	k	Fy^a	Fy^b	Jk^a	Jk^b	Serum Alb IS	37 C	AHG
1	0	+	0	+	+	+	0	0	+	0	+	0	0	+	0	+	0	+	0	0	0
2	+	+	0	0	+	0	+	0	+	+	0	+	0	+	+	0	0	+	0	0	2+
3	+	+	0	0	+	+	+	+	+	0	+	+	+	0	+	+	+	+	0	0	3+
4	+	+	+	+	0	0	+	+	0	0	+	+	0	+	0	+	0	+	0	1+	4+
5	0	0	+	+	+	0	+	0	+	0	+	+	0	+	+	+	+	+	0	1+	4+
6	0	0	0	+	+	+	0	0	+	0	0	+	0	+	0	0	+	0	0	0	0
7	0	0	0	+	+	0	+	0	+	0	+	+	+	+	0	+	0	+	0	0	2+
8	0	0	0	+	+	+	0	+	0	+	0	+	0	+	0	+	+	0	0	0	0
9	0	0	0	+	+	+	0	+	0	0	+	+	+	+	+	0	+	+	0	0	3+
10	+	+	+	0	+	+	0	+	0	+	0	0	0	+	+	0	+	0	0	1+	4+
Autocontrol																			0	0	0

Based on the results of the above panel, the most likely antibodies are:

    a. anti-M and anti-K
    b. anti-E, anti-Fy^a and anti-K
    c. anti-Fy^a and anti-M
    d. anti-E and anti-Le^b

---

6. A patient is group O, Rh-negative with anti-D and anti-K in her serum. What percentage of the general Caucasian donor population would be compatible with this patient?

    a. 0.5%
    b. 2.0%
    c. 3.0%
    d. 6.0%

7. A unit of very rare red cells has been deglycerolized for ten hours. The patient's condition has stabilized and transfusion of these cells is no longer necessary. Which of the following is the most appropriate course of action?

    a. Urge the attending physician to transfuse the patient due to the value of the rare cells.
    b. Discard the unit.
    c. Extend the expiration time and date an additional 24 hours.
    d. Document the value of the rare cells and refreeze before 20 hours have elapsed.

8. A poor increment in the platelet count one hour following platelet transfusion is most commonly caused by:

    a. fever
    b. splenomegaly
    c. alloimmunization to HLA antigens
    d. disseminated intravascular coagulation
    e. defective platelets

9. The phenomenon of an Rh-positive person whose serum contains anti-D is best explained by antigen:

    a. deletion
    b. mosaicism
    c. suppression
    d. inhibition

10. A mother types as Rh-positive and her serum contains anti-c (titer of 32 at AHG). Her baby has a negative DAT and is not affected by hemolytic disease of the newborn. What is the father's most likely Rh phenotype?

    a. rr
    b. $r''r$
    c. R_1r
    d. R_2r

11. Which of the following can cause the kidney to be unable to concentrate and/or dilute urine?

    a. radiographic dyes
    b. exercise
    c. diabetes mellitus
    d. hormone deficiency

12. In synovial fluid, the most characteristic microscopic finding in osteoarthritis is:

    a. neutrophils with 0.5 - 1.5 micron inclusions
    b. cartilage debris
    c. monosodium urate crystals
    d. hemosiderin-laden macrophages

13. In which of the following metabolic diseases will urine turn dark brown to black upon standing?

    a. phenylketonuria
    b. alkaptonuria
    c. maple syrup disease
    d. aminoaciduria

14. A four-year-old girl has edema that is most obvious in her eyelids. Laboratory studies reveal:

    Serum albumin   1.8 g/dL
    Serum cholesterol   450 mg/dL
    Serum urea nitrogen   20 mg/dL
    Urinalysis   Protein 4+; hyaline, granular
                             and fatty casts

    This is most compatible with:

    a. acute poststreptococcal glomerulonephritis
    b. minimal change glomerular disease
    c. acute pyelonephritis
    d. diabetes mellitus

15. A component seen during a microscopic urinalysis stains positively with Sudan III stain but does not polarize. This most likely is a:

    a. cholesterol ester
    b. neutral fat
    c. lipid
    d. leucine

16. Bilirubin, when dissolved in chloroform at 25°C, should have a molar absorptivity of 60,700 at 453 nm. What is the molar concentration of a solution of bilirubin which has an absorbance of 0.500 when measured in a 1 cm cuvette at 25°C and 453 nm?

    a. 3.035×10^4
    b. 1.214×10^5
    c. 8.237×10^{-6}
    d. 6.750×10^{-4}

17. A patient with malabsorption receives 25 g of d-xylose orally. During the subsequent five-hour period, the urine excretion of d-xylose is less than 3 g. This would indicate:

    a. pancreatic malabsorption
    b. chronic pancreatitis
    c. intestinal malabsorption
    d. absence of disease

18. Refer to the following data:

	Patient Values	Reference Range
Total Protein	7.3 g/dL	6.0-8.0 g/dL
Albumin	4.1 g/dL	3.5-5.0 g/dL
Calcium	9.6 mg/dL	8.5-10.5 mg/dL
Phosphorus	3.3 mg/dL	2.5-4.5 mg/dL
Glucose	95 mg/dL	65-110 mg/dL
BUN	16 mg/dL	10-20 mg/dL
Uric acid	6.0 mg/dL	2.5-8.0 mg/dL
Creatinine	1.2 mg/dL	0.7-1.4 mg/dL
Total Bilirubin	3.7 mg/dL	0.2-0.9 mg/dL
Alkaline phosphatase	275 U/L	30-80 U/L
Lactate dehydrogenase	185 U/L	100-225 U/L
AST	75 U/L	10-40 U/L

The above lab results are most consistent with:

    a. viral hepatitis
    b. hemolytic anemia
    c. common bile duct stone
    d. chronic active hepatitis

19. A 1-year-old girl with hyperlipoproteinemia and lipase deficiency has the following lipid profile:

Cholesterol	300 mg/dL	LDL	increased
Triglycerides	200 mg/dL	HDL	decreased
Chylomicrons	present		

A serum specimen from this patient that was refrigerated overnight would most likely be:

    a. clear
    b. cloudy
    c. creamy layer over cloudy serum
    d. creamy layer over clear serum

20. Which of the following serum proteins migrate in the beta-globulins on cellulose acetate at pH 8.6?

    a. ceruloplasmin
    b. hemoglobin
    c. haptoglobin
    d. C3 component of complement

21. The following laboratory results were obtained:

	Calcium	Phosphate	Alkaline Phosphatase
Serum	increased	decreased	normal or increased
Urine	increased	increased	

    These results are most compatible with:

    a. multiple myeloma
    b. milk-alkali syndrome
    c. sarcoidosis
    d. primary hyperparathyroidism

22. A patient in her 33rd week of pregnancy is hospitalized with toxemia. Her doctor would like to deliver the baby early because the toxemia is becoming more severe. The baby's best chance of delivery without respiratory distress due to lung immaturity is if:

    a. the L/S ratio is greater than 3.5
    b. the L/S ratio is greater than 2.5
    c. PG is absent
    d. creatinine is 1.3 mg/dL

23. The thyrotropin-releasing hormone (TRH) stimulation test rules out the diagnosis of mild or subclinical hyperthyroidism if TRH infusion causes:

    a. a rise in plasma TSH
    b. no rise in plasma TSH
    c. a rise in plasma growth hormone concentration
    d. no rise in plasma growth hormone concentration

24. Testing for the diagnosis of lead poisoning should include:

    a. ion-exchange analysis of urine for porphobilinogen
    b. analysis of morning urine for delta-aminolevulinic acid
    c. analysis of feces for porphyrin
    d. ion-exchange analysis of feces for protoporphyrin

25. The osmolal gap is defined as measured Osm/kg minus the calculated Osm/kg. The average osmolal gap is near:

   a. 0
   b. 2
   c. 4
   d. 6

26. In general, 60-70% of the operating expenses of laboratories are:

   a. labor or labor related
   b. reagents and supplies
   c. equipment replacement and maintenance
   d. safety supplies and disposables

27. A patient is admitted with a history of chronic bleeding secondary to peptic ulcer. Hematology workup reveals a severe microcytic, hypochromic anemia. Iron studies were requested. Which of the following would be expected in this case?

   a. decreased serum iron, increased TIBC, increased storage iron
   b. increased serum iron, decreased TIBC, increased storage iron
   c. decreased serum iron, increased TIBC, decreased storage iron
   d. increased serum iron, normal TIBC, decreased storage iron

28. In which of the following disease states are macrocytes and abnormal platelets most characteristically seen?

   a. chronic myelocytic leukemia
   b. multiple myeloma
   c. thalassemia
   d. myeloid metaplasia

29. Biochemical abnormalities characteristic of polycythemia vera include:

   a. increased serum B_{12} binding capacity
   b. hypouricemia
   c. hypohistaminemia
   d. decreased leukocyte alkaline phosphatase activity

30. A 60-year-old man has a painful right knee and a slightly enlarged spleen. Hematology results include:

Hemoglobin	15 g/dL
Absolute neutrophil count	10.0 x 10^3/µL (10.0 x 10^9/L)
Platelet count	900 x 10^3/µL (900 x 10^9/L)
Reticulocyte count	1%

-red cell morphology and indices were normal
-a slight increase in bands
-rare metamyelocyte and myelocyte
-giant and bizarre shaped platelets

This is most compatible with:

a. congenital spherocytosis
b. rheumatoid arthritis with reactive thrombocytosis
c. myelofibrosis
d. idiopathic thrombocythemia

31. Of the following, the disease most closely associated with pale blue inclusions in granulocytes and giant platelets is:

a. Gaucher's disease
b. Alder-Reilly anomaly
c. May-Hegglin anomaly
d. Pelger-Huĕt anomaly

32. A blood specimen is collected in a tube anticoagulated with EDTA, and an electronic cell counter gives a platelet count of 20 x 10^3/µL. Examination of a peripheral blood smear reveals that almost all of the platelets are found encircling neutrophils. The best course of action would be to:

a. collect another specimen in a different EDTA tube and report the platelet count
b. collect another specimen by direct finger puncture dilution and repeat the platelet count
c. report the platelet count as accurate
d. repeat the platelet count on the original specimen

33. Factor VIII activity following cryoprecipitate therapy of patients with von Willebrand's disease is best described by which of the following statements?

a. The activity is higher than would be predicted.
b. An immediate response is seen.
c. The activity disappears quickly.
d. The pattern is similar to that seen in hemophiliacs.

34. Which of the following is true of acute lymphoblastic leukemia (ALL)?

    a. occurs most commonly in children 1-2 years of age
    b. patient is asymptomatic
    c. massive accumulation of primitive lymphoid-appearing cells in bone marrow occurs
    d. children under 1 year of age have a good prognosis

35. A properly functioning electronic cell counter obtains the following results:

    WBC $5.1 \times 10^3/\mu L$ ($5.1 \times 10^9/L$)
    RBC $4.87 \times 10^6/\mu L$ ($4.87 \times 10^{12}/L$)
    HGB   16.1 g/dL
    HCT   39.3%
    MCV   82.0 fL
    MCH   33.1 pg
    MCHC 41.3 g/dL

    What is the most likely cause of these results?

    a. lipemia
    b. cold agglutinins
    c. increased WBC
    d. rouleaux

36. Which of the following findings is associated with a hereditary deficiency of C3?

    a. pneumococcal septicemia
    b. small bowel obstruction
    c. systemic lupus erythematosus
    d. gonococcemia

37. A 28-year-old man is seen by a physician because of several months of intermittent low back pain. The patient's symptoms are suggestive of ankylosing spondylitis. Which of the following laboratory studies would support this diagnosis?

    a. a decreased synovial fluid CH_{50} level
    b. low serum CH_{50} level
    c. positive HLA-B27 antigen test
    d. rheumatoid factor in the synovial fluid

38. Which of the following cells respond best to concanavalin A?

    a. T lymphocytes
    b. B lymphocytes
    c. macrophages
    d. eosinophils

39. Reaginic sensitivity is most commonly associated with:

    a. transfusion reaction
    b. anaphylactic reaction
    c. contact sensitivity to inorganic chemicals
    d. bacterial septicemia

40. A patient has the following test results:

    ANA - positive, 1:320   Complement - decreased
    ASO - 50 Todd units   RA - positive

    The above results would be seen in patients with:

    a. rheumatic fever
    b. rheumatoid arthritis
    c. lupus erythematosus
    d. glomerulonephritis

41. Legal pre-employment questions on an application are:

    a. medical history of an employee
    b. place of birth
    c. convictions unrelated to job requirements
    d. name and address of person to notify in case of emergency

42. A Gram stain of vaginal discharge reveals many squamous epithelial cells covered with gram-variable bacilli. After isolation of this organism on selective agar, which of the following tests should the technologist perform?

    a. alpha-glucosidase and starch hydrolysis
    b. penicillinase and bile esculin hydrolysis
    c. catalase and bile solubility
    d. oxidase and motility

43. A urine culture from a patient with a urinary tract infection yields a yeast with the following characteristics:

    - failure to produce germ tubes
    - hyphae not formed on cornmeal agar
    - urease-negative
    - assimilates trehalose

    The most likely identification is:

    a. *Saccharomyces cerevisiae*
    b. *Cryptococcus laurentii*
    c. *Candida pseudotropicalis*
    d. *Candida (Torulopsis) glabrata*

44. In cases of suspected infection with *Pneumocystis carinii*, the preferred specimen for a methenamine silver stain is:

    a. lung biopsy
    b. sputum
    c. bronchial brushings
    d. tracheobronchial aspirate

45. A culture from an infected dog bite yields a gram-negative, bipolar-staining bacillus. The organism is cytochrome oxidase and indole test positive. The most likely identification of this isolate is:

    a. *Aeromonas hydrophila*
    b. *Pasteurella haemolytica*
    c. *Pasteurella multocida*
    d. *Vibrio parahaemolyticus*

46. The agent used for processing specimens for mycobacterial culture contaminated with *Pseudomonas* is:

    a. N-acetyl-L-cystine and NaOH
    b. NaOH alone
    c. zephiran-trisodium phosphate
    d. oxalic acid

47. An unusual number of methicillin-resistant *Staphylococcus aureus* (determined by the Bauer-Kirby method) were isolated in the laboratory in the past month. Which of the following is the most likely explanation?

    a. incubation of the susceptibility plates at 35°C
    b. deterioration of the methicillin discs
    c. inoculation of plates 10 minutes after standardizing the inoculum
    d. standardization of the inoculum to a 0.5 McFarland turbidity standard

48. A jaundiced seven-year-old boy, with a history of playing in a pond in a rat-infested area, has a urine specimen submitted for a direct dark-field examination. No organisms are seen in the specimen. Which medium should be inoculated in an attempt to isolate the suspected organism?

    a. blood cysteine dextrose
    b. PPLO agar
    c. Fletcher's semisolid
    d. chopped meat glucose

49. The most appropriate clinical test for diagnosing *Clostridium difficile* is:

    a. tissue culture toxin assay
    b. gas-liquid chromatography
    c. routine fecal cultures
    d. anaerobic culture techniques

50. A 10-year-old boy was admitted to the emergency room with lower right quadrant pain and tenderness. The following laboratory results were obtained:

	Patient	Range
% Segmented Neutrophils	75	16-60
WBC count:	$200 \times 10^3/\mu L$	$4.0 \times 10^3 - 13.0 \times 10^3/\mu L$

The admitting diagnosis was appendicitis. During surgery the appendix appeared normal; an enlarged node was removed and cultured. Small gram-negative rods were isolated from the room temperature plate. The organism most likely is:

    a. *Bacteroides melaninogenicus*
    b. *Shigella sonnei*
    c. *Listeria monocytogenes*
    d. *Yersinia enterocolitica*

END OF MT PRACTICE EXAMINATION

MT Practice Examination Answer Key

1.	C	14.	B	27.	C	40.	C
2.	D	15.	B	28.	D	41.	D
3.	D	16.	C	29.	A	42.	A
4.	B	17.	C	30.	D	43.	D
5.	B	18.	C	31.	C	44.	A
6.	D	19.	D	32.	B	45.	C
7.	D	20.	D	33.	A	46.	D
8.	C	21.	D	34.	C	47.	B
9.	B	22.	A	35.	A	48.	C
10.	A	23.	A	36.	A	49.	A
11.	D	24.	B	37.	C	50.	D
12.	B	25.	A	38.	A		
13.	B	26.	A	39.	B		

BOARD OF REGISTRY

NAME: _____

EXAM TYPE: _____

DATE: _____

IDENTIFICATION NUMBER | **EXAM TYPE**

TEST BOOKLET NUMBER

IMPORTANT DIRECTIONS FOR MARKING ANSWERS

- Use black lead pencil only (No. 2½ or softer).
- Do NOT use ink, felt tip or ballpoint pens.
- Erase cleanly any answer you wish to change.
- Make no stray marks on the answer sheet.
- Make heavy black marks that fill the circle completely.

EXAMPLES

WRONG: Fill in the circle completely.

1 Ⓧ Ⓑ Ⓒ Ⓓ Ⓔ

2 Ⓐ Ⓒ Ⓓ Ⓔ

3 Ⓐ Ⓑ Ⓓ Ⓔ

WRONG: Make heavy black marks.

4 Ⓐ Ⓒ Ⓓ Ⓔ

RIGHT: Make heavy black marks that fill in the circle completely.

5 Ⓐ Ⓑ ● Ⓓ Ⓔ

BOARD OF REGISTRY
founded in 1928 by the
American Society of Clinical Pathologists

■ Representatives from:

American Society of Clinical Pathologists
Medical Technologists/Technicians
Pathologists
American Academy of Microbiology
■ American Association of Blood Banks
American Society of Cytology
National Registry in Clinical Chemistry
American Society of Hematology
■ National Society for Histotechnology

IMPORTANT DIRECTIONS
FOR MARKING ANSWERS

- Use black lead pencil only (No. 2½ or softer).
- Do NOT use ink, felt tip or ballpoint pens.
- Erase cleanly any answer you wish to change.
- Make no stray marks on the answer sheet.
- Make heavy black marks that fill the circle completely.

EXAMPLES

1 Ⓐ Ⓑ Ⓒ Ⓓ Ⓔ   WRONG: Fill in the circle completely.
2 Ⓐ Ⓑ Ⓒ Ⓓ Ⓔ
3 Ⓐ Ⓑ Ⓒ Ⓓ Ⓔ
4 Ⓐ Ⓑ Ⓒ Ⓓ Ⓔ   WRONG: Make heavy black marks.
5 Ⓐ Ⓑ ● Ⓓ Ⓔ   RIGHT: Make heavy black marks that fill in the circle completely.

121 Ⓐ Ⓑ Ⓒ Ⓓ Ⓔ	141 Ⓐ Ⓑ Ⓒ Ⓓ Ⓔ	161 Ⓐ Ⓑ Ⓒ Ⓓ Ⓔ	181 Ⓐ Ⓑ Ⓒ Ⓓ Ⓔ
122 Ⓐ Ⓑ Ⓒ Ⓓ Ⓔ	142 Ⓐ Ⓑ Ⓒ Ⓓ Ⓔ	162 Ⓐ Ⓑ Ⓒ Ⓓ Ⓔ	182 Ⓐ Ⓑ Ⓒ Ⓓ Ⓔ
123 Ⓐ Ⓑ Ⓒ Ⓓ Ⓔ	143 Ⓐ Ⓑ Ⓒ Ⓓ Ⓔ	163 Ⓐ Ⓑ Ⓒ Ⓓ Ⓔ	183 Ⓐ Ⓑ Ⓒ Ⓓ Ⓔ
124 Ⓐ Ⓑ Ⓒ Ⓓ Ⓔ	144 Ⓐ Ⓑ Ⓒ Ⓓ Ⓔ	164 Ⓐ Ⓑ Ⓒ Ⓓ Ⓔ	184 Ⓐ Ⓑ Ⓒ Ⓓ Ⓔ
125 Ⓐ Ⓑ Ⓒ Ⓓ Ⓔ	145 Ⓐ Ⓑ Ⓒ Ⓓ Ⓔ	165 Ⓐ Ⓑ Ⓒ Ⓓ Ⓔ	185 Ⓐ Ⓑ Ⓒ Ⓓ Ⓔ
126 Ⓐ Ⓑ Ⓒ Ⓓ Ⓔ	146 Ⓐ Ⓑ Ⓒ Ⓓ Ⓔ	166 Ⓐ Ⓑ Ⓒ Ⓓ Ⓔ	186 Ⓐ Ⓑ Ⓒ Ⓓ Ⓔ
127 Ⓐ Ⓑ Ⓒ Ⓓ Ⓔ	147 Ⓐ Ⓑ Ⓒ Ⓓ Ⓔ	167 Ⓐ Ⓑ Ⓒ Ⓓ Ⓔ	187 Ⓐ Ⓑ Ⓒ Ⓓ Ⓔ
128 Ⓐ Ⓑ Ⓒ Ⓓ Ⓔ	148 Ⓐ Ⓑ Ⓒ Ⓓ Ⓔ	168 Ⓐ Ⓑ Ⓒ Ⓓ Ⓔ	188 Ⓐ Ⓑ Ⓒ Ⓓ Ⓔ
129 Ⓐ Ⓑ Ⓒ Ⓓ Ⓔ	149 Ⓐ Ⓑ Ⓒ Ⓓ Ⓔ	169 Ⓐ Ⓑ Ⓒ Ⓓ Ⓔ	189 Ⓐ Ⓑ Ⓒ Ⓓ Ⓔ
130 Ⓐ Ⓑ Ⓒ Ⓓ Ⓔ	150 Ⓐ Ⓑ Ⓒ Ⓓ Ⓔ	170 Ⓐ Ⓑ Ⓒ Ⓓ Ⓔ	190 Ⓐ Ⓑ Ⓒ Ⓓ Ⓔ
131 Ⓐ Ⓑ Ⓒ Ⓓ Ⓔ	151 Ⓐ Ⓑ Ⓒ Ⓓ Ⓔ	171 Ⓐ Ⓑ Ⓒ Ⓓ Ⓔ	191 Ⓐ Ⓑ Ⓒ Ⓓ Ⓔ
132 Ⓐ Ⓑ Ⓒ Ⓓ Ⓔ	152 Ⓐ Ⓑ Ⓒ Ⓓ Ⓔ	172 Ⓐ Ⓑ Ⓒ Ⓓ Ⓔ	192 Ⓐ Ⓑ Ⓒ Ⓓ Ⓔ
133 Ⓐ Ⓑ Ⓒ Ⓓ Ⓔ	153 Ⓐ Ⓑ Ⓒ Ⓓ Ⓔ	173 Ⓐ Ⓑ Ⓒ Ⓓ Ⓔ	193 Ⓐ Ⓑ Ⓒ Ⓓ Ⓔ
134 Ⓐ Ⓑ Ⓒ Ⓓ Ⓔ	154 Ⓐ Ⓑ Ⓒ Ⓓ Ⓔ	174 Ⓐ Ⓑ Ⓒ Ⓓ Ⓔ	194 Ⓐ Ⓑ Ⓒ Ⓓ Ⓔ
135 Ⓐ Ⓑ Ⓒ Ⓓ Ⓔ	155 Ⓐ Ⓑ Ⓒ Ⓓ Ⓔ	175 Ⓐ Ⓑ Ⓒ Ⓓ Ⓔ	195 Ⓐ Ⓑ Ⓒ Ⓓ Ⓔ
136 Ⓐ Ⓑ Ⓒ Ⓓ Ⓔ	156 Ⓐ Ⓑ Ⓒ Ⓓ Ⓔ	176 Ⓐ Ⓑ Ⓒ Ⓓ Ⓔ	196 Ⓐ Ⓑ Ⓒ Ⓓ Ⓔ
137 Ⓐ Ⓑ Ⓒ Ⓓ Ⓔ	157 Ⓐ Ⓑ Ⓒ Ⓓ Ⓔ	177 Ⓐ Ⓑ Ⓒ Ⓓ Ⓔ	197 Ⓐ Ⓑ Ⓒ Ⓓ Ⓔ
138 Ⓐ Ⓑ Ⓒ Ⓓ Ⓔ	158 Ⓐ Ⓑ Ⓒ Ⓓ Ⓔ	178 Ⓐ Ⓑ Ⓒ Ⓓ Ⓔ	198 Ⓐ Ⓑ Ⓒ Ⓓ Ⓔ
139 Ⓐ Ⓑ Ⓒ Ⓓ Ⓔ	159 Ⓐ Ⓑ Ⓒ Ⓓ Ⓔ	179 Ⓐ Ⓑ Ⓒ Ⓓ Ⓔ	199 Ⓐ Ⓑ Ⓒ Ⓓ Ⓔ
140 Ⓐ Ⓑ Ⓒ Ⓓ Ⓔ	160 Ⓐ Ⓑ Ⓒ Ⓓ Ⓔ	180 Ⓐ Ⓑ Ⓒ Ⓓ Ⓔ	200 Ⓐ Ⓑ Ⓒ Ⓓ Ⓔ
201 Ⓐ Ⓑ Ⓒ Ⓓ Ⓔ			221 Ⓐ Ⓑ Ⓒ Ⓓ Ⓔ
202 Ⓐ Ⓑ Ⓒ Ⓓ Ⓔ			222 Ⓐ Ⓑ Ⓒ Ⓓ Ⓔ
203 Ⓐ Ⓑ Ⓒ Ⓓ Ⓔ			223 Ⓐ Ⓑ Ⓒ Ⓓ Ⓔ
204 Ⓐ Ⓑ Ⓒ Ⓓ Ⓔ			224 Ⓐ Ⓑ Ⓒ Ⓓ Ⓔ
205 Ⓐ Ⓑ Ⓒ Ⓓ Ⓔ			225 Ⓐ Ⓑ Ⓒ Ⓓ Ⓔ
206 Ⓐ Ⓑ Ⓒ Ⓓ Ⓔ			226 Ⓐ Ⓑ Ⓒ Ⓓ Ⓔ
207 Ⓐ Ⓑ Ⓒ Ⓓ Ⓔ			227 Ⓐ Ⓑ Ⓒ Ⓓ Ⓔ
208 Ⓐ Ⓑ Ⓒ Ⓓ Ⓔ			228 Ⓐ Ⓑ Ⓒ Ⓓ Ⓔ
209 Ⓐ Ⓑ Ⓒ Ⓓ Ⓔ			229 Ⓐ Ⓑ Ⓒ Ⓓ Ⓔ
210 Ⓐ Ⓑ Ⓒ Ⓓ Ⓔ			230 Ⓐ Ⓑ Ⓒ Ⓓ Ⓔ
211 Ⓐ Ⓑ Ⓒ Ⓓ Ⓔ			231 Ⓐ Ⓑ Ⓒ Ⓓ Ⓔ
212 Ⓐ Ⓑ Ⓒ Ⓓ Ⓔ			232 Ⓐ Ⓑ Ⓒ Ⓓ Ⓔ
213 Ⓐ Ⓑ Ⓒ Ⓓ Ⓔ			233 Ⓐ Ⓑ Ⓒ Ⓓ Ⓔ
214 Ⓐ Ⓑ Ⓒ Ⓓ Ⓔ			234 Ⓐ Ⓑ Ⓒ Ⓓ Ⓔ
215 Ⓐ Ⓑ Ⓒ Ⓓ Ⓔ			235 Ⓐ Ⓑ Ⓒ Ⓓ Ⓔ
216 Ⓐ Ⓑ Ⓒ Ⓓ Ⓔ			236 Ⓐ Ⓑ Ⓒ Ⓓ Ⓔ
217 Ⓐ Ⓑ Ⓒ Ⓓ Ⓔ			237 Ⓐ Ⓑ Ⓒ Ⓓ Ⓔ
218 Ⓐ Ⓑ Ⓒ Ⓓ Ⓔ			238 Ⓐ Ⓑ Ⓒ Ⓓ Ⓔ
219 Ⓐ Ⓑ Ⓒ Ⓓ Ⓔ			239 Ⓐ Ⓑ Ⓒ Ⓓ Ⓔ
220 Ⓐ Ⓑ Ⓒ Ⓓ Ⓔ			240 Ⓐ Ⓑ Ⓒ Ⓓ Ⓔ

SIDE TWO

BOARD OF REGISTRY

NAME: _____

EXAM TYPE: _____   DATE: _____

IMPORTANT DIRECTIONS FOR MARKING ANSWERS

- Use black lead pencil only (No. 2½ or softer).
- Do NOT use ink, felt tip or ballpoint pens.
- Erase cleanly any answer you wish to change.
- Make no stray marks on the answer sheet.
- Make heavy black marks that fill the circle completely.

EXAMPLES

1 WRONG: Fill in the circle completely.
   ⓧ Ⓑ Ⓒ Ⓓ Ⓔ

2 Ⓐ ⊘ Ⓒ Ⓓ Ⓔ

3 Ⓐ Ⓑ ⊘ Ⓓ Ⓔ

4 WRONG: Make heavy black marks.
   Ⓐ Ⓒ Ⓓ Ⓔ

5 RIGHT: Make heavy black marks that fill in the circle completely.
   Ⓐ Ⓑ Ⓒ Ⓓ ●

1 Ⓐ Ⓑ Ⓒ Ⓓ Ⓔ   21 Ⓐ Ⓑ Ⓒ Ⓓ Ⓔ   41 Ⓐ Ⓑ Ⓒ Ⓓ Ⓔ   61 Ⓐ Ⓑ Ⓒ Ⓓ Ⓔ   81 Ⓐ Ⓑ Ⓒ Ⓓ Ⓔ   101 Ⓐ Ⓑ Ⓒ Ⓓ Ⓔ
2 Ⓐ Ⓑ Ⓒ Ⓓ Ⓔ   22 Ⓐ Ⓑ Ⓒ Ⓓ Ⓔ   42 Ⓐ Ⓑ Ⓒ Ⓓ Ⓔ   62 Ⓐ Ⓑ Ⓒ Ⓓ Ⓔ   82 Ⓐ Ⓑ Ⓒ Ⓓ Ⓔ   102 Ⓐ Ⓑ Ⓒ Ⓓ Ⓔ
3 Ⓐ Ⓑ Ⓒ Ⓓ Ⓔ   23 Ⓐ Ⓑ Ⓒ Ⓓ Ⓔ   43 Ⓐ Ⓑ Ⓒ Ⓓ Ⓔ   63 Ⓐ Ⓑ Ⓒ Ⓓ Ⓔ   83 Ⓐ Ⓑ Ⓒ Ⓓ Ⓔ   103 Ⓐ Ⓑ Ⓒ Ⓓ Ⓔ
4 Ⓐ Ⓑ Ⓒ Ⓓ Ⓔ   24 Ⓐ Ⓑ Ⓒ Ⓓ Ⓔ   44 Ⓐ Ⓑ Ⓒ Ⓓ Ⓔ   64 Ⓐ Ⓑ Ⓒ Ⓓ Ⓔ   84 Ⓐ Ⓑ Ⓒ Ⓓ Ⓔ   104 Ⓐ Ⓑ Ⓒ Ⓓ Ⓔ
5 Ⓐ Ⓑ Ⓒ Ⓓ Ⓔ   25 Ⓐ Ⓑ Ⓒ Ⓓ Ⓔ   45 Ⓐ Ⓑ Ⓒ Ⓓ Ⓔ   65 Ⓐ Ⓑ Ⓒ Ⓓ Ⓔ   85 Ⓐ Ⓑ Ⓒ Ⓓ Ⓔ   105 Ⓐ Ⓑ Ⓒ Ⓓ Ⓔ
6 Ⓐ Ⓑ Ⓒ Ⓓ Ⓔ   26 Ⓐ Ⓑ Ⓒ Ⓓ Ⓔ   46 Ⓐ Ⓑ Ⓒ Ⓓ Ⓔ   66 Ⓐ Ⓑ Ⓒ Ⓓ Ⓔ   86 Ⓐ Ⓑ Ⓒ Ⓓ Ⓔ   106 Ⓐ Ⓑ Ⓒ Ⓓ Ⓔ
7 Ⓐ Ⓑ Ⓒ Ⓓ Ⓔ   27 Ⓐ Ⓑ Ⓒ Ⓓ Ⓔ   47 Ⓐ Ⓑ Ⓒ Ⓓ Ⓔ   67 Ⓐ Ⓑ Ⓒ Ⓓ Ⓔ   87 Ⓐ Ⓑ Ⓒ Ⓓ Ⓔ   107 Ⓐ Ⓑ Ⓒ Ⓓ Ⓔ
8 Ⓐ Ⓑ Ⓒ Ⓓ Ⓔ   28 Ⓐ Ⓑ Ⓒ Ⓓ Ⓔ   48 Ⓐ Ⓑ Ⓒ Ⓓ Ⓔ   68 Ⓐ Ⓑ Ⓒ Ⓓ Ⓔ   88 Ⓐ Ⓑ Ⓒ Ⓓ Ⓔ   108 Ⓐ Ⓑ Ⓒ Ⓓ Ⓔ
9 Ⓐ Ⓑ Ⓒ Ⓓ Ⓔ   29 Ⓐ Ⓑ Ⓒ Ⓓ Ⓔ   49 Ⓐ Ⓑ Ⓒ Ⓓ Ⓔ   69 Ⓐ Ⓑ Ⓒ Ⓓ Ⓔ   89 Ⓐ Ⓑ Ⓒ Ⓓ Ⓔ   109 Ⓐ Ⓑ Ⓒ Ⓓ Ⓔ
10 Ⓐ Ⓑ Ⓒ Ⓓ Ⓔ   30 Ⓐ Ⓑ Ⓒ Ⓓ Ⓔ   50 Ⓐ Ⓑ Ⓒ Ⓓ Ⓔ   70 Ⓐ Ⓑ Ⓒ Ⓓ Ⓔ   90 Ⓐ Ⓑ Ⓒ Ⓓ Ⓔ   110 Ⓐ Ⓑ Ⓒ Ⓓ Ⓔ

11 Ⓐ Ⓑ Ⓒ Ⓓ Ⓔ   31 Ⓐ Ⓑ Ⓒ Ⓓ Ⓔ   51 Ⓐ Ⓑ Ⓒ Ⓓ Ⓔ   71 Ⓐ Ⓑ Ⓒ Ⓓ Ⓔ   91 Ⓐ Ⓑ Ⓒ Ⓓ Ⓔ   111 Ⓐ Ⓑ Ⓒ Ⓓ Ⓔ
12 Ⓐ Ⓑ Ⓒ Ⓓ Ⓔ   32 Ⓐ Ⓑ Ⓒ Ⓓ Ⓔ   52 Ⓐ Ⓑ Ⓒ Ⓓ Ⓔ   72 Ⓐ Ⓑ Ⓒ Ⓓ Ⓔ   92 Ⓐ Ⓑ Ⓒ Ⓓ Ⓔ   112 Ⓐ Ⓑ Ⓒ Ⓓ Ⓔ
13 Ⓐ Ⓑ Ⓒ Ⓓ Ⓔ   33 Ⓐ Ⓑ Ⓒ Ⓓ Ⓔ   53 Ⓐ Ⓑ Ⓒ Ⓓ Ⓔ   73 Ⓐ Ⓑ Ⓒ Ⓓ Ⓔ   93 Ⓐ Ⓑ Ⓒ Ⓓ Ⓔ   113 Ⓐ Ⓑ Ⓒ Ⓓ Ⓔ
14 Ⓐ Ⓑ Ⓒ Ⓓ Ⓔ   34 Ⓐ Ⓑ Ⓒ Ⓓ Ⓔ   54 Ⓐ Ⓑ Ⓒ Ⓓ Ⓔ   74 Ⓐ Ⓑ Ⓒ Ⓓ Ⓔ   94 Ⓐ Ⓑ Ⓒ Ⓓ Ⓔ   114 Ⓐ Ⓑ Ⓒ Ⓓ Ⓔ
15 Ⓐ Ⓑ Ⓒ Ⓓ Ⓔ   35 Ⓐ Ⓑ Ⓒ Ⓓ Ⓔ   55 Ⓐ Ⓑ Ⓒ Ⓓ Ⓔ   75 Ⓐ Ⓑ Ⓒ Ⓓ Ⓔ   95 Ⓐ Ⓑ Ⓒ Ⓓ Ⓔ   115 Ⓐ Ⓑ Ⓒ Ⓓ Ⓔ
16 Ⓐ Ⓑ Ⓒ Ⓓ Ⓔ   36 Ⓐ Ⓑ Ⓒ Ⓓ Ⓔ   56 Ⓐ Ⓑ Ⓒ Ⓓ Ⓔ   76 Ⓐ Ⓑ Ⓒ Ⓓ Ⓔ   96 Ⓐ Ⓑ Ⓒ Ⓓ Ⓔ   116 Ⓐ Ⓑ Ⓒ Ⓓ Ⓔ
17 Ⓐ Ⓑ Ⓒ Ⓓ Ⓔ   37 Ⓐ Ⓑ Ⓒ Ⓓ Ⓔ   57 Ⓐ Ⓑ Ⓒ Ⓓ Ⓔ   77 Ⓐ Ⓑ Ⓒ Ⓓ Ⓔ   97 Ⓐ Ⓑ Ⓒ Ⓓ Ⓔ   117 Ⓐ Ⓑ Ⓒ Ⓓ Ⓔ
18 Ⓐ Ⓑ Ⓒ Ⓓ Ⓔ   38 Ⓐ Ⓑ Ⓒ Ⓓ Ⓔ   58 Ⓐ Ⓑ Ⓒ Ⓓ Ⓔ   78 Ⓐ Ⓑ Ⓒ Ⓓ Ⓔ   98 Ⓐ Ⓑ Ⓒ Ⓓ Ⓔ   118 Ⓐ Ⓑ Ⓒ Ⓓ Ⓔ
19 Ⓐ Ⓑ Ⓒ Ⓓ Ⓔ   39 Ⓐ Ⓑ Ⓒ Ⓓ Ⓔ   59 Ⓐ Ⓑ Ⓒ Ⓓ Ⓔ   79 Ⓐ Ⓑ Ⓒ Ⓓ Ⓔ   99 Ⓐ Ⓑ Ⓒ Ⓓ Ⓔ   119 Ⓐ Ⓑ Ⓒ Ⓓ Ⓔ
20 Ⓐ Ⓑ Ⓒ Ⓓ Ⓔ   40 Ⓐ Ⓑ Ⓒ Ⓓ Ⓔ   60 Ⓐ Ⓑ Ⓒ Ⓓ Ⓔ   80 Ⓐ Ⓑ Ⓒ Ⓓ Ⓔ   100 Ⓐ Ⓑ Ⓒ Ⓓ Ⓔ   120 Ⓐ Ⓑ Ⓒ Ⓓ Ⓔ

SIDE ONE

BOARD OF REGISTRY
founded in 1928 by the
American Society of Clinical Pathologists

Representatives from:

American Society of Clinical Pathologists
Medical Technologists/Technicians
Pathologists
American Academy of Microbiology
American Association of Blood Banks
American Society of Cytology
National Registry in Clinical Chemistry
American Society of Hematology
National Society for Histotechnology

IMPORTANT DIRECTIONS FOR MARKING ANSWERS

- Use black lead pencil only (No. 2½ or softer).
- Do NOT use ink, felt tip or ballpoint pens.
- Erase cleanly any answer you wish to change.
- Make no stray marks on the answer sheet.
- Make heavy black marks that fill the circle completely.

EXAMPLES

WRONG: Fill in the circle completely.

1 Ⓧ Ⓑ Ⓒ Ⓓ Ⓔ

2 Ⓐ Ⓑ Ⓒ Ⓓ Ⓔ

3 Ⓐ Ⓑ Ⓓ Ⓔ

WRONG: Make heavy black marks.

4 Ⓐ Ⓒ Ⓓ Ⓔ

RIGHT: Make heavy black marks that fill in the circle completely.

5 Ⓐ Ⓑ Ⓒ Ⓓ ● Ⓔ

Questions 121–240, answer options A B C D E:

121–140, 141–160, 161–180, 181–200, 201–220, 221–240 — each numbered item with bubbles Ⓐ Ⓑ Ⓒ Ⓓ Ⓔ

CHAPTER 10

Computer Practice Tests

The computer disk in the insert at the back of the Study Guide is programmed to administer many different practice tests. You may find these practice tests useful for self-assessment.

Each disk contains 1400 items from the Study Guide and programming which will select test questions based on your response pattern. Each computer practice test will contain between 50 and 100 questions. The distribution of the questions across content areas will be comparable to the MT or MLT content guidelines (Chapter 7). The tests vary in length because each test is tailored to the current level of knowledge of the examinee. This means that as you become more knowledgeable, you will get more difficult or complex questions. New tests will be constructed until all the items have been used. You will then be notified that the program will begin to reuse questions. You must answer each question when it is presented, so consider your answers carefully. Questions answered incorrectly will be presented again at the end of each test with the correct answers highlighted.

Suggestions for Taking a Computer Administered Test

1. Read the instructions carefully before beginning.

2. Read the questions carefully looking for words such as best, most, likely and not.

3. Read all the answer choices before answering. Sometimes what appears initially to be a correct answer may not be the best answer.

4. You must answer each question to the best of your ability when it is presented. You will not have a second opportunity to answer the question, so take as much time as you feel is necessary (within reason) to answer the question correctly.

5. You have the option of recording your answers in any one of 3 ways:

   - Press the "space bar" until the answer you wish to select is highlighted, then press the ENTER key to record the answer.

- Press the number of the answer you wish to select on the key pad (make sure "Number Lock" is turned on). When the answer you selected is highlighted, press the ENTER key to record your answer.
- Press the number of the answer you wish to select on the top row of the keyboard. When the answer you selected is highlighted, press the ENTER key to record your answer.

You may change your answer as many times as you wish before you record it permanently by pressing the ENTER key.

6. Some questions require an illustration. Refer to the appropriate illustration in the "Computer Practice Test Illustrations" section of this chapter.

7. Try to stay relaxed so that you can think through the problems presented clearly and logically.

Should You Guess?

This is no built-in-penalty for guessing. You _must_ answer all questions presented at the time they are presented to the best of your ability. Try to narrow the options to two answer choices if possible. The computer will _not_ allow you to continue to the next question until you select an answer and press the ENTER key.

Directions for Using the Computer Practice Test Disk

1. Turn on the IBM compatible computer and bring up the operating system (usually DOS). The specifics of invoking the operating system are unique for each computer.

2. At the back of the study guide, you will find the computer disk. Insert the disk in the appropriate disk drive and log onto that disk drive. You may run the computer Practice Test program from that drive or you may copy the program onto a hard disk drive and run the program on the hard drive. Use the DOS "COPY" command followed by "*.*". The program will run faster on the hard drive than it will on the "floppy" disk drive.

3. At the prompt, type MT to take an MT level test _OR_ MLT to take a MLT level test.

   Press ENTER (RETURN) to activate the program. A "Welcome" screen will appear (see Figure 4).

4. If your computer has a "keypad" (usually to the right), be sure it is set for number (NUM LOCK is on).

5. For help in using the program, press F1 at any time. The HELP screen is presented in Figure 5.

6. Read the instructions carefully before you begin the first test.

7. The answer you select should be highlighted on the screen. If it is not highlighted, adjust the BRIGHTNESS and CONTRAST on the monitor.

8. You may change your response as many times as you wish until you press the ENTER key. This causes the answer to be recorded and the next question to be presented. Each question must be answered when it is presented. You may not skip questions.

9. When you encounter a question that refers to an illustration, find the appropriate diagram at the end of this chapter under the heading "Computer Practice Test Illustrations"

10. In the Computer Practice Test, superscripts, subscripts and exponents are presented as follows:

> Superscripts: eg, Duffy a (Fy^a) will appear as Fy(a);
> Subscripts: eg, Sulfuric acid (H_2SO_4) will appear as H2SO4;
> Exponents: eg, 10 to the third power (10^3) will appear as 10^3

11. The computer will end your test automatically between 50 and 100 questions. The questions you answered incorrectly will be presented after you have completed the test. The answer you selected will be highlighted and the correct answer will be indicated at the bottom of the screen.

12. If you wish to stop testing, press ALT-Q (ALT key + letter Q simultaneously). This the will end test and any questions you answered incorrectly will be presented. To end the review of questions press ALT and Q again.

13. You may use the Computer Practice Test program as often as you wish (Type MT or MLT to activate the program). You will be presented with different questions until the entire database has been used. Then the questions will be presented a second time. You should expect to get more difficult questions as your level of knowledge increases.

Welcome to the Study Guide Practice-Test Program

Read each question carefully. Select the correct answer by pressing the key with the corresponding number. The response you select will be highlighted. To change your response, press the number of the new choice. When you are satisfied with your selection, press the "Enter/Return" key to move on to the next question.

You must answer all questions presented. Be sure you are satisfied with your answer before pressing the "Enter" key because you will not be able to make changes after you have completed the question.

When you encounter a question that refers to an illustration, find the appropriate diagram in the Study Guide under "Computer Practice Test Illustrations."

Superscripts, subscripts and exponents are presented as follows: Superscripts - Duffy a will appear as Fy(a); Subscripts - Sulfuric acid will appear as H2SO4; Exponents - 10 to the third power will appear as 10^3.

A help screen may be activated by pressing function key F1. The test will end automatically between 50 and 100 questions. To stop test before completion press the "ALTERNATE" key and "Q" simultaneously. You may review the items you answered incorrectly at the end of the test.

Figure 4: Directions Screen

a) Read the question at the top of the screen.
b) Select the correct answer from the choices listed.
c) Hit the number on the keyboard which corresponds to the correct answer.
d) To change you answer hit a different number.
e) When you are sure of your choice, press the "Enter/Return" key and next item will appear on the screen.
f) To stop a test before the end press the "ALTERNATE" key and the "Q" simultaneously to quit.
g) Superscripts, subscripts and exponents are presented as follows: Superscripts - Duffy a will appear as Fy(a); Subscripts - Sulfuric acid will appear as H_2SO_4; Exponents - 10 to the third power will appear as 10^3

Figure 5: Help Screen invoked by pressing F1 key

Computer Practice Test (CPT) Illustrations

Illustration 1: Reagent Red Cell Panel

Cell	D	C	E	c	e	M	N	S	s	Le^a	Le^b	P₁	K	k	Fy^a	Fy^b	Jk^a	Jk^b	Serum Alb IS	37 C	AHG
1	0	+	0	+	+	+	0	0	+	0	+	0	0	+	0	+	0	+	0	0	0
2	+	+	0	0	+	0	+	0	+	+	0	+	0	+	+	0	0	+	0	0	2+
3	+	+	0	0	+	+	+	+	+	0	+	+	+	0	+	+	+	+	0	0	3+
4	+	+	+	+	0	0	+	+	0	0	+	+	0	+	0	+	0	+	0	1+	4+
5	0	0	+	+	+	0	+	0	+	0	+	+	0	+	+	+	+	+	0	1+	4+
6	0	0	0	+	+	+	0	0	+	0	0	+	0	+	0	0	+	0	0	0	0
7	0	0	0	+	+	0	+	0	+	0	+	+	+	+	0	+	0	+	0	0	2+
8	0	0	0	+	+	+	0	+	0	+	0	+	0	+	0	+	+	0	0	0	0
9	0	0	0	+	+	+	0	+	0	0	+	+	+	+	+	0	+	+	0	0	3+
10	+	+	+	0	+	+	0	+	0	+	0	0	0	+	+	0	+	0	0	1+	4+
Autocontrol																			0	0	0

Illustration 2: Reagent Red Cell Panel

Cell	D	C	E	c	e	M	N	S	s	Le^a	Le^b	P₁	K	k	Fy^a	Fy^b	Jk^a	Jk^b	Xg^a	Serum IS	37 C	AHG
1	0	+	0	+	+	+	0	0	+	0	+	0	0	+	0	+	0	+	+	0	0	1+
2	+	+	0	0	+	0	+	0	+	+	0	+	0	+	+	0	+	+	+	0	0	0
3	+	+	0	0	+	+	+	+	+	0	+	+	0	+	0	+	0	+	+	0	0	0
4	+	0	+	+	0	+	+	+	0	0	+	0	+	+	0	+	+	0	+	0	0	1+
5	0	0	+	+	+	0	+	0	+	+	0	+	0	+	+	0	0	+	+	0	0	1+
6	0	0	0	+	+	+	0	0	+	0	0	+	0	+	0	0	+	0	+	0	0	1+
7	0	0	0	+	+	+	+	0	+	+	0	+	+	0	0	+	+	+	0	0	0	1+
8	0	0	0	+	+	+	0	0	+	0	+	0	0	+	+	0	+	+	+	0	0	1+
9	0	0	0	+	+	+	+	+	0	0	0	0	0	+	+	+	+	0	+	0	0	1+
10	0	0	0	+	+	+	0	+	+	0	+	0	0	+	+	0	+	0	+	0	0	1+
Patient																				0	0	0

Illustration 3: Reagent Red Cell Panel

		ANTIGENS					TEST RESULTS
		D	C	E	c	e	
P C A E N L E L L S	I	+	0	0	+	+	+
	II	0	0	+	0	+	0
	III	0	+	+	+	0	0
	IV	0	+	+	0	+	+
	V	+	+	+	0	0	+
	AUTO						0

Illustration 4: Pedigree

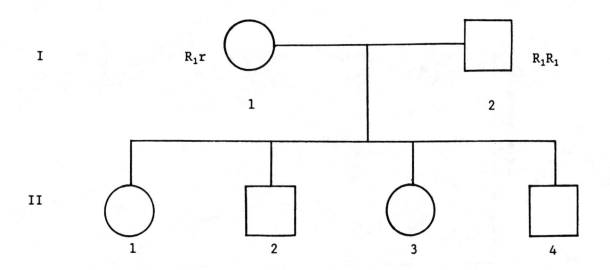

Illustration 5: Reagent Red Cell Panel

Cell	D	C	E	c	e	M	N	S	s	Leᵃ	Leᵇ	P₁	K	k	Fyᵃ	Fyᵇ	Jkᵃ	Jkᵇ	Serum Alb IS	Serum Alb 37 C	Serum Alb AHG	Enzyme AHG
1	0	+	0	+	+	+	0	0	+	0	+	0	0	+	0	+	0	+	0	0	2+	3+
2	+	+	0	0	+	+	+	+	+	0	+	+	0	+	+	0	0	+	0	0	3+	4+
3	+	+	0	+	+	+	0	+	+	+	0	+	+	0	+	+	+	0	0	0	2+	3+
4	+	+	0	0	+	+	0	+	0	0	+	+	0	+	0	+	+	+	0	0	3+	4+
5	0	0	0	+	+	+	0	+	+	0	+	0	0	+	+	+	+	+	0	0	2+	0
6	0	0	0	+	+	0	+	+	0	0	+	+	+	+	+	+	+	0	0	0	2+	0
7	+	0	0	+	+	0	+	+	+	0	+	+	0	+	0	0	+	+	0	0	0	0
8	+	0	+	+	0	0	+	0	+	+	0	+	0	+	0	+	0	+	0	0	0	0
9	+	0	+	+	+	+	+	0	+	0	+	+	0	+	+	+	+	+	0	0	2+	0
10	0	0	0	+	+	+	+	+	0	0	+	0	0	+	+	0	+	0	0	0	2+	0
Autocontrol																			0	0	0	0

Illustration 6: Amniotic Fluid Analysis

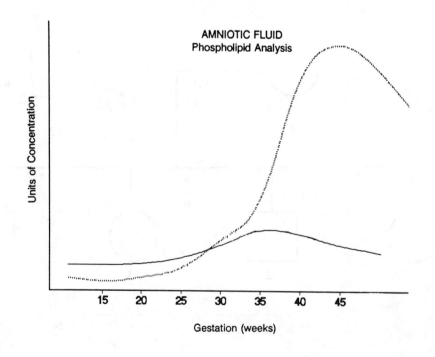

AMNIOTIC FLUID
Phospholipid Analysis

Units of Concentration

Gestation (weeks)

Illustration 7: Urine Crystals

Illustration 8: Serum Protein Electrophoresis

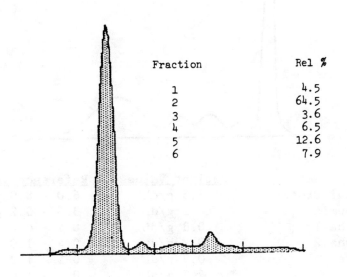

Fraction	Rel %
1	4.5
2	64.5
3	3.6
4	6.5
5	12.6
6	7.9

Illustration 9: Serum Protein Electrophoresis

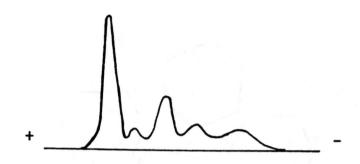

	Patient Values	Reference Values
Total Protein	7.8 g/dL	6.0 - 8.0 g/dL
Albumin	4.0 g/dL	3.6 - 5.2 g/dL
Alpha-1	0.4 g/dL	0.1 - 0.4 g/dL
Alpha-2	1.8 g/dL	0.4 - 1.0 g/dL
Beta	0.5 g/dL	0.5 - 1.2 g/dL
Gamma	1.1 g/dL	0.6 - 1.6 g/dL

Illustration 10: Serum Protein Electrophoresis

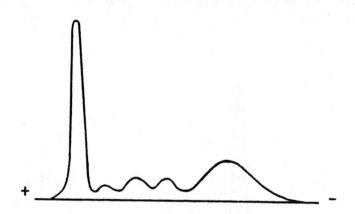

	Patient Values	Reference Values
Total Protein	8.5 g/dL	6.0 - 8.0 g/dL
Albumin	4.3 g/dL	3.6 - 5.2 g/dL
Alpha-1	0.3 g/dL	0.1 - 0.4 g/dL
Alpha-2	0.7 g/dL	0.4 - 1.0 g/dL
Beta	0.9 g/dL	0.5 - 1.2 g/dL
Gamma	2.3 g/dL	0.6 - 1.6 g/dL

Illustration 11: Graph

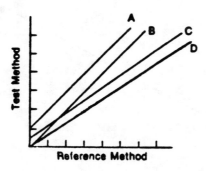

Illustration 12: Serum Protein Electrophoresis

Illustration 13: Graph

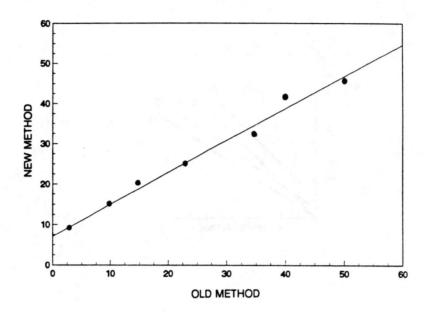

Illustration 14: Serum HCG Graph

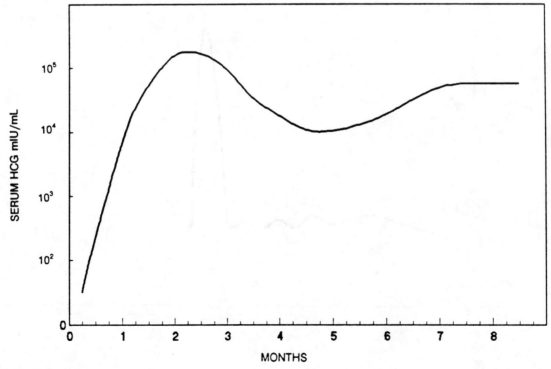

Illustration 15: Levy-Jennings Quality Control Chart

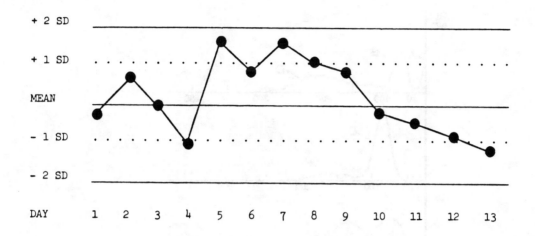

Illustration 16: Platelet Aggregation Curves

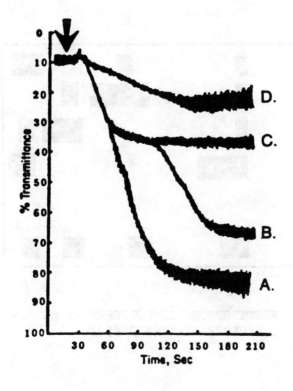

Illustration 17: Hematology Histogram

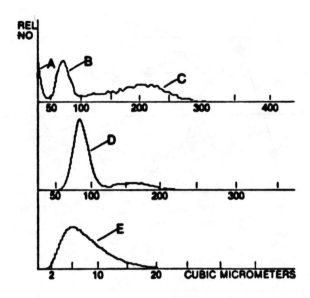

Illustration 18: Hemoglobin Electrophoresis Patterns

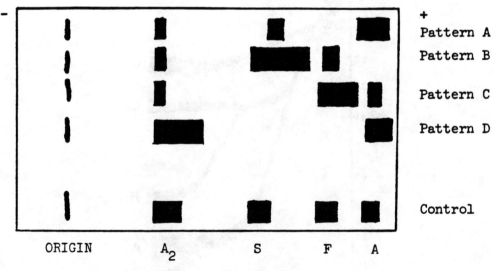

HEMOGLOBIN ELECTROPHORESIS PATTERNS AT pH 8.4
(CELLULOSE ACETATE STRIP)

Illustration 19: Antigen/Antibody Precipitation Graph

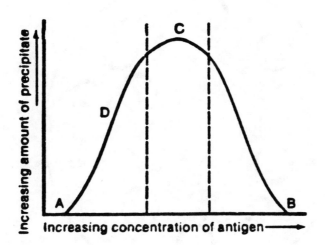

Illustration 20: Radial Immunodiffusion Results

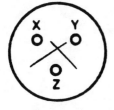

Figure #1

Figure #2

Figure #3

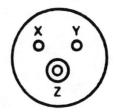

Figure #4

Illustration 21: Parasitology Illustration

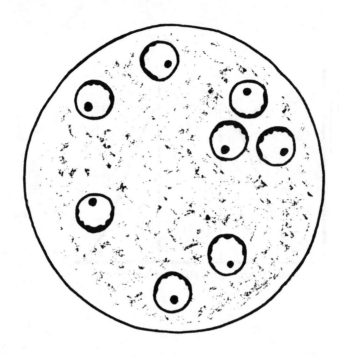

Illustration 22: Parasitology Illustration

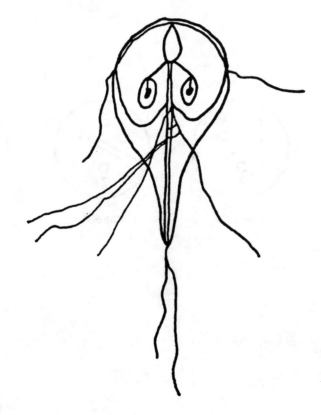

Illustration 23: Parasitology Illustration

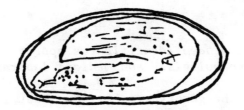

CHAPTER 11

Blood Bank

The following items have been identified as appropriate for both entry level medical technologists and medical laboratory technicians.

1. A blood donor has the genotype: *hh*, *AB*. What is his red blood cell phenotype?

   a. A
   b. B
   c. O
   d. AB

2. A donor is tested with Rh antisera, with the following results:

Anti-D	Anti-C	Anti-E	Anti-c	Anti-e	Rh Control
+	+	0	+	+	0

   What is his most probable Rh genotype?

   a. R_1R_1
   b. R_1r
   c. R_or
   d. R_2r

3. An individual has been sensitized to the Cellano (k) antigen and has produced anti-k. What is her most probable Kell genotype?

   a. *KK*
   b. *Kk*
   c. *kk*
   d. K_oK_o

4. Human blood groups were discovered in 1900 by:

   a. Jules Bordet
   b. Louis Pasteur
   c. Karl Landsteiner
   d. P. L. Mollison

5. What is the most probable racial origin of a donor with the following typing results?

    Le(a-b-); Fy(a-b-); Js(a+b+)

    a. Black
    b. Oriental
    c. American Indian
    d. Caucasian

6. Which of the following Rh antigens has the highest frequency in Caucasians?

    a. D
    b. C
    c. E
    d. c
    e. e

7. When the red cells of an individual fail to react with anti-U, they usually fail to react with:

    a. anti-M
    b. anti-Le^b
    c. anti-S
    d. anti-P$_1$

8. The antibody in the Lutheran system that is best detected at lower temperatures is:

    a. anti-Lu^a
    b. anti-Lu^b
    c. anti-Lu3
    d. anti-Lu

9. The Kell antigen is:

    a. absent from the red cells of neonates
    b. strongly immunogenic
    c. destroyed by enzymes
    d. has a frequency of 50% in the random population

10. Proteolytic enzyme treatment of red cells usually destroys which of the following antigens?

   a. Jk^a
   b. E
   c. Fy^a
   d. k

11. Which of the following antigens gives enhanced reactions with its corresponding antibody following treatment of the red cells with proteolytic enzymes?

   a. Fy^a
   b. E
   c. S
   d. M

12. Paroxysmal cold hemoglobinuria (PCH) is best associated with which of the following blood groups?

   a. Kell
   b. Duffy
   c. P
   d. I/i

13. Cold agglutinin syndrome is best associated with which of the following blood groups?

   a. Duffy
   b. P
   c. I/i
   d. Rh

14. Antibodies involved in warm autoimmune hemolytic anemia are often associated with which blood group system?

   a. Rh
   b. I
   c. P
   d. Duffy

15. An antibody that causes in vitro hemolysis and reacts with the red cells of three out of ten crossmatched donor units is most likely:

   a. anti-Le^a
   b. anti-s
   c. anti-k
   d. anti-E

16. Anti-Sd^a is strongly suspected if:

    a. the patient has been previously transfused
    b. the agglutinates are mixed-field and refractile
    c. the patient is group A or B
    d. only a small number of panel cells are reactive

17. Anti-Fy^a is:

    a. usually a cold-reactive agglutinin
    b. more reactive when tested with enzyme-treated red blood
       cells
    c. capable of causing hemolytic transfusion reactions
    d. often an autoagglutinin

18. Which of the following is a characteristic of anti-i?

    a. often associated with hemolytic disease of the newborn
    b. frequently a cold agglutinin
    c. reacts best at 37°C
    d. is usually IgG

19. Which of the following is a characteristic of anti-i?

    a. is often associated with warm autoimmune hemolytic
       anemia
    b. can often be found in the serum of patients with
       infectious mononucleosis
    c. can often be detected at lower temperatures in the
       serum of normal individuals
    d. is found only in the serum of group O individuals

20. HLA antigen typing is important in screening for:

    a. ABO incompatibility
    b. a kidney donor
    c. Rh incompatibility
    d. a blood donor

21. DR antigens in the HLA system are:

    a. significant in organ transplantation
    b. not detectable in the lymphocytotoxicity test
    c. expressed on platelets
    d. expressed on granulocytes

22. HLA antibodies are:

    a. naturally occurring
    b. induced by multiple transfusions
    c. directed against granulocyte antigens only
    d. frequently cause hemolytic transfusion reactions

23. One of the most useful techniques in the identification and classification of high-titer, low-avidity (HTLA) antibodies is:

    a. reagent red cell panels
    b. adsorption and elution
    c. titration and inhibition
    d. cold autoadsorption

24. Which of the following HTLA antibodies is considered to be most clinically significant?

    a. anti-Yt^a
    b. anti-Ch
    c. anti-Yk
    d. anti-Cs

25. Which of the following HTLA antibodies is neutralizable by pooled human plasma?

    a. anti-Yt^a
    b. anti-Ch
    c. anti-Yk
    d. anti-Cs

26. What is the most likely cause of the following ABO discrepancy?

Patient's cells vs:		Patient's serum vs:	
anti-A	anti-B	A$_1$ cells	B cells
O	O	O	O

    a. recent transfusion with group O blood
    b. antigen depression due to leukemia
    c. false-negative cell typing due to rouleaux
    d. hypogammaglobulinemia due to advanced patient age

27. Which of the following best reflects the discrepancy seen when a person's red cells demonstrate the acquired-B phenotype?

	Forward Grouping	Reverse Grouping
a.	B	O
b.	AB	A
c.	O	B
d.	B	AB

28. Which of the following is characteristic of Tn polyagglutinable red cells?

   a. If group O, they may appear to have acquired a group A antigen.
   b. They show strong reactions with anti A_1 lectin.
   c. They react with *Arachis hypogaea* lectin.
   d. The polyagglutination is a transient condition.

29. Examine the following results of ABO typing tests and state the most probable cause of the discrepancy

Patient's cells vs:			Patient's serum vs:		
Anti-A	Anti-B	Anti-A,B	A_1 cells	B cells	O cells
0	0	+/-	2+	4+	0

   a. acquired B antigen
   b. the patient is a newborn
   c. chimerism
   d. weak subgroup of A with anti-A_1

30. Mixed field agglutination encountered in ABO grouping would most likely be due to:

   a. Bombay phenotype (O_h)
   b. T activation
   c. A_3 red cells
   d. positive indirect Coombs test

31. Which of the following is a characteristic of polyagglutinable red cells?

   a. can be classified by reactivity with *Ulex europaeus*
   b. are agglutinated by most adult sera
   c. are always an acquired condition
   d. autocontrol is always positive

32. Cells of the A_3 subgroup will:

   a. react with *Dolichos biflorus*
   b. not be agglutinated by anti-A
   c. give a mixed field reaction with anti-A,B
   d. not be agglutinated by anti-H

33. The following results were obtained:

	Anti-A	Anti-B	Anti-D	D^u	DAT	Ab Screen
Infant:	0	0	0	NT	4+	NT
Mother:	4+	0	0	0	NT	Anti-D

NT = Not tested

Which of the following is the most probable explanation for these results?

    a. ABO hemolytic disease of the newborn
    b. Rh hemolytic disease of the newborn; infant has received intrauterine transfusions
    c. Rh hemolytic disease of the newborn; infant has a false-negative Rh typing
    d. large fetomaternal hemorrhage

34. Consider the following ABO typing results:

Patient's cells vs:		Patient's serum vs:	
anti-A	anti-B	A$_1$ cells	B cells
4+	0	1+	4+

Additional testing was performed using patient serum:

	IS	RT
Screening cell I	1+	2+
Screening cell II	1+	2+
Autocontrol	1+	2+

What is the MOST LIKELY cause of this discrepancy?

    a. A$_2$ with anti-A$_1$
    b. cold alloantibody
    c. cold autoantibody
    d. acquired-A phenomenon

35. Which of the following would most likely indicate that a patient's red cells are a subgroup of A?

    a. positive autocontrol
    b. heavy rouleaux in the serum
    c. positive antibody screening test
    d. discrepancy between cell and serum ABO grouping

36. Consider the following ABO typing results:

Patient's cell vs:		Patient's serum vs:	
anti-A	anti-B	A₁ cells	B cells
4+	0	1+	4+

Additional testing was performed using patient serum:

	IS	RT
Screening cell I	1+	2+
Screening cell II	1+	2+
Autocontrol	1+	2+

What should be done next?

    a. antibody identification
    b. neutralization
    c. cold autoadsorption
    d. elution

37. The following results were obtained on a patient's blood group and type during routine ABO and Rh testing:

CELL TESTING		SERUM TESTING	
anti-A	= neg	A₁ cells = 2+	
anti-B	= 4+	B cells = agglutination	
anti-D	= neg		
Dᵘ test	= neg		
Autocontrol	= neg		

Select the course of action to resolve this problem.

    a. Draw a new blood sample from the patient and repeat all test procedures
    b. Test the patient's serum with A₂ cells and the patient's red cells with anti-A₁ lectin
    c. Repeat the ABO antigen grouping using 3-time washed saline-suspended cells.
    d. Perform antibody screening procedure at immediate spin using group O cells.

38. Which one of the following is an indicator of polyagglutination?

    a. RBCs typing as Dᵘ positive
    b. presence of red cell autoantibody
    c. decreased serum bilirubin
    d. agglutination with normal adult ABO compatible sera

39. Which of the following situations could result in an ABO discrepancy that is caused by problems with the patient's red cells?

    a. an unexpected antibody
    b. rouleaux
    c. agammaglobulinemia
    d. Tn activation

40. The most appropriate laboratory test for early detection of acute hemolysis is:

    a. a visual inspection for free plasma hemoglobin
    b. plasma haptoglobin concentration
    c. Schumm's test on posttransfusion plasma
    d. examination for hematuria
    e. serum bilirubin concentration

41. The serum of a group O Cde/Cde donor contains anti-D. In order to prepare a specific anti-D reagent from this donor's serum, which of the following cells should be used for the adsorption?

    a. group O, cde/cde cells
    b. group O, Cde/cde cells
    c. group A$_2$B, CDe/cde cells
    d. group A$_1$B, cde/cde cells

42. Which of the following refers to chemically-modified anti-D?

    a. contains only IgM antibody
    b. is in a low protein medium
    c. contains macromolecular additives
    d. cannot be used to perform a D^u test

43. To prepare anti-Kell as a reagent from a serum containing anti-I and anti-Kell, the serum should be absorbed with:

    a. Kell-positive, I-positive cells at 22°C
    b. Kell-positive, I-negative cells at 4°C
    c. Kell-negative, I-positive cells at 4°C
    d. Kell-negative, I-positive cells at 37°C

44. In the direct (DAT) and indirect (IAT) antiglobulin techniques, false-negative reactions may result if the:

    a. red cell/AHG mixture is overcentrifuged
    b. patient's blood specimen was collected into tubes containing silicon gel
    c. saline used for washing the serum/cell mixture has been stored in glass or metal containers
    d. addition of AHG is delayed for 40 minutes or more after washing the serum/cell mixture

45. Which of the following might cause a false-negative indirect antiglobulin test (IAT)?

    a. over-reading
    b. IgG-coated screening cells
    c. over-centrifugation
    d. too heavy a cell suspension

46. Broad spectrum reagents used in the direct antiglobulin (Coombs) test should have specificity for:

    a. IgG and IgA
    b. IgG and C3d
    c. IgM and IgA
    d. IgM and C3d

47. In the direct antiglobulin test, the antiglobulin (Coombs) reagent is used to:

    a. mediate hemolysis of indicator red blood cells by providing complement
    b. precipitate anti-erythrocyte antibodies
    c. measure antibodies in a test serum by fixing complement
    d. detect preexisting antibodies on erythrocytes

48. AHG (Coombs) Control Cells:

    a. can be used as a positive control for anti-C3 reagents
    b. can be used only for the indirect Coombs test
    c. are coated only with IgG antibody
    d. must be used to confirm all positive Coombs reactions

49. The D^u test is performed by incubating patient's red cells with:

    a. several different dilutions of anti-D serum
    b. anti-D serum followed by washing and antiglobulin serum
    c. anti-D^u serum
    d. antiglobulin serum

50. Mixed-field agglutination at the antihuman globulin phase of a crossmatch may be attributed to:

    a. recently transfused cells
    b. intrauterine exchange transfusion
    c. an antibody such as anti-Sd[a]
    d. fetomaternal hemorrhage

51. The major crossmatch will detect a(n):

    a. group A patient mistyped as group O
    b. irregular antibody in the donor unit
    c. Rh-negative donor unit mislabeled as Rh-positive
    d. recipient antibody directed against antigens on the
       donor red cells

52. Pre-transfusion compatibility testing must include:

    a. antibody screening by antiglobulin test
    b. autocontrol
    c. minor crossmatch
    d. D^u test on recipient

53. The Western Blot is a confirmatory test for the presence of:

    a. CMV antibody
    b. anti-HIV-1
    c. HBsAg
    d. serum protein abnormalities

54. A commonly used screening method for anti-HIV-1 detection is:

    a. latex agglutination
    b. radioimmunoassay (RIA)
    c. flame photometry
    d. thin-layer-chromatography (TLC)
    e. enzyme-labeled immunosorbent assay (ELISA)

55. Which of the following is the correct storage temperature for
    the component listed?

    a. Cryoprecipitated AHF, 4°C
    b. Fresh Frozen Plasma (FFP), -20°C
    c. Red Blood Cells Frozen, -40°C
    d. Platelets, 37°C

56. A unit of Red Blood Cells is issued at 9:00 a.m. At 9:10 a.m.
    the unit is returned to the Blood Bank. The container has NOT
    been entered, but the unit has NOT been refrigerated during
    this time span. The best course of action for the technologist
    is to:

    a. culture the unit for bacterial contamination
    b. discard the unit if not used within 24 hours
    c. store the unit at room temperature
    d. record the return and place the unit back into inventory

57. The quality assurance program for Red Blood Cells Deglycerolized should include regularly scheduled monitoring to determine:

    a. sterility
    b. hematocrit
    c. potassium concentration
    d. acceptable glycerol removal

58. Rejuvenation of a unit of Red Blood Cells is a method used to:

    a. remove antibody attached to RBCs
    b. inactivate viruses and bacteria
    c. restore 2,3-DPG and ATP to normal levels
    d. prevent hemolytic transfusion reaction
    e. filter blood clots and other debris

59. A method currently in routine use for freezing red blood cells is:

    a. low concentration of glycerol (5% w/v)
    b. low concentration of glycerol (10% w/v)
    c. high concentration of glycerol (40% w/v)
    d. high concentration of glycerol (70% w/v)

60. The optimum storage temperature for Red Blood Cells Frozen is:

    a. 4°C
    b. -12°C
    c. -20°C
    d. -80°C

61. The optimum storage temperature for Whole Blood is:

    a. 4°C
    b. -12°C
    c. -20°C
    d. -80°C

62. If the seal is entered on a unit of Whole Blood stored at 1°C to 6°C, what is the maximum allowable storage period, in hours?

    a. 4
    b. 6
    c. 24
    d. 48
    e. 72

63. Each unit of Whole Blood will yield approximately how many units of Cryoprecipitated AHF?

    a. 40
    b. 80
    c. 130
    d. 250

64. The optimum storage temperature for Cryoprecipitated AHF is:

    a. 22°C
    b. 4°C
    c. -12°C
    d. -20°C

65. After thawing, reconstituted Cryoprecipitated AHF should be stored at:

    a. room temperature
    b. 37°C
    c. 10°C
    d. 1-6°C

66. The approximate percentage of the original plasma content of factor VIII recovered in Cryoprecipitated AHF is:

    a. 10-20%
    b. 20-40%
    c. 40-80%
    d. 80-100%

67. In a quality assurance program, at least 75% of the bags of Cryoprecipitated AHF must contain a minimum of how many International Units of factor VIII?

    a. 60
    b. 70
    c. 80
    d. 90

68. An assay of plasma from a bag of Cryoprecipitated AHF yields a concentration of 9 International Units (IU) of factor VIII per mL of Cryoprecipitated AHF. If the volume is 9 mL, what is the factor VIII content of the bag in IU?

    a. 9
    b. 18
    c. 27
    d. 81

69. According to AABB Standards, 75% of all Platelets Pheresis units tested shall contain how many platelets per µL?

    a. 5.5×10^{10}
    b. 6.5×10^{10}
    c. 3.0×10^{11}
    d. 5.0×10^{11}

70. According to AABB standards, Platelets prepared from Whole Blood shall have at least:

    a. 5.5×10^{10} platelets per unit in at least 75% of the units tested
    b. 6.5×11^{10} platelets per unit in 75% of the units tested
    c. 7.5×10^{10} platelets per unit in 100% of the units tested
    d. 8.5×10^{10} platelets per unit in 95% of the units tested

71. Platelets prepared in a polyolefin type container, stored at 22-24°C in 50 mL of plasma, and gently agitated can be used for up to:

    a. 24 hours
    b. 48 hours
    c. 3 days
    d. 5 days

72. Following the second spin in the preparation of Platelets, the platelets should be:

    a. allowed to sit undisturbed for 1 hour
    b. agitated immediately
    c. pooled immediately
    d. transfused within 48 hours

73. Which of the following is the proper procedure for the preparation of Platelets from Whole Blood?

    a. light spin followed by a hard spin
    b. light spin followed by two hard spins
    c. two light spins
    d. hard spin followed by a light spin

74. According to AABB standards, what is the minimum pH required for Platelets?

    a. 4
    b. 5
    c. 6
    d. 7

75. The optimum storage temperature for Platelets is:

   a. 22°C
   b. 4°C
   c. -12°C
   d. -20°C

76. An important determinant of platelet viability following storage is:

   a. plasma potassium concentration
   b. plasma pH
   c. prothrombin time
   d. activated partial thromboplastin time

77. According to AABB standards, platelets must be:

   a. gently agitated if stored at room temperature
   b. separated within 12 hours of Whole Blood collection
   c. suspended in sufficient plasma to maintain a pH of 5.0 or lower
   d. prepared only from Whole Blood units that have been stored at 4°C for 6 hours

78. Which of the following blood components must be prepared within eight hours after phlebotomy?

   a. Red Blood Cells
   b. Fresh Frozen Plasma
   c. Red Blood Cells Frozen
   d. Cryoprecipitated AHF

79. In the liquid state, plasma must be stored at:

   a. 56°C
   b. 37°C
   c. 22°C
   d. 1-6°C

80. According to AABB standards, Fresh Frozen Plasma must be infused within:

   a. 24 hours
   b. 36 hours
   c. 48 hours
   d. 72 hours

81. Fresh Frozen Plasma which was thawed at 37°C and then stored at 1-6°C for 30 hours:

    a. should be discarded and not used for transfusion
    b. could be used for treating von Willebrand's disease
    c. could be used as Single-Donor plasma
    d. can be refrozen and processed for Cryoprecipitated AHF

82. Quality control tests must be performed daily on:

    a. reagent red blood cells
    b. oral thermometers
    c. banked Whole Blood
    d. centrifuge timers

83. Addition of which one of the following will enhance the shelf-life of Whole Blood?

    a. heparin
    b. adenine
    c. hydroxyethyl starch
    d. lactated Ringer's solution

84. When removed from the refrigerator, a unit of donor blood was observed to have an accumulation of cream colored material at the top of the plasma. The most probable cause of the accumulation is:

    a. ingestion of a fatty meal shortly before blood donation
    b. fungal contamination of the anticoagulant solution
    c. bacterial contamination during collection of the blood
    d. failure to mix the blood with anticoagulant during collection

85. Microaggregates in stored blood:

    a. decrease in number upon prolonged storage
    b. are a common cause of allergic transfusion reactions
    c. can be dispersed by using a blood warmer
    d. can be effectively removed using filters with a pore size of 20-40 microns

86. During storage, the concentration of 2,3-diphosphoglycerate (2,3-DPG) decreases in a unit of:

    a. Platelets
    b. Fresh Frozen Plasma
    c. Red Blood Cells
    d. Cryoprecipitated AHF

87. A weakly reactive anti-D is detected in a postpartum serum specimen from an Rh-negative woman. During her prenatal period, all antibody screening tests were negative. These findings indicate:

    a. that she is a candidate for Rh immune globulin
    b. that she is NOT a candidate for Rh immune globulin
    c. a need for further investigation to determine candidacy for Rh immune globulin
    d. the presence of Rh-positive cells in her circulation

88. A group A, Rh-positive infant of a group O, Rh-positive mother has a weakly positive direct antiglobulin test and a moderately elevated bilirubin at birth. The most likely cause is:

    a. ABO incompatibility
    b. Rh incompatibility
    c. blood group incompatibility due to an antibody to a low frequency antigen
    d. neonatal jaundice NOT associated with blood group incompatibility

89. A mother has the red cell phenotype DCe with anti-c (titer of 32 at AHG) in her serum. The father has the phenotype DCce, and the baby is Rh-negative and not affected with hemolytic disease of the newborn. What is the baby's most probable Rh phenotype?

    a. dCe
    b. dCce
    c. DCe
    d. DCce

90. Isoimmunization to platelet antigen (Pl^{A1}) and the placental transfer of maternal antibodies would be expected to cause which one of the following effects in a newborn?

    a. erythroblastosis
    b. leukocytosis
    c. leukopenia
    d. thrombocytopenia

91. A mother is group A, with anti-D in her serum. What would be the preferred blood product if an intrauterine transfusion is indicated?

    a. O, Rh-negative Whole Blood
    b. O, Rh-negative Red Blood Cells
    c. O, Rh-negative Red Blood Cells, irradiated
    d. A, Rh-negative Red Blood Cells
    e. A, Rh-negative Red Blood Cells, irradiated

92. Laboratory studies of maternal and cord blood yield the following results:

Maternal Blood:	Cord Blood:
O, Rh-negative	B, Rh-positive
Anti-E in serum	DAT = 2+
	Anti-E in eluate

If exchange transfusion is necessary, the best choice of blood is:

    a. B, Rh-negative, E positive
    b. B, Rh-positive, E positive
    c. O, Rh-negative, E negative
    d. O, Rh-positive, E negative

93. A blood specimen from a pregnant woman is found to be group B, Rh-negative and the serum contains anti-D with a titer of 1:512. Which of the following would be the most appropriate type of blood to have available for a possible exchange transfusion for her infant?

    a. O, Rh-negative
    b. O, Rh-positive
    c. B, Rh-negative
    d. B, Rh-positive

94. Blood selected for exchange transfusion must:

    a. lack the red blood cell antigens corresponding to the maternal antibodies
    b. be less than three days old
    c. be negative for hemoglobin S
    d. be ABO compatible with the father

95. When the main objective of an exchange transfusion is to remove the infant's antibody-sensitized red blood cells and to control hyperbilirubinemia, the blood product of choice is ABO compatible:

    a. fresh Whole Blood
    b. Red Blood Cells Washed
    c. Fresh Frozen Plasma
    d. heparinized Red Blood Cells
    e. Cryoprecipitated AHF

96. As a preventive measure against graft-versus-host disease, Red Blood Cells prepared for infants who have received intrauterine transfusions should be:

    a. saline-washed
    b. irradiated
    c. frozen and deglycerolized
    d. group- and Rh-compatible with the mother

97. One week after birth, an infant with a positive DAT and a bilirubin level of 18.5 mg/dL is in need of an exchange transfusion. Since the mother could not be located at the time, the next course of action would be to:

    a. crossmatch blood using the baby's serum
    b. crossmatch blood using an eluate from baby's red cells
    c. locate the father as a potential donor
    d. use group O, Rh-positive blood for the exchange

98. The results of a Kleihauer-Betke stain indicate a fetomaternal hemorrhage of 35 mL of whole blood. How many vials of Rh immune globulin would be required?

    a. 1
    b. 2
    c. 3
    d. 4

99. A fetomaternal hemorrhage of 35 mL of fetal Rh-positive packed RBCs has been detected in an Rh-negative woman. How many vials of Rh immune globulin should be given?

    a. 0
    b. 1
    c. 2
    d. 3

100. Criteria determining Rh immune globulin eligibility include:

   a. mother is Rh-positive
   b. infant is Rh-negative
   c. mother has not been previously immunized to the D antigen
   d. infant has a positive direct antiglobulin test

101. While performing routine postpartum testing for an Rh immune globulin (RhIG) candidate, a weakly positive antibody screening test was found. Anti-D was identified. This antibody is most likely the result of:

   a. massive fetomaternal hemorrhage occurring at the time of this delivery
   b. antenatal administration of RhIG at 28 weeks gestation
   c. contamination of the blood sample with Wharton's jelly
   d. mother having a positive direct Coombs test

102. Rh immune globulin administration would NOT be indicated in an Rh-negative woman who has a(n):

   a. first trimester abortion
   b. husband who is Rh-positive
   c. anti-D titer of 1:4096
   d. positive direct Coombs test

103. Which of the following is the preferred specimen for the initial compatibility testing in exchange transfusion therapy?

   a. maternal serum
   b. eluate prepared from infant's red blood cells
   c. paternal serum
   d. infant's postexchange serum

104. An obstetrical patient has had three previous pregnancies. Her first baby was healthy, the second was jaundiced at birth and required an exchange transfusion, while the third was stillborn. Which of the following is the most likely cause?

   a. ABO incompatibility
   b. immune deficiency disease
   c. congenital spherocytic anemia
   d. Rh incompatibility

105. In suspected cases of hemolytic disease of the newborn, what significant information can be obtained from the baby's blood smear?

   a. estimation of WBC, RBC, and platelet counts
   b. marked increase in immature neutrophils (shift to the left)
   c. a differential to estimate the absolute number of lymphocytes present
   d. determination of the presence of spherocytes and elevated numbers of nucleated red blood cells

106. A 33-year-old woman is found to have a positive antibody screening test during a prenatal evaluation. Which of the following techniques would be most useful in determining if the antibody involved could cause hemolytic disease of the newborn?

   a. treating the serum with dithiothreitol (DTT)
   b. one-stage papain procedure
   c. two-stage papain procedure
   d. adsorption-elution technique

107. A specimen of cord blood is submitted to the Blood Bank for routine testing. The following results are obtained:

anti-A:	4+
anti-B:	negative
anti-A,B:	4+
anti-D:	3+
Rh-control	negative
Direct antiglobulin test:	2+

   It is known that the father is group B, with a genotype of *cde/cde*. Of the following four antibodies, which is the most likely cause of the positive direct antiglobulin test?

   a. anti-A
   b. anti-D
   c. anti-c
   d. anti-C

108. ABO-hemolytic disease of the newborn:

   a. usually requires an exchange transfusion
   b. most often occurs in first born children
   c. frequently results in stillbirth
   d. is usually seen only in the newborn of group O mothers

109. Which of the following antigens is MOST likely to be involved in hemolytic disease of the newborn?

    a. Le^a
    b. P$_1$
    c. M
    d. Kell

110. The following results were obtained:

	Anti-A	-B	-D	Rh Control	DAT	Ab. Screen	
Infant	4+	0	2+	0	0	NT	0
Mother	0	0	+^{w}(mf)	0	0		

(mf = mixed field)

Which of the following is the most probable explanation for these results?

    a. hemolytic disease of the newborn due to antibody against a high frequency antigen
    b. large fetomaternal hemorrhage
    c. hemolytic disease of the newborn due to anti-D
    d. mother's cells are polyagglutinable

111. A Kleihauer-Betke stain of a postpartum blood film revealed 0.3% fetal cells. What is the estimated volume (mL) of the fetomaternal hemorrhage expressed as whole blood?

    a. 5
    b. 15
    c. 25
    d. 35

112. Which of the following is the BEST screening method for the detection of large fetomaternal hemorrhage?

    a. indicator cell rosette test
    b. D^u test
    c. Kleihauer-Betke
    d. latex agglutination

113. Why are donors deferred for 6 months following receipt of blood products?

    a. to permit adequate screening for transfusion-acquired viral infections
    b. donation may cause recurrence of the condition which required transfusion
    c. to allow clearance of all transfused cells in the donor
    d. to allow donor recovery from the condition which required transfusion

114. During a medical history evaluation, a prospective donor indicates that she returned from a trip to Southeast Asia 3 months ago. Malaria is endemic there, but she did not take any prophylactic medications. For what additional period of time must she be deferred?

    a. 3 months longer
    b. 6 months longer
    c. 9 months longer
    d. 3 years from the date of return

115. Which of the following prospective donors would be accepted for donation?

    a. 32-year-old woman who received a transfusion in a complicated delivery five months ago
    b. 19-year-old sailor who has been stateside for one year and stopped taking his anti-malarial medication one year ago
    c. 22-year-old college student who has a temperature of 99.7°F and states that he feels well, but is nervous about donating
    d. 45-year-old woman who has just recovered from a bladder infection and is still taking antibiotics

116. Which of the following is a cause for temporary deferment of a Whole Blood donor?

    a. aspirin ingestion twelve hours previously
    b. antibiotics taken 4 weeks ago
    c. oral polio vaccine taken 4 weeks previously
    d. history of malaria: has been asymptomatic for last 2 years

117. Which of the following constitute permanent rejection status of a donor?

    a. a tattoo five months previously
    b. recent close contact with a patient with viral hepatitis
    c. two units of blood transfused four months previously
    d. confirmed positive test for HBsAg ten years previously

118. According to AABB standards, which of the following donors may be accepted as a blood donor?

    a. hip replacement five months ago
    b. spontaneous abortion at 2 months of pregnancy, 3 months ago
    c. resides with a known hepatitis patient
    d. received a blood transfusion twenty-two weeks ago

119. Which one of the following histories represents an acceptable donor?

	HCT	BP	Temp	Pulse	Age	Sex
a.	39	110/70	99.8	75	40	F
b.	37	135/85	98.6	80	35	M
c.	41	90/50	99.4	65	65	M
d.	45	115/80	98.6	102	17	M

120. Below are the results of the history obtained from a prospective female blood donor:

Age: 18
Temperature: 99.0
Pulse: 80 beats/min
Hct: 36% (0.36 L/L)
Hgb: 12.5 g/dL (125 g/L)

History: Tetanus toxoid immunization 1 week ago

How many of the above results will exclude this donor from giving blood for a routine transfusion?

    a. none
    b. one
    c. two
    d. three

121. A first time blood donor is noticed to experience rapid breathing and involuntary twitching of his fingers shortly after starting phlebotomy. The phlebotomist should:

    a. raise his feet above his head
    b. administer oxygen
    c. have him rebreathe air from a paper bag
    d. have him inhale from an ammonia capsule
    e. place padded tongue blades between his teeth

122. Which of the following measures should be employed if a donor experiences perioral paresthesia during an apheresis procedure?

    a. increase flow rate
    b. reduce flow rate
    c. elevate donor's feet
    d. have donor breathe into a paper bag

123. For serial plasmapheresis donors, the total serum protein must be at least:

   a. 4.5 g/dL
   b. 5.0 g/dL
   c. 5.5 g/dL
   d. 6.0 g/dL

124. Therapeutic plasmapheresis is performed in order to:

   a. harvest granulocytes
   b. harvest platelets
   c. treat patients with polycythemia
   d. treat patients with plasma abnormalities

125. Following plasmapheresis, how long must a person wait before being eligible to donate a unit of Whole Blood?

   a. eight weeks
   b. two weeks
   c. forty-eight hours
   d. twenty-four hours

126. Hydroxyethyl starch (HES) is a rouleaux-promoting agent which is used to:

   a. increase the harvest of granulocytes in leukopheresis
   b. treat patients following hemolytic transfusion reaction
   c. resolve ABO typing discrepancies
   d. stabilize the pH of stored platelets

127. Prior to blood donation, the intended venipuncture site must be cleaned with a scrub solution containing:

   a. hypochlorite
   b. isopropyl alcohol
   c. 10% acetone
   d. PVP iodine complex

128. The test which is currently used to detect donors who are infected with the AIDS virus is:

   a. anti-HBc
   b. anti-HIV 1
   c. HBsAg
   d. ALT

129. Current testing on all donor blood must include:

    a. complete Rh phenotyping
    b. indirect antiglobulin test
    c. test for hemoglobin S
    d. direct antiglobulin test
    e. serological test for syphilis

130. What is/are the minimum pretransfusion testing requirement(s) for autologous donations collected and transfused by the same facility?

    a. ABO and Rh typing only
    b. ABO/Rh type, antibody screen
    c. ABO/Rh type, antibody screen, crossmatch
    d. no pretransfusion testing is required for autologous donations

131. For Platelets Pheresis donors, the pretransfusion platelet count must be at least:

    a. $150 \times 10^3/\mu L$
    b. $200 \times 10^3/\mu L$
    c. $250 \times 10^3/\mu L$
    d. $300 \times 10^3/\mu L$

132. A 14-year-old male trauma victim is in need of three units of Red Blood Cells. The following results were obtained during pretransfusion testing:

	IS	37°C	IAT
Screening Cell I	0	0	0
Screening Cell II	0	0	0
Autocontrol	0	0	0
Crossmatch:			
donor 1	0	0	0
donor 2	0	0	±
donor 3	0	0	0

What is the FIRST step in resolving this problem?

    a. perform an enzyme panel on the patient's serum
    b. choose more donors to crossmatch
    c. confirm ABO and Rh on donors
    d. repeat the crossmatch
    e. perform a DAT on donor 2

133. A 42-year-old female is undergoing surgery tomorrow and her physician requests that 4 units of Red Blood Cells be crossmatched. The following results were obtained:

	IS	37°C	IAT
Screening Cell I	0	0	0
Screening Cell II	0	0	0
Autocontrol	0	0	0
Crossmatch:			
donor 1	4+	1+	+/-
donors 2,3,4	0	0	0

What is the most likely cause of the incompatibility of donor 1?

    a. single alloantibody
    b. multiple alloantibodies
    c. Rh incompatibility
    d. donor 1 has a positive DAT

134. A 26-year-old female is admitted with anemia of undetermined origin. Blood samples are received with a crossmatch request for 6 units of Red Blood Cells. The patient is group A, Rh-negative and has not history of transfusion or pregnancy. The following results were obtained in pretransfusion testing:

	IS	37°C	IAT
Screening Cell I	0	0	3+
Screening Cell II	0	0	3+
Autocontrol	0	0	3+
All 6 donors	0	0	3+

The best way to find compatible blood is to:

    a. do an antibody identification panel
    b. use the saline replacement technique
    c. use the pre-warm technique
    d. perform a warm autoadsorption

135. Which of the following would most likely be responsible for an incompatible major crossmatch?

    a. recipient's red cells possess a low frequency antigen
    b. anti-K (Kell) antibody in donor serum
    c. recipient's red cells are polyagglutinable
    d. donor red cells have a positive direct antiglobulin test

136. A 37-year-old female with systemic lupus erythematosus (SLE) is admitted with anemia. Blood samples are received with a crossmatch request for 4 units of Red Blood Cells. The patient is group B, Rh-negative. The following results were obtained in pretransfusion testing:

	IS	37°C	IAT
Screening Cell I	0	0	3+
Screening Cell II	0	0	3+
Autocontrol	0	0	3+

The most probable cause of these results is:

   a. rouleaux
   b. ABO incompatibility
   c. a warm autoantibody
   d. a cold autoantibody
   e. multiple alloantibodies

137. A patient is typed as group O, Rh-positive and crossmatched with 6 units of Red Blood Cells. At the indirect antiglobulin (IAT) phase of testing, both antibody screening cells and two crossmatched units are incompatible. What is the most likely cause of the incompatibility?

   a. recipient alloantibody
   b. recipient autoantibody
   c. donors have positive DATs
   d. rouleaux

138. A 56-year-old female with cold hemagglutinin disease has a positive direct antiglobulin test (DAT). When the DAT is repeated using monospecific antiglobulin sera, which of the following is most likely to be detected?

   a. IgM
   b. IgG
   c. C3d
   d. C4d

139. In which of the following situations would the phthalate ester separation technique be most useful?

   a. positive DAT due to methyldopa
   b. recently transfused patient with multiple alloantibodies
   c. incompatibility due to cold autoantibodies
   d. febrile transfusion reaction caused by leukocyte antibodies

140. Refer to the following data:

Hemoglobin: 7.4 g/dL (74 g/L)
Reticulocyte Count: 22%

Direct Antiglobulin Test   Antibody Screen - IAT

Polyspecific   3+   SC I   3+
IgG   3+   SC II   3+
C3   0   Auto   3+

Which clinical condition is consistent with the lab results shown above?

   a. cold hemagglutinin disease
   b. warm autoimmune hemolytic anemia
   c. penicillin-induced hemolytic anemia
   d. delayed hemolytic transfusion reaction

141. A group B patient has received 4 units of group O blood during an emergency. When can she be given group B units again?

   a. immediately, providing group O units will not be transfused again
   b. 3 months following the last group O unit transfusion
   c. when anti-B is not detectable in her serum by immediate spin
   d. when group B units are crossmatch-compatible in the antiglobulin phase

142. While performing an antibody screen, a test reaction is observed which is suspected to be rouleaux. A saline replacement test is done and the reaction remains. What is the best interpretation?

   a. The original reaction was rouleaux and may be ignored.
   b. The replacement test is invalid and should be repeated.
   c. The original reaction was due to true agglutination.
   d. The antibody screen is negative.

143. In an emergency situation, Rh-negative red cells are transfused into an Rh-positive person of the genotype CDe/CDe. The first antibody MOST likely to develop is:

   a. anti-c
   b. anti-d
   c. anti-e
   d. anti-E

144. A 10-year-old girl was hospitalized because her urine had a distinct red color. The patient had recently recovered from an upper respiratory infection and appeared very pale and lethargic. Tests were performed with the following results:

Hemoglobin:	5 g/dL
Reticulocyte count:	15%
DAT:	weak reactivity with poly-specific and anti-C3d only
Antibody screen:	negative
Methemalbumin:	present
Ham's test:	negative
Sucrose hemolysis test:	negative
Donath-Landsteiner test:	positive; P-cells showed no hemolysis

The patient probably has:

a. paroxysmal cold hemoglobinuria (PCH)
b. paroxysmal nocturnal hemoglobinuria (PNH)
c. warm autoimmune hemolytic anemia
d. hereditary erythroblastic multinuclearity with a positive acidified serum test (HEMPAS)

145. A patient has life-threatening anemia due to warm autoantibodies. The patient's serum was reactive 2+ in the antiglobulin phase of testing with all cells on a routine panel. A technique that would be beneficial in preparing the patient's serum for compatibility testing is:

a. autoadsorption using the patient's heat-eluted, enzyme-treated red cells
b. autoadsorption using the patient's LISS-treated red cells
c. adsorption using enzyme-treated red cells from a normal donor
d. adsorption using methyldopa-treated red cells

146. In the autoadsorption procedure for the removal of cold autoagglutinins from serum, pretreatment of the patient's red cells with which one of the following reagents is helpful?

a. ficin
b. phosphate-buffered saline at pH 9.0
c. low ionic strength saline (LISS)
d. albumin

147. A patient's serum results revealed weakly positive reactions (1+^{w}) in 16 of 16 group O panel cells only at the AHG phase of testing; however, no reaction was noted in the autocontrol. Further testing with ficin-treated panel cells demonstrated no reactivity at the AHG phase. Which one of the following antibodies is most likely responsible for these results?

    a. anti-Ch
    b. anti-k
    c. anti-e
    d. anti-Js^a

148. A patient received 2 units of Red Blood Cells and had a delayed hemolytic transfusion reaction. Records indicate that no agglutination was detected in antibody screening except after the addition of IgG sensitized cells. Repeat testing of the pretransfusion specimen detected an antibody at the antiglobulin phase. Which of the following is the most likely explanation for the original results?

    a. red cells were overwashed
    b. centrifugation time was prolonged
    c. patient's serum was omitted from the original testing
    d. antiglobulin reagent was neutralized

149. To confirm the specificity of a serum antibody identified as anti-P$_1$, a neutralization study was performed and the following results were obtained:

                                    __P$_1$+ RBCs__

    Serum + P$_1$ substance -   negative
    Serum + saline   -   negative

What conclusion can be made from these results?

    a. Anti-P$_1$ is confirmed.
    b. Anti-P$_1$ is ruled out.
    c. A second antibody is suspected due to the negative control.
    d. Anti-P$_1$ cannot be confirmed due to the negative control.

150. A reason why a patient's crossmatch may be incompatible while the antibody screen is negative is:

    a. the patient has a antibody against a high frequency antigen
    b. the incompatible donor unit has a positive direct Coombs test
    c. cold agglutinins are interfering in the crossmatch
    d. the patient's serum contains warm autoantibody

151. An antibody identification study is performed with the 5 cell panel shown below:

		ANTIGENS					TEST RESULTS
		1	2	3	4	5	
P A N E L	C E L L S						
	I	+	0	0	+	+	+
	II	0	0	+	0	+	0
	III	0	+	+	+	0	0
	IV	0	+	+	0	+	+
	V	+	+	+	0	0	+
	AUTO						0

An antibody against which of the following antigens could NOT be excluded?

    a. 1
    b. 2
    c. 3
    d. 4
    e. 5

152. A patient received 2 units of Red Blood Cells and had a delayed transfusion reaction. Antibody screening records indicate that no agglutination was detected during testing except after the addition of IgG sensitized cells. Repeat testing of the pretransfusion specimen detected an antibody at the antiglobulin phase. What is a possible explanation?

    a. red cells were overwashed
    b. centrifugation time was prolonged
    c. patient's serum was omitted from the original testing
    d. antiglobulin reagent was neutralized

For questions 153 to 155, refer to the following panel and information:

A 25-year-old Caucasian woman, gravida 3, para 2, required two units of Whole Blood. The antibody screen was positive and the results of the antibody panel are shown.

Cell	D	C	E	c	e	M	N	S	s	Le^a	Le^b	P$_1$	K	k	Fy^a	Fy^b	Jk^a	Jk^b	Xg^a	IS	37 C	AHG
1	0	+	0	+	+	+	0	0	+	0	+	0	0	+	0	+	0	+	+	0	0	1+
2	+	+	0	0	+	0	+	0	+	+	0	+	0	+	+	0	+	+	+	0	0	0
3	+	+	0	0	+	+	+	+	+	0	+	+	0	+	0	+	0	+	+	0	0	0
4	+	0	+	+	0	+	+	+	0	0	+	0	+	+	0	+	+	0	+	0	0	1+
5	0	0	+	+	+	0	+	0	+	+	0	+	0	+	+	0	0	+	+	0	0	1+
6	0	0	0	+	+	+	0	0	+	0	0	+	0	+	0	0	+	0	+	0	0	1+
7	0	0	0	+	+	+	+	0	+	+	0	+	+	0	0	+	+	+	0	0	0	1+
8	0	0	0	+	+	+	0	0	+	0	+	0	0	+	+	0	+	+	+	0	0	1+
9	0	0	0	+	+	+	+	+	0	0	0	0	0	+	+	+	+	0	+	0	0	1+
10	0	0	0	+	+	+	0	+	+	0	+	0	0	+	+	0	+	0	+	0	0	1+
Patient																				0	0	0

153. Which of the following antibodies may be the cause of the positive antibody screen?

        a. anti-M and anti-K
        b. anti-c and anti-E
        c. anti-s and anti-c
        d. anti-Fy^b and anti-c

154. What is the most probable genotype of this patient?

        a. *rr*
        b. *r'r'*
        c. *R$_o$r*
        d. *R$_1$R$_1$*

155. Which of the following antibodies has NOT been ruled out
by the panel?

    a. anti-S
    b. anti-Le^a
    c. anti-Jk^a
    d. anti-K

156. The following compatibility testing results were obtained:

	22°C	37°C	AHG
Donor:	0	0	0
Screening Cells:	0	0	0
Autocontrol:	0	0	3+

The most probable explanation for these findings is that the:

    a. patient has an antibody directed against an antigen
present on donor RBCs
    b. donor has an antibody directed against an antigen
present on patient RBCs
    c. patient has a positive direct antiglobulin test
    d. donor has a positive direct antiglobulin test

157. A blood specimen was found to be A, Rh-positive. The antibody
screen and the direct antiglobulin tests were negative. Six
units of group A, Rh-positive Red Blood Cells were crossmatched
and one unit was incompatible in the antiglobulin phase. The
same result was obtained when the test was repeated. Which
of the following should be done first?

    a. repeat the ABO grouping on the incompatible unit using a
more sensitive technique
    b. test a panel of red cells which possess low-frequency
antigens
    c. perform a direct antiglobulin test on the donor unit
    d. obtain a new specimen and repeat the crossmatch

158. Under extreme emergency conditions when there is no time to
determine ABO group for transfusion, the technologist should:

    a. refuse to release any blood until the patient's sample
has been typed
    b. release O Rh-negative Whole Blood
    c. release O Rh-negative Red Blood Cells
    d. release O Rh-positive Red Blood Cells

159. A 29-year-old male is hemorrhaging severely. He is AB, Rh-negative. Six units of blood are required STAT. Of the following types available in the blood bank, which would be most preferable for crossmatch?

    a. AB, Rh-positive
    b. A, Rh-negative
    c. A, Rh-positive
    d. O, Rh-negative

160. A patient is group A_2B, Rh-positive and has a Coombs-reacting anti-A_1 in his serum. He is bleeding profusely in the operating room and group A_2B Red Blood Cells are NOT available. Which of the following types of blood should be given as a first choice?

    a. B, Rh-positive
    b. B, Rh-negative
    c. A_1B, Rh-positive
    d. O, Rh-negative

161. A request is received to crossmatch five units of Red Blood Cells on a man who is group AB, Rh-positive. The blood inventory shows the following:

    A, Rh-positive: 23 units   B, Rh-positive: 4 units
    A, Rh-negative: 6 units   AB, Rh-positive: 2 units
    O, Rh-positive: 30 units
    O, Rh-negative: 4 units

    Assuming all the blood crossmatched to be compatible, the desirable sequence of blood units that can be issued for transfusion would be:

    a. 5 units of group O, Rh-positive
    b. 5 units of group A, Rh-positive
    c. 2 units of group AB, Rh-positive; 3 units of group A, Rh-positive
    d. 2 units of group AB, Rh-positive; 3 units of group B, Rh-positive

162. A 22-year-old man is admitted to the emergency room in shock following massive hemorrhage from knife wounds to his chest and abdomen. An emergency transfusion is required. Which of the following is the product of choice?

    a. O, Rh-positive Red Blood Cells
    b. O, Rh-negative Red Blood Cells
    c. O, Rh-positive Whole Blood
    d. O, Rh-negative Whole Blood

163. An adult male patient who is actively bleeding has the following test results:

ABO: AB
Rh: negative
Antibody Screening: negative

Six units of Red Blood Cells are ordered STAT. The blood bank has the following Red Blood Cells units available:

A, Rh-positive: 12   B, Rh-positive: 2   AB Rh-positive: 4
A, Rh-negative: 4   B, Rh-negative: 2

Which of the following should be crossmatched for this patient while more blood is being ordered?

    a. 6 A, Rh-positive
    b. 4 A, Rh-negative and 2 A, Rh-positive
    c. 4 AB, Rh-positive and 2 A, Rh-negative
    d. 4 A, Rh-negative and 1 O, Rh-negative and 1 B, Rh-
       negative

164. A bone marrow transplant recipient with *Bacteroides* sp. septicemia has a PMN count of 350/µL. A 24 hour trial of antibiotic therapy has not proven effective. The blood component of choice is:

    a. Platelets
    b. Granulocytes Pheresis
    c. Cryoprecipitated AHF
    d. fresh Whole Blood

165. A 40-year-old man with autoimmune hemolytic anemia due to anti-E has a hemoglobin level of 10.8 gm/dL. This patient will most likely be treated with:

    a. Whole Blood
    b. Red Blood Cells
    c. Fresh Frozen Plasma
    d. no transfusion

166. Which of the following blood components contains the most factor VIII concentration relative to volume?

    a. Single-Donor Plasma
    b. Cryoprecipitated AHF
    c. Fresh Frozen Plasma
    d. Platelets

167. Which of the following blood components is the best source of fibrinogen for transfusion to a patient with hypofibrinogenemia?

    a. Fresh Frozen Plasma
    b. Whole Blood
    c. Platelets
    d. Cryoprecipitated AHF

168. A patient has had massive trauma involving replacement of one blood volume with Red Blood Cells and crystalloid. She is currently experiencing oozing from mucous membranes and surgical incisions. Laboratory values are as follows:

PT: Normal
APTT: Normal
Bleeding Time: Prolonged
Platelet Count: $20 \times 10^3/\mu L$ ($20 \times 10^9/L$)
Hemoglobin: 11.4 g/dL (114 g/L)

What is the blood component of choice for this patient?

    a. Red Blood Cells
    b. Platelets
    c. Cryoprecipitated AHF
    d. Fresh Frozen Plasma
    e. Prothrombin Complex

169. Transfusion of which of the following is needed to help correct hypofibrinogenemia due to DIC?

    a. Whole Blood
    b. Fresh Frozen Plasma
    c. Cryoprecipitated AHF
    d. Platelets

170. Which of the following blood components is the best source of factor IX?

    a. Platelets
    b. Whole Blood
    c. Cryoprecipitated AHF
    d. Single-Donor Plasma

171. A 24-year-old man with hemophilia is involved in an auto accident and is actively bleeding. Factor VIII assay results are 8%. The blood product of choice is:

    a. Single-Donor Plasma
    b. Fresh Frozen Plasma
    c. Whole Blood
    d. Cryoprecipitated AHF

172. Which of the following would be the component of choice for treatment of von Willebrand's disease?

    a. Platelets
    b. Factor IX concentrate
    c. Cryoprecipitated AHF
    d. Fresh Frozen Plasma

173. A 35-year-old man with von Willebrand's disease has an acute nose bleed and a hemoglobin level of 9.9 gm/dL. From the following list, select the blood component which is the MOST appropriate choice for transfusion to this patient.

    a. Platelets
    b. Fresh Frozen Plasma
    c. Cryoprecipitated AHF
    d. Red Blood Cells

174. The most effective component to treat a patient with fibrinogen deficiency is:

    a. Fresh Frozen Plasma
    b. Platelets
    c. fresh Whole Blood
    d. Cryoprecipitated AHF

175. A blood component used in the treatment of hemophilia A is:

    a. Factor VIII concentrate
    b. Fresh Frozen Plasma
    c. Platelets
    d. Whole Blood

176. Although ABO compatibility is preferred, ABO incompatible product may be administered when transfusing:

    a. Single-Donor-Plasma
    b. Cryoprecipitated AHF
    c. Fresh Frozen Plasma
    d. Granulocytes

177. Which of the following blood products is most appropriate to transfuse to an 8-year-old male hemophiliac who is about to undergo minor surgery?

    a. Cryoprecipitated AHF
    b. Red Blood Cells
    c. Platelets
    d. heat-treated Factor VIII concentrate

178. Leukocyte-Poor Red Blood Cells would most likely be indicated for patients with a history of:

    a. febrile transfusion reaction
    b. iron deficiency anemia
    c. hemophilia A
    d. von Willebrand's disease

179. Transfusion of Platelets Pheresis from HLA-compatible donors is the preferred treatment for:

    a. recently diagnosed cases of aplastic anemia with severe thrombocytopenia
    b. acute leukemia in relapse with neutropenia, thrombocytopenia and sepsis
    c. immune thrombocytopenic purpura
    d. severely thrombocytopenic patients, known to be refractory to random donor platelets

180. Plasma exchange is recommended in the treatment of patients with macroglobulinemia in order to remove:

    a. antigen
    b. excess IgM
    c. excess IgG
    d. abnormal platelets

181. A Whole Blood unit from a donor which contains a clinically significant red cell alloantibody should be:

    a. discarded
    b. adsorbed with antigen-positive red cells before issue
    c. processed into components containing minimal plasma
    d. labeled with the antibody specificity

182. The most important step in the safe administration of blood is to:

    a. perform a careful crossmatch
    b. take a careful history from the recipient
    c. exclude disqualified donors
    d. accurately identify the donor unit and intended recipient

183. During the issue of an autologous unit of Whole Blood, the supernatant plasma is observed to be dark red in color. What would be the best course of action?

    a. The unit may be issued only for autologous use.
    b. Remove the plasma and issue the unit as Red Blood Cells.
    c. Issue the unit only as Washed Red Blood Cells.
    d. Quarantine the unit until further testing determines disposition.

184. What information is essential on the label of recipient blood samples drawn for compatibility testing?

    a. biohazard sticker for AIDS patients
    b. patient's room number
    c. patient's hospital identification number
    d. identification of phlebotomist

185. Which of the following patients should receive CMV antibody-negative blood products?

    a. pregnant woman in the third trimester
    b. newborn weighing 1400 gms
    c. renal dialysis patient
    d. bone marrow transplant recipient

186. Granulocytes for transfusion should:

    a. be administered through a microaggregate filter
    b. be ABO and Rh compatible with the recipient's serum
    c. be infused within 72 hours of collection
    d. never be transfused to patients with a history of febrile transfusion reactions

187. A patient has a positive antibody screen. Prior to transfusion, granulocytes MUST be:

    a. washed to remove the plasma
    b. retyped for Rh antigen only
    c. crossmatched with the recipient's serum
    d. filtered to remove RBCs and lymphocytes

188. A granulocyte transfusion is indicated if the patient has:

    a. leukemia
    b. an absolute granulocyte count of 500/µL or less
    c. a viral infection
    d. a leukocyte count of 1,000/µL

189. Cryoprecipitated AHF:

    a. is indicated for fibrinogen deficiencies
    b. should be stored at 4°C prior to administration
    c. will not transmit hepatitis B virus
    d. is indicated for the treatment of hemophilia B

190. The use of Red Blood Cells Deglycerolized would be most beneficial when transfusing a patient:

    a. with sickle cell anemia
    b. who is at high risk for hepatitis B infection
    c. who is sensitized to platelet antigens
    d. with warm autoantibody

191. Washed Red Blood Cells are indicated in which of the following situations?

    a. an IgA-deficient patient with a history of transfusion-associated anaphylaxis
    b. a pregnant woman with a history of hemolytic disease of the newborn
    c. a patient with a positive DAT and red cell autoantibody
    d. a newborn with a hematocrit of less than 30%

192. A 42-year-old male of average body mass has a history of chronic anemia requiring transfusion support. Two units of Red Blood Cells are transfused. If the pretransfusion hemoglobin was 7.0 g/dL (70 g/L), the expected posttransfusion hemoglobin concentration should be:

    a. 8.0 g/dL (80 g/L)
    b. 9.0 g/dL (90 g/L)
    c. 10.0 g/dL (100 g/L)
    d. 11.0 g/dL (110 g/L)
    e. 12.0 g.dL (120 g/L)

193. How many units of Red Blood Cells are required to raise the hematocrit of a 70 kg nonbleeding man from 24% to 30%?

   a. 1
   b. 2
   c. 3
   d. 4

194. Which of the following is consistent with standard blood bank procedure governing the infusion of Fresh Frozen Plasma?

   a. Only blood group-specific plasma may be administered.
   b. Group O may be administered to recipients of all blood groups.
   c. Group AB may be administered to AB recipients only.
   d. Group A may be administered to both A and O recipients.

195. A patient who is group AB, Rh-negative needs 2 units of Fresh Frozen Plasma. Which of the following units of plasma would be MOST acceptable for transfusion?

   a. group O, Rh-negative
   b. group A, Rh-negative
   c. group B, Rh-positive
   d. group AB, Rh-positive

196. Fresh Frozen Plasma from a group A, Rh-positive donor may be safely transfused to a patient who is group:

   a. A, Rh-negative
   b. B, Rh-negative
   c. AB, Rh-positive
   d. AB, Rh-negative

197. A patient admitted to the trauma unit requires emergency release of Fresh Frozen Plasma (FFP). His blood donor card states that he is group AB, Rh-positive. Which of the following blood groups of FFP should be issued?

   a. A
   b. B
   c. AB
   d. O

198. Fresh Frozen Plasma:

   a. contains all labile coagulation factors except Cryoprecipitated AHF
   b. has a higher risk of transmitting hepatitis than does Whole Blood
   c. should be transfused within 24 hours of thawing
   d. need not be ABO-compatible

199. An Rh-positive patient's serum is known to contain anti-LW. Red Blood Cells selected for crossmatch should be from which of the following genotypes?

   a. R_1R_1
   b. R_2R_2
   c. R_0R_0
   d. rr

200. What increment of platelets/µL, per m^2 body surface area, is expected to result from each single unit of Platelets transfused into a non-HLA-sensitized recipient?

   a. 3,000
   b. 10,000
   c. 20,000
   d. 30,000
   e. 50,000

201. Platelet transfusions are of most value in treating:

   a. hemolytic transfusion reaction
   b. posttransfusion purpura
   c. functional platelet abnormalities
   d. immune thrombocytopenic purpura

202. Posttransfusion anaphylactic reactions occur most often in patients with:

   a. leukocyte antibodies
   b. erythrocyte antibodies
   c. IgA deficiency
   d. factor VIII deficiency

203. Posttransfusion purpura is caused by:

   a. anti-A
   b. white cell antibodies
   c. plasma antigens
   d. anti-Pl^{A1}
   e. platelet wash-out

204. An unexplained fall in hemoglobin and mild jaundice in a patient transfused with Red Blood Cells 1 week ago would most likely indicate:

    a. paroxysmal nocturnal hemoglobinuria
    b. posttransfusion hepatitis infection
    c. presence of HLA antibodies
    d. delayed hemolytic transfusion reaction

205. In investigating a hemolytic transfusion reaction, the pre- and posttransfusion samples should be:

    a. tested for HBsAg and anti-HIV-1
    b. crossmatched against the suspected unit(s)
    c. tested against a reagent red cell panel
    d. autoadsorbed and tested against screening cells

206. Which of the following transfusion reactions occurs after infusion of only a few milliliters of blood and gives no history of fever?

    a. febrile
    b. circulatory overload
    c. anaphylactic
    d. hemolytic

207. Which of the following transfusion reactions is characterized by high fever, shock, hemoglobinuria, DIC and renal failure?

    a. bacterial contamination
    b. circulatory overload
    c. hemolytic
    d. anaphylactic

208. Fever and chills are symptoms of which of the following transfusion reactions?

    a. citrate toxicity
    b. circulatory overload
    c. allergic
    d. febrile

209. Hemoglobinuria, hypotension and generalized bleeding are symptoms of which of the following transfusion reactions?

    a. allergic
    b. circulatory overload
    c. hemolytic
    d. anaphylactic

210. Coughing, cyanosis and difficult breathing are symptoms of which of the following transfusion reactions?

    a. febrile
    b. allergic
    c. circulatory overload
    d. hemolytic

211. Hives and itching are symptoms of which of the following transfusion reactions?

    a. febrile
    b. allergic
    c. circulatory overload
    d. anaphylactic

212. Hypotension, nausea, flushing, fever and chills are symptoms of which of the following transfusion reactions?

    a. allergic
    b. circulatory overload
    c. hemolytic
    d. anaphylactic

213. When evaluating a suspected transfusion reaction, which of the following is the ideal sample collection time for a bilirubin determination?

    a. 6 hours posttransfusion
    b. 12 hours posttransfusion
    c. 24 hours posttransfusion
    d. 48 hours posttransfusion

214. Which of the following is an immediate nonimmunologic adverse effect of a transfusion?

    a. hemolytic reaction
    b. febrile nonhemolytic reaction
    c. congestive heart failure
    d. urticaria

215. The most frequent transfusion-associated disease complication of blood transfusions is:

    a. cytomegalovirus (CMV)
    b. syphilis
    c. hepatitis
    d. AIDS

216. In a delayed transfusion reaction, the causative antibody is generally too weak to be detected in routine compatibility testing and antibody screening tests, but becomes detectable at what point after transfusion?

    a. 3 to 6 hours
    b. 1 to 5 days
    c. 60 to 90 days
    d. after 120 days

217. The most serious transfusion reactions are due to incompatibility in which of the following blood group systems?

    a. ABO
    b. Rh
    c. MN
    d. Duffy

218. Congestive heart failure, severe headache and/or peripheral edema occurring soon after transfusion is indicative of which type of transfusion reaction?

    a. hemolytic
    b. febrile
    c. anaphylactic
    d. circulatory overload

219. Which of the following is the first step in hemoglobin clearance from the plasma following an intravascular hemolytic transfusion reaction?

    a. reduction in plasma haptoglobin concentration
    b. increase in plasma hemoglobin
    c. urinary excretion of hemosiderin
    d. urinary excretion of hemoglobin

220. Severe intravascular hemolysis is most likely caused by antibodies of which blood group system?

    a. ABO
    b. Rh
    c. Kell
    d. Duffy

221. Which of the following blood group systems is most commonly associated with delayed hemolytic transfusion reactions?

    a. Lewis
    b. Kidd
    c. MNS
    d. I
    e. P

222. A patient whose saline and albumin crossmatches were compatible had a severe hemolytic reaction. Of the following antibodies, the one most likely present is anti-:

    a. Le^b
    b. K
    c. M
    d. P

223. After receiving a unit of Whole Blood, a patient immediately developed flushing, nervousness, fever spike of 102°F, shaking, chills and back pain. The plasma hemoglobin was elevated and there was hemoglobinuria. Laboratory investigation of this adverse reaction would most likely show:

    a. an error in ABO grouping
    b. an error in Rh typing
    c. presence of anti-Jk^a antibody in patient's serum
    d. presence of gram-negative bacteria in blood bag

224. In paternity testing, a "direct exclusion" is established when a genetic marker is:

    a. absent in the child, but present in the mother and alleged father
    b. absent in the child, present in the mother and absent in the alleged father
    c. present in the child, absent in the mother and present in the alleged father
    d. present in the child, but absent in the mother and alleged father

225. With regard to inheritance, most blood group systems are:

    a. sex-linked dominant
    b. sex-linked recessive
    c. autosomal recessive
    d. autosomal codominant

226. The observed phenotypic frequencies at the Jk locus in a particular population are:

Phenotype	Number of persons
Jk(a+b-)	122
Jk(a+b+)	194
Jk(a-b+)	84

What is the gene frequency of the Jk^a in this population?

   a. 0.31
   b. 0.45
   c. 0.55
   d. 0.60

227. A paternity investigation produces the following red cell phenotyping results. What conclusions may be made?

	ABO	Rh
Alleged Father:	B	DcE
Mother:	O	DCe
Child:	O	DCce

   a. There is no exclusion of paternity.
   b. Paternity may be excluded on the basis of ABO typing.
   c. Paternity may be excluded on the basis of Rh typing.
   d. Paternity may be excluded on the basis of both ABO and Rh typing.

228. The mating of an Xg(a+) man and an Xg(a-) woman will ONLY produce:

   a. Xg(a-) sons and Xg(a-) daughters
   b. Xg(a+) sons and Xg(a+) daughters
   c. Xg(a-) sons and Xg(a+) daughters
   d. Xg(a+) sons and Xg(a-) daughters

229. Irradiation of a unit of Red Blood Cells is done to prevent the replication of donor:

   a. granulocytes
   b. lymphocytes
   c. red cells
   d. platelets
   e. viruses

230. Refer to the following data:

Antisera	Reactions
Anti-C	+
Anti-D	+
Anti-E	+
Anti-c	+
Anti-e	+

Which of the following is a possible genotype for an individual whose red cells gives the reactions shown above?

    a. R_1R_1
    b. R_1r'
    c. R_0r''
    d. R_1R_2

---

231. Refer to the following diagram:

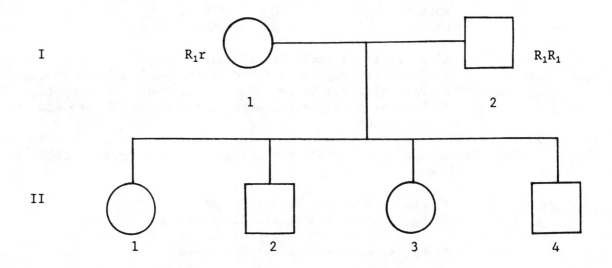

Given the most probable genotypes of the parents, which of the following statements best describes the most probable Rh genotypes of the four children?

    a. two are R_1r, two are R_1R_1
    b. three are R_1r, one is rr
    c. one is R_0r, one is R_1r, two are R_1R_1
    d. one is R_0r, two are R_1r
    e. all four are R_1R_1

232. Refer to the following data:

Rh Genotype

Mother: cde/cde
Father: CDe/cde

These parents would most likely have a child with the genotype:

a. R_1R_1
b. R_0r
c. $r'r$
d. rr

233. The linked HLA genes on each chromosome constitute a(n):

a. allele
b. trait
c. phenotype
d. haplotype

234. Genes of the major histocompatibility complex (MHC):

a. code for HLA-A, HLA-B, and HLA-C antigens only
b. are linked to genes in the ABO system
c. are the primary genetic sex-determinants
d. contribute to the coordination of cellular and humoral immunity

235. A family has been typed for HLA because one of the children needs a bone marrow donor. Typing results are listed below:

Father: A1,3;B8,35
Mother: A2,23;B12,18
Child #1: A1,2;B8,12
Child #2: A1,23;B8,18
Child #3: A3,23;B18,?

What expected antigen is missing in child #3?

a. A1
b. A2
c. B8
d. B12
e. B35

236. Which of the following is the best source of HLA-compatible leukocytes or platelets?

    a. mother
    b. father
    c. siblings
    d. cousins

237. The enzyme responsible for conferring H activity on the red cell membrane is alpha-:

    a. galactosyl transferase
    b. N-acetylgalactosaminyl transferase
    c. L-fucosyl transferase
    d. glucosyl transferase

238. Which of the following immunoglobulins is present in the highest concentration in normal human serum?

    a. IgM
    b. IgG
    c. IgA
    d. IgD
    e. IgE

239. Hemolysis of the red cell occurs when which components of complement are attached?

    a. C1
    b. C3
    c. C4-C2
    d. C8-C9

240. The mechanism that best explains hemolytic anemia due to penicillin is:

    a. drug adsorption
    b. membrane modification
    c. immune complex formation
    d. autoantibody production

241. Use of EDTA plasma prevents activation of the classical complement pathway by:

    a. causing rapid decay of complement components
    b. chelating Mg^{++} ions which prevents the assembly of C6
    c. chelating Ca^{++} ions which prevents assembly of C1
    d. preventing chemotaxis

The following items (*) have been identified as more appropriate for the entry level medical technologist.

*242. The red cells of a non-secretor (se/se) will most likely type as:

        a. Le(a-b-)
        b. Le(a+b+)
        c. Le(a+b-)
        d. Le(a-b+)

*243. Which of the following phenotypes will react with anti-f?

        a. rr
        b. R_1R_1
        c. R_2R_2
        d. R_1R_2

*244. Red cells of which of the following genotypes have the least amount of LW antigen?

        a. CDe/CDe
        b. Cde/cDE
        c. cDE/cde
        d. cde/cde

*245. Glycophorin B is associated with which one of the following blood groups' antigenic activity?

        a. MN
        b. Ss
        c. Wr^a/Wr^b
        d. Lu^a/Lu^b

*246. In chronic granulomatous disease (CGD), granulocyte function is impaired. An association exists between this clinical condition and a depression of which of the following antigen systems?

        a. Rh
        b. P
        c. Kell
        d. Duffy

*247. Mixed field agglutination is a characteristic observation for which of the following antibodies?

        a. anti-K
        b. anti-Sd^a
        c. anti-Js^a
        d. anti-e

*248. Even in the absence of prior transfusion or pregnancy, individuals with the Bombay phenotype (O_h) will always have naturally occurring:

    a. anti-Rh
    b. anti-K_o
    c. anti-U
    d. anti-H
    e. anti-Ku

*249. Inhibition testing can be used to confirm antibody specificity for which of the following antibodies?

    a. anti-Lu^a
    b. anti-M
    c. anti-Le^a
    d. anti-Fy^a

*250. Resistance to malaria is best associated with which of the following blood groups?

    a. Rh
    b. I/i
    c. P
    d. Duffy

*251. The HLA complex shows strong associations with which blood group?

    a. MN
    b. Bg
    c. Duffy
    d. Rodgers

*252. Which of the following red cell antigens are found on glycophorin-A?

    a. M, N
    b. Le^a, Le^b
    c. S, s
    d. P, P_1, P^k

*253. Mixed Leukocyte Culture (MLC) is a biological assay for detecting which of the following?

    a. HLA-A antigens
    b. HLA-B antigens
    c. HLA-D antigens
    d. complement components C2, C4a, C4b
    e. immunoglobulins

*254. Which of the following medications is most likely to cause production of autoantibodies?

   a. penicillin
   b. cephalothin
   c. methyldopa
   d. tetracycline

*255. Transfusion of Ch+ (Chido-positive) red cells to a patient with anti-Ch has been reported to cause:

   a. no clinically significant red cell destruction
   b. clinically significant immune red cell destruction
   c. decreased ^{51}Cr red cell survival
   d. febrile transfusion reactions

*256. Results of a serum sample tested against a panel of reagent red cells gives presumptive evidence of an alloantibody directed against a high incidence antigen. Further investigation to confirm the specificity should include which of the following?

   a. serum testing against red cells from random donors
   b. serum testing against red cells known to lack high incidence antigens
   c. serum testing against enzyme-treated autologous red cells
   d. testing of an eluate prepared from the patient's red cells

*257. In a case of cold autoimmune hemolytic anemia, the patient's serum would most likely react 4+ at immediate spin with:

   a. group A cells, B cells and O cells, but not his own cells
   b. cord cells but not his own or other adult cells
   c. all cells of a group O cell panel and his own cells
   d. only penicillin-treated panel cells, not his own cells

*258. Anti-A_1 lectin (*Dolichos biflorus*) will react with which of the following red cells?

   a. T-activated
   b. Tn-activated
   c. O_h
   d. A_x

Refer to the following panel:

Cell	D	C	E	c	e	M	N	S	s	Le^a	Le^b	P₁	K	k	Fy^a	Fy^b	Jk^a	Jk^b	Serum Alb IS	37 C	AHG
1	0	+	0	+	+	+	0	0	+	0	+	0	0	+	0	+	0	+	0	0	0
2	+	+	0	0	+	0	+	0	+	+	0	+	0	+	+	0	0	+	0	0	2+
3	+	+	0	0	+	+	+	+	+	0	+	+	+	0	+	+	+	+	0	0	3+
4	+	+	+	+	0	0	+	+	0	0	+	+	0	+	0	+	0	+	0	1+	4+
5	0	0	+	+	+	0	+	0	+	0	+	+	0	+	+	+	+	+	0	1+	4+
6	0	0	0	+	+	+	0	0	+	0	0	+	0	+	0	0	+	0	0	0	0
7	0	0	0	+	+	0	+	0	+	0	+	+	+	+	0	+	0	+	0	0	2+
8	0	0	0	+	+	+	0	+	0	+	0	+	0	+	0	+	+	0	0	0	0
9	0	0	0	+	+	+	0	+	0	0	+	+	+	+	+	0	+	+	0	0	3+
10	+	+	+	0	+	+	0	+	0	+	0	0	0	+	+	0	+	0	0	1+	4+
Autocontrol																			0	0	0

Based on the results of the above panel, which technique would be most helpful in determining antibody specificity?

   a. proteolytic enzyme treatment
   b. urine neutralization
   c. autoadsorption
   d. saliva inhibition

---

*260. Which of the following occurs to the patient's antibody in an in vitro neutralization study when a soluble antigen preparation is added?

   a. inhibition
   b. dilution
   c. complement fixation
   d. hemolysis

For questions 261 and 262, refer to the following data:

Forward Group			Reverse Group		
Anti-A	Anti-B	Anti-A$_1$ lectin	A$_1$ cells	A$_2$ Cells	B Cells
4+	neg	4+	neg	2+	4+

*261. The ABO discrepancy seen above is most likely due to:

   a. anti-A$_1$
   b. rouleaux
   c. anti-H
   d. unexpected IgG antibody present

*262. Which of the following antibody screen results would you expect
   with the ABO discrepancy seen above?

   a. negative
   b. positive with all screen cells at the 37°C phase
   c. positive with all screen cells at the RT phase;
      autocontrol is negative
   d. positive with all screen cells and the autocontrol
      at the RT phase

---

*263. To confirm the specificity of a serum containing anti-Le^b
   an inhibition study using Lewis substance was performed and
   the following results were obtained:

	Le(b+) cells
Patient serum + Lewis Substance:	+
Patient serum + Saline Control:	0

   What conclusion can be made from these results?

   a. Anti-Le^b is confirmed.
   b. Anti-Le^b is not confirmed.
   c. A second antibody is suspected due to the positive
      control.
   d. Anti-Le^b cannot be confirmed due to the positive control.

*264. Serologic testing of a patient with no history of transfusion
   revealed the following results:

Antibody Screening:	negative
Direct Antiglobulin Test:	3+
Ether eluate:	negative

   Which of the following drugs would most likely be involved?

   a. methyldopa
   b. aspirin
   c. insulin
   d. cephalothin

*265. A patient who has been typed as Rh-negative has a negative antibody screen. However, crossmatching reveals an antibody that reacts 4+ in the AHG phase with 1 out of 10 Rh-negative donors. What is the most likely cause of this incompatibility?

    a. The patient has an antibody to a low-frequency antigen.
    b. The donor has been mistyped for ABO.
    c. The donor is actually Rh-positive.
    d. The donor's RBCs are polyagglutinable.

---

*266. Refer to the following cell panel:

Cell	D	C	E	c	e	M	N	S	s	Le^a	Le^b	P$_1$	K	k	Fy^a	Fy^b	Jk^a	Jk^b	IS	37 C	AHG	Enzyme AHG
1	0	+	0	+	+	+	0	0	+	0	+	0	0	+	0	+	0	+	0	0	2+	3+
2	+	+	0	0	+	+	+	+	+	0	+	+	0	+	+	0	0	+	0	0	3+	4+
3	+	+	0	+	+	+	0	+	+	+	0	+	+	0	+	+	+	0	0	0	2+	3+
4	+	+	0	0	+	+	0	+	0	0	+	+	0	+	0	+	+	+	0	0	3+	4+
5	0	0	0	+	+	+	0	+	+	0	+	0	0	+	+	+	+	+	0	0	2+	0
6	0	0	0	+	+	0	+	+	0	0	+	+	+	+	+	+	+	0	0	0	2+	0
7	+	0	0	+	+	0	+	+	+	0	+	+	0	+	0	0	+	+	0	0	0	0
8	+	0	+	+	0	0	+	0	+	+	0	+	0	+	0	+	0	+	0	0	0	0
9	+	0	+	+	+	+	+	0	+	0	+	+	0	+	+	+	+	+	0	0	2+	0
10	0	0	0	+	+	+	+	+	0	0	+	0	0	+	+	0	+	0	0	0	2+	0
Autocontrol																			0	0	0	0

Based on these results which of the following antibodies is MOST likely present?

    a. anti-C
    b. anti-E
    c. anti-D
    d. anti-Kell

*267. A patient's red blood cells gave the following reactions:

Anti-D	Anti-C	Anti-E	Anti-c	Anti-e	Anti-f
+	+	+	+	+	0

The most probable genotype of this patient is:

a. R_1R_2
b. $R_2r"$
c. R_zr
d. R_zR_z

*268. Refer to the following data:

Indicator Cells

	A	B	O
Saliva plus anti-A	+	0	0
Saliva plus anti-B	0	+	0
Saliva plus anti-H	0	0	0

Which of the following is the correct interpretation of the results of this saliva neutralization testing?

a. group A secretor
b. group B secretor
c. group AB secretor
d. group O secretor
e. nonsecretor

---

*269. A person's saliva incubated with the following antibodies and tested with the appropriate A_2, O, and B indicator cells, gives the following test results:

Antibody Specificity	Test Results
anti-A	reactive
anti-B	inhibited
anti-H	inhibited

The person's red cell ABO phenotype is:

a. A
b. AB
c. B
d. O

*270. Which of the following would be most useful for removing
autoantibody from red cells to permit D^u testing ?

    a. bromelin
    b. chloroquine
    c. LISS
    d. phthalate esters

*271. Anti-D and anti-C are identified in the serum of a 35-year-old
woman, gravida 1, para 1, who has never been transfused. Nine
months ago she received Rh immune globulin (RhIG) after
delivery. Testing of the patient, her husband and the child
revealed the following:

	Anti-D	Anti-C	Anti-E	Anti-c	Anti-e
Patient	neg	neg	neg	+	+
Father	+	neg	neg	+	+
Child	+	neg	neg	+	+

The most likely explanation for the presence of anti-C is that
this antibody:

    a. is actually anti-C^w
    b. is from the RhIG dose
    c. is actually anti-G
    d. is naturally occurring

*272. In a prenatal workup, the following results were obtained:

Forward Group				Reverse Group	
Anti-A	Anti-B	Anti-D	Rh Control	A_1 Cells	B Cells
4+	2+	4+	neg	neg	3+

DAT: negative
Antibody Screen: negative

ABO discrepancy was thought to be due to an antibody directed
against acriflavin. Which of the following tests would
resolve this discrepancy?

    a. A_1 lectin
    b. wash patient's RBCs and repeat typing
    c. anti-A,B and extend incubation of the reverse group
    d. repeat reverse group using A_2 cells

*273. A newborn demonstrates petechiae, ecchymosis and mucosal bleeding. The preferred blood component for this infant would be:

    a. Red Blood Cells
    b. Fresh Frozen Plasma
    c. Platelets
    d. Cryoprecipitated AHF

*274. Based upon Kleihauer-Betke test results, which of the following formulas is used to determine the volume of fetomaternal hemorrhage in mL of whole blood?

    a. % of fetal cells x 30

    b. % of fetal cells x 50

    c. % of maternal cells x 50

    d. % of maternal cells x 30

*275. An acid elution stain was made using a one-hour post-delivery maternal blood sample. Two thousand cells were counted and thirty of these cells appeared to contain fetal hemoglobin. It is the policy of the medical center to add one vial of Rh immune globulin to the calculated dose when the estimated volume of the hemorrhage exceeds 20 mL of whole blood. Calculate the number of vials of Rh immune globulin that would be indicated under these circumstances.

    a. 2
    b. 3
    c. 4
    d. 5

*276. A neonate is to be transfused for the first time with group O Red Blood Cells. Which of the following is appropriate when compatibility testing is performed?

    a. screen and crossmatch with mother's serum
    b. screen and crossmatch with baby's serum
    c. crossmatch is NOT necessary if initial screening of mother's or baby's serum was negative
    d. screening or crossmatching is NOT necessary; issue group and Rh compatible blood

*277. The Liley method of predicting the severity of hemolytic disease of the newborn is based on the amniotic fluid:

    a. bilirubin concentration by standard methods
    b. change in optical density measured at 450 nm
    c. Rh determination
    d. ratio of lecithin to sphingomyelin

*278. Which of the following is the proper storage requirement for Granulocytes?

    a. 1° to 6°C
    b. 10° to 18°C
    c. room temperature with constant agitation
    d. room temperature without agitation

*279. Once collected, Granulocytes MUST be administered within:

    a. 6 hours
    b. 24 hours
    c. 7 days
    d. 35 days

*280. The purpose of a low dose irradiation of blood components is to:

    a. prevent posttransfusion purpura
    b. prevent graft-versus-host (GVH) disease
    c. sterilize components
    d. prevent non-cardiogenic pulmonary edema

*281. A 65-year-old woman experienced shaking, chills, and a fever of 103°F approximately 40 minutes following the transfusion of a second unit of Red Blood Cells. The most likely explanation for the patient's symptoms is:

    a. transfusion of bacterially contaminated blood
    b. congestive heart failure due to fluid overload
    c. anaphylactic transfusion reaction
    d. severe febrile transfusion reaction

*282. A patient has become refractory to platelet transfusion. Which of the following is the most probable cause?

    a. transfusion of Rh-incompatible platelets
    b. decreased pH of the Platelets
    c. development of an alloantibody with anti-D specificity
    d. development of antibodies to HLA antigen

*283. A unit of Fresh Frozen Plasma was inadvertently thawed and then immediately refrigerated at 4°C on Monday morning. On Tuesday evening this unit may still be transfused as a replacement for:

   a. all coagulation factors
   b. factor V
   c. factor VIII
   d. factor IX

*284. A patient diagnosed as having mild hemophilia A (8% factor VIII:C) was transfused with factor VIII concentrates in preparation for abdominal surgery. It was calculated that he would require 1200 units of factor VIII to raise his plasma concentration to 50%. Following infusion his factor VIII concentration rose to 65%, and remained at 50% for approximately 30 hours without further infusion. What would be the most likely explanation for this observation?

   a. patient really had von Willebrand's disease
   b. factor VIII concentrates had twice the specified factor VIII concentration
   c. patient had an inhibitor to the Factor VIII complex
   d. patient had idiopathic thrombocytopenic purpura

*285. Cryoprecipitated AHF, if maintained in the frozen state at -18°C or below, has a shelf life of:

   a. 42 days
   b. 6 months
   c. 12 months
   d. 36 months

*286. Washed Red Blood Cells would be the product of choice for patients with:

   a. multiple red cell alloantibodies
   b. an increased risk of hepatitis infection
   c. warm autoimmune hemolytic anemia
   d. a very elevated serum potassium level

*287. Which of the following would be the best source of platelets for transfusion in a case of alloimmune neonatal thrombocytopenia?

   a. father
   b. mother
   c. pooled platelet-rich plasma
   d. polycythemic donor

*288. A patient presented with the following laboratory data:

-decreased levels of factor VIII antigen
-decreased levels of factor VIII clotting activity
-prolonged template bleeding time
-impaired aggregation of platelets in response to ristocetin

What is the treatment of choice for this disease?

a. Platelets
b. lyophilized Factor VIII concentrate
c. Factor IX complex
d. Cryoprecipitated AHF

*289. Which of the following components requires compatibility testing prior to transfusion?

a. Fresh Frozen Plasma
b. Granulocytes
c. Platelets
d. Cryoprecipitated AHF

*290. What percent of group O donors would be compatible with a serum sample that contained anti-X and anti-Y if X antigen is present on red cells of 5 of 20 donors, and Y antigen is present on red cells of 1 of 10 donors?

a. 2.5
b. 6.8
c. 25.0
d. 68.0

*291. In a random population, 16% of the people are Rh-negative (rr). What percentage of the Rh-positive population would be heterozygous for the D antigen?

a. 36
b. 48
c. 57
d. 66

*292. How may Caucasians in a population of 100,000 will have the following combination of phenotypes?

System	Phenotype	Phenotype Frequency (%)
ABO	0	45
Gm	Fb	48
PGM$_1$	2-1	37
EsD	2-1	18

    a.   1
    b.   14
    c. 144
    d. 1,438

*293. What is the approximate probability of finding compatible blood among random Rh-positive units for a patient who has anti-c and anti-K? (Consider that 20% of Rh-positive donors are E-negative and 90% are K-negative)

    a. 1%
    b. 10%
    c. 18%
    d. 45%
    e. 80%

*294. In a paternity case, the child has a genetic marker that is absent in the mother and cannot be demonstrated in the alleged father. What type of paternity exclusion is this known as?

    a. indirect (second order)
    b. direct (first order)
    c. prior probability
    d. Hardy-Weinberg

*295. Anti-N is identified in a patient's serum. If random crossmatches are performed on 10 donor units, how many would be expected to be compatible?

    a. 0
    b. 3
    c. 7
    d. 10

*296. For a patient who has suffered an acute hemolytic transfusion reaction, the primary treatment goal should be to:

    a. prevent alloimmunization
    b. diminish chills and fever
    c. prevent hemoglobinemia
    d. reverse hypotension and minimize renal damage

*297. A panel of tests composed of HBsAg, anti-HAV-IgM, and anti-HBc is designed to:

   a. indicate immunity to hepatitis
   b. estimate the degree of infectivity
   c. aid in the diagnosis of past hepatitis infection
   d. aid in the diagnosis of acute viral hepatitis

*298. In a hematologically stable adult with a 1.8 m² body surface area, one unit of Platelets should increase the platelet count by:

   a. 500-1,000/µL
   b. 1,500-3,000/µL
   c. 5,000-10,000/µL
   d. 15,000-20,000/µL

*299. The drug cephalosporin can cause a positive direct antiglobulin test by which of the following mechanisms?

   a. immune-complex formation
   b. complement fixation
   c. autoantibody production
   d. membrane modification

*300. Examination of immune parameters during the course of HIV infection reveals:

   a. a progressive decrease in T-helper cell numbers as clinical disease worsens
   b. qualitative defects in B-cell function
   c. a progressive increase in T-helper cell numbers as clinical disease worsens
   d. normal B-cell function

Blood Bank Answer Key

1.	C	48.	C	95.	A	142.	C
2.	B	49.	B	96.	B	143.	A
3.	A	50.	C	97.	B	144.	A
4.	C	51.	D	98.	B	145.	A
5.	A	52.	A	99.	D	146.	A
6.	C	53.	B	100.	C	147.	A
7.	C	54.	E	101.	B	148.	C
8.	A	55.	B	102.	C	149.	D
9.	B	56.	D	103.	A	150.	B
10.	C	57.	D	104.	D	151.	A
11.	B	58.	C	105.	D	152.	C
12.	C	59.	C	106.	A	153.	B
13.	C	60.	D	107.	C	154.	D
14.	A	61.	A	108.	D	155.	D
15.	A	62.	C	109.	D	156.	C
16.	B	63.	B	110.	B	157.	C
17.	C	64.	D	111.	B	158.	C
18.	B	65.	A	112.	A	159.	B
19.	C	66.	C	113.	A	160.	A
20.	B	67.	C	114.	A	161.	C
21.	A	68.	D	115.	C	162.	B
22.	B	69.	C	116.	D	163.	B
23.	C	70.	A	117.	D	164.	B
24.	A	71.	D	118.	B	165.	D
25.	B	72.	A	119.	C	166.	B
26.	D	73.	A	120.	A	167.	D
27.	B	74.	C	121.	C	168.	B
28.	A	75.	A	122.	B	169.	C
29.	D	76.	B	123.	D	170.	D
30.	C	77.	A	124.	D	171.	D
31.	B	78.	B	125.	C	172.	C
32.	C	79.	D	126.	A	173.	C
33.	C	80.	A	127.	D	174.	D
34.	C	81.	C	128.	B	175.	A
35.	D	82.	A	129.	B	176.	B
36.	C	83.	B	130.	A	177.	D
37.	D	84.	A	131.	A	178.	A
38.	D	85.	D	132.	E	179.	D
39.	D	86.	C	133.	A	180.	B
40.	A	87.	C	134.	D	181.	C
41.	D	88.	A	135.	D	182.	D
42.	B	89.	A	136.	C	183.	D
43.	C	90.	D	137.	A	184.	C
44.	D	91.	C	138.	C	185.	D
45.	D	92.	D	139.	C	186.	B
46.	B	93.	A	140.	B	187.	C
47.	D	94.	A	141.	D	188.	B

189.	A	217.	A	245.	B	273.	C
190.	C	218.	D	246.	C	274.	B
191.	A	219.	A	247.	B	275.	C
192.	B	220.	A	248.	D	276.	C
193.	B	221.	B	249.	C	277.	B
194.	D	222.	B	250.	D	278.	D
195.	D	223.	A	251.	C	279.	B
196.	A	224.	D	252.	A	280.	B
197.	C	225.	D	253.	C	281.	D
198.	C	226.	C	254.	C	282.	D
199.	D	227.	C	255.	A	283.	D
200.	B	228.	C	256.	B	284.	A
201.	C	229.	B	257.	C	285.	C
202.	C	230.	D	258.	B	286.	D
203.	D	231.	A	259.	A	287.	B
204.	D	232.	D	260.	A	288.	D
205.	A	233.	D	261.	C	289.	B
206.	C	234.	D	262.	C	290.	D
207.	A	235.	E	263.	A	291.	B
208.	D	236.	C	264.	D	292.	D
209.	C	237.	C	265.	A	293.	C
210.	C	238.	B	266.	A	294.	B
211.	B	239.	D	267.	C	295.	C
212.	C	240.	A	268.	D	296.	D
213.	A	241.	C	269.	C	297.	D
214.	C	242.	C	270.	B	298.	C
215.	C	243.	A	271.	C	299.	D
216.	B	244.	D	272.	B	300.	A

CHAPTER 12

Body Fluid

The following items have been identified as appropriate for both entry level medical technologists and medical laboratory technicians.

1. Which of the following inorganic substances are excreted in the urine in the largest amount?

   a. urea and NaCl
   b. creatine and NaCl
   c. creatine and ammonia
   d. urea and glucose

2. Normal urine primarily consists of:

   a. water, protein and sodium
   b. water, urea and protein
   c. water, urea and sodium chloride
   d. water, urea and bilirubin

3. An abdominal fluid is submitted from surgery. The physician wants to determine if this fluid could be urine. The technologist should:

   a. perform a culture
   b. smell the fluid
   c. test for urea, creatinine, sodium and chloride
   d. test for protein, glucose and Ph

4. Antidiuretic hormone regulates the reabsorption of:

   a. water
   b. glucose
   c. potassium
   d. calcium

5. The clarity of a urine sample should be determined:

   a. using glass tubes only - never plastic
   b. following thorough mixing of the specimen
   c. after addition of sulfosalicylic acid
   d. after the specimen cools to room temperature

6. A milky colored urine from a 24-year-old woman would most likely contain:

    a. spermatozoa
    b. many WBCs
    c. red blood cells
    d. bilirubin

7. A brown-black colored urine would most likely contain:

    a. bile pigment
    b. porphyrin
    c. melanin
    d. blood cells

8. The amber yellow color of urine is primarily due to:

    a. urochrome pigment
    b. methemoglobin
    c. bilirubin
    d. homogentisic acid

9. Red colored urine may be due to:

    a. bilirubin
    b. excess urobilin
    c. myoglobin
    d. homogentisic acid

10. The normal kidney does NOT:

    a. remove metabolic waste products from the blood
    b. regulate the acid-base balance in the body
    c. remove excess protein from the blood
    d. regulate the water content in the body

11. Which of the following components are present in serum but NOT present in the glomerular filtrate?

    a. glucose
    b. amino acids
    c. urea
    d. large molecular weight proteins

12. While performing a urinalysis, a technologist notices the urine specimen to have a fruity odor. This patient's urine most likely contains:

    a. acetone
    b. bilirubin
    c. coliform bacilli
    d. porphyrin

13. Which of the following is the average volume of urine excreted by an adult in 24 hours?

    a. 750 mL
    b. 1000 mL
    c. 1500 mL
    d. 2000 mL

14. Oliguria is usually correlated with:

    a. acute glomerulonephritis
    b. diabetes mellitus
    c. hepatitis
    d. tubular damage

15. Cessation of urine flow is defined as:

    a. azotemia
    b. dysuria
    c. diuresis
    d. anuria

16. Patients with diabetes mellitus have urine with:

    a. decreased volume and decreased specific gravity
    b. decreased volume and increased specific gravity
    c. increased volume and decreased specific gravity
    d. increased volume and increased specific gravity

17. A patient with uncontrolled diabetes mellitus will most likely have:

    a. pale urine with a high specific gravity
    b. concentrated urine with a high specific gravity
    c. pale urine with a low specific gravity
    d. dark urine with a high specific gravity

18. A urine's specific gravity is directly proportional to its:

    a. turbidity
    b. dissolved solids
    c. salt content
    d. sugar content

19. Isosthenuria is associated with a specific gravity which is usually:

    a. variable between 1.001 and 1.008
    b. variable between 1.015 and 1.022
    c. fixed around 1.010
    d. fixed around 1.020

20. The fluid leaving the glomerulus normally has a specific gravity of:

    a. 1.001
    b. 1.010
    c. 1.020
    d. 1.030

21. An antidiuretic hormone deficiency is associated with a:

    a. specific gravity around 1.031
    b. low specific gravity
    c. high specific gravity
    d. variable specific gravity

22. A standard water-load dilution test is performed on a patient. A specific gravity measurement made on the urine specimen at 18.6°C using the refractometer method is 1.012. A reagent strip analysis of the specimen includes the following:

    pH   8.0
    Glucose 1 g/dL
    Protein 1 g/dL

The corrected specific gravity to be reported is:

    a. 1.004
    b. 1.005
    c. 1.007
    d. 1.012

23. Use of a refractometer over a urinometer is preferred due to the fact that the refractometer uses:

    a. large volume of urine and compensates for temperature
    b. small volume of urine and compensates for glucose
    c. small volume of urine and compensates for temperature
    d. small volume of urine and compensates for protein

24. Calibration of refractometers is done by measuring the specific gravity of:

    a. distilled water and protein
    b. distilled water and glucose
    c. distilled water and sodium chloride
    d. distilled water and urea

25. The pH of a urine specimen measures the:

    a. free sodium ions
    b. free hydrogen ions
    c. total acid excretion
    d. volatile acids

26. The normal value for pH on a healthy adult is:

    a. 4.5
    b. 5.0
    c. 6.0
    d. 8.0

27. Upon standing at room temperature a urine pH typically:

    a. decreases
    b. increases
    c. remains the same
    d. changes depending on bacterial concentration

28. A 28-year-old woman is taking an antibiotic for a urinary tract infection and was told that the antibiotic would be most effective if her urine pH was acidic. This woman should be on a diet rich in:

    a. vegetables
    b. protein
    c. citrus fruits
    d. milk

29. Urine reagent strips should be stored in a(n):

    a. refrigerator (4-7°C)
    b. incubator (37°C)
    c. cool dry area
    d. open jar exposed to air

30. The principle of the reagent strip test for urine protein depends on:

    a. an enzyme reaction
    b. protein error of indicators
    c. copper reduction
    d. the toluidine reaction

31. The protein section of the urine reagent strip is MOST sensitive to:

    a. albumin
    b. mucoprotein
    c. Bence Jones protein
    d. globulin

32. When performing a routine urinalysis, the technologist notes a 2+ protein result. He should:

    a. request another specimen
    b. confirm with the acid precipitation test
    c. test for Bence Jones protein
    d. report the result obtained without further testing

33. The confirmatory test for a positive protein result by the reagent strip method uses:

    a. Ehrlich's reagent
    b. a diazo reaction
    c. sulfosalicylic acid
    d. a copper reduction tablet

34. A patient with multiple myeloma submits a specimen for urinalysis immediately after having IVP radiologic studies. Which of the following is the method of choice for performing a protein screening test?

    a. reagent strip
    b. sulfosalicylic acid
    c. heat and acetic acid
    d. protein electrophoresis

35. After receiving a 24 hour urine for quantitative total protein analysis, the technician must first:

    a. subculture the urine for bacteria
    b. add the appropriate preservative
    c. screen for albumin using a dipstick
    d. measure the total volume

36. Routine screening of urine samples for glycosuria is performed primarily to detect:

    a. glucose
    b. galactose
    c. bilirubin
    d. ketones

37. Glycosuria testing typically is done by:

    a. yeast fermentation and glucose oxidase
    b. glucose oxidase and copper reduction
    c. chromatography and copper reduction
    d. copper reduction and yeast fermentation

38. A urine specimen is analyzed for glucose by a glucose oxidase reagent strip and a copper reduction test. If both results are positive, which of the following interpretations is correct?

    a. galactose is present
    b. glucose is present
    c. lactose is not present
    d. sucrose is not present

39. Some regional and public health laboratories carry out mass screening tests on the urine of newborns for a genetic disorder involving metabolism of:

    a. fructose
    b. galactose
    c. glucose
    d. lactose

40. A woman in her ninth month of pregnancy has a urine sugar which is negative with the urine reagent strip, but gives a positive reaction with the copper reduction method. The sugar most likely responsible for these results is:

    a. maltose
    b. galactose
    c. glucose
    d. lactose

41. A urinalysis performed on a two week-old infant with diarrhea shows a negative reaction with the glucose oxidase reagent strip. A copper reduction tablet test should be performed to check the urine sample for the presence of:

    a. glucose
    b. galactose
    c. bilirubin
    d. ketones

42. Ketones in urine are due to:

    a. complete utilization of fatty acids
    b. incomplete fat metabolism
    c. high carbohydrate diets
    d. renal tubular dysfunction

43. Which of the following reagents is used to react with ketones in the urine?

    a. sodium nitroprusside
    b. acetoacetic acid
    c. acetone
    d. beta-hydroxybutyric acid

44. A test area of a urine reagent strip is impregnated with buffered sodium nitroprusside. This section will react with:

   a. acetoacetic acid
   b. acetone
   c. beta-hydroxybutyric acid
   d. ferric chloride

45. Which of the following ketone bodies is excreted in the largest amount in ketonuria?

   a. acetone
   b. acetoacetic acid
   c. cholesterol
   d. beta-hydroxybutyric acid

46. A reagent strip area impregnated with stabilized, diazotized 2,4-dichloroaniline will yield a positive reaction with:

   a. bilirubin
   b. hemoglobin
   c. ketones
   d. urobilinogen

47. Bilirubinuria is most often associated with:

   a. strenuous exercise
   b. increased destruction of platelets
   c. infectious hepatitis
   d. CMV infection

48. The following are compounds formed in the synthesis of heme:

   1. Coproporphyrinogen
   2. Porphobilinogen
   3. Uroporphyrinogen
   4. Protoporphyrinogen

Which of the following responses lists these compounds in the order in which they are formed?

   a. 4, 3, 1, 2
   b. 2, 3, 1, 4
   c. 2, 4, 3, 1
   d. 2, 1, 3, 4

49. False results in urobilinogen testing may occur if the urine specimen is:

   a. exposed to light
   b. adjusted to a neutral pH
   c. cooled to room temperature
   d. collected in a non-sterile container

50. Which of the following factors will NOT interfere with the reagent strip test for leukocytes?

   a. ascorbic acid
   b. formaldehyde
   c. nitrite
   d. urinary protein level of 300 mg/dL

51. The presence of leukocytes in urine is known as:

   a. chyluria
   b. hematuria
   c. leukocytosis
   d. pyuria

52. Myoglobinuria is MOST likely to be noted in urine specimens from patients with which of the following disorders?

   a. hemolytic anemia
   b. lower urinary tract infections
   c. myocardial infarctions
   d. paroxysmal nocturnal hemoglobinuria

53. A clean catch urine is submitted to the laboratory for routine urinalysis and culture. The routine urinalysis is done first, and the specimen is then sent to microbiology for culture. The specimen should:

   a. be centrifuged, and the supernatant cultured
   b. be rejected due to possible contamination from routine urinalysis
   c. not be cultured if no bacteria are seen
   d. be immediately processed for culture regardLess of urinalysis results

54. A clean catch urine specimen is to be collected for culture and routine analysis. A preservative is added since the specimen cannot be submitted to the laboratory within one hour. Which of the following determinations may be affected by this?

    a. culture
    b. glucose
    c. bilirubin
    d. specific gravity

55. A urine specimen contaminated with bacteria is left standing unrefrigerated for seven hours. If this specimen was not preserved which of the following tests will be most accurate?

    a. pH
    b. leukocyte esterase
    c. urobilinogen
    d. glucose

56. The following results were obtained on an unpreserved urine specimen at 8:00 a.m.:

pH	5.5
Protein	2+
Glucose	3+
Ketones	3+
Blood	negative
Bilirubin	positive
Nitrite	positive

If this specimen is reanalyzed at 3:00 p.m., which of the following results is most apt to be changed by exposure to light?

    a. pH
    b. protein
    c. ketones
    d. bilirubin

57. Urinalysis testing is performed on a urine specimen which was left at 25°C for eight hours prior to testing. If bacteria are seen in the microscopic analysis, which of the following test results will most likely be inaccurate?

    a. protein
    b. glucose
    c. blood
    d. specific gravity

58. Urine samples should be examined within one hour of voiding because:

    a. red blood cells, leukocytes and casts agglutinate on standing for several hours at room temperature
    b. urobilinogen increases and bilirubin decreases after prolonged exposure to light
    c. bacterial contamination will cause alkalinization of the urine
    d. ketones will increase due to bacterial and cellular metabolism

59. The following results were obtained on a urine specimen at 8:00 a.m.:

pH	5.5
Protein	2+
Glucose	3+
Ketones	3+
Blood	negative
Bilirubin	positive
Nitrite	positive

    If this urine specimen was stored uncapped at 5°C without preservation and retested at 2 p.m., which of the following test results would be changed due to these storage conditions?

    a. glucose
    b. ketones
    c. protein
    d. nitrite

60. A urine specimen comes to the laboratory 7 hours after it is obtained. It is acceptable for culture only if the specimen has been stored:

    a. at room temperature
    b. at 4-7°C
    c. frozen
    d. with a preservative additive

61. The results of a urinalysis on a first morning specimen are:

Specific gravity	1.024
pH	8.5
Protein	negative
Glucose	negative
Microscopic	uric acid crystals

The next step is to repeat the:

    a. microscopic examination
    b. protein and glucose
    c. specific gravity
    d. pH and microscopic examination

62. Which of the following is an abnormal crystal described as a hexagonal plate?

    a. cystine
    b. tyrosine
    c. leucine
    d. cholesterol

63. Urinary calculi most often consist of:

    a. calcium
    b. uric acid
    c. leucine
    d. cystine

For questions 64 and 65, refer to the following illustration.

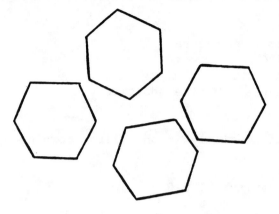

64. Colorless crystals, such as those depicted above, were
    seen in a urine specimen. This patient is most likely
    to have which of the following clinical conditions?

        a. gout
        b. renal damage
        c. bilirubinuria
        d. cystinosis

65. The colorless crystals depicted above would be found in a urine
    which has a(n):

        a. acid pH
        b. alkaline pH
        c. neutral pH
        d. variable pH

---

66. After warming to 60°C, a cloudy urine clears. This is due to
    the presence of:

        a. urates
        b. phosphates
        c. WBCs
        d. bacteria

67. Tiny colorless, dumbbell shaped crystals were found in an alka-
    line urine sediment. They most likely are:

        a. calcium oxalate
        b. calcium carbonate
        c. calcium phosphate
        d. amorphous phosphate

68. Which of the following crystals may be found in acidic urine?

    a. calcium carbonate
    b. calcium oxalate
    c. calcium phosphate
    d. triple phosphate

69. Using polarized light microscopy, which of the following urinary elements are birefringent?

    a. cholesterol
    b. triglycerides
    c. crystals
    d. neutral fats

70. Oval fat bodies are defined as:

    a. squamous epithelial cells that contain lipids
    b. renal tubular epithelial cells that contain lipids
    c. free-floating fat droplets
    d. white blood cells with phagocytized lipids

71. Round refractile globules noted on bright-light microscopy of a urinary sediment were birefringent with polarized-light and appeared as perfect Maltese crosses. These globules are most likely:

    a. neutral fats
    b. starch
    c. triglycerides
    d. cholesterol

72. All casts typically contain:

    a. albumin
    b. globulin
    c. immunoglobulins G and M
    d. Tamm-Horsfall glycoprotein

73. Hyaline casts are usually found:

    a. in the center of the coverslip
    b. under subdued light
    c. under very bright light
    d. in the supernatant

74. Which of the following casts is most likely to be found in healthy people?

   a. hyaline
   b. red blood cell
   c. waxy
   d. white blood cell

75. Which of the following casts is characteristically associated with acute pyelonephritis?

   a. red cell
   b. white cell
   c. waxy
   d. fatty

76. White blood cells casts are most likely to indicate disease of the:

   a. bladder
   b. ureter
   c. urethra
   d. kidney

77. Which of the following casts is most indicative of severe renal disease?

   a. hemoglobin
   b. granular
   c. cellular
   d. waxy

78. Waxy casts are most easily differentiated from hyaline casts by their:

   a. color
   b. size
   c. granules
   d. refractivity

79. Broad waxy casts are LEAST likely to be associated with:

   a. advanced tubular atrophy
   b. end-stage renal disease
   c. fatty degeneration tubular disease
   d. formation in a pathologically dilated tubule

80. The type of urinary cast that is most characteristically associated with glomerular injury is a(n):

    a. epithelial cell
    b. white cell
    c. red cell
    d. fatty

81. A technologist is having trouble differentiating between red blood cells, oil droplets and yeast cells on a urine microscopy. Acetic acid should be added to the sediment to:

    a. lyse the yeast cells
    b. lyse the red blood cells
    c. dissolve the oil droplets
    d. crenate the red blood cells

82. Small round objects found in a urine sediment that dissolve after addition of dilute acetic acid and do not polarize are most likely:

    a. air bubbles
    b. calcium oxalate
    c. red blood cells
    d. yeast cells

83. A microscopic examination of a urine sediment reveals ghost cells. These red blood cells were most likely lysed due to:

    a. greater than 2% glucose concentrations
    b. specific gravity less than 1.007
    c. large amounts of ketone bodies
    d. neutral pH

84. Glitter cells are a microscopic finding of:

    a. red blood cells in hypertonic urine
    b. red blood cells in hypotonic urine
    c. white blood cells in hypertonic urine
    d. white blood cells in hypotonic urine

85. What cell is MOST commonly associated with vaginal contamination?

    a. WBC
    b. transitional epithelial
    c. squamous epithelial
    d. glitter

86. Which of the following cells is the largest?

    a. glitter
    b. WBC
    c. transitional epithelial
    d. renal epithelial

87. In synovial fluid, the most characteristic microscopic finding in gout is:

    a. calcium pyrophosphate crystals
    b. cartilage debris
    c. monosodium urate crystals
    d. hemosiderin-laden macrophages

88. A synovial fluid specimen is diluted with saline and placed in a counting chamber. How can the leukocytes best be separated from erythrocytes?

    a. light microscopy
    b. phase contrast microscopy
    c. darkfield microscopy
    d. polarized light microscopy

89. In amniotic fluid, the procedure used to determine fetal lung maturity is:

    a. lecithin/sphingomyelin ratio
    b. creatinine
    c. measurement of absorbance at 450 nm
    d. alpha-fetoprotein

90. Of the following containers, the one best suited for collection of a cell count on peritoneal fluid is a:

    a. sterile plastic container
    b. test tube containing NaF
    c. capped syringe on ice
    d. tube containing EDTA

The following items (*) have been identified as more appropriate for the entry level medical technologist.

* 91. While performing an analysis of a baby's urine, the techno-
      logist notices the specimen to have a "mousy" odor. Of the
      following substances that may be excreted in urine, the one that
      MOST characteristically produces this odor is:

      a. phenylketone
      b. acetone
      c. coliform bacilli
      d. porphyrin

* 92. An ammonia-like odor is characteristically associated with
      urine from patients who:

      a. are diabetic
      b. have hepatitis
      c. have an infection with *Proteus* sp.
      d. have a yeast infection

* 93. The method of choice for performing a specific gravity measure-
      ment of urine following administration of x-ray contrast dyes
      is:

      a. reagent strip
      b. refractometer
      c. urinometer
      d. densitometer

* 94. Which of the following urinary parameters are measured during
      the course of concentration and dilution tests to assess renal
      tubular function?

      a. urea, nitrogen and creatinine
      b. osmolality and specific gravity
      c. sodium and chloride
      d. sodium and osmolality

* 95. Refractive index is a comparison of:

      a. light velocity in solutions to light velocity in
         solids
      b. light velocity in air to light velocity in solutions
      c. light scattering by air to light scattering by
         solutions
      d. light scattering by particles in solution

* 96. A patient with renal tubular acidosis would most likely excrete a urine with a:

    a. low pH
    b. high pH
    c. neutral pH
    d. variable pH

* 97. Excess urine on the reagent test strip can turn a normal pH result into an acidic pH when which of the following reagents interferes?

    a. tetrabromphenol blue
    b. citrate buffer
    c. glucose oxidase
    d. alkaline copper sulfate

* 98. When employing the urine reagent strip method, a false-positive protein result may occur in the presence of:

    a. large amounts of glucose
    b. x-ray contrast media
    c. Bence Jones protein
    d. highly alkaline urine

* 99. When using the sulfosalicylic acid test, false-positive protein results may occur in the presence of:

    a. ketones
    b. alkali
    c. glucose
    d. radiographic contrast media

*100. Which of the following is the primary reagent in the copper reduction tablet?

    a. sodium carbonate
    b. copper sulfate
    c. glucose oxidase
    d. polymerized diazonium salt

*101. A reagent strip test for hemoglobin has been reported positive. Microscopic examination fails to yield red blood cells. This patient's condition can be called:

    a. hematuria
    b. hemoglobinuria
    c. oliguria
    d. hemosiderinuria

*102. A 34-year-old man with diabetes mellitus has a blood sugar of 450 mg/dL. The following urinalysis results were obtained:

Specific gravity	1.030	Tablet Method:
pH	5.0	Reducing substance 3+
Protein	4+	
Glucose	trace	
Ketones	large	
Bilirubin	negative	
Blood	negative	
Nitrite	negative	
Urobilinogen	1.0 EU/dL	

Which of the following is the MOST likely explanation for the difference in glucose reactions by the two method?

a. The tablet method is more sensitive.
b. The high specific gravity falsely elevated the tablet results.
c. Ketones interfered with the reagent strip reaction.
d. Proteins interfered with the reagent strip reaction.

*103. The following urinalysis results were obtained from a 18-year-old woman in labor:

pH	6.5	Copper reduction test	1.0 g/dL
Protein	30 gm/dL	Sulfosalicylic acid	
Glucose	0.25 g/dL	test for protein	30 mg/dL
Ketones	negative		
Bilirubin	small (color slightly abnormal)		
Blood	negative		
Nitrite	negative		
Urobilinogen	0.1 EU/dL		
Specific gravity	1.025		

Which of the following is the MOST likely explanation for the patient's positive copper reduction test?

a. only glucose is present
b. only lactose is present
c. glucose and possibly other reducing substances/sugars are present
d. results are false-positive due to the presence of protein

*104. A 24-year-old obese diabetic woman had the following blood and urine test results from specimens obtained at the same time.

pH	7.5	Microscopic:	
Protein	30 mg/dL	Epithelial cells	3-5
Glucose	negative	Bacteria	many
Ketones	15 mg/dL	Yeast	many
Bilirubin	negative	Amorphous	moderate
Blood	negative		
Nitrite	negative	Blood sugar	195 mg/dL
Urobilinogen	1 EU/dL		
Specific gravity	1.008		

Which of the following is the MOST likely explanation for the negative urine glucose finding?

    a. There is a false-negative glucose due to oxidizing contaminants.

    b. There is a false-negative glucose due to the alkaline pH.

    c. The specimen is probably old and the bacteria and yeast have consumed the glucose.

    d. Glucose would not be present in the urine specimen since the blood sugar was normal.

*105. A 52-year-old man has urine glucose measurements performed as part of a three (3) hour glucose tolerance test. The test results are as follows:

TIME	SERUM GLUCOSE	URINE GLUCOSE
Fasting	82 mg/dL	negative
1/2 hour	120 mg/dL	negative
1 hour	190 mg/dL	negative
2 hours	115 mg/dL	1+
3 hours	95 mg/dL	trace

The best explanation for these findings is:

    a. The serum level must exceed the threshold level before glucose is filtered by the renal glomeruli.

    b. The serum level must exceed the threshold level before reabsorption of glucose is exceeded.

    c. The patient probably has renal glucosuria.

    d. The patient probably has diabetes mellitus.

*106. Glycosuria may be due to:

    a. hypoglycemia
    b. increased renal threshold
    c. renal tubular dysfunction
    d. increased glomerular filtration rate

*107. A 17-year-old woman decided to go on a starvation diet. After one week of starving herself, what substance would most likely be found in her urine?

    a. protein
    b. ketones
    c. glucose
    d. blood

*108. A 2-year-old child had a positive urine ketone. This would most likely be caused by:

    a. dehydration
    b. anemia
    c. hypoglycemia
    d. biliary tract obstruction

*109. A patient's urinalysis revealed a positive bilirubin and a decreased urobilinogen level. These results are associated with:

    a. hemolytic disease
    b. biliary obstruction
    c. hepatic disease
    d. urinary tract infection

*110. A urine specimen which displays an elevated urobilinogen and a negative bilirubin may indicate:

    a. obstruction of the biliary tract
    b. hepatic damage
    c. hemolytic jaundice
    d. cirrhosis

*111. Microscopic analysis of a urine specimen yields a moderate amount of red blood cells in spite of a negative result for occult blood using a reagent strip. The technologist should determine if this patient has taken:

    a. vitamin C
    b. a diuretic
    c. high blood pressure medicine
    d. antibiotics

*112. A 42-year-old man is admitted to the emergency room with multiple abrasions, several broken bones, a fractured pelvis and a crushed femur. The following urinalysis results are obtained:

Clarity	hazy	Microscopic:
Color	red-brown	Hemoglobin granular casts 3-5
Specific gravity	1.026	
pH	6.0	
Protein	300 mg/dL	
Glucose	negative	
Ketones	negative	
Blood	4+	
Bilirubin	negative	
Nitrite	negative	
Urobilinogen	0.1 EU/dL	

What is the MOST likely explanation for the discrepancy between the 4+ blood result, hemoglobin granular casts, and the complete absence of red cells on the microscopic?

    a. There is a false positive reaction for blood on the urine strip due to the large amount of protein
    b. The blood portion of the urine reagent strip is more sensitive to hemoglobin than intact red cells.
    c. Red blood cells have been lysed due to the pH and the specific gravity.
    d. The hemoglobin granular casts which were reported may actually be myoglobin granular casts.

*113. A technologist performed a STAT microscopic urinalysis and reported the following:

WBCs	10 to 13
RBCs	2 to 6
Hyaline casts	5 to 7
Bacteria	1+

The centrifuge tube was not discarded and the urine sediment was reevaluated microscopically five hours after the above results were reported. A second technologist reported the same results, except 2+ bacteria and no hyaline casts were found. The most probable explanation for the second technologist's findings is:

a. sediment was not agitated before preparing the microscope slide
b. casts dissolved due to decrease in urine pH
c. casts dissolved due to increase in urine pH
d. casts were never present in this specimen

*114. The following urine results were obtained on a 25-year-old female:

Color	amber	Microscopic:	
Appearance	cloudy	Bacteria	many
Specific gravity	1.015	WBC casts	few
pH	5.0	WBC/HPF	30-40
Protein	1+		
Glucose	negative		
Blood	slightly positive		

These results are most compatible with:

a. glomerulonephritis
b. renal calculus
c. vaginitis
d. pyelonephritis

For questions 115 and 116, refer to the following results:

A urinalysis performed on a 27-year-old woman yields the following results:

Specific gravity	1.008	Microscopic:
pH	5.0	WBC/HPF 20-30
Protein	2+	RBC/HPF 30-55
Glucose	negative	Casts/LPF
Ketones	negative	Hyaline 5-7
Bilirubin	negative	RBC 0-2
Blood	3+	Epithelial 1-3
Nitrite	negative	Coarse granular 2-3
Leukocytes	positive	Waxy 1-3
Urobilinogen	0.1 EU/dL	Uric acid crystals moderate

*115.   The above data is MOST consistent with:

    a. yeast infections
    b. pyelonephritis
    c. bacterial cystitis
    d. glomerulonephritis

*116.   The above data is consistent with:

    a. a vegetarian diet
    b. gout
    c. biliary obstruction
    d. chronic renal disease

---

*117.   A 62-year-old patient with hyperlipoproteinemia has a large amount of protein in his urine. Microscopic analysis yields moderate to many fatty, waxy, granular and cellular casts. Many oval fat bodies are also noted. This is most consistent with:

    a. nephrotic syndrome
    b. viral infection
    c. cystitis
    d. acute glomerulonephritis

*118. A patient has two separate urinalysis reports which contain the following data:

	Report A	Report B
Specific gravity:	1.004	1.017
pH:	5.5	7.0
Protein:	negative	trace
Glucose:	negative	trace
Blood:	negative	negative
Microscopic:	Rare epithelial cells	Occasional granular cast Rare hyaline cast Moderate epithelial cells

Which of the following statements best explains these results?

    a. The protein, glucose and microscopic of A are falsely negative because of the specific gravity.
    b. The protein and glucose are falsely positive in B due to the specific gravity.
    c. The microscopic of A is falsely negative because of the pH.
    d. The microscopic of B is falsely positive because of the pH.

*119. A 24-hour urine from a man who had no evidence of kidney impairment was sent to the laboratory for hormone determination. The volume was 600 mL, but there was some question as to the completeness of the 24 hour collection. The next step would be to:

    a. perform the hormone determination since 600 mL is a normal 24 hour urine volume
    b. check the creatinine level; if it is less than 1 gram do the procedure
    c. report the hormone determination in mg per deciliter in case the specimen was incomplete
    d. check the creatinine level; if it is greater than 1 gram do the procedure

*120. A 27-year-old woman with severe lower back pain, has the following urinalysis test results:

pH	5.5	Specific gravity	1.018
Protein	trace	Sulfosalicylic acid	
Glucose	negative	for protein	20 mg/dL
Ketones	negative	Microscopic:	
Blood	negative	WBC	3 to 5
Bilirubin	negative	RBC	25 to 50
Nitrite	negative	Epithelial cells	3 to 5
Urobilinogen	0.1 EU/dL	Mucous strands	moderate

Which of the following is the MOST likely explanation for the discrepancy in the blood portion of the urine reagent strip and the microscopic RBC finding?

   a. Oxidizing contaminants are causing a false-negative blood on the urine reagent strip.
   b. More red blood cells must be present in order for the blood portion to react.
   c. The red blood cells reported may actually be the round form of calcium oxalate crystals.
   d. The urine reagent strip is more sensitive to red blood cells than hemoglobin.

*121. A urine specimen collected on an apparently healthy 25-year-old man shortly after he finished eating lunch, was cloudy but showed normal results on a multiple reagent strip analysis. The most likely cause of the turbidity is:

   a. fat
   b. white blood cells
   c. urates
   d. phosphates

*122. On bright-light microscopic examination of a urinary sediment round refractile globules are noted in cells encapsulated within a hyaline matrix. A polarized-light microscopic examination of the urinary structure showed the globules to be birefringent in the shape of Maltese crosses. These urinary structures can be identified as:

   a. waxy casts associated with advanced tubular atrophy
   b. granular casts containing plasma protein aggregates
   c. crystal casts associated with obstruction due to tubular damage
   d. fatty casts containing lipid-laden renal tubular cells

*123. Which of the following fails to encourage the formation
of casts in the renal tubules?

    a. acid pH
    b. increased protein concentration
    c. diminished urine flow
    d. diluted urine

*124. In synovial fluid, the most characteristic finding in rheuma-
toid arthritis is:

    a. cartilage debris
    b. monosodium urate crystals
    c. hemosiderin-laden macrophages
    d. neutrophils with 0.5 - 1.5 micron inclusions

*125. In synovial fluid, the most characteristic finding in
pseudogout is:

    a. calcium pyrophosphate dihydrate crystals
    b. cartilage debris
    c. monosodium urate crystals
    d. hemosiderin-laden macrophages

*126. In synovial fluid, the most characteristic finding in
traumatic arthritis is:

    a. monosodium urate crystals
    b. cartilage debris
    c. calcium pyrophosphate dihydrate crystals
    d. hemosiderin-laden macrophages

*127. In amniotic fluid, the procedure most closely related
to fetoplacental function is:

    a. measurement of absorbance at 450 nm
    b. creatinine
    c. lecithin/sphingomyelin ratio
    d. estriol

For questions 128 and 129, refer to the following illustration:

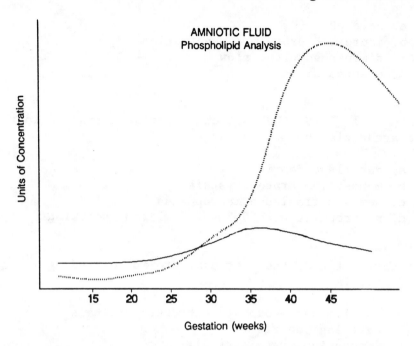

*128. Which class of phospholipid surfactants associated with pulmonary maturity is represented by the dotted line on the amniotic fluid analysis shown above?

    a. sphingomyelin
    b. choline
    c. lecithin
    d. phosphatidic acid

*129. The class of phospholipid surfactants represented by the dotted line on the amniotic fluid analysis shown above is thought to originate in what fetal organ system?

    a. cardiovascular
    b. pulmonary
    c. hepatic
    d. placental

*130. Technical problems encountered during the collection of an amniotic fluid specimen caused doubt as to whether the specimen was amniotic in origin. Which one of the following procedures would establish that the fluid is amniotic in origin?

    a. measurement of absorbance at 450 nm
    b. creatinine measurement
    c. lecithin/sphingomyelin ratio
    d. human amniotic placental lactogen (HPL)

*131. The procedure used to determine the presence of neural tube defects is:

    a. lecithin/sphingomyelin ratio
    b. amniotic fluid creatinine
    c. measurement of absorbance at 450 nm
    d. alpha fetoprotein

*132. Which one of the following is NOT a risk associated with amniocentesis?

    a. premature delivery
    b. maternal red cell immunization
    c. genetic defects
    d. fetal infection

*133. In amniotic fluid, the procedure used to detect Rh isosensitization is:

    a. human amniotic placental lactogen (HPL)
    b. alpha fetoprotein
    c. measurement of absorbance at 450 nm
    d. creatinine

*134. The glucose level in normal peritoneal fluid should be:

    a. near zero
    b. the same as the plasma glucose
    c. twice the plasma glucose
    d. ten times the plasma glucose

*135. A yellow peritoneal fluid specimen produced the following cell counts:

Total WBC	- 1,600/mm³
Total RBC	- 200/mm³
Segmented neutrophils	- 2%
Lymphocytes	- 5%
Large mononuclear cells	- 93%

Subsequent testing procedures should include:

a. blood cultures
b. serological studies
c. cytology examination
d. tissue culture

*136. In gastric analysis, milliequivalence/liter (degrees of acidity) is defined as the number of milliliters of:

a. NaOH required to neutralize a liter of gastric fluid
b. NaOH required to neutralize 100 mL of gastric fluid
c. 0.1N NaOH required to neutralize 100 mL of gastric fluid
d. gastric juice required to neutralize 100 mL of 0.1N NaOH

Body Fluid Answer Key

1.	A	35.	D	69.	A	103.	C
2.	C	36.	A	70.	B	104.	C
3.	C	37.	B	71.	D	105.	B
4.	A	38.	B	72.	D	106.	C
5.	B	39.	B	73.	B	107.	B
6.	B	40.	D	74.	A	108.	A
7.	C	41.	B	75.	B	109.	B
8.	A	42.	B	76.	D	110.	C
9.	C	43.	A	77.	D	111.	A
10.	C	44.	A	78.	D	112.	B
11.	D	45.	D	79.	C	113.	C
12.	A	46.	A	80.	C	114.	D
13.	C	47.	C	81.	B	115.	D
14.	A	48.	B	82.	C	116.	D
15.	D	49.	A	83.	B	117.	A
16.	D	50.	C	84.	D	118.	A
17.	A	51.	D	85.	C	119.	D
18.	B	52.	C	86.	C	120.	C
19.	C	53.	B	87.	C	121.	D
20.	B	54.	A	88.	B	122.	D
21.	B	55.	B	89.	A	123.	D
22.	B	56.	D	90.	D	124.	D
23.	C	57.	B	91.	A	125.	A
24.	C	58.	C	92.	C	126.	B
25.	B	59.	B	93.	A	127.	D
26.	C	60.	B	94.	B	128.	C
27.	B	61.	D	95.	B	129.	B
28.	B	62.	A	96.	B	130.	B
29.	C	63.	A	97.	B	131.	D
30.	B	64.	D	98.	D	132.	C
31.	A	65.	A	99.	D	133.	C
32.	B	66.	A	100.	B	134.	B
33.	C	67.	B	101.	B	135.	C
34.	C	68.	B	102.	C	136.	C

CHAPTER 13

Chemistry

The following items have been identified as appropriate for both entry level medical technologists and medical laboratory technicians.

1. Which of the following inhibits glycolysis and glucose uptake by muscle cells, and causes a rise in blood glucose concentration?

    a. parathyroid hormone
    b. calcitonin
    c. growth hormone
    d. gastrin

2. The different water content of erythrocytes and plasma makes true glucose concentrations in whole blood a function of the:

    a. hematocrit
    b. leukocyte count
    c. erythrocyte count
    d. erythrocyte indices

3. In the fasting state, the arterial and capillary blood glucose concentration varies from the venous glucose concentration by approximately how many mg/dL?

    a. 2 mg/dL higher
    b. 5 mg/dL higher
    c. 10 mg/dL lower
    d. 12 mg/dL lower

4. Total glycosylated hemoglobin levels in a hemolysate reflect the:

    a. average blood glucose levels of the past 2-3 months
    b. average blood glucose levels for the past week
    c. blood glucose level at the time the sample is drawn
    d. hemoglobin A_1C level at the time the sample is drawn

5. Which of the following hemoglobins has glucose-6-phosphate on the amino-terminal valine of the beta chain?

    a. S
    b. C
    c. A_2
    d. A_{1c}

6. In a specimen collected for plasma glucose analysis, sodium fluoride:

    a. serves as a coenzyme of hexokinase
    b. prevents reactivity of non-glucose reducing substances
    c. precipitates proteins
    d. inhibits glycolysis

7. Which of the following would be an example of a glucose-specific colorimetric method?

    a. alkaline ferricyanide
    b. glucose oxidase
    c. hexokinase
    d. o-toluidine

8. Increased concentrations of ascorbic acid inhibit chromogen production in which of the following glucose methods?

    a. ferricyanide
    b. ortho-toluidine
    c. glucose oxidase (peroxidase)
    d. hexokinase

9. In the hexokinase method for glucose determination, the actual endproduct measured is the:

    a. amount of hydrogen peroxide produced
    b. NADH produced from the reduction of NAD
    c. amount of glucose combined with bromcresol purple
    d. condensation of glucose with an aromatic amine

10. The function of the major lipid components of the very low density lipoproteins (VLDL) is to transport:

    a. cholesterol from peripheral cells to the liver
    b. cholesterol and phospholipids to peripheral cells
    c. exogenous triglycerides
    d. endogenous triglycerides

11. A 9-month-old boy from Israel has gradually lost the ability
to sit up and develops seizures. He has an increased amount
of a phospholipid called GM_2-ganglioside in his neurons, and
he lacks the enzyme hexosaminidase A in his leukocytes.
These findings suggest:

   a. Niemann-Pick disease
   b. Tay-Sachs disease
   c. phenylketonuria
   d. Hurler's syndrome

12. Turbidity in serum suggests elevation of:

   a. cholesterol
   b. total protein
   c. chylomicrons
   d. albumin

13. Storage of serum at low temperatures or in a lyophilized
condition usually insures the stability of each of the
following EXCEPT:

   a. serum lipoprotein
   b. cholinesterase
   c. gamma globulin
   d. alanine aminotransferase

14. The substance that is measured to estimate the serum
concentration of triglycerides by MOST methods is:

   a. phospholipids
   b. glycerol
   c. fatty acids
   d. pre-beta lipoprotein

15. Which of the following lipid results would be expected to
be falsely elevated on a serum specimen from a nonfasting
patient?

   a. cholesterol
   b. triglyceride
   c. HDL
   d. LDL

16. Which of the following is NOT a stain for lipids?

   a. Congo red
   b. Sudan IV
   c. oil red 0
   d. Coomassie brilliant blue

17. In lipoprotein electrophoresis at pH 8.6 using agarose gel, which fraction migrates the fastest toward the anode?

    a. chylomicrons
    b. alpha lipoprotein
    c. pre-beta lipoprotein
    d. beta lipoprotein

18. As part of a hyperlipidemia screening program, the following results were obtained on a 25-year-old woman 6 hours after eating:

    Triglycerides   260 mg/dL
    Cholesterol   120 mg/dL

Which of the following is the BEST interpretation of these results?

    a. Both results are normal, and not affected by the recent meal.
    b. The cholesterol is normal, but the triglycerides are elevated which may be attributed to the recent meal.
    c. Both results are elevated, indicating a metabolic problem in addition to the nonfasting state.
    d. Both results are below normal despite the recent meal, indicating a metabolic problem.

19. The most widely used support media for electrophoretic separation of lipoprotein is:

    a. agar gel
    b. starch gel
    c. paper
    d. agarose gel

20. Blood was collected in a serum separator tube on a patient who has been fasting since midnight. The time of collection was 7:00 a.m. The laboratory test(s) which should be recollected is (are):

    a. triglycerides
    b. iron
    c. LD
    d. Na/K

21. In the liver, bilirubin is converted to:

    a. urobilinogen
    b. urobilin
    c. bilirubin-albumin complex
    d. bilirubin glucuronide

22. In the Malloy and Evelyn method for the determination of bilirubin, the reagent that is reacted with bilirubin to form a purple azobilirubin is:

    a. dilute sulfuric acid
    b. diazonium sulfate
    c. sulfobromophthalein
    d. diazotized sulfanilic acid

23. If the total bilirubin is 4.3 mg/dL and the conjugated bilirubin is 2.1 mg/dL, the unconjugated bilirubin is:

    a. 1.1 mg/dL
    b. 2.2 mg/dL
    c. 4.2 mg/dL
    d. 6.3 mg/dL

24. In which of the following disease states is conjugated bilirubin a major serum component?

    a. biliary obstruction
    b. hemolysis
    c. neonatal jaundice
    d. erythroblastosis fetalis

25. Kernicterus is an abnormal accumulation of bilirubin in:

    a. heart tissue
    b. brain tissue
    c. liver tissue
    d. kidney tissue

26. In the Jendrassick-Grof method for the determination of serum bilirubin concentration, quantitation is obtained by measuring the green color of:

    a. azobilirubin
    b. bilirubin glucuronide
    c. urobilin
    d. urobilinogen

27. The fast hemoglobin fraction is:

    a. Hgb A
    b. Hgb A_2
    c. Hgb A_1
    d. Hgb F

28. The hemoglobin that is resistant to alkali (KOH) denaturation is:

    a. A
    b. A_2
    c. C
    d. F

29. A patient with hemolytic anemia will:

    a. show a decrease in glycosylated Hgb values
    b. show an increase in glycosylated Hgb values
    c. show little or no change in glycosylated Hgb values
    d. demonstrate an elevated Hgb A_1

30. Toxic effects of lead poisoning are manifested by each of the following EXCEPT:

    a. increased excretion of delta-aminolevulinic acid
    b. increased excretion of coproporphyrins
    c. increased excretion of porphobilinogen
    d. increased erythrocyte protoporphyrins

31. The pH that is most suitable for storing urine for porphyrin analysis is:

    a. 2
    b. 5
    c. 7
    d. 9

32. Fecal porphyrin analysis by talc thin-layer chromatography can detect:

    a. hereditary coproporphyria
    b. carrier state of acute intermittent porphyria
    c. erythrocytic protoporphyria
    d. acute porphyria attack

33. A urine screening test for porphobilinogen is positive. The MOST likely disease state is:

    a. lead poisoning
    b. porphyria cutanea tarda
    c. acute porphyria attack
    d. erythrocytic protoporphyria

34. Zinc protoporphyrin or free erythrocyte protoporphyrin in measurements are useful to assess blood concentrations of:

   a. lead
   b. mercury
   c. arsenic
   d. beryllium

35. Conditions in which erythrocyte protoporphyrin is increased include:

   a. acute intermittent porphyria
   b. iron deficiency anemia
   c. porphyria cutanea tarda
   d. acute porphyria attack

36. The normal concentration of proteins in cerebrospinal fluid, relative to serum protein, is:

   a. less than 1%
   b. 5-10%
   c. 25-30%
   d. 50-60%

37. Loss of renal function is demonstrated by high serum concentrations in each of the following analytes EXCEPT:

   a. creatinine
   b. phosphate
   c. protein
   d. uric acid

38. The protein that has the highest dye-binding capacity is:

   a. albumin
   b. alpha globulin
   c. beta globulin
   d. gamma globulin

39. Refer to the following illustration:

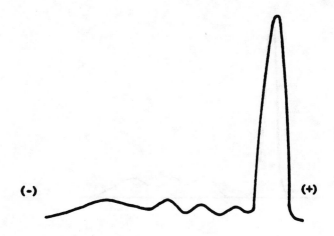

The serum protein electrophoresis pattern shown above was obtained on cellulose acetate at pH 8.6. Identify the serum protein fraction on the far right of the illustration.

a. gamma globulin
b. albumin
c. alpha-1 globulin
d. alpha-2 globulin

---

40. Which of the following serum protein fractions is most likely to be elevated in patients with nephrotic syndrome?

a. alpha-1 globulin
b. alpha-1 globulin and alpha-2 globulin
c. alpha-2 globulin and beta globulin
d. beta globulin and gamma globulin

41. Refer to the following illustration:

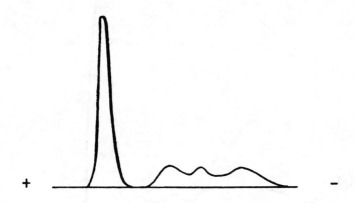

	Patient Values	Reference Values
Total Protein	7.3 g/dL	6.0-8.0 g/dL
Albumin	4.2 g/dL	3.6-5.2 g/dL
Alpha-1	0.0 g/dL	0.1-0.4 g/dL
Alpha-2	0.8 g/dL	0.4-1.0 g/dL
Beta	1.4 g/dL	0.5-1.2 g/dL
Gamma		0.6-1.6 g/dL

This electrophoresis pattern is consistent with:

    a. cirrhosis
    b. monoclonal gammopathy
    c. polyclonal gammopathy (e.g., chronic
       inflammation)
    d. alpha-1 antitrypsin deficiency; severe
       emphysema

---

42. The biuret reaction for the analysis of serum protein
depends on the number of:

    a. free amino groups
    b. free carboxyl groups
    c. peptide bonds
    d. tyrosine residues

43. Refer to the following illustration:

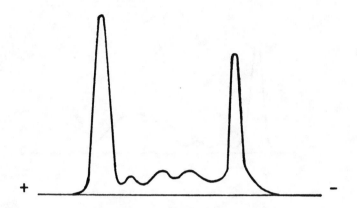

	Reference Values	Patient Values
Total Protein	8.9 g/dL	6.0-8.0 g/dL
Albumin	4.8 g/dL	3.6-5.2 g/dL
Alpha-1	0.3 g/dL	0.1-0.4 g/dL
Alpha-2	0.7 g/dL	0.4-1.0 g/dL
Beta	0.8 g/dL	0.5-1.2 g/dL
Gamma	2.3 g/dL	0.6-1.6 g/dL

The serum protein electrophoresis pattern is consistent with:

a. cirrhosis
b. acute inflammation
c. monoclonal gammopathy
d. polyclonal gammopathy (e.g., chronic
   inflammation)

---

44. A 24-hour urine specimen (total volume = 1,136 mL) is
submitted to the laboratory for quantitative urine protein.
Calculate the amount of protein excreted per day if the
total protein is 52 mg/dL.

a. 591 mg
b. 487 mg
c. 282 mg
d. 220 mg

45. Refer to the following pattern:

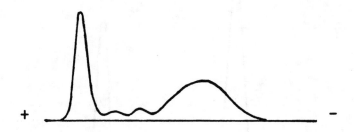

	Reference Values	Patient Values
Total Protein	6.1 g/dL	6.0-8.0 g/dL
Albumin	2.3 g/dL	3.6-5.2 g/dL
Alpha-1	0.2 g/dL	0.1-0.4 g/dL
Alpha-2	0.5 g/dL	0.4-1.0 g/dL
Beta	1.2 g/dL	0.5-1.2 g/dL
Gamma	1.9 g/dL	0.6-1.6 g/dL

This pattern is consistent with:

    a. cirrhosis
    b. acute inflammation
    c. polyclonal gammopathy (e.g., chronic inflammation)
    d. alpha-1 antitrypsin deficiency; severe emphysema

---

46. A characteristic of the Bence Jones protein that is used to distinguish it from other urinary proteins is its solubility:

    a. in ammonium sulfate
    b. in sulfuric acid
    c. at 40-60°C
    d. at 100°C

47. Which of the following is an example of a peptide bond?

a. [structure: R_1-C-H with NH_2 above boxed, $C=O$ and NH_2 below]

c. [structure: $HO-C-$ (with O double bond) boxed $C=C$ with H, H above, $-C-OH$ with O]

b. [structure: $R-C-C-N-C-C-OH$ with H, O, H, O and NH_2, H, R_1 groups, box around central $C-N$ portion]

d. [structure: COOH, boxed $C=O$, CH_2, COOH]

---

48. In electrophoresis of proteins, when the sample is placed in an electric field connected to a buffer of pH 8.6, all of the proteins:

    a. have a positive charge
    b. have a negative charge
    c. are electrically neutral
    d. migrate toward the cathode

49. The electrophoretic pattern of a plasma sample as compared to a serum sample shows a:

    a. broad prealbumin peak
    b. sharp fibrinogen peak
    c. diffuse pattern because of the presence of anticoagulants
    d. decreased globulin fraction

50. At a pH of 8.6 the gamma globulins move toward the cathode, despite the fact that they are negatively charged. What is this phenomenon called?

    a. reverse migration
    b. molecular sieve
    c. endosmosis
    d. migratory inhibition factor

51. The relative migration rate of proteins on cellulose acetate is based on:

    a. molecular weight
    b. concentration
    c. ionic charge
    d. particle size

52. The cellulose acetate electrophoresis at pH 8.6 of serum proteins will show an order of migration beginning with the fastest migration as follows:

    a. albumin, alpha-1 globulin, alpha-2 globulin, beta globulin, gamma globulin
    b. alpha-1 globulin, alpha-2 globulin, beta globulin, gamma globulin, albumin
    c. albumin, alpha-2 globulin, alpha-1 globulin, beta globulin, gamma globulin
    d. gamma globulin, beta globulin, alpha-2 globulin, alpha-1 globulin, albumin

53. Which of the following amino acids is associated with sulfhydryl group?

    a. cysteine
    b. glycine
    c. serine
    d. tyrosine

54. Maple syrup urine disease is characterized by an increase in which of the following urinary amino acids?

    a. phenylalanine
    b. tyrosine
    c. valine, leucine and isoleucine
    d. cystine and cysteine

55. The protein portion of an enzyme complex is called the:

    a. apoenzyme
    b. coenzyme
    c. holoenzyme
    d. proenzyme

56. The most sensitive enzymatic indicator for liver damage from ethanol intake is:

    a. alanine aminotransferase (ALT)
    b. aspartate aminotransferase (AST)
    c. gamma-glutamyl transferase (GGT)
    d. alkaline phosphatase

57. When myocardial infarction occurs, the first enzyme to become elevated is:

    a. CK
    b. LD
    c. AST
    d. ALT

58. A scanning of a CK isoenzyme fractionation revealed two peaks: a slow cathodic peak (CK-MM) and an intermediate peak (CK-MB). A possible interpretation for this pattern is:

    a. brain tumor
    b. muscular dystrophy
    c. myocardial infarction
    d. viral hepatitis

59. The isoenzyme(s) of creatine kinase found in the myocardium is(are):

    a. MB
    b. MB and BB
    c. MM and BB
    d. MM and MB

60. Aspartate aminotransferase (AST) and alanine aminotransferase (ALT) are both elevated in which of the following diseases?

  a. muscular dystrophy
  b. viral hepatitis
  c. pulmonary emboli
  d. infectious mononucleosis

61. In the determination of lactate dehydrogenase at 340 nm, using pyruvate as the substrate, one actually measures the:

  a. decrease in pyruvate
  b. decrease in NADH
  c. increase in lactate
  d. increase in NADH

62. An electrophoretic separation of lactate dehydrogenase isoenzymes that demonstrates an elevation in LD-1 and LD-2 in a "flipped" pattern may indicate:

  a. myocardial infarction
  b. viral hepatitis
  c. pancreatitis
  d. renal failure

63. Increased total serum lactic dehydrogenase (LD) activity, confined to fractions 4 and 5 is most likely to be associated with:

  a. pulmonary infarction
  b. hemolytic anemia
  c. myocardial infarction
  d. acute viral hepatitis

64. In the assay of lactate dehydrogenase (LD), the reaction is dependent upon which of the following coenzyme systems?

  a. NAD/NADH
  b. ATP/ADP
  c. Fe^{++}/Fe^{+++}
  d. Cu/Cu^{++}

65. Refer to the following illustration:

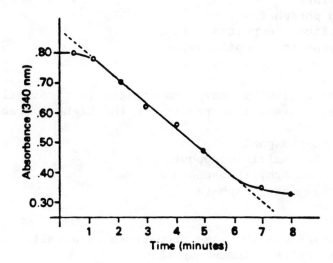

This illustration represents the change in absorbance at 340 nm over a period of 8 minutes in an assay for lactate dehydrogenase. True statements about this figure include:

   a. the reaction follows zero order kinetics between 5 and 8 minutes
   b. the reaction is proceeding from lactate to pyruvate
   c. non-linearity after 6 minutes is due to substrate exhaustion
   d. the change in absorbance is due to reduction of NAD to NADH

66. Which of the following chemical determinations may be of help in establishing the presence of seminal fluid?

   a. lactate dehydrogenase (LD)
   b. isocitrate dehydrogenase (ICD)
   c. acid phosphatase
   d. alkaline phosphatase

67. A 75-year-old man has prostatic cancer which has metastasized widely throughout his body. Which of the following serum enzymes would be elevated?

    a. aldolase
    b. acid phosphatase
    c. alkaline phosphatase
    d. leucine aminopeptidase

68. Which of the following enzyme substrates for prostatic acid phosphatase determination results in the highest specificity?

    a. phenyl-phosphate
    b. thymolphthalein monophosphate
    c. alpha-naphthyl-phosphate
    d. beta-glycerophosphate

69. Regan isoenzyme has the same properties as alkaline phosphatase that originates in the:

    a. skeleton
    b. kidney
    c. intestine
    d. placenta

70. An important metallic activator of alkaline phosphatase and creatine kinase is:

    a. iron
    b. zinc
    c. copper
    d. magnesium

71. An elevated aldolase level may indicate:

    a. portal cirrhosis
    b. lymphocytic leukemia
    c. obstructive jaundice
    d. progressive muscular dystrophy

72. Which of the following enzymes are used in the diagnosis of acute pancreatitis?

    a. amylase and lipase
    b. aspartate aminotransferase (AST) and alanine aminotransferase (ALT)
    c. 5'-Nucleotidase (5'N) and gamma-glutamyl transferase (GGT)
    d. aspartate aminotransferase (AST) and lactate dehydrogenase (LD)

73. Which of the following enzymes catalyzes the conversion of starch to glucose and maltose?

    a. malate dehydrogenase (MD)
    b. amylase (AMS)
    c. creatine kinase (CK)
    d. isocitrate dehydrogenase (ICD)

74. Which of the following sets of results would be consistent with macroamylasemia?

    a. normal serum amylase and elevated urine amylase values
    b. increased serum amylase and normal urine amylase values
    c. increased serum and urine amylase values
    d. normal serum and urine amylase values

75. A patient with glomerulonephritis would present the following serum results:

    a. creatinine decreased
    b. calcium increased
    c. phosphorous decreased
    d. BUN increased

76. The principle excretory form of nitrogen is:

    a. amino acids
    b. creatinine
    c. urea
    d. uric acid

77. Gout is a pathologic condition that is characterized by the accumulation of which of the following in joints and other body tissues?

    a. calcium
    b. phosphorous
    c. urea nitrogen
    d. uric acid

78. Which of the following represents the endproduct of nucleic acid and purine metabolism in man?

    a. AMP and GMP
    b. DNA and RNA
    c. allantoin
    d. uric acid

79. Fluoride additive to a blood specimen may lower the results of which of the following analyses?

    a. sodium by flame photometry
    b. urease method for urea
    c. atomic absorption spectroscopy for calcium
    d. atomic absorption spectroscopy for lithium

80. In the Jaffe reaction, creatinine reacts with:

    a. alkaline sulfasalazine solution to produce an orange-yellow complex
    b. potassium iodide to form a reddish-purple complex
    c. sodium nitroferricyanide to yield a reddish-brown color
    d. alkaline picrate solution to yield an orange-red complex

81. Creatinine clearance is used to estimate the:

    a. tubular secretion of creatinine
    b. glomerular secretion of creatinine
    c. renal glomerular and tubular mass
    d. glomerular filtration rate

82. The following results were obtained:

Urine creatinine   90 mg/100 mL
Serum creatinine   0.90 mg/100 mL
Patient's total body surface   1.73 m^2 (average = 1.73m^2)

Total urine volume in 24 hours 1500 mL

Given the above data, calculate the patient's creatinine clearance, in mL/min.

    a. 104
    b. 124
    c. 144
    d. 150

83. A 45-year-old male of average height and weight was admitted to the hospital for renal function studies. He had the following lab results:

Urine creatinine   120 mg/dL
Serum creatinine   1.5 mg/dL

Total urine volume in 24 hours   1800 mL

Calculate the creatinine clearance for this patient in mL/min.

    a. 100
    b. 144
    c. 156
    d. 225

84. A blood creatinine value of 5.0 mg/dL is most likely to be found with which of the following blood values?

    a. uric acid   1.7 mg/dL
    b. uric acid   5.8 mg/dL
    c. urea nitrogen   15 mg/dL
    d. urea nitrogen   80 mg/dL

85. One international unit of enzyme activity is the amount of enzyme that will, under specified reaction conditions of substrate concentration, pH and temperature, cause utilization of substrate at the rate of:

    a. 1 mole/min
    b. 1 millimole/min
    c. 1 micromole/min
    d. 1 nanomole/min

86. Enzyme-multiplied immunoassay techniques (EMIT) DIFFER from all other types of enzyme immunoassays in that:

   a. lysozyme is the only enzyme used to label the hapten molecule
   b. no separation of bound and free antigen is required
   c. inhibition of the enzyme label is accomplished with polyethylene glycol
   d. antibody absorption to polystyrene tubes precludes completion to labeled and unlabeled antigen

87. Which of the following statements about immunoassays using enzyme labeled antibodies or antigens is correct?

   a. Inactivation of the enzyme is required.
   b. The enzyme label is less stable than an isotopic label.
   c. Quantitation of the label can be carried out with a spectrophotometer.
   d. The enzyme label is not an enzyme found naturally in serum.

88. The bicarbonate and carbonic acid ratio is calculated from an equation by:

   a. Siggaard-Andersen
   b. Gibbs-Donnan
   c. Natelson
   d. Henderson-Hasselbalch

89. Most of the carbon dioxide present in blood is in the form of:

   a. dissolved CO_2
   b. carbonate
   c. bicarbonate ion
   d. carbonic acid

90. Arterial blood collected in a heparinized syringe but exposed to room air would cause which of the following changes in the specimen?

	pO_2	pCO_2	pH
a.	elevated	decreased	elevated
b.	decreased	elevated	decreased
c.	unchanged	elevated	unchanged
d.	decreased	decreased	decreased

91. Specimens for blood gas determination should be drawn into a syringe containing:

    a. no preservative
    b. heparin
    c. EDTA
    d. oxalate

92. Unless blood gas measurements are made immediately after sampling, in vitro glycolysis of the blood causes a:

    a. rise in pH and pCO_2
    b. fall in pH and a rise in pO_2
    c. rise in pH and a fall in pO_2
    d. fall in pH and a rise in pCO_2

93. Serum anion gap is increased in patients with:

    a. renal tubular acidosis
    b. diabetic alkalosis
    c. metabolic acidosis due to diarrhea
    d. lactic acidosis

94. The anion gap is useful for quality control of laboratory results for:

    a. amino acids and proteins
    b. blood gas analyses
    c. sodium, potassium, chloride, and total CO_2
    d. calcium, phosphorus and magnesium

95. At blood pH 7.40 what is the ratio between bicarbonate and carbonic acid?

    a. 15:1
    b. 20:1
    c. 25:1
    d. 30:1

96. The reference range for the pH of arterial blood measured at 37°C is:

    a. 7.28-7.34
    b. 7.33-7.37
    c. 7.35-7.45
    d. 7.45-7.50

97. Hydrogen ion concentration (pH) in blood is usually determined by means of which of the following electrodes?

    a. silver
    b. glass
    c. platinum
    d. platinum-lactate

98. The buffering capacity of blood is maintained by a reversible exchange process between bicarbonate and:

    a. sodium
    b. potassium
    c. calcium
    d. chloride

99. A 68-year-old man arrives in the emergency room with a glucose level of 722 mg/dL and serum acetone of 4+ undiluted. An arterial blood gas from this patient is likely to indicate which of the following?

    a. low pH
    b. high pH
    c. low pO_2
    d. high pO_2

100. A fire victim is being treated in the emergency room for smoke inhalation. No other injuries are noted. Which of the following tests would be most helpful in the treatment of this patient?

    a. hemoglobin
    b. pH
    c. base excess
    d. pO_2

101. A patient is admitted to the emergency room in a state of metabolic alkalosis. Which of the following would be consistent with this diagnosis?

    a. high TCO_2, increased HCO_3
    b. low TCO_2, increased HCO_3
    c. high TCO_2, decreased H_2CO_3
    d. low TCO_2, decreased H_2CO_3

102. A person suspected of having metabolic alkalosis would have which of the following laboratory findings?

   a. CO_2 content and pCO_2 elevated, pH decreased
   b. CO_2 content decreased and pH elevated
   c. CO_2 content, pCO_2 and pH decreased
   d. CO_2 content and pH elevated

103. Metabolic acidosis is described as a(n):

   a. increase in CO_2 content and pCO_2 with a decreased pH
   b. decrease in CO_2 content with an increased pH
   c. increase in CO_2 with an increased pH
   d. decrease in CO_2 content and pCO_2 with a decreased pH

104. Respiratory acidosis is described as a(n):

   a. increase in CO_2 content and pCO_2 with a decreased pH
   b. decrease in CO_2 content with an increased pH
   c. increase in CO_2 content with an increased pH
   d. decrease in CO_2 content and pCO_2 with a decreased pH

105. In respiratory acidosis, a compensatory mechanism is the decrease in:

   a. respiration rate
   b. ammonia formation
   c. blood pCO_2
   d. plasma bicarbonate concentration

106. A common cause of respiratory alkalosis is:

   a. vomiting
   b. starvation
   c. asthma
   d. hyperventilation

107. Acidosis and alkalosis are best defined as fluctuations in blood pH and CO_2 content due to changes in:

   a. Bohr's effect
   b. O_2 content
   c. bicarbonate buffer
   d. carbonic anhydrase

108. Which of the following is characteristic of ammonia?

    a. a waste product of amino acid and protein
       metabolism
    b. obtained from hydrolysis of urea in the kidney
    c. obtained from ingested carbohydrates
    d. found in low concentrations in red blood cells

109. The method in which ammonia is eluted and measured
colorimetrically with the phenol-hypochlorite
reaction is a(n):

    a. ion-selective method
    b. enzymatic method
    c. diffusion method
    d. ion-exchange method

110. Erroneous ammonia levels can be eliminated by all of the
following EXCEPT:

    a. assuring water and reagents are ammonia-free
    b. separating plasma from cells and performing
       test analysis as soon as possible
    c. drawing the specimen in a prechilled tube and
       immersing the tube in ice
    d. storing the specimen at room temperature until
       the analysis is done

111. The method by which ammonia is converted to glutamate and
changes NADH to NAD^+ is:

    a. ammonia electrode method
    b. enzymatic method
    c. diffusion method
    d. resin absorption method

112. Which percentage of total serum calcium is nondiffusible
protein bound?

    a. 80-90%
    b. 51-60%
    c. 40-50%
    d. 10-30%

113. Calcium concentration in the serum is regulated by:

    a. insulin
    b. parathyroid hormone
    c. thyroxine
    d. vitamin C

114. The regulation of calcium and phosphorous metabolism is accomplished by which of the following glands:

    a. thyroid
    b. parathyroid
    c. adrenal glands
    d. pituitary

115. Each of the following factors influences the serum calcium concentration EXCEPT:

    a. vitamin D
    b. calcitonin
    c. proteins
    d. tyrosine

116. Which of the following calcium procedures utilizes lanthanum chloride to eliminate interfering substances?

    a. o-cresolphthalein complexone
    b. precipitation with chloranilic acid
    c. chelation with EDTA
    d. atomic absorption spectrophotometry

117. A patient has the following test results: increased serum calcium levels, decreased serum phosphorus levels, increased levels of parathyroid hormone.

    This patient most likely has:

    a. hyperparathyroidism
    b. hypoparathyroidism
    c. nephrosis
    d. steatorrhea

118. A hospitalized patient is experiencing increased neuromuscular irritability (tetany). Which of the following tests should be ordered immediately?

    a. calcium
    b. phosphorous
    c. BUN
    d. glucose

119. Which of the following is most likely to be ordered in addition to serum calcium to determine the cause of tetany?

    a. magnesium
    b. phosphorus
    c. sodium
    d. vitamin D

120. A reciprocal relationship exists between:

   a. sodium and potassium
   b. calcium and phosphorus
   c. chloride and CO_2
   d. calcium and magnesium

121. Fasting serum phosphate concentration is controlled primarily by the:

   a. pancreas
   b. skeleton
   c. parathyroid glands
   d. small intestine

122. Which of the following electrolytes is the chief plasma cation whose main function is maintaining osmotic pressure?

   a. chloride
   b. calcium
   c. potassium
   d. sodium

123. 90% of the copper present in the blood is bound to:

   a. transferrin
   b. ceruloplasmin
   c. albumin
   d. cryoglobulin

124. A potassium level of 6.8 mEq/L is obtained. Before reporting the results the technologist should:

   a. check the serum for hemolysis
   b. rerun the test
   c. check the age of the patient
   d. do nothing, simply report out the result

125. The stimulant that causes localized sweating for the sweat test is:

   a. polyvinyl alcohol
   b. lithium sulfate
   c. potassium sulfate
   d. pilocarpine nitrate

126. In the sweat test, the sweating stimulant is introduced to the skin by application of:

    a. filter paper moistened with pilocarpine nitrate
    b. an electric current
    c. copper electrodes
    d. filter paper moistened in deionized water

127. A patient's blood was drawn at 8 a.m. for a serum iron determination. The result was 85 µg/dL. A repeat specimen was drawn at 8 p.m.; the serum was stored at 4°C and run the next morning. The result was 40 µg/dL. These results are most likely due to:

    a. iron deficiency anemia
    b. improper storage of the specimen
    c. possible liver damage
    d. the time of day the second specimen was drawn

128. Magnesium carbonate is added in an iron binding capacity determination in order to:

    a. allow color to develop
    b. precipitate protein
    c. bind with hemoglobin iron
    d. remove excess unbound iron

129. An elevated serum iron with normal iron binding capacity is most likely associated with:

    a. iron deficiency anemia
    b. renal damage
    c. pernicious anemia
    d. septicemia

130. Decreased serum iron associated with increased TIBC is compatible with which of the following disease states?

    a. anemia of chronic infection
    b. iron deficiency anemia
    c. chronic liver disease
    d. nephrosis

131. Total iron-binding capacity measures the serum iron transporting capacity of:

    a. hemoglobin
    b. ceruloplasmin
    c. transferrin
    d. ferritin

132. The degree to which the kidney concentrates the glomerular filtrate can be determined by:

   a. urine creatine
   b. serum creatinine
   c. creatinine clearance
   d. urine to serum osmolality ratio

133. The formula for calculating serum osmolality that incorporates a correction for the water content of plasma is:

   a. $2Na \times \dfrac{Glucose}{20} \times \dfrac{BUN}{3}$

   b. $Na + \dfrac{(2 \times Glucose)}{20} \times \dfrac{BUN}{3}$

   c. $2Na + \dfrac{Glucose}{20} + \dfrac{BUN}{3}$

   d. $2Na + \dfrac{Glucose}{3} + \dfrac{BUN}{20}$

134. Calculate the serum osmolality in mOsmol/kg H_2O, based on the following serum data:

Sodium	140 mEq/L
Potassium	4.0 mEq/L
Glucose	120 mg/dL
BUN	60 mg/dL

   a. 234
   b. 252
   c. 289
   d. 306

135. Osmolal gap is:

   a. the difference between the ideal and real osmolality values
   b. the difference between the calculated and measured osmolality values
   c. the difference between plasma and water osmolality values
   d. the difference between molality and molarity at 4°C

136. Iodine-125 has a physical half-life of 60.0 days. A sample tested today had activity of 10,000 CPM/mL. How many days from today will the count be 1250 CPM/mL?

    a. 60
    b. 180
    c. 240
    d. 1250

137. The major fraction of organic iodine in the circulation is in the form of:

    a. thyroglobulin
    b. thyroxine
    c. triiodothyronine
    d. diiodotyrosine

138. Which one of the following statements about triiodothyronine (T_3) is NOT true?

    a. It is thought to be the active thyroid hormone.
    b. It may be elevated to a greater extent than T_4 in hyperthyroidism.
    c. It is not bound to serum proteins.
    d. It is commonly decreased in patients with nonthyroidal illness.

139. Which of the following methods employs a highly specific antibody to thyroxine?

    a. total T-4 by competitive protein binding
    b. T-4 by RIA
    c. T-4 by column
    d. T-4 by equilibrium dialysis

140. The triiodothyronine uptake ratio is used in the estimation of:

    a. T-3 by RIA
    b. T-4 by column
    c. T-4 by displacement analysis
    d. free thyroxine

141. The T-3 resin uptake test is a measure of:

    a. circulating T-3
    b. bound T-3
    c. binding capacity of thyroxine-binding globulin
    d. total thyroxine-binding globulin

142. A patient's values are as follows:

	Patient	Reference Range
T-4 (RIA):	4 μg/dL	5-12 μg/dL
T-3 Uptake (RIA):	40%	25-35%

What is the patient's Free Thyroxine Index (T-7)?

   a. 0.1
   b. 1.6
   c. 10.0
   d. 36.0

143. Which of the following steroids is an adrenal cortical hormone?

   a. angiotensinogen
   b. corticosterone
   c. progesterone
   d. pregnanetriol

144. The parent substance in the biosynthesis of androgens and estrogens is:

   a. cortisol
   b. catecholamines
   c. progesterone
   d. cholesterol

145. The biologically most active, naturally occurring androgen is:

   a. androstenedione
   b. dehydroepiandrosterone
   c. epiandrosterone
   d. testosterone

146. In the normal person, which of the following increases in the peripheral circulation during the insulin tolerance test?

   a. growth hormone
   b. luteinizing hormone (LH)
   c. follicle-stimulating hormone (FSH)
   d. thyrotropin (TSH)

147. During an evaluation of adrenal function, a patient had plasma
     cortisol determinations in the morning after awakening and
     in the evening. Laboratory results indicated that the morning
     value was higher than the evening concentration. These
     findings represent:

     a. a normal finding
     b. Cushing's syndrome
     c. Addison's disease
     d. hypopituitarism

148. The Porter-Silber method (phenylhydrazine in alcohol
     and sulfuric acid) involves which part of the steroid
     molecule?

     a. ketone group
     b. hydroxyl group
     c. dihydroxyacetone side chain
     d. steroid ring

149. The Porter-Silber reaction measures:

     a. androgen steroids
     b. 17-ketosteroids
     c. 17-hydroxycorticosteroids
     d. cortisol specifically

150. Which family of steroid hormones is characterized by an
     unsaturated A ring?

     a. progestins
     b. estrogens
     c. androgens
     d. glucocorticoids

151. The formation of estriol in a pregnant woman is dependent on:

     a. maternal ovarian function
     b. fetal and placental function
     c. fetal adrenal function
     d. maternal liver function

152. For the past three weeks serum estriol levels on a pregnant
     woman have been steadily increasing. This is consistent with:

     a. a normal pregnancy
     b. hemolytic disease of the newborn
     c. fetal death
     d. congenital cytomegalovirus infection

153. Which of the following is secreted by the placenta and used for the early detection of pregnancy?

    a. follicle-stimulating hormone (FSH)
    b. human chorionic gonadotropin (HCG)
    c. luteinizing hormone (LH)
    d. progesterone

154. Night blindness is associated with deficiency of which of the following vitamins:

    a. A
    b. C
    c. niacin
    d. thiamine

155. Which of the following vitamins is NOT fat-soluble?

    a. A
    b. B Complex
    c. D
    d. E

156. Beriberi is associated with deficiency of vitamin:

    a. A
    b. C
    c. niacin
    d. thiamine

157. Scurvy is associated with deficiency of vitamin:

    a. A
    b. C
    c. niacin
    d. thiamine

158. Rickets is associated with deficiency of vitamin:

    a. B_1
    b. C
    c. niacin
    d. D

159. Pellagra is associated with deficiency of vitamin:

    a. A
    b. C
    c. niacin
    d. thiamine

160. Major actions of angiotensin II include:

  a. increased pituitary secretion of petressin
  b. increased vasoconstriction
  c. increased parathormone secretion by the parathyroid
  d. decreased adrenal secretion of aldosterone

161. The urinary excretion product measured as an indicator of epinephrine production is:

  a. dopamine
  b. dihydroxyphenylalanine (DOPA)
  c. homovanillic acid
  d. vanillylmandelic acid

162. The main reason for suboptimal drug levels in therapeutic drug monitoring is:

  a. renal failure
  b. liver failure
  c. improper dosage prescribed
  d. patient noncompliance with dosage regimen

163. Bioavailability of a drug refers to the:

  a. availability for therapeutic administration
  b. availability of the protein-bound fraction of the drug
  c. drug transformation
  d. extent and rate at which the active drug reaches target tissues

164. Carbonate salt used to control manic-depressive disorders is:

  a. digoxin
  b. acetaminophen
  c. lithium
  d. phenytoin

165. The anticonvulsant used to control tonic-clonic (grand mal) seizures is:

  a. digoxin
  b. acetaminophen
  c. lithium
  d. phenytoin

166. A drug that relaxes the smooth muscles of the bronchial passages is:

   a. acetaminophen
   b. lithium
   c. phenytoin
   d. theophylline

167. A cardiac glycoside that is used in the treatment of congenital heart failure and arrhythmias by increasing the force and velocity of myocardial contraction is:

   a. digoxin
   b. acetaminophen
   c. lithium
   d. phenytoin

168. An analgesic that alleviates pain without causing loss of consciousness is:

   a. digoxin
   b. acetaminophen
   c. lithium
   d. phenytoin

169. Which of the following elevates carboxyhemoglobin?

   a. nitrite poisoning
   b. exposure to carbon monoxide
   c. sulfa drug toxicity
   d. sickle cell anemia

170. The reason carbon monoxide is so toxic is because it:

   a. is a protoplasmic poison
   b. combines with cytochrome oxidase
   c. has 200 times the affinity of oxygen for hemoglobin binding sites
   d. sensitizes the myocardium

171. The reference range for methanol is:

   a. 0   mg/dL
   b. 2-4 mg/dL
   c. 5-9 mg/dL
   d. greater than 10 mg/dL

172. The first step to be taken when attempting to repair a piece of electronic equipment is:

   a. check all the electronic connections
   b. reseat all the printed circuit boards
   c. turn the instrument off
   d. replace all the fuses

173. In a continuous flow system, the pump tubing for the sample has a rate of 1.5 mL/min. The sampling rate is 90 samples/hr and the sample-to-wash ratio of the cam is 3:1. The minimum amount (mL) of serum necessary for analysis on the instrument is:

   a. 0.5
   b. 0.75
   c. 1.0
   d. 1.25

174. The most widely employed screening technique for drug abuse is:

   a. high-performance liquid chromatography
   b. gas-liquid chromatography
   c. thin layer chromatography
   d. UV spectrophotometry

175. An automated method for measuring chloride which generates silver ions in the reaction is:

   a. coulometry
   b. mass spectroscopy
   c. chromatography
   d. polarography

176. The nanometer is used as a measure of:

   a. absorbance
   b. % transmittance
   c. intensity of radiant energy
   d. wavelength of radiant energy

177. An instrument suitable for use in reading quantitative porphyrin analyses is:

   a. UV spectrophotometer
   b. colorimeter
   c. nephelometer
   d. filter photometer

178. The function of lithium in the flame emission method for sodium analysis is to:

    a. enhance dialysis
    b. act as an internal standard
    c. stabilize electrode potential
    d. act as a quality control precision check

179. In a flame photometer, the concentration of sodium is determined by measuring the light:

    a. absorbed by the atoms
    b. emitted by the atoms
    c. transmitted by the atoms
    d. absorbed by the sodium atoms and water vapor

180. Spectrophotometers isolate a narrow band pass by means of:

    a. filters and prisms
    b. prisms and grating
    c. barrier layer cells and filters
    d. gratings and lanier layer cells

181. Which of the following is used to verify wavelength settings for narrow bandwidth spectrophotometers?

    a. didymium filter
    b. prisms
    c. holmium oxide glass
    d. diffraction gratings

182. Absorbance (A) of a solution may be converted to percent transmittance (%T) using the formula:

    a. 1 + log %T
    b. 2 + log %T
    c. 1 - log %T
    d. 2 - log %T

183. In electrophoretic analysis, buffers:

    a. stabilize electrolytes
    b. maintain basic pH
    c. act as a carrier for ions
    d. produce an effect on protein configuration

184. Ion selective electrodes are called selective rather than specific because they actually measure the:

    a. activity of one ion only
    b. concentration of one ion
    c. activity of one ion much more than other ions present
    d. concentration and activity of one ion only

185. The centrifugal analyzer:

    a. employs the concept of sequential analysis
    b. employs the concept of discrete sample analysis
    c. is limited to kinetic analysis
    d. is limited to endpoint analysis

186. In the atomic absorption method for calcium, lanthanum is used:

    a. as an internal standard
    b. to bind calcium
    c. to eliminate protein interference
    d. to prevent phosphate interference

187. The usual radiant energy source in atomic absorption instruments is the:

    a. xenon arc
    b. deuterium lamp
    c. tungsten lamp
    d. hollow cathode lamp

188. To be analyzed by gas liquid chromatography a compound must:

    a. be volatile or made volatile
    b. not be volatile
    c. be water-soluble
    d. contain a nitrogen atom

189. Which of the following statements about fluorometry is true?

    a. A compound is said to fluoresce when it absorbs light at one wavelength and emits light at a second wavelength.
    b. Detectors in fluorometers are plated at 180° from the excitation source.
    c. It is less sensitive than spectrophotometry.
    d. It avoids the necessity for complexing of components because fluorescence is a native property.

190. A true statement about high performance liquid chromatography (HPLC) is that it:

    a. utilizes a flame ionization detector
    b. requires derivation of non-volatile compounds
    c. can be used to separate gases, liquids or soluble solids
    d. can be used for adsorption, partition, ion exchange and gel permeation chromatography

191. Thin-layer chromatography is of particular use in the identification of:

    a. lipids
    b. drugs
    c. inorganic ions
    d. enzyme inhibitors

192. In thin layer chromatography, the R_f value for a compound is given by the:

    a. ratio of distance moved by compound: distance moved by solvent
    b. rate of movement of compound through the adsorbent
    c. distance between the compound spot and solvent front
    d. distance moved by compound from the origin

193. The measurement of light scattered by particles in the sample is the principle of:

    a. spectrophotometry
    b. fluorometry
    c. nephelometry
    d. atomic absorption

194. The measurement of the amount of electricity passing between two electrodes in an electrochemical cell is the principle of:

    a. electrophoresis
    b. amperometry
    c. nephelometry
    d. coulometry

195. Coulometry is used to measure:

    a. chloride
    b. pH
    c. bicarbonate
    d. ammonia

196. Fluctuation of the needle on a coulometric type titrator is most probably due to:

    a. common ion effect
    b. lack of indicator
    c. faulty reference voltage
    d. dirty electrodes

197. The osmolality of a urine or serum specimen is measured by a change in the:

    a. vapor pressure
    b. sedimentation point
    c. midpoint
    d. osmotic pressure

198. The solute that contributes the most to the total serum osmolality is:

    a. glucose
    b. sodium
    c. chloride
    d. urea

199. In the potentiometric measurement of hydrogen ion concentration, reference electrodes that may be used include:

    a. silver-silver chloride
    b. quinhydrone
    c. hydroxide
    d. hydrogen

200. Which of the following electrodes is based on the principle of amperometric measurement?

    a. pCO_2 electrode
    b. pO_2 electrode
    c. pH electrode
    d. ionized calcium electrode

201. Most automated blood gas analyzers directly measure:

    a. pH, HCO_3^- and % O_2 saturation
    b. pH, pCO_2 and pO_2
    c. HCO_3^-, pCO_2 and pO_2
    d. pH, pO_2 and % O_2 saturation

202. The blood gas analyzer had been calibrating well all day.
However, the last two patient blood gases had pHs of 6.843
and 6.992. You immediately run a control. The pH is reading
low and on the next calibration the pH has ???? on the
printout. All other parameters of the calibration and control
are acceptable. What is the most likely cause of the problem?

    a. protein on the pH electrode tip
    b. low level of salt bridge solution
    c. low level of rinse solution
    d. patient syringe contained too much heparin

203. In automated methods utilizing a bichromatic analyzer, dual
wavelengths are employed to:

    a. minimize the effect of interference (e.g., from
       turbidity)
    b. improve precision
    c. facilitate dialysis
    d. monitor temperature changes

204. Which of the following is the formula for calculating the
unknown concentration based on Beer's Law?
(A = absorbance, C = concentration)

    a. $\dfrac{(A\ unknown\ )}{(A\ standard)}$ x C standard

    b. C standard x A unknown
    c. A standard x A unknown

    d. $\dfrac{(C\ standard)}{(A\ standard)}$ x 100

205. In spectrophotometric determination, which of the following
is the formula for calculating the absorbance of a solution?

    a. $\dfrac{absorptivity\ x\ light\ path}{concentration}$

    b. $\dfrac{absorptivity\ x\ concentration}{light\ path}$

    c. absorptivity x light path x concentration

    d. $\dfrac{light\ path\ x\ concentration}{absorptivity}$

206. Which of the following is the formula for calculating absorbance given the percent transmittance (%T) of a solution?

        a. 1 - log of %T
        b. $\dfrac{\text{log of \% T}}{2}$
        c. 2 x log of %T
        d. 2 - log of %T

207. Which of the following is the Henderson-Hasselbalch equation?

        a. $pKa = pH + \log \dfrac{acid}{salt}$

        b. $pKa = pH + \log \dfrac{salt}{acid}$

        c. $pH = pKa + \log \dfrac{acid}{salt}$

        d. $pH = pKa + \log \dfrac{salt}{acid}$

208. Which of the following is the formula for calculating the dilution of a solution?
(V = volume, C = concentration)

        a. V1 + C1 = V2 + C2
        b. V1 + C2 = V2 + C1
        c. V1 x C1 = V2 x C2
        d. V1 x V2 = V1 x C2

209. A colorimetric method calls for the use of 0.1 mL serum, 5 mL of reagent and 4.9 mL of water. What is the dilution of the serum in the final solution?

        a. 1:5
        b. 1:10
        c. 1:50
        d. 1:100

210. Four mL of water are added to one mL of serum. This represents which of the following serum dilutions?

        a. 1:3
        b. 1:4
        c. 1:5
        d. 1:6

211. Which of the following is the formula for calculating a percent (w/v) solution?

    a. $\dfrac{\text{grams of solute}}{\text{volume of solvent}} \times 100$

    b. grams of solute x volume of solvent x 100

    c. $\dfrac{\text{volume of solvent} \times 100}{\text{grams of solute}}$

    d. $\dfrac{\text{grams of solute x volume of solvent}}{100}$

212. A solution contains 20 g of solute dissolved in 0.5 L of water. What is the percentage of this solution?

    a. 2%
    b. 4%
    c. 6%
    d. 8%

213. How many grams of sulfosalicylic acid (MW = 254) are required to prepare 1 L of a 3% (w/v) solution?

    a.   3
    b. 30
    c. 254
    d. 300

214. How many milliliters of a 3% solution can be made if 6 grams of solute are available?

    a. 100 mL
    b. 200 mL
    c. 400 mL
    d. 600 mL

215. Which of the following is the formula for calculating the gram-equivalent weight of a chemical?

    a. MW x oxidation number

    b. $\dfrac{\text{MW}}{\text{oxidation number}}$

    c. MW + oxidation number
    d. MW - oxidation number

216. Eighty grams of NaOH (MW = 40) is equal to how many gram-equivalents?

    a. 1
    b. 2
    c. 3
    d. 4

217. A serum potassium is 19.5 mg/100 mL. This value is equal to how many mEq/L?
(MW of K = 39)

    a. 3.9
    b. 4.2
    c. 5.0
    d. 8.9

218. Which of the following is the formula for calculating the amount of moles of a chemical?

    a. $\dfrac{g}{GMW}$

    b. g x GMW

    c. $\dfrac{GMW}{g}$

    d. $\dfrac{g \times 100}{GMW}$

219. A one molal solution is equivalent to:

    a. a solution containing one mole of solute per kg of solvent
    b. 1000 mL of solution containing one mole of solute
    c. a solution containing one gram-equivalent weight of solute in one liter of solution
    d. a one liter solution containing 2 moles of solute

220. Which of the following is the formula for calculating the molarity of a solution?

    a. number of moles of solute/L of solution
    b. number of moles of solute x 100
    c. 1 GEW of solute x 10
    d. 1 GEW of solute/L of solution

221. What is the molarity of a solution that contains 18.7 g of KCl (MW = 74.5) in 500 mL of water?

    a. 0.1
    b. 0.5
    c. 1.0
    d. 5.0

222. 25 grams of NaOH (MW = 40) are added to a 0.5 L of water. What is the molarity of this solution if an additional 0.25 L of water are added to this solution?

    a. 0.25 M
    b. 0.50 M
    c. 0.75 M
    d. 0.83 M

223. In an alkaline picrate procedure to measure creatinine concentration in serum, the sodium hydroxide solution used contains 30 g NaOH/L. One milliliter of this solution is added to 1.5 mL of water, 1.5 mL of serum and 1 mL of picric acid. The concentration of NaOH in the final solution is equivalent to: (Atomic weights: NA = 23, H = 1, 0 = 16)

    a. 1.5 mol/L
    b. 0.75 mol/L
    c. 0.3 mol/L
    d. 0.15 mol/L

224. A one normal solution is equivalent to:

    a. a solution containing one mole of solute per kg of solvent
    b. 1000 mL of solution containing one mole of solute
    c. a solution containing one gram-equivalent weight of solute in one liter of solution
    d. a one liter solution containing 2 moles of solute

225. What is the normality of a solution which contains 280 grams of NaOH (MW = 40) in 2000 mL of solution?

    a. 3.5 N
    b. 5.5 N
    c. 7.0 N
    d. 8.0 N

226. Which of the following solutions has a normality of 1?

    a. 1 mole of H_2SO_4
    b. 2 moles of HCl
    c. 2 moles of H_2CO_3
    d. 1 mole of H_3PO_4

227. How many grams of H_2SO_4 (MW = 98) are in 750 mL of 3N H_2SO_4?

    a. 36 gm
    b. 72 gm
    c. 110 gm
    d. 146 gm

228. How many milliliters of 0.25 N NaOH are needed to make 100 mL of a 0.05 N solution of NaOH?

    a. 5 mL
    b. 10 mL
    c. 15 mL
    d. 20 mL

229. The extent to which measurements agree with the true value of the quantity being measured is known as:

    a. reliability
    b. accuracy
    c. reproducibility
    d. precision

230. An index of precision is statistically known as the:

    a. median
    b. mean
    c. standard deviation
    d. coefficient of variation

231. The statistical term for the average value is the:

    a. mode
    b. median
    c. mean
    d. coefficient of variation

232. Refer to the following graph:

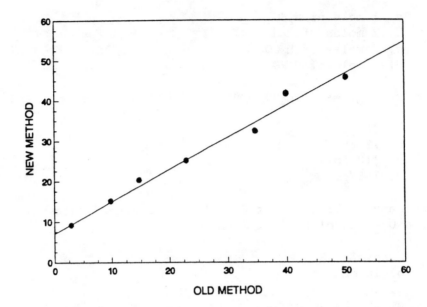

A new methodology for amylase has been developed and compared with the existing method as illustrated in the graph shown above. The new method can be described as:

a. poor correlation with constant bias
b. good correlation with constant bias
c. poor correlation with no bias
d. good correlation with no bias

---

233. The most frequent value in a collection of data, is statistically known as:

a. mode
b. median
c. mean
d. standard deviation

234. The middle value of a data set is statistically known as the:

a. mean
b. median
c. mode
d. standard deviation

235. Which of the following is the formula for arithmetic mean?

    a. square root of the sum of values

    b. sum of values x number of values

    c. $\dfrac{\text{number of values}}{\text{sum of values}}$

    d. $\dfrac{\text{sum of values}}{\text{number of values}}$

236. Given the following values:

    100
    120
    150
    140
    130

What is the mean?

    a. 100
    b. 128
    c. 130
    d. 640

237. Which of the following is the formula for coefficient of variation?

    a. $\dfrac{\text{standard deviation x 100}}{\text{standard error}}$

    b. $\dfrac{\text{mean x 100}}{\text{standard deviation}}$

    c. $\dfrac{\text{standard deviation x 100}}{\text{mean}}$

    d. $\dfrac{\text{variance x 100}}{\text{mean}}$

238. Which of the following is the formula for standard deviation?

    a. square root of the mean

    b. square root of $\frac{\underline{\text{sum of squared differences}}}{(N-1)}$

    c. square root of the variance

    d. square root of $\left(\frac{\text{mean}}{\text{sum of squared differences}}\right)$

239. Two standard deviations is the acceptable limit of error in the chemistry laboratory. If you run the normal control 100 times, how many of the values would be out of control due to random error?

    a. 1
    b. 5
    c. 10
    d. 20

240. A mean value of 100 and a standard deviation of 1.8 mg/dL were obtained from a set of glucose measurements on a control solution. The 95% confidence interval in mg/dL would be:

    a. 94.6 to 105.4
    b. 96.4 to 103.6
    c. 97.3 to 102.7
    d. 98.2 to 101.8

The following items (*) have been identified as more appropriate for the entry level medical technologist.

*241. The conversion of glucose or other hexoses into lactate or pyruvate is called:

a. glycogenesis
b. glycogenolysis
c. gluconeogenesis
d. glycolysis

*242. Which of the following hormones is <u>NOT</u> important in the regulation of blood glucose concentration?

a. insulin
b. hydrocortisone
c. thyroxine
d. prolactin

*243. The serum glucose concentration of a diabetic patient undergoing a two-hour glucose tolerance test should return to the baseline (fasting level) after a minimum of:

a. 30 minutes
b. 60 minutes
c. 90 minutes
d. 120 minutes

*244. A fasting serum sample from an 43-year-old woman is examined visually and chemically with the following results:

Initial appearance of serum:	milky
Appearance of serum after overnight refrigeration:	cream layer over turbid serum
Triglyceride level:	2,000 mg/dL
Cholesterol level:	550 mg/dL

A lipoprotein electrophoresis of this serum specimen would show:

a. a heavy band at the origin
b. a heavy beta band
c. heavy beta and pre-beta bands
d. heavy bands at the origin and at the pre-beta region

*245. Which of the following diseases results from a familial absence of high density lipoprotein (HDL)?

a. Krabbe's
b. Gaucher's
c. Tangier
d. Tay-Sachs

*246. With which of the following methods for measuring serum triglycerides is use of lyophilized quality control materials LEAST satisfactory?

    a. nephelometry following ultrafiltration of diluted serum
    b. alkaline saponification, periodate oxidation, and condensation with acetylacetone
    c. alkaline saponification, with enzymatic analysis of liberated glycerol
    d. enzymatic hydrolysis, with enzymatic analysis of liberated glycerol

*247. In which of the following conditions does decreased activity of glucuronyl transferase result in increased unconjugated bilirubin and kernicterus in neonates?

    a. Gilbert's disease
    b. Rotor's syndrome
    c. Dubin-Johnson syndrome
    d. Crigler-Najjar syndrome

*248. A 21-year-old man with nausea, vomiting, and jaundice has the following laboratory findings:

Total serum bilirubin level: 8.5 mg/dL (normal: 0-1.0 mg/dL)
Direct serum bilirubin level: 6.1 mg/dL (normal: 0-0.5 mg/dL)
Urine urobilinogen: increased
Fecal urobilinogen: decreased
Urine bilirubin: positive
AST: 300 U/L (normal: 0-50 U/L)
Alkaline phosphatase: 170 U/L (normal: 0-150 U/L)

These can best be explained as representing:

    a. unconjugated hyperbilirubinemia, probably due to hemolysis
    b. unconjugated hyperbilirubinemia, probably due to toxic liver damage
    c. conjugated hyperbilirubinemia, probably due to biliary tract disease
    d. conjugated hyperbilirubinemia, probably due to hepatocellular obstruction

*249. Which of the following allows separation of Hgb A_{1a} and Hgb A_{1b} from Hgb A_{1c} and Hgb A?

    a. HPLC
    b. electrophoresis
    c. chromatography
    d. spectrophotometry

*250. In using ion-exchange chromatographic methods, falsely decreased levels of Hgb A_{1c} will be demonstrated in the presence of:

a. Hgb F
b. pernicious anemia
c. thalassemias
d. Hgb S

*251. Quantitative analysis of urine for delta-aminolevulinic acid is associated with:

a. lead poisoning
b. hereditary coproporphyria
c. carrier state of acute intermittent porphyria
d. erythrocytic protoporphyria

*252. Detection of carriers of hereditary coproporphyria should include analysis of:

a. 24-hour urine for porphobilinogen
b. fresh morning urine for delta-aminolevulinic acid
c. erythrocyte protoporphyrin
d. 24-hour urine for porphyrin

*253. A test request slip indicates that an acute porphyria attack is suspected clinically. Analysis should include:

a. quantitative delta-aminolevulinic acid
b. porphyrin screen
c. quantitative 24-hour porphobilinogen
d. porphobilinogen screen

*254. A fresh urine sample is received for analysis for "porphyrins" or "porphyria" without further information or specifications. Initial analysis should include:

a. porphyrin screen and quantitative total porphyrin
b. quantitative total porphyrin and porphobilinogen screen
c. porphyrin screen and porphobilinogen screen
d. porphobilinogen screen and ion-exchange analysis for porphobilinogen

*255. The method of choice for diagnosis of a protracted attack of porphyria is:

    a. screening a fresh morning urine for porphobilinogen
    b. analysis of delta-aminolevulinic acid in a morning urine
    c. screening a fresh morning urine for porphyrin
    d. ion-exchange analysis of porphobilinogen on a 24-hour urine

*256. The urinary excretion of porphobilinogen is increased in patients with:

    a. erythropoietic protoporphyria
    b. porphyria cutanea tarda
    c. hemolytic anemia
    d. acute intermittent porphyria

*257. Analysis of erythrocytes for uroporphyrinogen synthetase detects:

    a. acute porphyria attack
    b. lead poisoning
    c. hereditary coproporphyria
    d. carrier state of acute intermittent porphyria

*258. Which of the following enzymes of heme biosynthesis is inhibited by lead?

    a. aminolevulinate synthetase
    b. porphobilinogen synthetase
    c. uroporphyrinogen synthetase
    d. bilirubin synthetase

*259. Fasting and postprandial bile acid concentrations are useful to assess:

    a. diabetes mellitus
    b. hepatobiliary disease
    c. intestinal malabsorption
    d. kidney function

*260. Each of the following statements about alpha-1-antitrypsin is true EXCEPT:

    a. it constitutes the major portion of the alpha-1 globulin fraction
    b. deficiency is associated with chronic obstructive lung disease
    c. serum concentrations can be decreased while hepatocyte concentrations are increased
    d. serum concentrations frequently are decreased in conditions associated with inflammation

*261. In an electrophoretic separation, the zones appear artifactually crescent-shaped. The most likely cause is:

    a. insufficient amount of sample
    b. overload of sample
    c. use of phosphate-borate buffer
    d. inadequate fixation prior to staining

*262. The electrophoretic resolution of serum globulins can be improved by:

    a. using high ionic strength buffer
    b. using a buffer with high osmolality
    c. adding calcium ions to the buffer
    d. using Tris rather than barbital buffer

*263. Increased serum albumin concentrations are seen in which of the following conditions:

    a. nephrotic syndrome
    b. acute hepatitis
    c. chronic inflammation
    d. dehydration

*264. In electrophoresis of serum proteins, artifacts at the application point are most frequently caused by:

    a. endosmosis
    b. prestaining with tracer dye
    c. overloading of serum sample
    d. dirty applicators

*265. Refer to the following illustration:

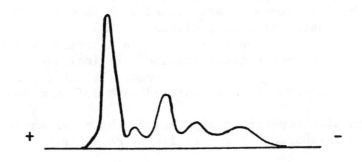

	Patient Values	Reference Values
Total Protein	7.8 g/dL	6.0-8.0 g/dL
Albumin	3.0 g/dL	3.6-5.2 g/dL
Alpha-1	0.4 g/dL	0.1-0.4 g/dL
Alpha-2	1.8 g/dL	0.4-1.0 g/dL
Beta	0.5 g/dL	0.5-1.2 g/dL
Gamma	1.1 g/dL	0.6-1.6 g/dL

The serum protein electrophoresis pattern is consistent with:

    a. cirrhosis
    b. acute inflammation
    c. polyclonal gammopathy (e.g., chronic inflammation)
    d. alpha-1-antitrypsin deficiency; severe emphysema

---

*266. The buffer pH most effective at allowing amphoteric proteins to migrate toward the cathode in an electrophoretic system would be:

    a. 4.5
    b. 7.5
    c. 8.6
    d. 9.5

*267. Refer to the following illustration:

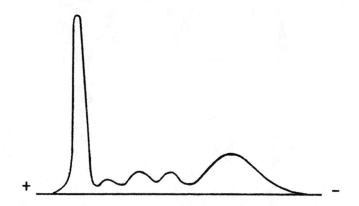

	Reference Values	Patient Values
Total Protein	8.5 g/dL	6.0-8.0 g/dL
Albumin	4.3 g/dL	3.6-5.2 g/dL
Alpha-1	0.3 g/dL	0.1-0.4 g/dL
Alpha-2	0.7 g/dL	0.4-1.0 g/dL
Beta	0.9 g/dL	0.5-1.2 g/dL
Gamma	2.3 g/dL	0.6-1.6 g/dL

The above serum protein electrophoresis pattern is consistent with:

    a. cirrhosis
    b. monoclonal gammopathy
    c. polyclonal gammopathy (e.g., chronic inflammation)
    d. alpha-1-antitrypsin deficiency; severe emphysema

---

*268. Analysis of CSF for oligoclonal bands is used to screen for which of the following disease states?

    a. multiple myeloma
    b. multiple sclerosis
    c. myasthenia gravis
    d. von Willebrand's disease

*269. The identification of Bence Jones protein is best accomplished by:

    a. a sulfosalicylic acid test
    b. urine reagent strips
    c. immunofixation
    d. electrophoresis

*270. Below are the results of a protein electrophoresis:

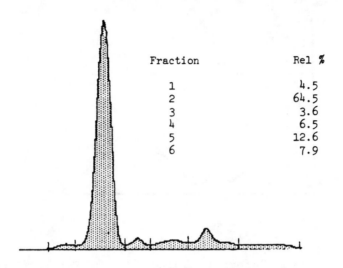

Fraction	Rel %
1	4.5
2	64.5
3	3.6
4	6.5
5	12.6
6	7.9

These results are consistent with a(n):

    a. normal serum protein pattern
    b. normal CSF protein pattern
    c. abnormal serum protein pattern
    d. abnormal CSF protein pattern

---

*271. In competitive inhibition of an enzyme reaction the:

    a. inhibitor binds to the enzyme at the same site
       as does the substrate
    b. inhibitor often has a chemical structure
       different to that of the substrate
    c. activity of the reaction can be decreased by
       increasing the concentration of the substrate
    d. activity of the reaction can be increased by
       decreasing the temperature

*272. A 36-week-pregnant woman was admitted to the hospital with
a diagnosis of possible liver disease. Which of the following
enzyme determinations would be LEAST useful in confirming the
diagnosis?

    a. alkaline phosphatase
    b. alanine aminotransferase
    c. gamma-glutamyl transferase
    d. isocitrate dehydrogenase

For questions 273 and 274, refer to the following illustration:

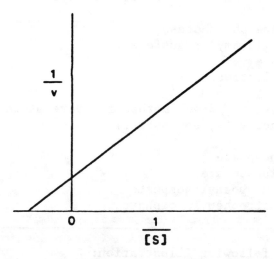

*273. The above figure shows the reciprocal of the measured velocity
of an enzyme reaction plotted against the reciprocal of the
substrate concentration. True statements about this figure
include:

    a. the intercept of the line on the abscissa (x
       axis) can be used to calculate the V_{max}
    b. the straight line indicates that the enzyme
       reaction proceeds according to zero order kinetics
    c. the intercept on the abscissa (x axis) can be
       used to calculate the Michaelis-Menten constant
    d. the fact that the substrate concentration is
       plotted on both sides of the zero point indicates
       that the reaction is reversible

*274. The figure above shows the reciprocal of the measured velocity
of an enzyme reaction plotted against the reciprocal of the
substrate concentration. True statements about this figure
include:

    a. the intercept of the line on the ordinate (y
       axis) can be used to calculate the V_{max}
    b. the straight line indicates that the enzyme
       reaction proceeds according to zero order kinetics
    c. the intercept on the ordinate (y axis) can be
       used to calculate the Michaelis-Menten constant
    d. the fact the substrate concentration is plotted
       on both sides of the zero point indicates that the
       reaction is reversible

*275. Each of the enzymes listed is included in the hepatobiliary panel for assessing liver function EXCEPT:

    a. alkaline phosphatase
    b. gamma-glutamyl transferase
    c. aldolase
    d. 5'-nucleotidase

*276. In the Bessey-Lowry-Brock method for determining alkaline phosphatase activity, the substrate used is:

    a. monophosphate
    b. phenylphosphate
    c. disodium phenylphosphate
    d. para-nitrophenylphosphate

---

*277. Refer to the following illustration:

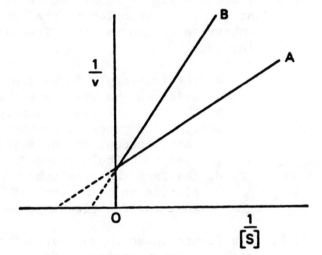

v   = reaction rate
[S] = substrate concentration

The illustration above represents a Lineweaver-Burk plot of 1/v versus 1/[S] in an enzyme reaction. The following assumptions should be made:

The enzyme concentration was the same for reactions A and B. The substrate concentration was in excess for reactions A and B. Reaction A occurred under ideal conditions. Which of the following statements about reaction B is true?

    a. It illustrates noncompetitive inhibition.
    b. It illustrates competitive inhibition.
    c. It illustrates neither competitive nor noncompetitive inhibition.
    d. It could be the result of heavy metal contamination.

*278. A 10-year-old child was admitted to pediatrics with an initial diagnosis of skeletal muscle disease. The best confirmatory tests would be:

    a. creatine kinase and isocitrate dehydrogenase
    b. gamma-glutamyl transferase and alkaline phosphatase
    c. aldolase and creatine kinase
    d. lactate dehydrogenase and malate dehydrogenase

*279. Which of the following glycolytic enzymes catalyzes the cleavage of fructose-1, 6-diphosphate to glyceraldehyde-3-phosphate and dihydroxyacetone phosphate?

    a. aldolase
    b. phosphofructokinase
    c. pyruvate kinase
    d. fumarase

*280. The most heat labile fraction of alkaline phosphatase is obtained from:

    a. liver
    b. bone
    c. intestine
    d. placenta

*281. A 48-year-old woman with mild jaundice has the following serum enzyme results:

Alkaline phosphatase
        (untreated):   600 U/L (normal: 0-150 U/L)
Gamma-glutamyl transferase: 230 U/L (normal: 0-55 U/L)
Alkaline phosphatase after 10
  minutes incubation at 56°C: 300 U/L (50% of original activity)
AST :   400 U/L (normal: 0-50 U/L)

Which of the following sources contributes most to the patient's serum alkaline phosphatase activity?

    a. bone
    b. liver
    c. placenta
    d. Regan isoenzyme

*282. In the immuno-inhibition phase of the CK-MB procedure:

    a. M subunit is inactivated
    b. B subunit is activated
    c. MB is inactivated
    d. BB is activated

*283. The greatest activities of serum AST and ALT are seen in:

    a. acute hepatitis
    b. primary biliary cirrhosis
    c. metastatic hepatic carcinoma
    d. alcoholic cirrhosis

*284. The presence of increased CK-MB activity on a CK electrophoresis pattern is most likely found in a patient suffering from:

    a. acute muscular stress following strenuous exercise
    b. malignant liver disease
    c. myocardial infarction
    d. severe head injury

---

*285. Refer to the illustration:

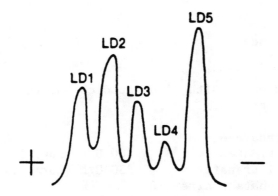

Which of the following is the most likely interpretation of the LD isoenzyme scan illustrated above?

    a. myocardial infarction
    b. megaloblastic anemia
    c. acute pancreatitis
    d. viral hepatitis

---

*286. In a severely hemolyzed specimen, the fluorescence observed cathodal to the CK-MM isoenzyme is caused by:

    a. hemoglobin
    b. adenylate kinase
    c. CK-BB
    d. CK-MB

*287. In the "reverse reaction" of creatine kinase (Creatine Phosphate + ADP → Creatine + ATP), thiol compounds such as cysteine, glutathione, and dithiothreitol serve to:

    a. predictably inhibit enzyme activity
    b. enhance enzyme activity
    c. bind ADP
    d. precipitate proteins

*288. The prostatic fraction of acid phosphatase is inhibited by:

    a. acetic acid
    b. citric acid
    c. sodium nitrite
    d. tartrate

*289. Which of the following is a characteristic shared by lactate dehydrogenase, malate dehydrogenase, isocitrate dehydrogenase, and hydroxybutyrate dehydrogenase?

    a. They are liver enzymes.
    b. They are cardiac enzymes.
    c. They catalyze oxidation-reduction reactions.
    d. They are class III enzymes.

*290. Increased serum lactate dehydrogenase activity due to elevation of fast fraction (1 and 2) on electrophoretic separation is caused by:

    a. nephrotic syndrome
    b. hemolytic anemia
    c. pancreatitis
    d. hepatic damage

*291. A serum sample drawn in the emergency room from a 42-year-old man yielded the following laboratory results:

    CK   185 Units   (Normal = 15-160)
    AST   123 Units   (Normal = 0-48)
    CK-MB 6 Units   (Normal = 2-12)

Which of the following conditions might account for these values?

    a. crush injury to the thigh
    b. cerebrovascular accident
    c. pulmonary infarction
    d. early acute hepatitis

*292. Malic dehydrogenase is added to the aspartate aminotrans-
aminase (AST) reaction to catalyze the conversion of:

a. alpha-ketoglutarate to aspartate
b. alpha-ketoglutarate to malate
c. aspartate to oxalacetate
d. oxalacetate to malate

*293. In acute pancreatitis, the relative increase in urinary amylase
activity is greater than that of serum amylase activity because:

a. salivary isoamylases are increased
b. there are fewer inhibitors of amylase in urine
c. there is an increased renal clearance of amylase
d. measurements exhibit greater linearity in urine

*294. Given the following results:

Alkaline Phosphatase	Aspartate amino- transferase	Alanine amino- transferase	Gamma-glutamyl transferase
Slight Increase	Marked Increase	Marked Increase	Slight Increase

This is most consistent with:

a. acute hepatitis
b. chronic hepatitis
c. obstructive jaundice
d. liver hemangioma

*295. Given the following results:

Alkaline Phosphatase	Aspartate amino- transferase	Alanine amino- transferase	Gamma-glutamyl transferase
Marked Increase	Slight Increase	Slight Increase	Marked Increase

This is most consistent with:

a. acute hepatitis
b. osteitis fibrosa
c. chronic hepatitis
d. obstructive jaundice

*296. Given the following results:

Alkaline Phosphatase	Aspartate amino-transferase	Alanine amino-transferase	Gamma-glutamyl transferase
Slight Increase	Slight Increase	Slight Increase	Slight Increase

This is most consistent with:

a. acute hepatitis
b. chronic hepatitis
c. obstructive jaundice
d. liver hemangioma

*297. Assay of transketolase activity in blood is used to detect deficiency of:

a. thiamine
b. folic acid
c. ascorbic acid
d. riboflavin

*298. Creatinine metabolism in patients with decreased renal function is characterized by:

a. linear increase in serum concentrations (mg/dL) as creatinine clearance (in mL/min) decreases
b. decrease excretion into the gut
c. enzymatic conversion of creatine to creatinine
d. increased renal tubular secretion of creatinine

*299. A blood creatinine value of 5.0 mg/dL is most likely to be found with which of the following blood values?

a. osmolality   292 mOsm/L
b. uric acid   8 mg/dL
c. urea nitrogen   180 mg/dL
d. ammonia   80 µg/dL

*300. The following results were obtained in a creatinine clearance evaluation:

Urine concentration   84 mg/dL (7.43 mEq/L)
Urine volume   1440 mL/24 hr
Serum concentration   1.4 mg/dL (124 μmol/L)
Body surface area   1.60 m² (average = 1.73 m²)

The creatinine clearance in mL/min is:

    a. 0.006
    b. 0.022
    c. 0.60
    d. 64.9

*301. Serum haptoglobin:

    a. is decreased in patients with tissue injury and neoplasia
    b. is increased in patients with prosthetic heart valves
    c. can be separated into distinct phenotypes by starch-gel electrophoresis
    d. binds heme

*302. Which of the following methods offers the greatest sensitivity for HB_sAg testing?

    a. counterimmunoelectrophoresis
    b. enzyme immunoassay
    c. flow cytometry
    d. spectrophotometry

*303. In the international System of Units serum urea is expressed in millimoles per liter. A serum urea nitrogen concentration of 28 mg/dL would be equivalent to what concentration of urea?

(Urea: NH_2CONH_2; atomic wt. N=14, C=12, O=16, H=1)

    a. 4.7 mEq/L
    b. 5.0 mEq/L
    c. 10.0 mEq/L
    d. 20.0 mEq/L

*304. The urea nitrogen concentration of a serum sample was measured to be 15 mg/dL (5.36 mEq/L). The urea concentration of the same sample, in mg/dL, is:

(Atomic weights: carbon = 12, oxygen = 16, nitrogen = 14, hydrogen = 1)

    a. 15
    b. 24
    c. 32
    d. 40

*305. Patients who have a certain defective enzyme are unable to hydrolyze succinyl choline and may suffer from respiratory paralysis for up to 24 hours after administration of the muscle relaxant. This phenomenon is referred to as:

    a. pharmacogenetic variability
    b. enzyme induction
    c. drug-protein interaction
    d. drug-drug interaction

*306. A blood gas was sent to the lab on ice, but there was a bubble in the syringe. The blood has been exposed to room air for at least 30 minutes. The following change in blood gases will occur:

    a. CO_2 content increased/pCO_2 decreased
    b. CO_2 content and pO_2 increased/pH increased
    c. CO_2 content and pCO_2 decreased/pH decreased
    d. pO_2 increased/HCO_3- decreased

*307. A pH of 7.0 represents a H+ concentration of:

    a. 70 mEq/L
    b. 10 µmol/L
    c. 7 nmol/L
    d. 100 nmol/L

*308. Normally the bicarbonate concentration is about 24 mEq/L and the carbonic acid concentration is about 1.2; pK = 6.1, log 20 = 1.3. Using the equation pH = pK + log[salt] calculate the pH.   [acid]

    a. 7.28
    b. 7.38
    c. 7.40
    d. 7.42

*309. A patient with metabolic acidosis has the following arterial blood values:

$$pH\ 7.1,\ pCO_2\ 20\ mm\ Hg$$

If pK $(H_2CO_3 - HCO_3) = 6.1$, and $[H_2CO_3] = 0.03 \times pCO_2$, what is the bicarbonate concentration of the sample?

    a. 0.6 mEq/L
    b. 1.67 mEq/L
    c. 6 mEq/L
    d. 16.7 mEq/L

*310. Blood pCO_2 may be measured by:

    a. direct colorimetric measurement of dissolved CO_2
    b. calculations of blood pH and total CO_2 concentration
    c. measurement of CO_2-saturated hemoglobin
    d. measurement of CO_2 consumed at the cathode

*311. A potentiometric electrode which measures an analyte that passes through a selectively permeable membrane and rapidly enters into an equilibrium with an electrolyte solution is:

    a. pH
    b. pCO_2
    c. pO_2
    d. HCO_3^-

*312. The following laboratory results were obtained:

Serum Electrolytes		Arterial Blood
Sodium	136 mEq/L	pH 7.32
Potassium	4.4 mEq/L	pCO_2 79 mm Hg
Chloride	92 mEq/L	
Bicarbonate	40 mEq/L	

These results are most compatible with:

    a. respiratory alkalosis
    b. respiratory acidosis
    c. metabolic alkalosis
    d. metabolic acidosis

*313. An arterial blood specimen is submitted for blood gas analysis.
The specimen was obtained at 8:30 a.m. but was not received
in the laboratory until 11:00 a.m. The technologist should:

   a. perform the test immediately upon receipt
   b. perform the test only if the specimen was
      submitted in ice water
   c. request a venous blood specimen
   d. request a new arterial specimen be obtained

*314. In various colorimetric methods for determining inorganic
phosphorus concentrations, reagents such as stannous chloride,
ferrous sulfate, and ascorbic acid function as:

   a. oxidizing agents
   b. reducing agents
   c. stabilizing agents
   d. catalysts

*315. A low concentration of serum phosphorus is commonly found in:

   a. patients who are receiving carbohydrate hyperalimentation
   b. chronic renal disease
   c. hypoparathyroidism
   d. patients with pituitary tumors

*316. Serum and urine copper levels are run on a hospital patient
with the following results:

	Patients Values	Reference Values
Serum Cu	58 µg/dL	70-140 µg/dL
Urine Cu	83 µg/dL	<40 µg/dL

These results are most consistent with:

   a. normal copper levels
   b. Wilm's tumor
   c. Wilson's disease
   d. Addison's disease

*317. In the urea cycle:

   a. mitochondria carbamyl phosphate synthetase
      (ammonia) is activated by N-acetyl glutamate
   b. urea is formed by the action of arginase on
      arginosuccinate synthetase
   c. hepatic ornithine levels are determined by
      ornithine transcarbamylase
   d. ammonia, CO_2, and ATP are unnecessary for
      the first step of the urea cycle

*318. A critically ill patient becomes comatose. The physician believes the coma is due to hepatic failure. The assay most helpful in this diagnosis is:

     a. ammonia
     b. ALT
     c. AST
     d. GGT

*319. A patient has the following results:

	Patient Values	Reference Values
Serum iron -	250 µg/dL	60-150 µg/dL
TIBC -	350 µg/dL	300-350 µg/dL

The best conclusion is that this patient has:

     a. normal iron status
     b. iron deficiency anemia
     c. chronic disease
     d. iron hemochromatosis

*320. Blood samples were collected at the beginning of an exercise class and after thirty minutes of aerobic activity. Which of the following would be most consistent with the post-exercise sample?

     a. normal lactic acid, low pyruvate
     b. low lactic acid, elevated pyruvate
     c. elevated lactic acid, low pyruvate
     d. elevated lactic acid, elevated pyruvate

*321. A sweat chloride result of 55 mEq/L and a sweat sodium of 52 mEq/L were obtained on a patient who has a history of respiratory problems. The best interpretation of these results is:

     a. normal results
     b. normal sodium and an abnormal chloride, test should be repeated
     c. abnormal results
     d. borderline results, the tests should be repeated

*322. Which of the following is a trophic hormone?

     a. thyroxine
     b. estriol
     c. parathyroid hormone
     d. growth hormone

*323. A two-year-old child with a decreased serum T-4 is described as being somewhat dwarfed, stocky, overweight, and having coarse features. Of the following, the most informative additional laboratory test would be the serum:

   a. thyroxine-binding globulin (TBG)
   b. thyroid-stimulating hormone (TSH)
   c. triiodothyronine (T-3)
   d. cholesterol

*324. In a normal individual, injection of thyrotropin-releasing hormone (TRH) causes an increase in blood concentrations of which of the following hormones?

   a. growth hormone
   b. prolactin
   c. ACTH
   d. insulin

*325. The TRH (Thyrotropin Releasing Hormone) Stimulation test is useful in assessing which of the following:

   a. TRH concentration
   b. iodine deficiency
   c. depression
   d. hyperthyroidism

*326. Hyperthyroidism has been associated with each of the following EXCEPT:

   a. increased T-4
   b. increased T-3
   c. decreased serum cholesterol
   d. decreased serum calcium

*327. Total T-4 by competitive protein binding or displacement is based on the specific binding properties of:

   a. thyroxine-binding prealbumin
   b. albumin
   c. thyroxine-binding globulin
   d. thyroid-stimulating hormone

*328. When taken by a euthyroid individual, oral contraceptives containing estrogens will have which of the following effects on the thyroid function studies?

   a. increase total circulating T-4
   b. increase T-3 resin uptake
   c. decrease thyroxine-binding globulin
   d. decrease circulating T-3

*329. The most common type of congenital adrenal hyperplasia
associated with increased plasma concentrations of
17α-hydroxyprogesterone and increased urinary excretion of
pregnanetriol is:

    a. 17α-hydroxylase deficiency
    b. 11ß-hydroxylase deficiency
    c. 21-hydroxylase deficiency
    d. 18-hydroxysteroid dehydrogenase deficiency

*330. Chronic fetal metabolic distress is demonstrated by:

    a. decreased estrogen concentrations in maternal
       plasma and increased estriol concentrations in
       amniotic fluid
    b. increased estradiol concentrations in maternal
       plasma with a corresponding increase of estriol in
       amniotic fluid
    c. increased urinary estriol excretion and
       increased maternal serum estriol concentrations
    d. decreased urinary estriol excretion and
       decreased maternal serum estriol concentrations

*331. Androgen secretion by the testes is stimulated by:

    a. interstitial cell-stimulating hormone (ICSH)
    b. follicle-stimulating hormone(FSH)
    c. testosterone
    d. gonadotropins

*332. Progesterone:

    a. is produced by Leydig's cells of the adult
       testes and is responsible for genital development,
       beard growth, muscle development, and sexual drive
    b. is produced by the placenta during pregnancy;
       the highest concentration is seen at the time of
       conception and then steadily decreases to nondetectable
       levels at term
    c. plasma concentrations are lowest during the luteal phase
       of the menstrual cycle and highest during the follicular
       phase
    d. parallels the activity of the corpus luteum by rapidly
       increasing following ovulation and then abruptly falling
       to initial low concentrations prior to the onset of
       menstruation

*333. In the uncontrolled diabetic patient, urine glucose may give false elevations in the colorimetric assay of:

    a. androgens
    b. estrogens
    c. 17-hydroxycorticosteroids
    d. 17-ketosteroids

*334. The color reagent for the determination of 17-ketosteroids by the Zimmerman reaction is:

    a. dihyroxyacetone
    b. phenylhydrazine
    c. m-dinitrobenzene
    d. m-dinitrophenol

*335. The definitive diagnosis of primary adrenal insufficiency requires demonstration of:

    a. decreased urinary 17-keto- and 17-hydroxysteroids
    b. decreased cortisol production
    c. impaired response to ACTH stimulation
    d. increased urinary cortisol excretion after metyrapone

*336. The test for adrenal cortical hyperfunction that has the greatest diagnostic sensitivity is measurement of:

    a. urinary free cortisol
    b. plasma cortisol
    c. urinary 17-hydroxycorticosteroids
    d. plasma corticosterone

*337. Oral administration of L-dopa in children provokes stimulation of:

    a. insulin
    b. growth hormone
    c. estrogen
    d. pituitary gonadotropin

*338. A patient has signs and symptoms suggestive of acromegaly. The diagnosis would be confirmed if the patient had which of the following?

    a. an elevated serum phosphate concentration
    b. a decreased serum growth hormone releasing factor concentration
    c. no decrease in serum growth hormone concentration 90 minutes after oral glucose administration
    d. an increased serum somatostatin concentration

*339. Patients with Cushing's syndrome exhibit:

   a. decreased plasma 17-hydroxysteroid concentration
   b. decreased urinary 17-hydroxysteroid excretion
   c. serum cortisol concentrations greater than 15 mg/dL
   d. decreased cortisol secretory rate

*340. Urinary estrogen in pregnant women consists chiefly of:

   a. estradiol
   b. estriol
   c. estrone
   d. pregnanediol

*341. Estrogen and progesterone receptor assays are useful in assessing prognosis in which of the following?

   a. ovarian cancer
   b. breast cancer
   c. endometriosis
   d. amenorrhea

---

*342. Refer to the following graph:

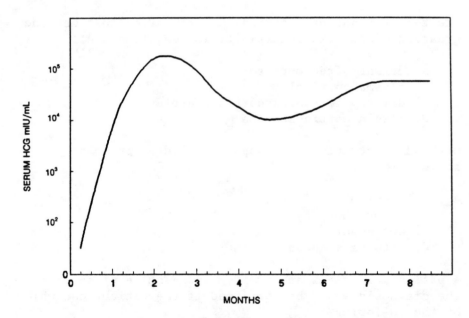

The HCG levels shown in the above graph most probably represent:

   a. hydatiform mole following miscarriage at 4 months
   b. normal pregnancy
   c. development of hydatiform mole
   d. miscarriage at 2 months with retained placenta

*343.   Blood specimens for digoxin assays should be obtained
        8 hours or more after drug administration because:

        a. adequate time for tissue distribution and
           equilibration with serum levels must be allowed
        b. serum digoxin concentration will be falsely low
           prior to six hours
        c. all of the digoxin is in the cellular fraction
           prior to six hours
        d. digoxin protein-binding interactions are
           minimal prior to six hours

*344.   If a drug has a half-life of 7 hours, how many doses given at
        7-hour intervals does it usually take to achieve a steady
        state or plateau level?

        a. one
        b. three
        c. five
        d. eight

*345.   When clinical response does not agree with total drug
        concentration, free drug levels may be of clinical use
        in all of the following cases, EXCEPT:

        a. uremia
        b. hypoalbuminemia
        c. ingestion of other drugs
        d. patient noncompliance

*346.   Most drugs and intracellular metabolites measured by radio-
        immunoassay have molecular weights between 200 and 1000 and
        can be made immunogenic by:

        a. attaching them to protein molecules
        b. frequent injections of the compound mixed with
           Freund's adjuvant
        c. sensitizing the animal with another antigen first
        d. treating the animals with glucocorticoids

*347.   Nortriptyline is a metabolite of:

        a. amitriptyline
        b. protriptyline
        c. butriptyline
        d. norbutriptyline

*348. A psychiatric patient was experiencing severe depression, but responded to treatment with amitriptyline with no apparent side effects. A blood sample was sent to the laboratory for therapeutic monitoring. Which of the following drug levels would be MOST reflective of this patient's condition?

a. Amitriptyline = 237 µg/L
b. Amitriptyline = 104 µg/L
c. Protriptylene = 76 µg/L
d. Imipramine = 103 µg/L

*349. Phenobarbital is toxic above the level of:

a. 20 mg/L
b. 30 mg/L
c. 40 mg/L
d. 60 mg/L

*350. Both phenobarbital and phenylethylmalonamide (PEMA) are metabolites of:

a. primidone
b. phenytoin
c. amobarbital
d. secobarbital

*351. Currently the most common method for specific identification and quantitation of serum barbiturates is:

a. immunoassay
b. thin-layer chromatography
c. gas-liquid chromatography
d. ultraviolet absorption spectroscopy

*352. In acid solution, 5,5-disubstituted barbiturates exist in which state of ionization?

a. first ionized species
b. second ionized species
c. non-ionized
d. an equilibrium mixture of non-ionized and the first species

*353.   A blood sample was received from the emergency room with
        a request for narcotic analysis. The request slip indicated
        that the patient (a known heroin addict) responded to
        naloxone administration. The serum was negative for morphine
        by EIA. What other tests should be performed in assessing
        suspected opiate abuse?

            a.   heroin
            b.   salicylate
            c.   alcohol
            d.   methadone

*354.   Cocaine is metabolized to:

            a. carbamazepine
            b. codeine
            c. hydrocodone
            d. benzoylecgonine

*355.   The cyclic antidepressants are:

            a. basic drugs
            b. neutral drugs
            c. acidic drugs
            d. structurally cycloparaffinic

*356.   Gas chromatography with the nitrogen/phosphorus detector is
        the most commonly used technique for the analysis of:

            a. digoxin
            b. acetylsalicylic acid
            c. ethyl alcohol
            d. cyclic antidepressants

*357.   Certain enzymes are activated to metabolize drugs as a result
        of another drug action. This is referred to as:

            a. substrate depletion
            b. enzyme depletion
            c. enzyme induction
            d. enzyme inhibition

*358.   The trade name for chlordiazepoxide is:

            a. Librium
            b. Valium
            c. Tegretol
            d. Luminal

*359. About 90% of phenytoin is excreted in the urine as:

    a. phenobarbital
    b. para-hydroxyphenyl phenylhydantoin
    c. primidone
    d. procainamide

*360. Serum concentrations of vitamin B_{12} are elevated in:

    a. pernicious anemia in relapse
    b. patients on chronic hemodialysis
    c. chronic granulocytic leukemia
    d. Hodgkin's disease

*361. Absorption of vitamin B_{12} requires the presence of:

    a. intrinsic factor
    b. gastrin
    c. secretin
    d. folic acid

*362. The concentration of serum carotene is affected MOST by which of the following?

    a. diet
    b. hepatic function
    c. drawing time of specimen
    d. age

*363. Which of the following in NOT commonly used as a tumor marker?

    a. prostate specific antigen
    b. alpha-fetoprotein
    c. carcinoembryonic antigen
    d. cortisol

*364. Clinical assays for tumor markers are most important for:

    a. screening for the presence of cancer
    b. monitoring the course of a known cancer
    c. confirming the absence of disease
    d. identifying patients at risk for cancer

*365. Acidification of the urine specimen (to pH 2) is essential during 24-hour collection for which one of the following compounds?

    a. ketosteroids
    b. hydroxycorticosteroids
    c. catecholamines
    d. calcium

*366. Characteristics of malabsorption syndrome due to pancreatic insufficiency include:

    a. fecal fat excretion greater than 10 g/day
    b. urinary excretion of 2.0 g of d-xylose within five hours after the patient has received 24 g orally
    c. marked changes of secretion into the duodenum following injection of secretin
    d. normal or elevated serum carotene concentration

*367. A course of instruction is being planned to teach laboratory employees to correct simple malfunctions in selected laboratory instruments. In writing the objectives for this course, which one of the following would be most appropriate?

    a. learn how to repair 9 of 10 simple instrument malfunctions
    b. correctly answer 9 of 10 test questions dealing with simple instrument malfunctions
    c. be able to detect 9 of 10 simple instrument malfunctions

*368. Which of the following are very sensitive to the pH and ionic strength of eluting buffers?

    a. chromatography
    b. spectrophotometry
    c. HPLC
    d. colorimetry

*369. In addition to its use as an internal standard in the flame emission method for sodium and potassium analyses, lithium:

    a. minimizes interference
    b. improves precision
    c. increases flame temperature
    d. acts as a radiation buffer

*370. Valinomycin enhances the selectivity of the electrode used to quantitate:

 a. sodium
 b. chloride
 c. potassium
 d. calcium

*371. The selectivity of an ion-selective electrode is determined by:

 a. the properties of the membrane used
 b. the solution used to fill the electrode
 c. the magnitude of the potential across the membrane
 d. the internal reference electrode

*372. On electrophoresis, distorted zones of protein separation are usually due to:

 a. presence of therapeutic drugs in serum sample
 b. dirty applicators
 c. overloading of serum sample
 d. prestaining with tracer dye

*373. On electrophoresis, spurious bisalbuminemia is associated with:

 a. dirty applicators
 b. presence of therapeutic drugs in serum sample
 c. endosmosis
 d. prestaining with tracer dye

*374. Macroenzymes are occasionally seen as persistent aberrant bands on electrophoresis with larger molecular weight than their corresponding normal form. They generally represent:

 a. production of large enzyme molecules
 b. enzymes bound to immunoglobulins
 c. media artifact seen on cellulose acetate electrophoresis
 d. autosomal recessive variants

*375. The three general types of interference in atomic absorption spectrophotometry:

 a. are chemical, ionization and matrix interference
 b. only occur in organic solvents
 c. can all be overcome by the addition of certain competing cations
 d. significantly hinder method specificity

*376. Gas-liquid chromatography is the current method of choice for qualitative and quantitative analysis of:

    a. benzodiazepines
    b. barbiturates
    c. antibiotics
    d. drugs of abuse

*377. In gas-liquid chromatography (GLC), actual separation of compounds occurs in the column by the:

    a. inert phase
    b. solid phase
    c. liquid phase
    d. mobile phase

*378. Reverse phase high-performance liquid chromatography is being increasingly utilized in therapeutic drug monitoring. The term reverse phase implies that the column eluant is:

    a. pumped up the column
    b. more polar than the stationary phase
    c. always nonpolar
    d. less polar than the stationary phase

*379. Which of the following applies to cryoscopic osmometry?

    a. The temperature at equilibrium is a function of the number of particles in solution
    b. The temperature plateau for a solution is horizontal.
    c. The freezing point of a sample is absolute.
    d. The initial freezing of a sample produces an immediate solid state.

*380. Which of the following DOES NOT detect volatiles such as alcohol:

    a. vapor pressure osmometry
    b. ideal osmolality values
    c. cryoscopic osmometry
    d. freezing point depression osmometry

*381. A chemiluminescent EIA:

    a. measures absorption of light
    b. is less sensitive than radioisotopic reactions
    c. is monitored by the use of a gamma counter
    d. is quantitated by the amount of light produced by the reaction

*382. The volume of specimen required for microassays can be decreased by:

   a. using reactions that decrease the molar absorptivity of the reaction products
   b. increasing the sensitivity of the signal detection method
   c. increasing the diameters of the manifolds to the continuous flow analyzers
   d. using concentration techniques

*383. A benefit of microassays is:

   a. increased analytical reliability
   b. reduced reagent requirements
   c. increased diagnostic specificity
   d. reduced numbers of repeated tests

---

*384. Refer to the following illustration:

The above symbol posted in an area would indicate which of the following hazards?

   a. flammable
   b. electrical
   c. radiation
   d. biohazard

*385. Diagnostic specificity is defined as the percentage of individuals:

    a. with a given disease who have a positive result by a given test
    b. without a given disease who have a negative result by a given test
    c. with a given disease who have a negative result by a given test
    d. without a given disease who have a positive result by a given test

*386. The predictive value of a test is defined as:

    a. $\dfrac{\text{true positives + true negatives}}{\text{true positives}}$

    b. $\dfrac{\text{true positives}}{\text{true positives + false positives}}$

    c. $\dfrac{\text{true positives + true negatives}}{\text{true negatives}}$

    d. $\dfrac{\text{true negatives}}{\text{true negatives + false positives}}$

*387. Relative standard deviation is the preferred term for the:

    a. correlation coefficient
    b. variance
    c. f test
    d. coefficient of variation

*388. A cholesterol QC chart has the following data for the normal control:

x = mean of data

x = 137 mg/dL Σx = 1,918 mg/dL
2SD = 6 mg/dL   N = 14

The coefficient of variation for this control is:

    a. 1.14%
    b. 2.19%
    c. 4.38%
    d. 9.49%

*389. If the correlation coefficient (r) of two variables is zero:

    a. there is complete correlation between the variables
    b. there is an absence of correlation
    c. as one variable increases, the other decreases
    d. as one variable decreases, the other increases

---

*390. Refer to the following diagram:

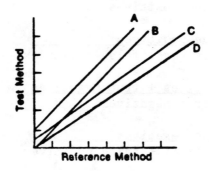

The line which demonstrates a proportional error relationship is:

    a. line A
    b. line B
    c. line C
    d. line D

*391. **Refer to the following illustration:**

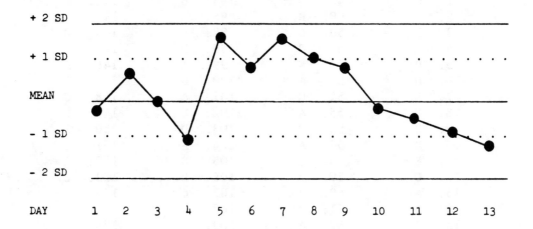

Shown above is a Levy-Jennings quality control chart which represents control values for 13 consecutive analyses for a particular serum constituent. If the 14th value is below the -2SD limit, which of the following should be done?

    a. The control should be repeated to see if it will fall within the established interval.
    b. The analysis system should be checked for a deteriorating component.
    c. The analysis system should be checked for a change in reagent lot number.
    d. It is not necessary to take any action.

Chemistry Answer Key

1.	C	48.	B	95.	B	142.	B
2.	A	49.	B	96.	C	143.	B
3.	B	50.	C	97.	B	144.	D
4.	A	51.	C	98.	D	145.	D
5.	D	52.	A	99.	A	146.	A
6.	D	53.	A	100.	D	147.	A
7.	B	54.	C	101.	A	148.	C
8.	C	55.	A	102.	D	149.	C
9.	B	56.	C	103.	D	150.	B
10.	D	57.	A	104.	A	151.	B
11.	B	58.	C	105.	C	152.	A
12.	C	59.	D	106.	D	153.	B
13.	A	60.	B	107.	C	154.	A
14.	B	61.	B	108.	A	155.	B
15.	B	62.	A	109.	D	156.	D
16.	A	63.	D	110.	D	157.	B
17.	B	64.	A	111.	B	158.	B
18.	B	65.	C	112.	C	159.	C
19.	D	66.	C	113.	B	160.	B
20.	A	67.	B	114.	B	161.	D
21.	D	68.	B	115.	D	162.	D
22.	D	69.	D	116.	D	163.	D
23.	B	70.	D	117.	A	164.	C
24.	A	71.	D	118.	A	165.	D
25.	B	72.	A	119.	A	166.	D
26.	A	73.	B	120.	B	167.	A
27.	C	74.	B	121.	C	168.	B
28.	D	75.	D	122.	D	169.	B
29.	A	76.	C	123.	B	170.	C
30.	C	77.	D	124.	A	171.	A
31.	C	78.	D	125.	D	172.	C
32.	C	79.	B	126.	B	173.	B
33.	C	80.	D	127.	D	174.	C
34.	A	81.	D	128.	D	175.	A
35.	B	82.	A	129.	C	176.	D
36.	A	83.	A	130.	B	177.	A
37.	C	84.	D	131.	C	178.	B
38.	A	85.	C	132.	D	179.	B
39.	B	86.	B	133.	C	180.	B
40.	C	87.	C	134.	D	181.	C
41.	D	88.	D	135.	B	182.	D
42.	C	89.	C	136.	B	183.	C
43.	C	90.	A	137.	B	184.	C
44.	A	91.	B	138.	C	185.	B
45.	A	92.	D	139.	B	186.	D
46.	D	93.	D	140.	D	187.	D
47.	B	94.	C	141.	C	188.	A

189.	A	236.	B	283.	A	330.	D
190.	D	237.	C	284.	C	331.	A
191.	B	238.	B	285.	D	332.	D
192.	A	239.	B	286.	B	333.	C
193.	C	240.	B	287.	B	334.	C
194.	D	241.	D	288.	D	335.	C
195.	A	242.	D	289.	C	336.	A
196.	D	243.	D	290.	B	337.	B
197.	A	244.	D	291.	A	338.	C
198.	B	245.	C	292.	D	339.	C
199.	A	246.	A	293.	C	340.	B
200.	B	247.	D	294.	A	341.	B
201.	B	248.	D	295.	D	342.	B
202.	A	249.	A	296.	B	343.	A
203.	A	250.	D	297.	A	344.	C
204.	A	251.	A	298.	D	345.	D
205.	C	252.	B	299.	C	346.	A
206.	D	253.	D	300.	D	347.	A
207.	D	254.	C	301.	C	348.	B
208.	C	255.	D	302.	B	349.	D
209.	D	256.	D	303.	C	350.	A
210.	C	257.	D	304.	C	351.	C
211.	A	258.	B	305.	A	352.	C
212.	B	259.	B	306.	D	353.	D
213.	B	260.	D	307.	D	354.	D
214.	B	261.	B	308.	C	355.	A
215.	B	262.	C	309.	C	356.	D
216.	B	263.	D	310.	B	357.	C
217.	C	264.	D	311.	B	358.	A
218.	A	265.	B	312.	B	359.	B
219.	A	266.	A	313.	D	360.	C
220.	A	267.	C	314.	B	361.	A
221.	B	268.	B	315.	A	362.	A
222.	D	269.	C	316.	C	363.	D
223.	D	270.	B	317.	A	364.	B
224.	C	271.	A	318.	A	365.	C
225.	A	272.	A	319.	D	366.	A
226.	C	273.	C	320.	D	367.	C
227.	C	274.	A	321.	D	368.	A
228.	D	275.	C	322.	D	369.	D
229.	B	276.	D	323.	B	370.	C
230.	D	277.	B	324.	B	371.	A
231.	C	278.	C	325.	D	372.	C
232.	B	279.	A	326.	D	373.	B
233.	A	280.	B	327.	C	374.	B
234.	B	281.	B	328.	A	375.	A
235.	D	282.	A	329.	C	376.	B

377.	C	381.	D	385.	B	389.	B
378.	B	382.	B	386.	B	390.	D
379.	A	383.	B	387.	D	391.	B
380.	A	384.	A	388.	B		

CHAPTER 14

Hematology

The following items have been identified as appropriate for both entry level medical technologists and medical laboratory technicians.

1. After the removal of red blood cells from the circulation, hemoglobin is broken down into:

    a. iron, porphyrin, and amino acids
    b. iron, protoporphyrin, and globin
    c. heme, protoporphyrin, and amino acids
    d. heme, hemosiderin, and globin

2. The majority of the iron in an adult is found as a constituent of:

    a. hemoglobin
    b. hemosiderin
    c. myoglobin
    d. transferrin

3. Cells for the transport of O_2 and CO_2 are:

    a. erythrocytes
    b. granulocytes
    c. lymphocytes
    d. thrombocyte

4. Erythropoietin acts to:

    a. shorten the replication time of the granulocytes
    b. stimulate RNA synthesis of erythroid cells
    c. increase colony-stimulating factors produced by the B-lymphocytes
    d. decrease the release of marrow reticulocytes

5. What cell shape is MOST commonly associated with an increased MCHC?

    a. teardrop cells
    b. target cells
    c. spherocytes
    d. sickle cells

6. Heinz bodies are:

   a. readily identified with polychrome stains
   b. rarely found in glucose-6-phosphate
      dehydrogenase deficient erythrocytes
   c. closely associated with spherocytes
   d. denatured hemoglobin inclusions that are
      readily removed by the spleen

7. Blood collected in EDTA undergoes which of the following
   changes if kept at room temperature for 6-24 hours?

   a. increased hematocrit and MCV
   b. increased ESR and MCV
   c. increased MCHC and MCV
   d. decreased reticulocyte count and hematocrit

8. A heparinized blood sample is collected from a patient during
   open-heart surgery. The surgeon requests a complete blood count
   on the specimen. The most appropriate course of action is:

   a. perform the complete blood count as requested
   b. report only the hemoglobin and hematocrit on
      heparinized blood
   c. report only the white cell and platelet counts
      on heparinized blood
   d. report the white cell and red cell counts on
      heparinized blood

9. Which of the following technical factors will cause a decreased
   erythrocyte sedimentation rate?

   a. gross hemolysis
   b. small fibrin clots in the sample
   c. increased room temperature
   d. tilting of the tube

10. The mean value of a reticulocyte count on specimens of cord
    blood from healthy, full-term newborns is about:

    a. 0.5%
    b. 2.0%
    c. 5.0%
    d. 8.0%

11. Which of the following tests is used to monitor red cell production?

   a. packed cell volume
   b. total iron-binding capacity
   c. Schilling test
   d. reticulocyte count

12. Which of the following is used for staining reticulocytes?

   a. Giemsa stain
   b. Wright's stain
   c. new methylene blue
   d. Prussian blue

13. The most appropriate screening test for detecting hemoglobin F is:

   a. osmotic fragility
   b. dithionite solubility
   c. Kleihauer-Betke
   d. heat instability test

14. The most appropriate screening test for hemoglobin H is:

   a. dithionite solubility
   b. osmotic fragility
   c. sucrose hemolysis
   d. heat instability test

15. The most appropriate screening test for hemoglobin S is:

   a. Kleihauer-Betke
   b. dithionite solubility
   c. osmotic fragility
   d. sucrose hemolysis

16. Which of the following stains is used to demonstrate iron, ferritin and hemosiderin?

   a. peroxidase
   b. Sudan black B
   c. periodic acid-Schiff (PAS)
   d. Prussian blue

17. Refer to the following illustration:

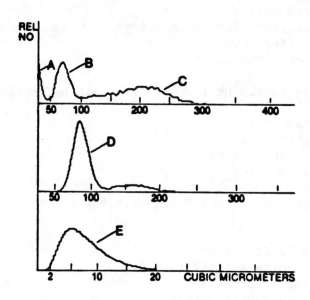

Which area in the automated cell counter histogram represents the RBC distribution curve?

a. A
b. B
c. C
d. D

18. A patient has a high cold agglutinin titer. Automated cell counter results reveal an elevated MCV, MCH and MCHC. Individual erythrocytes appear normal on a stained smear, but agglutinates are noted. The appropriate course of action would be to:

a. Perform the RBC, HGB, and HCT determinations using manual methods.
b. Perform the RBC determination by a manual method; use the automated results for the HGB and HCT
c. Repeat the determinations using a microsample of diluted blood.
d. Repeat the determinations using a prewarmed microsample of diluted blood.

19. A blood sample from a patient with a high-titer cold agglutinin, analyzed at room temperature, with an electronic cell counter would cause an error in the:

   a. hemoglobin and MCV
   b. MCHC and WBC
   c. WBC and RBC
   d. MCV and MCHC

20. When using an electronic cell counter, which of the following results can occur in the presence of a cold agglutinin?

   a. increased MCV and decreased RBC
   b. increased MCV and normal RBC
   c. decreased MCV and increased MCHC
   d. decreased MCV and RBC

21. The following results were obtained on an electronic particle counter:

   WBC $6.5 \times 10^3/\mu L$ ($6.5 \times 10^9/L$)
   RBC $4.55 \times 10^6/\mu L$ ($4.55 \times 10^{12}/\mu L$)
   HGB   18.0 g/dL
   HCT   41.5%
   MCV   90.1 fL
   MCH   39.6 pg
   MCHC 43.4 g/dL

   The first step in obtaining valid results is to:

   a. perform a microhematocrit
   b. correct the hemoglobin for lipemia
   c. dilute the blood
   d. replace the lysing agent

22. On an electronic particle counter, if the RBC is erroneously increased, how will other parameters be affected?

   a. increased MCHC
   b. increased hemoglobin
   c. decreased MCH
   d. increased MCV

23. On setting up the electronic particle counter in the morning, one of the controls is slightly below the range for the MCV. Which of the following is indicated?

   a. call for service
   b. adjust the MCV up slightly
   c. shut down the instrument
   d. repeat the control

24. Hematology standards include:

    a. stabilized red blood cell suspension
    b. latex particles
    c. stabilized avian red blood cells
    d. certified cyanmethemoglobin solution

25. Megaloblastic asynchronous development in the bone marrow indicates which one of the following?

    a. proliferation of erythrocyte precursors
    b. impaired synthesis of DNA
    c. inadequate production of erythropoietin
    d. deficiency of G-6-PD

26. Which of the following are found in association with megaloblastic anemia?

    a. neutropenia and thrombocytopenia
    b. decreased LD activity
    c. increased erythrocyte folate levels
    d. decreased plasma bilirubin levels

27. The characteristic morphologic feature in folic acid deficiency is:

    a. macrocytosis
    b. target cells
    c. basophilic stippling
    d. rouleaux formation

28. Which of the following is most closely associated with iron deficiency anemia?

    a. iron overload in tissue
    b. target cells
    c. basophilic stippling
    d. chronic blood loss

29. The anemia found in myeloproliferative disorders is usually:

    a. microcytic, hypochromic
    b. macrocytic, normochromic
    c. normocytic, normochromic
    d. microcytic, normochromic

30. The anemia of chronic infection is characterized by:

   a. decreased iron stores in the reticuloendothelial system
   b. decreased serum iron levels
   c. macrocytic erythrocytes
   d. increased serum iron binding capacity

31. The characteristic morphologic feature in multiple myeloma is:

   a. basophilic stippling
   b. rouleaux formation
   c. spherocytosis
   d. macrocytosis

32. Anemia secondary to uremia characteristically is:

   a. microcytic, hypochromic
   b. hemolytic
   c. normocytic, normochromic
   d. macrocytic

33. Which of the following is most closely associated with idiopathic hemochromatosis?

   a. iron overload in tissue
   b. target cells
   c. basophilic stippling
   d. ringed sideroblast

34. Factors commonly involved in producing anemia in patients with chronic renal disease include:

   a. marrow hypoplasia
   b. ineffective erythropoiesis
   c. vitamin B_{12} deficiency
   d. increased erythropoietin production

35. A 20-year-old woman with sickle cell anemia whose usual hemoglobin concentration is 8 gm/dL develops fever, increased weakness and malaise. The hemoglobin concentration is 4 gm/dL and the reticulocyte count is 0.1%. The most likely explanation for this clinical picture is:

   a. increased hemolysis due to hypersplenism
   b. aplastic crisis
   c. thrombotic crisis
   d. occult blood loss

36. The most appropriate screening test for hereditary spherocytosis is:

    a. osmotic fragility
    b. sucrose hemolysis
    c. heat instability test
    d. Kleihauer-Betke

37. Laboratory findings in hereditary spherocytosis do NOT include:

    a. decreased osmotic fragility
    b. increased autohemolysis corrected by glucose
    c. reticulocytosis
    d. shortened erythrocyte survival

38. Which of the following is a congenital non-spherocytic hemolytic anemia in which there are red cell inclusions when blood smears are stained with Prussian blue?

    a. paroxysmal nocturnal hemoglobinuria
    b. pyruvate kinase deficiency
    c. thalassemia
    d. G-6-PD deficiency

39. A characteristic morphologic feature in hemoglobin C disease is:

    a. macrocytosis
    b. spherocytosis
    c. rouleaux formation
    d. target cells

40. Thalassemias are characterized by:

    a. structural abnormalities in the hemoglobin molecule
    b. absence of iron in hemoglobin
    c. decreased rate of heme synthesis
    d. decreased rate of globin synthesis

41. Which of the following is seen most often in thalassemia?

    a. chronic blood loss
    b. target cells
    c. basophilic stippling
    d. ringed sideroblasts

42. A patient has the following blood values:

RBC $6.5 \times 10^6/\mu L$ ($6.5 \times 10^{12}/L$)
HGB   14.0 g/dL
HCT   42.0%
MCV   65 fL
MCH   21.5 pg
MCHC   33 g/dL

These results are compatible with:

a. iron deficiency
b. pregnancy
c. thalassemia minor
d. beta thalassemia major

---

43. Refer to the following pattern:

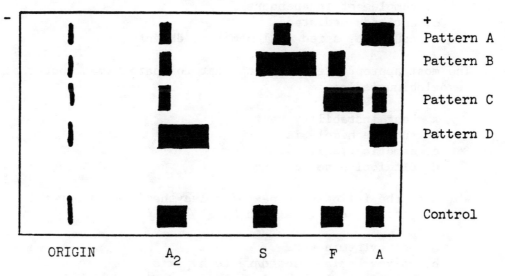

HEMOGLOBIN ELECTROPHORESIS PATTERNS AT pH 8.4
(CELLULOSE ACETATE STRIP)

Which pattern is consistent with thalassemia major?

a. pattern A
b. pattern B
c. pattern C
d. pattern D

44. In an adult with rare homozygous delta-beta thalassemia, the hemoglobin produced is:

    a. A
    b. Bart's
    c. F
    d. H

45. The morphologic feature most characteristic of hemolytic anemia is:

    a. spherocytosis
    b. rouleaux formation
    c. basophilic stippling
    d. target cells

46. Hemolysis in paroxysmal nocturnal hemoglobinuria (PNH) is:

    a. temperature-dependent
    b. complement-independent
    c. antibody-mediated
    d. caused by a red cell membrane defect

47. The most appropriate screening test for paroxysmal nocturnal hemoglobinuria is:

    a. heat instability test
    b. sucrose hemolysis
    c. osmotic fragility
    d. dithionite solubility

48. Which of the following types of polycythemia is a severely burned patient most likely to have?

    a. polycythemia vera
    b. polycythemia, secondary to hypoxia
    c. relative polycythemia associated with dehydration
    d. polycythemia associated with renal disease

49. Decreased to normal erythropoietin production is most likely to be associated with:

    a. polycythemia vera
    b. polycythemia, secondary to hypoxia
    c. relative polycythemia associated with dehydration
    d. polycythemia associated with renal disease

50. A patient with polycythemia vera who is treated by phlebotomy is most likely to develop a deficiency of:

   a. iron
   b. vitamin B_{12}
   c. folic acid
   d. erythropoietin

51. Which of the following are characteristic of polycythemia vera?

   a. elevated urine erythropoietin levels
   b. increased oxygen affinity of hemoglobin
   c. "teardrop" poikilocytosis
   d. decreased or absent bone marrow iron stores

52. In polycythemia vera, the leukocyte alkaline phosphatase activity is:

   a. elevated
   b. normal
   c. decreased

53. In polycythemia vera, the hemoglobin, hematocrit, red blood cell count and red cell mass are:

   a. elevated
   b. normal
   c. decreased

54. The M:E ratio in polycythemia vera is usually:

   a. normal
   b. high
   c. low
   d. variable

55. Many microspherocytes, schistocytes and budding off of spherocytes can be seen on peripheral blood smears of patients with:

   a. hereditary spherocytosis
   b. disseminated intravascular coagulation (DIC)
   c. acquired autoimmune hemolytic anemia
   d. extensive burns

56. A Wright's stained peripheral smear reveals the following:

   -erythrocytes enlarged 1½ to twice normal size
   -Schüffner's dots
   -parasites with irregular "spread-out" trophozoites,
    golden brown pigment
   -12-24 merozoites
   -wide range of stages

   This is consistent with *Plasmodium*:

       a. *falciparum*
       b. *malariae*
       c. *ovale*
       d. *vivax*

57. Which of the following is most likely to be seen in lead poisoning?

       a. iron overload in tissue
       b. target cells
       c. basophilic stippling
       d. ringed sideroblasts

58. A term that means varying degrees of leukocytosis with a shift to the left and occasional nucleated red cells in the peripheral blood is:

       a. polycythemia vera
       b. erythroleukemia
       c. leukoerythroblastosis
       d. megaloblastoid

59. Phagocytosis is a function of:

       a. erythrocytes
       b. granulocytes
       c. lymphocytes
       d. thrombocytes

60. Cells that produce antibodies and lymphokines are:

       a. erythrocytes
       b. granulocytes
       c. lymphocytes
       d. thrombocytes

61. Which of the following cells contains hemosiderin?

    a. megakaryocyte
    b. osteoclast
    c. histiocyte
    d. mast cell

62. Which of the following is the largest cell in the bone marrow:

    a. megakaryocyte
    b. histiocyte
    c. osteoblast
    d. mast cell

63. The peripheral blood monocyte is an intermediate stage in the formation of the:

    a. plasmacyte
    b. Turk irritation cell
    c. histiocyte
    d. hairy cell

64. Specific (secondary) granules of the neutrophilic granulocyte:

    a. appear first at the myelocyte stage
    b. contain lysosomal enzymes
    c. are formed on the mitochondria
    d. are derived from azurophil (primary) granules

65. Precursors of tissue macrophages of the reticuloendothelial system most likely are:

    a. T lymphocytes
    b. B lymphocytes
    c. monocytes
    d. mast cells

66. In normal adult bone marrow, the most common granulocyte is the:

    a. basophil
    b. myeloblast
    c. eosinophil
    d. metamyelocyte

For questions 67 and 68, refer to the following illustration:

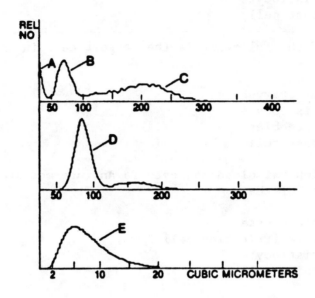

67. Which area of the automated cell counter histogram indicates the lymphocyte curve?

       a. A
       b. B
       c. C
       d. D

68. Which area of the automated cell counter histogram indicates the non-lymphocyte curve?

       a. A
       b. B
       c. C
       d. D

69. The most characteristic morphologic features of atypical lymphocytes include:

   a. coarse nuclear chromatin and basophilic cytoplasm
   b. cytoplasmic RNA and indentation by erythrocytes
   c. nucleoli and deep blue RNA-rich cytoplasm
   d. a stretched nucleus and cytoplasmic indentations

70. The specimen of choice for preparation of blood films for manual differential leukocyte counts is whole blood collected in:

   a. EDTA
   b. oxalate
   c. citrate
   d. heparin

71. Which cell type shows the most intense staining with peroxidase?

   a. segmented neutrophil
   b. basophil
   c. band
   d. monocyte

72. The granules in Alder-Reilly anomaly will stain positively with:

   a. Sudan black B
   b. periodic acid-Schiff
   c. myeloperoxidase
   d. naphthol-AS-D chloroacetate esterase

73. Which of the following may be used to stain glycogen, polysaccharides, and glycoproteins?

   a. peroxidase
   b. Sudan black B
   c. periodic acid-Schiff (PAS)
   d. nitroblue tetrazolium (NBT)

74. The stain that identifies intracellular carbohydrate, glycogen, mucopolysaccharide, mucoprotein, glycoprotein, and glycolipid is:

   a. Sudan black B
   b. leukocyte alkaline phosphatase (LAP)
   c. periodic acid-Schiff (PAS)
   d. peroxidase

75. Which of the following may be used to stain neutral fats, phospholipids and sterols?

   a. peroxidase
   b. Sudan black B
   c. periodic acid-Schiff (PAS)
   d. Prussian blue

76. The stain that selectively identifies phospholipid in the membranes of primary and secondary granules within myeloid cells is:

   a. Sudan black B
   b. leukocyte alkaline phosphatase (LAP)
   c. periodic acid-Schiff (PAS)
   d. peroxidase

77. Which substrate is used for the detection of specific esterase?

   a. acetate
   b. chloracetate
   c. pararosanalin acetate
   d. phenylene diacetate

78. The accuracy of automated differential leukocyte counts yielding histograms can be determined by:

   a. cell-by-cell comparisons
   b. slide-by-slide comparisons
   c. specimen-by-specimen comparisons

79. The following results were obtained on an electronic cell counter:

WBC	++++
RBC	2.01 x 10^6/µL (2.01 x 10^{12}/L)
HGB	7.7 g/dL
HCT	28.2%
MCV	141 fL
MCH	38.5 pg
MCHC	23.3 g/dL

   What step should be taken before recycling the sample?

   a. clean the apertures
   b. warm the specimen
   c. replace the lysing agent
   d. dilute the specimen

80. A leukocyte count and differential on a 40-year-old Caucasian man revealed:

WBC 5.4 x 10^3/μL (5.4 x 10^9/L)
Differential:
   segs   20%
   lymphs 58%
   monos 20%
   eos   2%

This data represents:

   a. absolute lymphocytosis
   b. relative neutrocytosis
   c. absolute neutropenia
   d. leukopenia

81. Neutropenia is NOT usually associated with:

   a. viral infections
   b. Hodgkin's disease
   c. select antibiotics
   d. chemotherapy

82. Long-term exposure to certain antibiotics such as penicillin has been found to result in:

   a. leukopenia
   b. thrombocytosis
   c. lymphocytosis
   d. polycythemia

83. Elevation of the total granulocyte count above 9 x 10^9/L is termed:

   a. relative lymphocytosis
   b. leukocytosis
   c. relative neutrophilic leukocytosis
   d. absolute neutrophilic leukocytosis

84. Elevation of the total white cell count above 12 x 10^9/L is termed:

   a. relative lymphocytosis
   b. absolute lymphocytosis
   c. leukocytosis
   d. relative neutrophilic leukocytosis

85. Elevation of the granulocyte percentage above 75% is termed:

    a. absolute lymphocytosis
    b. leukocytosis
    c. relative neutrophilic leukocytosis
    d. absolute neutrophilic leukocytosis

86. Elevation of the lymphocyte percentage above 47% is termed:

    a. relative lymphocytosis
    b. absolute lymphocytosis
    c. leukocytosis
    d. absolute neutrophilic leukocytosis

87. A leukocyte count and differential on a 40-year-old Caucasian man revealed:

    WBC: 5.4 x 10^3/μL (5.4 x 10^9/L)
    Differential:
        segs   20%
        lymphs   58%
        monos   20%
        eos   2%

    This represents:

    a. relative lymphocytosis
    b. absolute lymphocytosis
    c. relative neutrocytosis
    d. leukopenia

88. Of the following, the disease most closely associated with cytoplasmic granule fusion is:

    a. Chediak-Higashi syndrome
    b. Pelger-Huĕt anomaly
    c. May-Hegglin anomaly
    d. Alder-Reilly anomaly

89. Which of the following anomalies is an autosomal dominant disorder characterized by irregularly sized inclusions in polymorphonuclear neutrophils, abnormal giant platelets and often thrombocytopenia?

    a. Pelger-Huĕt
    b. Chediak-Higashi
    c. Alder-Reilly
    d. May-Hegglin

90. Of the following, the disease most closely associated with granulocyte hyposegmentation is:

   a. May-Hegglin anomaly
   b. Pelger-Huĕt anomaly
   c. Chediak-Higashi syndrome
   d. Gaucher's disease

91. Which of the following cell types is characteristic of Pelger-Huĕt anomaly?

   a. band form
   b. pince-nez form
   c. normal neutrophil
   d. myelocyte

92. Which of the following is associated with pseudo-Pelger-Huĕt anomaly?

   a. aplastic anemia
   b. iron deficiency anemia
   c. granulocytic leukemia
   d. Chediak-Higashi syndrome

93. Which of the following is associated with Chediak-Higashi syndrome?

   a. membrane defect of lysosome
   b. Dŏhle bodies and giant platelets
   c. two-lobed neutrophils
   d. mucopolysaccharidosis

94. Which of the following is associated with Alder-Reilly inclusions?

   a. membrane defect of lysosome
   b. Dŏhle bodies and giant platelets
   c. two-lobed neutrophils
   d. mucopolysaccharidosis

95. Which of the following is associated with May-Hegglin anomaly?

   a. membrane defect of lysosome
   b. Dŏhle bodies and giant platelets
   c. chronic granulocytic leukemia
   d. mucopolysaccharidosis

96. A bone marrow shows foam cells ranging from 20 to 100 μm in size, vacuolated cytoplasm containing sphingomyelin and is faintly PAS positive.

This cell type is most characteristic of:

   a. Gaucher's disease
   b. myeloma with Russell bodies
   c. DiGuglielmo disease
   d. Niemann-Pick disease

97. In an uncomplicated case of infectious mononucleosis, which of the following cells are affected?

   a. erythrocytes
   b. lymphocytes
   c. monocytes
   d. thrombocytes

98. Leukocyte alkaline phosphatase activity is decreased in:

   a. acute infections
   b. pregnant women
   c. polycythemia vera
   d. paroxysmal nocturnal hemoglobinuria

99. The leukocyte alkaline phosphatase activity is increased in:

   a. erythroleukemia
   b. leukemoid reaction
   c. chronic granulocytic leukemia
   d. acute granulocytic leukemia

100. Auer rods are most likely present in which of the following?

   a. chronic granulocytic leukemia
   b. myelofibrosis with myeloid metaplasia
   c. erythroleukemia
   d. acute granulocytic leukemia

101. Which of the following are characteristic of Auer rods?

   a. They contain lactoferrin.
   b. They are lysosome and acid phosphatase positive.
   c. They are found in the leukemic phase of lymphoma.
   d. They are found in acute lymphocytic leukemia.

102. Auer bodies are:

    a. a normal aggregation of lysosomes or primary
       (azurophilic) granules
    b. predominately found in acute myelogenous leukemia
    c. peroxidase negative
    d. alkaline phosphatase positive

103. Which of the following conditions are NOT associated with
a high incidence of leukemia?

    a. paroxysmal nocturnal hemoglobinuria
    b. Fanconi's anemia
    c. aplastic anemia
    d. megaloblastic anemia

104. All stages of neutrophils are most likely to be seen in the
peripheral blood of a patient with:

    a. chronic granulocytic leukemia
    b. myelofibrosis with myeloid metaplasia
    c. erythroleukemia
    d. acute granulocytic leukemia

105. The type of leukemia seen most commonly as a terminal event
in plasma cell myeloma is:

    a. acute lymphoblastic leukemia
    b. acute monocytic leukemia
    c. acute myelomonocytic leukemia
    d. acute myelogenous leukemia

106. All of the following conditions are myeloproliferative
disorders EXCEPT:

    a. granulocytic leukemia
    b. lymphocytic leukemia
    c. polycythemia vera
    d. idiopathic thrombocythemia

107. Giant, bizarre-shaped, multinucleated erythroid precursors
are present in which of the following?

    a. chronic granulocytic leukemia
    b. myelofibrosis with myeloid metaplasia
    c. erythroleukemia
    d. acute granulocytic leukemia

108. Which of the following is true of acute lymphoblastic leukemia (ALL)?

    a. occurs most commonly in children 1-2 years of age
    b. patient is asymptomatic
    c. massive accumulation of primitive lymphoid-appearing cells in bone marrow occurs
    d. children under 1 year of age have a good prognosis

109. The most frequent type of acute lymphocytic leukemia (ALL) is:

    a. T-cell
    b. common childhood
    c. B-cell
    d. undifferentiated

110. Chronic lymphocytic leukemia is defined as:

    a. a malignancy of the thymus
    b. an accumulation of prolymphocytes
    c. an accumulation of hairy cells in the spleen
    d. an accumulation of monoclonal B cells with a block in cell maturation

111. Hairy cell leukemia (leukemic reticuloendotheliosis) is:

    a. an acute myelocytic leukemia
    b. a chronic leukemia of myelocytic origin
    c. a chronic leukemia of mononuclear origin
    d. an acute myelocytic monocytic-type leukemia

112. A useful chemical test for the diagnosis of hairy cell leukemia is the:

    a. peroxidase test
    b. Sudan black test
    c. periodic acid-Schiff test
    d. tartrate-resistant acid phosphatase test

113. Which of the following is NOT a characteristic usually associated with hairy cell leukemia?

    a. pancytopenia
    b. mononuclear cells with ruffled edges
    c. splenomegaly
    d. increased resistance to infection

114. 50%-90% myeloblasts in a peripheral blood is typical of which of the following?

    a. chronic granulocytic leukemia
    b. myelofibrosis with myeloid metaplasia
    c. erythroleukemia
    d. acute granulocytic leukemia

115. The M:E ratio in acute granulocytic leukemia is usually:

    a. normal
    b. high
    c. low
    d. variable

116. Which of the following is most closely associated with acute promyelocytic leukemia?

    a. ringed sideroblasts
    b. disseminated intravascular coagulation
    c. micromegakaryocytes
    d. Philadelphia chromosome

117. Which of the following is most closely associated with chronic monocytic leukemia?

    a. Philadelphia chromosome
    b. disseminated intravascular coagulation
    c. micromegakaryocytes
    d. lysozymuria

118. Cytochemical stains were performed on bone marrow smears from an acute leukemia patient. All blasts were periodic acid-Schiff (PAS) negative. The majority of the blasts showed varying amounts of Sudan black B positivity. Some of the blasts stained positive for naphthol AS-D acetate esterase, some were positive for naphthol AS-D chloracetate esterase, and some blasts stained positive for both esterases. What type of leukemia is indicated?

    a. lymphocytic
    b. granulocytic
    c. myelomonocytic
    d. erythroleukemia

119. The absence of intermediate maturing cells between the blast and mature neutrophil commonly seen in acute myelocytic leukemia and preleukemic states is called:

   a. subleukemia
   b. aleukemic leukemia
   c. leukemic hiatus
   d. leukemoid reaction

120. The absence of the Philadelphia chromosome in granulocytic leukemia suggests:

   a. rapid progression of the disease
   b. a polyclonal origin to the disease
   c. excellent response to therapy
   d. conversion from another myeloproliferative disorder

121. A 50-year-old woman who has been receiving busulfan for three years for chronic granulocytic leukemia becomes anemic. Laboratory tests reveal:

   Thrombocytopenia
   Many peroxidase-negative blast cells in the peripheral blood
   Bone marrow hypercellular in blast transformation
   Markedly increased bone marrow TdT

   Which of the following complications is this patient most likely to have?

   a. acute lymphocytic leukemia
   b. acute granulocytic leukemia
   c. acute myelomonocytic leukemia
   d. busulfan toxicity

122. Which of the following tests can be useful in differentiating leukemoid reactions from chronic granulocytic leukemias?

   a. peroxidase stain
   b. Sudan black B stain
   c. surface membrane markers
   d. leukocyte alkaline phosphatase

123. The M:E ratio in chronic granulocytic leukemia is usually:

   a. normal
   b. high
   c. low
   d. variable

124. Which of the following is a significant feature of erythro-leukemia (DiGuglielmo's syndrome)?

    a. persistently increased M:E ratio
    b. megaloblastoid erythropoiesis
    c. marked thrombocytosis
    d. decreased stainable iron in the marrow

125. The M:E ratio in erythroleukemia is usually:

    a. normal
    b. high
    c. low
    d. variable

126. Which of the following is most closely associated with erythroleukemia?

    a. ringed sideroblasts
    b. disseminated intravascular coagulation
    c. micromegakaryocytes
    d. lysozymuria

127. Normal platelets have a circulating life-span of approximately:

    a. 5 days
    b. 10 days
    c. 20 days
    d. 30 days

128. Which of the following detects or measures platelet function?

    a. bleeding time
    b. prothrombin time
    c. thrombin time
    d. partial thromboplastin time

129. In an electronic or laser particle cell counter, clumped platelets may interfere with which of the following parameters?

    a. white blood cell count
    b. red blood cell count
    c. hemoglobin
    d. hematocrit

130. Irregular clumping of platelets is usually due to:

    a. inadequate mixing of blood and anticoagulant
    b. hemorrhage
    c. poorly made wedge smear
    d. hypersplenism

131. A platelet determination was performed on an automated instrument and a very low value was obtained. The platelets appeared adequate when estimated from the stained blood film. Possible explanations for this discrepancy include:

   a. many platelets are abnormally large
   b. blood sample was hemolyzed
   c. white cell fragments are present in the blood
   d. red cell fragments are present in the blood

132. When platelets concentrate at the edges and feathered end of a blood smear, it is usually due to:

   a. abnormal proteins
   b. inadequate mixing of blood and anticoagulant
   c. hemorrhage
   d. poorly made wedge smear

133. Which of the following will not cause erroneous results when using a darkfield optical system for enumerating platelets?

   a. incipient clotting
   b. decreased hematocrit
   c. Howell Jolly bodies
   d. leukocyte cytoplasmic fragments

134. The chamber counting method of platelet enumeration:

   a. allows direct visualization of the particles being counted
   b. has a high degree of precision
   c. has a high degree of reproducibility
   d. is the method of choice for the performance of 50-60 counts per day

135. Platelet aggregation is dependent in vitro on the presence of:

   a. calcium ions
   b. sodium citrate
   c. fibrinogen
   d. potassium

136. Platelet satellitosis is usually due to:

   a. abnormal proteins
   b. inadequate mixing of blood and anticoagulant
   c. hemorrhage
   d. poorly made wedge smear

137. On a smear made directly from a finger stick, no platelets were found in the counting area. The first thing to do is:

    a. examine the slide for clumping
    b. obtain another smear
    c. perform a total platelet count
    d. request another finger stick

---

138. Refer to the following illustration:

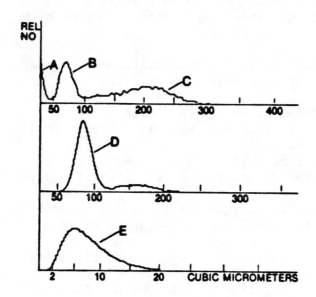

Which area of the automated cell counter histogram represents the platelet distribution curve?

    a. A
    b. B
    c. C
    d. E

---

139. In polycythemia vera, the platelet count is:

    a. elevated
    b. normal
    c. decreased

140. Thrombocytopenia is a characteristic of:

    a. classic von Willebrand's disease
    b. hemophilia A
    c. Glanzmann's thrombasthenia
    d. May-Hegglin anomaly

141. Which of the following platelet responses is most likely associated with Glanzmann's thrombasthenia?

    a. decreased platelet aggregation to ristocetin
    b. defective ADP release; normal response to ADP
    c. decreased amount of ADP in platelets
    d. markedly decreased aggregation to epinephrine, ADP and collagen

142. Which of the following is a true statement about acute idiopathic thrombocytopenic purpura (ITP)?

    a. It is found primarily in adults.
    b. Spontaneous remission usually occurs within several weeks.
    c. Women are more commonly affected.
    d. Peripheral destruction of platelets is decreased.

143. Which of the following platelet responses is most likely associated with classic von Willebrand's disease?

    a. decreased platelet aggregation to ristocetin
    b. normal platelet aggregation to ristocetin
    c. absent aggregation to epinephrine, ADP and collagen
    d. decreased amount of ADP in platelets

144. Which of the following platelet responses is most likely associated with hemophilia A (factor VIII deficiency)?

    a. defective ADP release; normal response to ADP
    b. decreased amount of ADP in platelets
    c. absent aggregation to epinephrine, ADP and collagen
    d. normal platelet aggregation

145. Which of the following is characteristic of platelet disorders?

    a. deep muscle hemorrhages
    b. retroperitoneal hemorrhages
    c. mucous membrane hemorrhages
    d. severely prolonged clotting times

146. Cells involved in hemostasis are:

    a. erythrocytes
    b. granulocytes
    c. lymphocytes
    d. thrombocytes

147. Which of the following is vitamin-K dependent?

    a. factor XII
    b. fibrinogen
    c. antithrombin III
    d. factor VII

148. Which of the following factors is used only in the extrinsic coagulation pathway?

    a. II
    b. V
    c. VII
    d. VIII

149. A hemophiliac male and a normal female can produce a:

    a. female carrier
    b. male carrier
    c. male hemophiliac
    d. normal female

150. Coagulation factors affected by coumarin drugs are:

    a. VIII, IX and X
    b. I, II, V and VII
    c. II, VII, IX and X
    d. II, V and VII

151. Which factor has the highest concentration in the peripheral blood?

    a. factor XII
    b. fibrinogen
    c. Fitzgerald factor
    d. antithrombin III

152. Which one of the following statements concerning vitamin K is NOT true?

    a. There are two sources of vitamin K: vegetable and bacterial.
    b. Vitamin K converts precursor molecules into active coagulation factors.
    c. Heparin inhibits the action of vitamin K.
    d. Vitamin K is fat soluble.

153. The most potent plasminogen activator in the contact phase of coagulation is:

    a. kallikrein
    b. streptokinase
    c. factor XIIa
    d. fibrinogen

154. The anticoagulant of choice for routine coagulation procedures is:

    a. sodium oxalate
    b. sodium citrate
    c. heparin
    d. sodium fluoride

155. The most accurate bedside test used to monitor heparin activity is the:

    a. activated clotting time
    b. Stypven time
    c. Reptilase time
    d. partial thromboplastin time

156. The prothrombin time test requires that the patient's citrated plasma be combined with:

    a. platelet lipids
    b. thromboplastin
    c. Ca^{++} and platelet lipids
    d. Ca^{++} and thromboplastin

157. A test used to monitor streptokinase therapy is:

    a. reptilase time
    b. euglobulin clot lysis
    c. staphylococcal clumping test
    d. thrombin generation time

158. Using automated coagulation instruments, duplication of normal tests is no longer necessary because:

   a. the laboratory can document precision by collecting data to reflect precision performance
   b. all technologists on all shifts can be taught quality control
   c. it is difficult to have duplicates done in a blind fashion
   d. one technologist can monitor quality control

159. A prolonged thrombin time and a normal reptilase-R time are characteristic of:

   a. dysfibrinogenemia
   b. increased fibrin split products
   c. fibrin monomer-split product complexes
   d. therapeutic heparinization

160. Which of the following is most useful in differentiating hemophilias A and B?

   a. pattern of inheritance
   b. clinical history
   c. whole blood clotting time and partial thromboplastin time
   d. mixing studies (substitution studies)

161. In manual or visual endpoint coagulation tests, duplicates are needed because:

   a. reagents and samples must be paired
   b. coagulation controls are expensive
   c. high precision is less attainable in manual methodology
   d. the CAP requires duplicate testing

162. A patient develops severe unexpected bleeding following four transfusions. The following test results were obtained:

   PT and APTT: prolonged
   Platelets: 50 x 10^3/μL
   Fibrinogen: 30 mg/dL
   Fibrin Split Products: increased

   Given these results, which of the following blood products should be recommended to the physician for this patient?

   a. Platelets
   b. Factor IX concentrate
   c. Cryoprecipitated AHF
   d. Fresh Frozen Plasma

163. Which of the following is the most common cause of an abnormality in hemostasis?

    a. decreased plasma fibrinogen level
    b. decreased factor VIII level
    c. decreased factor IX level
    d. quantitative abnormality of platelets

164. Which of the following laboratory procedures is most helpful in differentiating severe liver disease and accompanying secondary fibrinolysis from disseminated intravascular coagulation?

    a. presence of fibrin split products
    b. accelerated euglobulin clot lysis
    c. factor VIII activity
    d. fibrinogen level

165. Which of the following is a characteristic of factor XII deficiency?

    a. negative bleeding history
    b. normal clotting times
    c. decreased risk of thrombosis
    d. epistaxis

166. An abnormal Stypven time is associated with deficiency of factor:

    a. VII
    b. X
    c. XI
    d. XIII

167. Acute disseminated intravascular coagulation is characterized by:

    a. hypofibrinogenemia
    b. thrombocytosis
    c. negative plasma protamine paracoagulation test (PPP test)
    d. shortened thrombin time

168. Which of the following is the standard calibration method for hematology instrumentation against which other methods must be verified?

    a. latex particles of known dimension
    b. stabilized red cell suspensions
    c. stabilized 7 parameter reference controls
    d. normal whole blood

169. If a RBC count is performed on a 1:100 dilution and the number of cells in one fifth of a square mm is 600, the total RBC count is:

    a. $1.5 \times 10^6/\mu L$ ($1.5 \times 10^{12}/L$)
    b. $2.0 \times 10^6/\mu L$ ($2.0 \times 10^{12}/L$)
    c. $3.0 \times 10^6/\mu L$ ($3.0 \times 10^{12}/L$)
    d. $3.5 \times 10^6/\mu L$ ($3.5 \times 10^{12}/L$)

170. If a RBC count is performed on a 1:200 dilution and the number of cells in one fifth of a square mm is 150, the total RBC count is:

    a. $1.5 \times 10^6/\mu L$ ($1.5 \times 10^{12}/L$)
    b. $2.0 \times 10^6/\mu L$ ($2.0 \times 10^{12}/L$)
    c. $3.0 \times 10^6/\mu L$ ($3.0 \times 10^{12}/L$)
    d. $3.5 \times 10^6/\mu L$ ($3.5 \times 10^{12}/L$)

171. Which of the following is the formula for absolute cell count?

    a. $\dfrac{\text{number of cells counted}}{\text{total count}}$

    b. $\dfrac{\text{total count}}{\text{number of cells counted}}$

    c. 10 x total count
    d. % of cells counted x total count

172. The most common cause of error when using automated cell counters is:

    a. contamination of the diluent
    b. inadequate mixing of the sample prior to testing
    c. variation in voltage of the current supply
    d. a calibrating error

173. Which of the following is the formula for mean corpuscular hemoglobin (MCH)?

    a. $\dfrac{\text{Hct} \times 100}{\text{RBC}}$

    b. $\dfrac{\text{Hgb}}{\text{Hct}}$

    c. $\dfrac{\text{RBC}}{\text{Hct}}$

    d. $\dfrac{\text{Hgb} \times 10}{\text{RBC}}$

174. What is the MCH if the Hct is 20%, the RBC is $2.4 \times 10^6/\mu L$ the Hgb is 5 g/dL?

    a. 21 pg
    b. 23 pg
    c. 25 pg
    d. 84 pg

175. What is the MCH if the Hct is 20%, the RBC is $1.5 \times 10^6/\mu L$ and the Hgb is 6 g/dL?

    a. 28 pg
    b. 30 pg
    c. 40 pg
    d. 75 pg

176. Which of the following is the formula for MCHC?

    a. $\dfrac{\text{Hgb} \times 100}{\text{Hct}}$

    b. $\dfrac{\text{Hgb}}{\text{RBC}}$

    c. $\dfrac{\text{RBC}}{\text{Hct}}$

    d. $\dfrac{\text{Hct} \times 1000}{\text{RBC}}$

177. What is the MCHC if the Hct is 20%, the RBC is $2.4 \times 10^6/\mu L$ and the Hgb is 5 g/dL?

    a. 21 g/dL
    b. 25 g/dL
    c. 30 g/dL
    d. 34 g/dL

178. What is the MCHC if the Hct is 20%, the RBC is $1.5 \times 10^6/\mu L$ and the Hgb is 6 g/dL?

    a. 28 g/dL
    b. 30 g/dL
    c. 40 g/dL
    d. 75 g/dL

For questions 179 and 180, refer to the following data:

WBC   8.5 x 10^3/μL (8.5 x 10^9/L)
Differential:
  segs   56%
  bands   2%
  lymphs   30%
  monos   6%
  eos   6%

179. Given the above data, what is the absolute lymphocyte count?

      a.   170
      b.   510
      c. 2,550
      d. 4,760

180. Given the above data, what is the absolute eosinophil count?

      a.   170
      b.   510
      c. 2,550
      d. 4,760

---

181. Which of the following is the formula for manual white cell count?

      a. <u>number of cells counted x dilution x 10</u>
            number of squares counted

      b. <u>number of cells counted x dilution</u>
          10 x number of squares counted

      c. number of cells counted x dilution

      d. number of cells counted x number of squares
         counted

182. If a WBC count is performed on a 1:10 dilution and the number of cells counted in 8 squares is 120, the total WBC count is:

      a. 1,200/μL
      b. 1,500/μL
      c. 12,000/μL
      d. 15,000/μL

183. If a WBC count is performed on a 1:100 dilution and the number
     of cells counted in eight squares is 50, the total WBC
     count is:

     a. 5,000/µL
     b. 6,250/µL
     c. 50,000/µL
     d. 62,500/µL

184. An automated leukocyte count is 22.5 x 10^3/µL (22.5 x 10^9/L).
     The differential reveals 200 normoblasts/100 leukocytes.
     What is the actual leukocyte count per microliter?

     a. 7,500/µL
     b. 11,500/µL
     c. 14,400/µL
     d. 22,300/µL

185. A total leukocyte count is 10.0 x 10^3/µL and 25 NRBCs are seen
     per 100 leukocytes on the differential. What is the corrected
     leukocyte count?

     a. 2,000/µL
     b. 8,000/µL
     c. 10,000/µL
     d. 12,000/µL

186. If the total leukocyte count is 20.0 x 10^3/µL and 50 NRBCs are seen
     per 100 leukocytes on the differential, what is the corrected
     leukocyte count?

     a. 6,666/µL
     b. 10,000/µL
     c. 13,333/µL
     d. 26,666/µL

187. A blood smear shows 80 nucleated red cells per 100 leukocytes.
     The total leukocyte count is 18 x 10^3/µL (18 x 10^9/L). The
     true white cell count expressed in SI units is:

     a. 17.2 x 10^9/L
     b. 9.0 x 10^9/L
     c. 10.0 x 10^9/L
     d. 13.4 x 10^9/L

188. Which of the following is the formula for mean corpuscular volume (MCV)?

    a. $\dfrac{\text{Hgb} \times 10}{\text{RBC}}$

    b. $\dfrac{\text{Hgb}}{\text{Hct}}$

    c. $\dfrac{\text{Hct} \times 10}{\text{RBC}}$

    d. $\dfrac{\text{RBC}}{\text{Hct}}$

189. Given the following data:

    Hemoglobin   8 g/dL
    Hematocrit   28%
    RBC $3.6 \times 10^6/\mu L$ ($3.6 \times 10^{12}/L$)

    The MCV is:

    a. 28 fL
    b. 35 fL
    c. 40 fL
    d. 78 fL

190. What is the MCV if the hematocrit is 20%, the RBC is $2.4 \times 10^6/\mu L$ and the hemoglobin is 5 g/dL?

    a.   68 fL
    b.   83 fL
    c. 100 fL
    d. 120 fL

191. What is the MCV if the hematocrit is 20%, the RBC is $1.5 \times 10^6/\mu L$ and the hemoglobin is 6 g/dL?

    a.   68 fL
    b.   75 fL
    c. 115 fL
    d. 133 fL

192. The mean for hemoglobin is 13.0 and the standard deviation is 0.15. The acceptable control range is ±2 standard deviations. What are the allowable limits for the control?

    a. 13.0 - 14.0
    b. 12.9 - 13.1
    c. 12.7 - 13.3
    d. 12.5 - 13.5

193. The mean for hemoglobin is 14.0 and the standard deviation is 0.20. The acceptable control range is ± 2 standard deviations. What are the allowable limits for the control?

    a. 13.8 - 14.2
    b. 13.6 - 14.4
    c. 13.4 - 14.6
    d. 13.0 - 14.0

194. On Monday a patient's hemoglobin determination was 11.3 gm/dL and on Tuesday it measured 11.8 gm/dL. The standard deviation of the method used is ± 0.2 gm/dL. Which of the following can be concluded about the hemoglobin values given?

    a. One value probably resulted from laboratory error.
    b. There is poor precision; daily quality control charts should be checked.
    c. The second value is out of range and should be repeated.
    d. There is no significant change in the patient's hemoglobin concentration.

195. Blood is diluted 1:200 and a platelet count is performed. 180 platelets were counted in the red cell counting area on one side of the hemocytometer and 186 on the other side. The total platelet count is:

    a. 146 x 10^3/µL (146 x 10^9/L)
    b. 183 x 10^3/µL (183 x 10^9/L)
    c. 366 x 10^3/µL (366 x 10^9/L)
    d. 732 x 10^3/µL (732 x 10^9/L)

The following items (*) have been identified as more appropriate for the entry level medical technologist.

*196. The main function of the hexose monophosphate shunt in the erythrocyte is to:

    a. regulate the level of 2,3-DPG
    b. provide reduced glutathione to prevent oxidation of hemoglobin
    c. prevent the reduction of heme iron
    d. provide energy for membrane maintenance

For questions 197 to 201, refer to the following illustration:

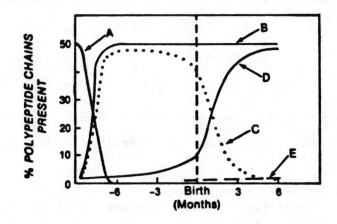

*197. Which curve represents the production of alpha polypeptide chains of hemoglobin?

    a. A
    b. B
    c. C
    d. D

*198. Which curve represents the production of beta polypeptide chains of hemoglobin?

    a. B
    b. C
    c. D
    d. E

*199. Which curve represents the production of gamma polypeptide chains of hemoglobin?

    a. A
    b. B
    c. C
    d. D

*200. Which curve represents the production of delta polypeptide chains of hemoglobin?

    a. B
    b. C
    c. D
    d. E

*201. Which curve represents the production of epsilon polypeptide chains of hemoglobin?

    a. A
    b. B
    c. C
    d. D

---

*202. In order for hemoglobin to combine reversibly with oxygen, the iron must be:

    a. completed with haptoglobin
    b. freely circulating in the cytoplasm
    c. attached to transferrin
    d. in the ferrous state

*203. Increased plasma iron turnover is a sign of:

    a. decreased red cell life span
    b. intravascular hemolysis
    c. increased heme catabolism
    d. increased erythropoiesis

*204. Which of the following stains can be used to differentiate siderotic granules (Pappenheimer bodies) from basophilic stippling?

    a. Wright's
    b. Prussian blue
    c. crystal violet
    d. periodic acid-Schiff

*205. On an electronic cell counter, hemoglobin determinations may be falsely elevated due to the presence of:

    a. lipemia or elevated bilirubin concentration
    b. a decreased WBC or lipemia
    c. an elevated bilirubin concentration or rouleaux
    d. rouleaux or lipemia

*206. The calculated erythrocyte indices on an adult man are MCV = 89 fL, MCH = 29 pg and MCHC = 38 g/dL. The calculations have been rechecked; erythrocytes on the peripheral blood smear appear normocytic and normochromic with no abnormal forms. The next step is to:

    a. report the results
    b. examine another smear
    c. repeat the hemoglobin and hematocrit
    d. repeat the erythrocyte count and hematocrit

*207. A 40-year-old man had an erythrocyte count of 2.5 x 10^3/μL, hematocrit of 22% and a reticulocyte count of 2.0%. Which of the following statements best describes his condition?

    a. The absolute reticulocyte count is 50 x 10^3/μL (50 x 10^9/L) indicating that the bone marrow is not adequately compensating for the anemia.
    b. The reticulocyte count is greatly increased indicating an adequate bone marrow response for this anemia.
    c. The absolute reticulocyte count is 500 x 10^3/μL (500 x 10^9/L) indicating that the bone marrow is adequately compensating for the anemia.
    d. The reticulocyte count is slightly increased indicating an adequate response to the slight anemia.

*208. A 50-year-old patient was found to have the following lab results:

Hgb 7.0 gm/dL; Hct 20%; and RBC 2.0 x 10^6/μL

It was determined that the patient was suffering from pernicious anemia. Which of the following sets of data most likely was obtained on the patient?

	WBCs	PLATELETS	RETICULOCYTES
a.	17,500	350,000	5.2%
b.	7,500	80,000	4.1%
c.	5,000	425,000	2.9%
d.	3,500	80,000	0.8%

*209. The most likely cause of the macrocytosis that often accompanies anemia of myelofibrosis is:

    a. folic acid deficiency
    b. increased reticulocyte count
    c. inadequate B_{12} absorption
    d. pyridoxine deficiency

*210. In an uncomplicated case of severe iron deficiency anemia, which of the following sets represents the typical pattern of results?

↓ - decrease
↑ - increase

	Serum Iron	Serum TIBC	% Saturat.	Marrow % Sidero-blasts	Marrow Iron Stores	Serum Ferritin	Hgb A_2
a.	↓	↑	↓	↓	↓	↑	↑
b.	↓	↓	↓	↓	↓	↓	↓
c.	↓	↑	↓	↓	↓	↓	↓
d.	↓	↓	↑	↑	↓	↑	↑

*211. A 56-year-old man was admitted to the hospital for treatment of a bleeding ulcer. The following laboratory data were obtained:

RBC $4.2 \times 10^6/\mu L$ ($4.2 \times 10^{12}/L$)   Serum iron   40 µg/dL
WBC $5.0 \times 10^3/\mu L$ ($5.0 \times 10^9/L$)   TIBC   460 µg/dL
HCT 30% (0.30 L/L)   Serum Ferritin 12 ng/mL
HGB 8.5 g/dL (85 g/L)

Examination of the bone marrow revealed the absence of iron stores. This data is most consistent with which of the following conditions?

    a. iron deficiency anemia
    b. anemia of chronic disease
    c. hemochromatosis
    d. acute blood loss

*212. A 40-year-old white male was admitted to the hospital for treatment of anemia, lassitude, weight loss, and loss of libido. The patient presented with the following laboratory data:

WBC   5.8 x 10³/μL (5.8 x 10⁹/L)   Serum iron   220 μg/dL
RBC   3.7 x 10³/μL (3.7 x 10¹²/L)   TIBC   300 μg/dL
HGB   10.0 g/dL   Serum ferritin 2,800 ng/mL
HCT   32%
MCV   86 fL
MCH   26 pg
MCHC   32 g/dL

Examination of the bone marrow revealed erythroid hyperplasia with a shift to the left of erythroid precursors. Prussian blue staining revealed markedly elevated iron stores noted with occasional sideroblasts seen. This data is most consistent with which of the following conditions?

   a. iron deficiency anemia
   b. anemia of chronic disease
   c. hemochromatosis
   d. acute blood loss

*213. Which of the following represents characteristic features of iron metabolism in patients with anemia of a chronic disorder?

   a. serum iron is normal, transferrin saturation is normal, TIBC is normal
   b. serum iron is increased, transferrin saturation is increased, TIBC is normal or slightly increased
   c. serum iron is normal, transferrin saturation is markedly increased, TIBC is normal
   d. serum iron is decreased, transferrin saturation is decreased, TIBC is normal or decreased

*214. The hypoproliferative red cell population in the bone marrow of uremic patients is caused by:

   a. infiltration of bone marrow by toxic waste products
   b. decreased levels of circulating erythropoietin
   c. defective globin synthesis
   d. overcrowding of bone marrow space by increased myeloid precursors

*215. An 89-year-old white female was transferred to the hospital from a nursing facility for treatment of chronic urinary tract infection with proteinuria. The patient presented with the following laboratory data:

WBC	10.0 x 10³/μL (10.0 x 10⁹/L)	Serum iron	29 μg/dL
RBC	3.1 x 10³/μL (3.1 x 10¹²/L)	TIBC	160 μg/dL
HGB	7.2 g/dL	Serum ferritin	100 ng/mL
HCT	24%		
MCV	78 fL		
MCH	23 pg		
MCHC	31 g/dL		

Examination of the bone marrow revealed a slightly fatty marrow with increased storage iron as detected by the Prussian blue technique. These data are most consistent with which of the following conditions?

   a. iron deficiency anemia
   b. anemia of chronic disease
   c. hemochromatosis
   d. acute blood loss

*216. The anemia in chronic renal failure is associated with all of the following EXCEPT:

   a. erythropoietin deficiency
   b. increased hemolysis of erythrocytes in the uremic environment
   c. blood loss
   d. elevated erythropoietin levels in tumor extracts

*217. Which of the following sets of laboratory findings is consistent with hemolytic anemia?

   a. normal or slightly increased erythrocyte survival; normal osmotic fragility
   b. decreased erythrocyte survival; increased catabolism of heme
   c. decreased serum lactate dehydrogenase activity; normal catabolism of heme
   d. normal concentration of haptoglobin; marked hemoglobinuria

*218. Which of the following characteristics are common to hereditary spherocytosis, hereditary elliptocytosis, hereditary stomatocytosis, and paroxysmal nocturnal hemoglobinuria?

a. autosomal dominant inheritance
b. red cell membrane defects
c. positive direct antiglobulin test
d. measured platelet count

*219. Patients with (A-) type G-6-PD deficiency are LEAST likely to have hemolytic episodes in which of the following situations?

a. following the administration of oxidizing drugs
b. the neonatal period
c. during infections
d. spontaneously

*220. A patient has a congenital nonspherocytic hemolytic anemia. After exposure to anti-malarial drugs the patient experiences a severe hemolytic episode. This episode is characterized by red cell inclusions caused by hemoglobin denaturation. Which of the following conditions is most consistent with these findings?

a. G-6-PD deficiency
b. thalassemia major
c. pyruvate kinase deficiency
d. paroxysmal nocturnal hemoglobinuria

*221. Which of the following is increased in erythrocytosis secondary to congenital heart defect?

a. arterial oxygen saturation
b. serum vitamin B_{12}
c. leukocyte alkaline phosphatase activity
d. erythropoietin

*222. Which of the following are NOT useful in distinguishing thalassemia minor from iron deficiency anemia?

a. free erythrocyte protoporphyrins (FEP)
b. serum ferritin
c. hemoglobin electrophoresis
d. osmotic fragility

*223. Refer to the following illustration:

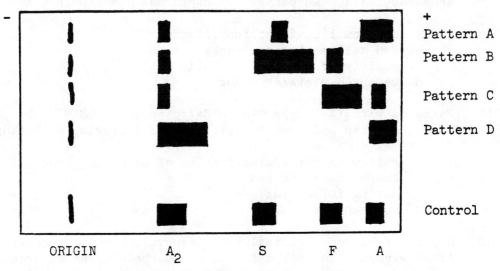

HEMOGLOBIN ELECTROPHORESIS PATTERNS AT pH 8.4
(CELLULOSE ACETATE STRIP)

Which electrophoresis pattern is consistent with sickle cell trait?

    a. pattern A
    b. pattern B
    c. pattern C
    d. pattern D

---

*224. A native of Thailand has a normal hemoglobin level. Hemoglobin electrophoresis on cellulose acetate shows 45% Hgb A and approximately 40% of a hemoglobin with the mobility of Hgb A_2. This is most consistent with:

    a. Hgb C trait
    b. Hgb E trait
    c. Hgb O trait
    d. Hgb D trait

*225. All of the following are characteristic of hemoglobin H EXCEPT:

   a. it is a tetramer of beta chains
   b. it is relatively unstable and thermolabile
   c. electrophoretically, it represents a fast hemoglobin
   d. its oxygen affinity is lower than that of Hgb A

*226. When using the turbidity (solubility) method for detecting the presence of hemoglobin S, an incorrect interpretation may be made when there is a(n):

   a. unusually high concentration of hemoglobin
   b. glucose concentration greater than 150 mg/dL
   c. blood specimen greater than 2 hours old
   d. increased total serum protein

*227. In most cases of hereditary persistence of fetal hemoglobin (HPFH):

   a. Hgb F is unevenly distributed throughout the erythrocytes
   b. the black heterozygote has 75% Hgb F
   c. beta and gamma chain synthesis is decreased
   d. gamma chain production equals alpha chain production

*228. Hemoglobin H disease results from:

   a. absence of 3 of 4 alpha genes
   b. absence of 2 of 4 alpha genes
   c. absence of 1 of 1 alpha genes
   d. absence of all four alpha genes

*229. Which one of the following hypochromic anemias is usually associated with a normal free erythrocyte protoporphyrin level?

   a. anemia of chronic disease
   b. iron deficiency
   c. lead poisoning
   d. thalassemia minor

*230. Evidence indicates that the genetic defect in thalassemia usually results in:

   a. the production of abnormal globin chains
   b. a quantitative deficiency in RNA resulting in decreased globin chain production
   c. a structural change in the heme portion of the hemoglobin
   d. an abnormality in the alpha or beta chain binding or affinity

*231. A 20-year-old Black man has peripheral blood changes
suggesting thalassemia minor. The quantitative hemoglobin
A_2 level is normal, but the hemoglobin F level is 5% (normal
less than 2%). This is most consistent with:

a. alpha thalassemia minor
b. beta thalassemia minor
c. delta-beta thalassemia minor
d. hereditary persistence of fetal hemoglobin

*232. The following results were obtained on a 55-year-old man
complaining of headaches and blurred vision:

Differential:

WBC   19.0 x 10^3/μL (19.0 x 10^9/L)   segs   84%
RBC   7.2 x 10^6/μL (7.2 x 10^{12}/L)   bands 10%
PLT   1,056 x 10^3/μL (1.1 x 10^{12}/L)   lymphs 3%
Uric Acid 13.0 mg/dL (0.78 mmol/L)   monos 2%
O_2 saturation 93%   eos   1%
Rh^1 negative
Red cell volume 3,911 mL (normal = 1,600)

These results are consistent with:

a. neutrophilic leukemoid reaction
b. polycythemia vera
c. chronic granulocytic leukemia
d. leukoerythroblastosis in myelofibrosis

*233. A patient has a tumor which concentrates erythropoietin.
Which of the following types of polycythemia does he most
likely have?

a. polycythemia vera
b. polycythemia, secondary to hypoxia
c. benign familial polycythemia
d. polycythemia associated with renal disease

*234. Which of the following types of polycythemia is most often
associated with emphysema?

a. polycythemia vera
b. polycythemia, secondary to hypoxia
c. relative polycythemia associated with dehydration
d. polycythemia associated with renal disease

*235. Hemorrhage in polycythemia vera is the result of:

   a. increased plasma viscosity
   b. persistent thrombocytosis
   c. splenic sequestration of platelets
   d. abnormal platelet function

*236. A patient diagnosed with polycythemia vera 5 years ago now
has a normal hematocrit, decreased hemoglobin and
microcytic, hypochromic red cells. What is the most probable
cause for the current blood picture?

   a. phlebotomy
   b. myelofibrosis
   c. preleukemia
   d. aplastic anemia

*237. A patient has been treated for polycythemia vera for several
years. His blood smear now shows:

   Oval macrocytes
   Howell-Jolly bodies
   Hypersegmented neutrophils
   Large, agranular platelets

The most probable cause of this blood picture is:

   a. iron deficiency
   b. alcoholism
   c. dietary B_{12} deficiency
   d. chemotherapy

*238. In comparison to malignant lymphoma cells, reactive
lymphocytes:

   a. have a denser nuclear chromatin
   b. are known to be T cells
   c. have more cytoplasm and more mitochondria
   d. are morphologically more variable throughout the smear

*239. Muramidase (lysozyme) is present in:

   a. granulocytes and their precursors
   b. monocytes and their precursors
   c. granulocytes, monocytes and their precursors
   d. lymphocytes and their precursors

*240. Terminal deoxynucleotidyl transferase (TdT) is a marker found on:

        a. hairy cells
        b. myeloblasts
        c. monoblasts
        d. lymphoblasts

*241. Which one of the following is a true statement about megakaryocytes in a bone marrow aspirate?

        a. An average of 1 to 3 should be found in each low power field (10 x).
        b. The majority of forms are the MK_1 stage.
        c. Morphology must be determined from the biopsy section.
        d. Quantitative estimation is done using the 100 x oil immersion lens.

*242. A bone marrow report described cells containing 1-2 nucleoli, moderately coarse nuclear chromatin, a high N/C ratio and a coarse staining pattern with PAS. These cells are most likely:

        a. myeloblasts
        b. lymphocytes
        c. monoblasts
        d. lymphoblasts

*243. Morphologic variants of plasma cells do NOT include:

        a. flame cells
        b. thesaurocytes
        c. grape cells
        d. Gaucher's cells

*244. Pluripotent stem cells are capable of producing:

        a. daughter cells of only one cell line
        b. only T-lymphocytes and B-lymphocytes
        c. erythropoietin, thrombopoietin, and leukopoietin
        d. lymphoid and myeloid stem cells

*245. The Philadelphia chromosome is formed by a translocation between the:

   a. long arm of chromosome 22 and long arm of chromosome 9
   b. long arm of chromosome 21 and long arm of chromosome 9
   c. long arm of chromosome 21 and short arm of chromosome 6
   d. long arm of chromosome 22 and short arm of chromosome 6

*246. In addition to a Romanowsky stain, routine evaluation of a bone marrow should include which of the following stains?

   a. chloroacetate esterase
   b. periodic acid-Schiff (PAS)
   c. Prussian blue
   d. Sudan black B

*247. Which of the following stains is closely associated with the lysosomal enzyme in primary (azurophilic) granules?

   a. peroxidase
   b. Sudan black B
   c. periodic acid-Schiff (PAS)
   d. Prussian blue

*248. The primary use of the toluidine blue stain is to distinguish between:

   a. myeloblasts and lymphoblasts
   b. "hairy cells" and lymphocytes
   c. leukemoid reactions and chronic granulocytic leukemia (CGL)
   d. progranulocytes and basophils

*249. Which of the following cells contain granules that stain with toluidine blue?

   a. megakaryocyte
   b. osteoclast
   c. histiocyte
   d. mast cell

*250. An EDTA blood sample has a white count of 7.0 x 10^3/μL. The specimen is selected as a patient precision control. It is refrigerated and run 7 times within a 24 hour period, being inverted by hand 10 times before each run. The following results are obtained (commercial control in range):

Time-from-collection-(hours)	WBC-Count
0	7,200
2	9,600
6	5,400
8	8,300
12	9,200
15	6,400
20	5,900
23	7,400

The best explanation for these results is:

a. the patient specimen was inadequately mixed
b. the white cells have deteriorated due to prolonged exposure to EDTA
c. the above represents normal random variation within the sample
d. the white blood cell values are only valid for a 12-hour period

*251. A characteristic of cyclic neutropenia is:

a. episodes of neutropenia beginning in infancy and recurring at three-week intervals
b. presence of leukoagglutinins in the serum
c. presence of serum neutropenic factors
d. production of neutropenia in persons transfused with plasma from an affected patient

*252. Mechanism of cortisol-induced neutrophilia includes:

a. an acute shift in granulocytes from the marginating pool to the circulating pool
b. an increased exit of granulocytes from the circulation
c. a decrease exit of granulocytes from the bone marrow
d. granulocyte return from the tissues to the circulating pool

*253. What feature would NOT be expected in pseudo-Pelger Huĕt cells?

      a. hyperclumped chromatin
      b. decreased granulation
      c. normal peroxidase activity
      d. normal neutrophils

*254. The cytoplasmic abnormality of the white blood cell of Alder-Reilly anomaly is found in the:

      a. endoplasmic reticulum
      b. lysosomes
      c. mitochondria
      d. ribosomes

*255. Of the following, the disease most closely associated with mucopolysaccharidosis is:

      a. Pelger-Huĕt anomaly
      b. Chediak-Higashi syndrome
      c. Gaucher's disease
      d. Alder-Reilly anomaly

*256. Of the following, the disease most closely associated with glucocerebrosidase deficiency is:

      a. Gaucher's disease
      b. Chediak-Higashi syndrome
      c. Pelger-Huĕt anomaly
      d. May-Hegglin anomaly

*257. A patient has a white blood count of 50 x 10^3/μL. To distinguish between bacterial infection and chronic granulocytic leukemia the most useful test is:

      a. Wright's stain
      b. peroxidase
      c. periodic acid-Schiff (PAS)
      d. leukocyte alkaline phosphatase (LAP)

*258. Increased numbers of basophils are often seen in:

      a. acute infections
      b. chronic granulocytic leukemia
      c. chronic lymphocytic leukemia
      d. erythroblastosis fetalis (hemolytic disease of the newborn)

*259. The following results were obtained on a leukocyte alkaline phosphatase stain:

Score	4+	3+	2+	1+	0
No. of cells counted	35	33	28	2	4

These reactions are most consistent with:

    a. leukemoid reaction
    b. nephrotic syndrome
    c. chronic granulocytic leukemia
    d. progressive muscular dystrophy

*260. A 30-year-old woman was admitted to the hospital for easy bruising and menorrhagia. Laboratory findings included the following:

WBC $3.5 \times 10^3/\mu L$ ($3.5 \times 10^9/L$)   Differential:
RBC $2.48 \times 10^6/\mu L$ ($2.48 \times 10^{12}/L$) polys   3%
PLT $30 \times 10^3/\mu L$ ($30 \times 10^9/L$)   lymphs 2%
Hgb 8.6 g/dL   monos   2%
HCT 25.0%   myelos   4%
MCV 100.7 fL   abnormal
MCH 34.7 pg   immature 58%
MCHC 34.3 g/dL   blasts   31%
PT   34.0 sec   NRBC   1%
APTT 62.5 sec   auer bodies,
TT   15.0 sec   1+ macrocytes,
FSP >40 µg/mL   1+ polychromasia
Fibrinogen 315 mg/dL (control 200-400)

The cells identified as "abnormal immature" were described as having lobulated nuclei (figure 8, reniform or kidney shaped) with prominent nucleoli; the cytoplasm had intense azurophilic granulation over the nucleus, with some cells containing 1 to 20 Auer bodies-frequently grouped in bundles. A 15-17 chromosomal translocation was noted. Cells were SBB, peroxidase and NAS-D-chloroacetate positive, PAS negative.

Which of the following types of acute leukemia is most likely?

    a. myeloblastic
    b. promyelocytic
    c. myelomonocytic
    d. monocytic

*261. Which of the following leukemias is characterized by immature
cells that are Sudan black B positive with discrete fine
granules, peroxidase negative, PAS variable, strongly alpha
naphthyl acetate esterase positive, and muramidase positive?

    a. acute lymphocytic
    b. chronic lymphocytic
    c. acute granulocytic
    d. acute myelomonocytic

*262. A hypercellular marrow with an M:E ratio of 6:1 is most
commonly due to:

    a. lymphoid hyperplasia
    b. granulocytic hyperplasia
    c. normoblastic hyperplasia
    d. myeloid hypoplasia

*263. The following results were obtained:

WBC 5.0 x 10^3/µL (5.0 x 10^9/L)
RBC 1.7 x 10^6/µL (1.7 x 10^{12}/L)
MCV 84 fL
PLT 89 x 10^3/µL (89 x 10^9/L)

Differential:
segs	16%
bands	22%
lymphs	28%
monos	16%
eos	1%
basos	1%
metamyelos	4%
myelos	3%
promyelos	4%
blasts	5%

1 megakaryoblast; 30 nucleated erythrocytes; teardrops;
schistocytes; polychromasia; giant, bizarre platelets noted

LAP: 142
Philadelphia chromosome: negative

This is consistent with:

    a. idiopathic thrombocythemia
    b. polycythemia vera
    c. chronic granulocytic leukemia
    d. leukoerythroblastosis in myelofibrosis

*264. A 50-year-old man was admitted into the hospital with acute leukemia. Laboratory findings included the following:

Myeloperoxidase stain   - blast cells negative
PAS stain   - blast cells demonstrate a blocking
                          pattern

Terminal deoxynucleotidyl
  transferase(TdT)   - blast cells positive
Surface immunoglobulin - blast cells negative
E rosettes   - blast cells negative
Philadelphia chromosome - positive

These results are most consistent with:

    a. acute myelogenous leukemia
    b. chronic lymphocytic leukemia in lymphoblastic
       transformation
    c. T cell acute lymphocytic leukemia
    d. chronic myelogenous leukemia in lymphoblastic
       transformation

*265. A 30-year-old man who had been diagnosed as having leukemia two years previously was readmitted because of cervical lymphadenopathy. Laboratory findings included the following:

		Differential:	
WBC 39.6 x 10³/µL (39.6 x 10⁹/L)		polys	7%
RBC 3.25 x 10⁶/µL (3.25 x 10¹²/L)		lymphs	4%
Hgb 9.4 g/dL (94 g/L)		monos	2%
HCT 28.2% (0.28 L/L)		eos	3%
MCV 86.7 fL		basos	48%
MCH 29.0 pg		myelos	13%
MCHC 33.4 g/dL		promyelos	2%
PLT 53 x 10³/µL (53 x 10⁹/L)		metamyelos	8%
		blasts	13%
		NRBCs	11%
		megakaryoblast	3%

Bone Marrow: 95% cellularity, 50% blast cells
             (some with peroxidase and SBB positivity)
LAP: 11
Philadelphia chromosome: positive

These results are most consistent with:

    a. acute myeloid leukemia
    b. erythroleukemia
    c. chronic granulocytic leukemia (CGL)
    d. CGL in blast transformation

*266. The following results were obtained on a 35-year-old woman complaining of fatigue and weight loss:

WBC: $1.8 \times 10^3/\mu L$ $(1.8 \times 10^9/L)$
RBC: $4.6 \times 10^6/\mu L$ $(4.6 \times 10^{12}/L)$
PLT: $903 \times 10^3/\mu L$ $(903 \times 10^9/L)$
Uric Acid: 6.4 ng/dL
LAP: 0
Philadelphia chromosome: positive

Differential:

segs	30%
bands	17%
lymphs	13%
monos	3%
eos	4%
basso	6%
metamyelos	3%
myelos	20%
promyelos	3%
blasts	1%

These results are consistent with:

a. neutrophilic leukemoid reaction
b. idiopathic thrombocythemia
c. chronic granulocytic leukemia
d. leukoerythroblastosis in myelofibrosis

*267. The bone marrow in the terminal stage of erythroleukemia is often indistinguishable from that seen in:

a. myeloid metaplasia
b. polycythemia vera
c. acute granulocytic leukemia
d. aplastic anemia

*268. The greatest activity of serum muramidase occurs with:

a. cancer of the prostate
b. myeloproliferative disease
c. myelomonocytic leukemia
d. Gaucher's disease

*269. The type of leukemia seen most commonly as a terminal event in plasma cell myeloma is:

a. acute lymphoblastic leukemia
b. acute monocytic leukemia
c. acute myelomonocytic leukemia
d. chronic myelogenous leukemia

*270. The atypical lymphocyte seen in the peripheral smear of patients with infectious mononucleosis is probably derived from which of the following?

        a. T lymphocytes
        b. B lymphocytes
        c. monocytes
        d. mast cells

*271. Which of the following cells is the atypical lymphocyte seen on the peripheral blood smear of patients with infectious mononucleosis?

        a. T lymphocytes
        b. B lymphocytes
        c. monocytes
        d. mast cells

*272. In the immunologic classification of acute lymphocytic leukemia (ALL), the acid phosphatase stain is usually positive for:

        a. null cell ALL
        b. T cell ALL
        c. common ALL
        d. B cell ALL

*273. T cell acute lymphocytic leukemia (ALL) is closely related to:

        a. chronic lymphocytic leukemia (CLL)
        b. autoimmune disease
        c. lymphoblastic lymphoma
        d. acute granulocytic leukemia (AGL)

*274. Bone marrow examination reveals a hypercellular marrow consisting of probable lymphoblasts with receptors for sheep rosettes and TdT; however, the lymphoblasts are negative for SIgs, Ia antigen, CALLA, Fc, and complement receptors. The most likely diagnosis is:

        a. null-cell acute lymphocytic leukemia (non-B, non-T cell ALL)
        b. chronic lymphocytic leukemia (CLL)
        c. T cell leukemia (T-ALL)
        d. hairy-cell leukemia

*275. In the French-American-British (FAB) classification, acute lymphocytic leukemia is divided into groups according to:

a. prognosis
b. immunology
c. cytochemistry
d. morphology

*276. A 10-year-old patient's bone marrow is classified morphologically by the French-American-British (FAB) system as an L3 ALL. Which of the following results support this diagnosis?

a. terminal deoxynucleotidyl transferase (TdT) positive
b. Pelger-Hüet-like neutrophils are found
c. surface immunoglobulin positive
d. E-rosette positive

*277. Increased levels of TdT activity are indicative of:

a. Burkitt's lymphoma
b. acute granulocytic leukemia
c. acute lymphocytic leukemia
d. eosinophilia

*278. In the French-American-British (FAB) classification myelomonocytic leukemia would be:

a. M1 & M2
b. M3
c. M4
d. M5

*279. In acute granulocytic leukemia, the myeloblasts stain positive with all of the following EXCEPT:

a. specific esterase
b. Sudan black
c. peroxidase
d. PAS

*280. In chronic myelocytic leukemia, blood histamine concentrations tend to reflect the:

a. number of platelets present
b. serum uric acid concentrations
c. number of basophils present
d. the total number of granulocytes

*281. Patients with chronic granulomatous disease suffer from frequent pyogenic infections due to the inability of:

a. lymphocytes to produce bacterial antibodies
b. eosinophils to degranulate in the presence of bacteria
c. neutrophils to kill phagocytized bacteria
d. basophils to release histamine in the presence of bacteria

*282. Which of the following stains is helpful to diagnosis suspected erythroleukemia?

a. peroxidase
b. non-specific esterase
c. periodic acid-Schiff (PAS)
d. acid phosphatase

*283. Abnormalities found in erythroleukemia include:

a. rapid DNA synthesis
b. marrow fibrosis
c. megaloblastoid development
d. increased erythrocyte survival

*284. The following results were obtained on a 45-year-old man complaining of chills and fever:

WBC 23.0 x $10^3/\mu L$ (23.0 x $10^9/L$)
Differential:
  segs   60%
  bands   21%
  lymphs   11%
  monos   3%
  metamyelos 2%
  myelos   3%
Toxic granulation, Döhle bodies and vacuoles

LAP: 200
Philadelphia chromosome: negative

These results are consistent with:

a. neutrophilic leukemoid reaction
b. polycythemia vera
c. chronic granulocytic leukemia
d. leukoerythroblastosis in myelofibrosis

*285. Which of the following will distinguish early myeloid metaplasia from chronic granulocytic leukemia?

a. bone marrow hyperplasia
b. bone marrow fibrosis
c. increased leukocytic alkaline phosphatase (LAP)
d. megaloblastosis

*286. Which of the following bone marrow findings favor the diagnosis of multiple myeloma?

a. presence of Reed-Sternberg cells
b. sheaths of immature plasma cells
c. presence of flame cells and Russell bodies
d. presence of plasmacytic satellitosis

*287. The disease most frequently present in patients with atypical lymphocytosis and persistently negative tests is:

a. toxoplasmosis
b. cytomegalovirus (CMV) infection
c. herpes virus infection
d. viral hepatitis

*288. Which of the following have a B cell origin?

a. Sezary syndrome
b. malignant lymphoma, lymphoblastic type
c. Sternberg sarcoma
d. Waldenström's macroglobulinemia

*289. Which of the following cells is most likely identified in lesions of mycosis fungoides?

a. T lymphocytes
b. B lymphocytes
c. monocytes
d. mast cells

*290. Aspirin affects platelet function by interfering with platelets' metabolism of:

a. prostaglandins
b. lipids
c. carbohydrates
d. nucleic acids

*291. A phase-platelet count was performed and the total platelet count was 356 x 10³/µL. Ten fields on the stained blood smear were examined for platelets and the results per field were:

16, 18, 15, 20, 19, 17, 19, 18, 20, 16

The next step would be to:

a. report the phase-platelet count since it correlated well with the slide
b. repeat the phase-platelet count on a recollected specimen and check for clumping
c. check ten additional fields on the blood smear
d. repeat the platelet count using a different method

---

*292. Refer to the following diagram:

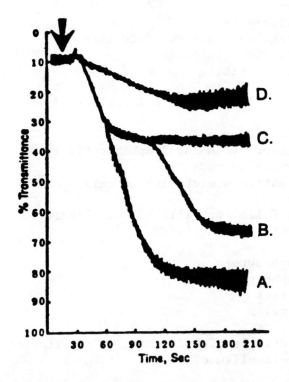

In the platelet aggregation curves shown above, the aggregating agent was added at the point indicated by the arrow. Select the appropriate aggregation curve for recent aspirin ingestion. (aggregating agent is ADP or epinephrine)

a. A
b. B
c. C
d. D

*293. The automated platelet count on an EDTA specimen is 58 x $10^3/\mu L$. The platelet estimate on the blood smear appears normal, but it was noted that the platelets were all surrounding the neutrophils. The next step should be to:

    a. report the automated platelet count since it is more accurate than a platelet estimate
    b. warm the EDTA tube and repeat the automated platelet count
    c. rerun the original specimen since the platelet count and blood smear estimate do not match
    d. recollect a specimen for a platelet count not using EDTA

*294. Platelet aggregation will occur with the endproduction of:

    a. cyclo-oxygenase
    b. arachidonic acid
    c. prostacyclin
    d. thromboxane A_2

*295. A 53-year-old man was in recovery following a triple bypass operation. Oozing was noted from his surgical wound. The following laboratory data were obtained:

Hemoglobin	12.5 g/dL
Hematocrit	37% (0.37 L/L)
Prothrombin time	12.3 seconds
APTT	34 seconds
Platelet count	40.0 x $10^3/\mu L$ (40.0 x $10^9/L$)
Fibrinogen	250 mg/dL

The most likely cause of bleeding would be:

    a. dilution of coagulation factors due to massive transfusion
    b. intravascular coagulation secondary to microaggregates
    c. hypofibrinogenemia
    d. dilutional thrombocytopenia

*296. Which of the following is characteristic of Bernard-Soulier syndrome?

    a. giant platelets
    b. normal bleeding time
    c. abnormal aggregation with ADP
    d. increased platelet count

*297. Which of the following is associated with Glanzmann's thrombasthenia?

     a. normal bleeding time
     b. normal ADP aggregation
     c. abnormal initial wave ristocetin aggregation
     d. absence of clot retraction

*298. Abnormal platelet retention in von Willebrand's disease is:

     a. due to defective nucleotide release
     b. related to a plasma factor deficiency
     c. one of the most important criteria in making the diagnosis
     d. improved following aspirin ingestion

*299. The combination of increased capillary fragility, prolonged bleeding time and prolonged clot retraction suggests a deficiency in:

     a. thromboplastin
     b. prothrombin
     c. platelets
     d. fibrinogen

*300. Hageman factor (XII) is involved in each of the following reactions EXCEPT:

     a. activation of C1 to C1 esterase
     b. activation of plasminogen
     c. activation of factor XI
     d. transformation of fibrinogen to fibrin

*301. The following coagulation results were obtained on a newborn:

		Reference Ranges
Prothrombin Time	12.8 sec	9.5 - 14.5 sec
Activated Partial Thromboplastin Time	34.5 sec	20-35 sec
Thrombin Time	14.0 sec	9-13 sec
Fibrinogen	380 mg/dL	200-400 mg/dL

The results are most suggestive of:

     a. factor VII deficiency
     b. normal newborn results
     c. hyperfibrinogenemia
     d. vitamin K deficiency

*302. A 54-year-old man was admitted with pulmonary embolism and given streptokinase. Which of the following would be most useful in monitoring this therapy?

    a. activated partial thromboplastin time
    b. bleeding time
    c. prothrombin time
    d. thrombin time

*303. The following laboratory data were obtained from a 27-year-old man with a long history of abnormal bleeding:

Prothrombin time:	normal
Activated partial thromboplastin time	markedly prolonged
Factor VIII coagulant activity:	markedly decreased
Factor VIII related antigen:	normal
Platelet count:	normal
Template bleeding time:	normal

Which of the following disorders does this man most likely have:

    a. classic hemophilia
    b. von Willebrand's disease
    c. Christmas disease
    d. disseminated intravascular coagulation (DIC)

*304. The following laboratory data were obtained from a 40-year-old woman with a long history of abnormal bleeding:

Prothrombin time:	normal
Activated partial thromboplastin time:	prolonged
Factor VIII-coagulant activity:	decreased
Factor VIII-related antigen:	markedly decreased
Platelet count:	normal
Template bleeding time:	prolonged

Which of the following disorders does this woman most likely have:

    a. classic hemophilia
    b. von Willebrand's disease
    c. Christmas disease
    d. disseminated intravascular coagulation (DIC)

*305. In von Willebrand's disease, platelets give an abnormal aggregation result in the presence of:

   a. adenosine diphosphate
   b. epinephrine
   c. collagen
   d. ristocetin

*306. A patient has a normal prothrombin time and a prolonged activated partial thromboplastin time (APTT) using a kaolin activator. The APTT corrects to normal when the incubation time is increased. These results suggest that the patient has:

   a. hemophilia A (factor VIII deficiency)
   b. Hageman factor (XII) deficiency
   c. Fletcher factor deficiency (prekallikrein)
   d. factor V deficiency

*307. A patient has a history of mild hemorrhagic episodes. Laboratory results include a prolonged prothrombin time and partial thromboplastin time. The abnormal prothrombin time was corrected by normal and adsorbed plasma, but not aged serum. Which of the following coagulation factors is deficient?

   a. prothrombin
   b. factor V
   c. factor VII
   d. factor X

*308. The following data were obtained on a patient:

PT: 20 seconds
Thrombin time: 13 seconds
APTT: 55 seconds
APTT plus aged serum: corrected
APTT plus adsorbed plasma: not corrected
Circulatory inhibitor: none present

   a. factor V
   b. factor VIII
   c. factor X
   d. factor XI

*309. A 56-year-old woman was admitted to the hospital with a history of a moderate to severe bleeding tendency of several years duration. Epistaxis and menorrhagia were reported. Prolonged APTT was corrected with fresh normal plasma, adsorbed plasma and aged serum. Deficiency of which of the following factors is most likely?

    a. factor VIII
    b. factor IX
    c. factor XI
    d. factor XII

*310. Which of the following laboratory findings is associated with factor XIII deficiency?

    a. prolonged activated partial thromboplastin time
    b. clot solubility in a 5 molar urea solution
    c. prolonged thrombin time
    d. prolonged prothrombin time

*311. A patient develops unexpected bleeding following three transfusions. The following test results were obtained:

    prolonged PT and APTT
    decreased fibrinogen
    increased fibrin split products
    decreased platelets

What is the most probable cause of these results?

    a. familial afibrinogenemia
    b. primary fibrinolysis
    c. DIC
    d. liver disease

*312. The preferred blood product for a bleeding patient with von Willebrand's disease is transfusion with:

    a. factor II, VII, IX, X concentrates
    b. commercial factor VIII concentrates
    c. Fresh Frozen Plasma and Platelets
    d. Cryoprecipitated AHF

*313. The following results were obtained on an electronic cell counter:

WBC   61.3 x 10³/μL (61.3 x 10⁹/L)
RBC   1.19 x 10⁶/μL (1.19 x 10⁹/L)
Hgb   9.9 g/dL
HCT   21%
MCV   125 fL
MCHC 54.1 g/dL

What action should be taken to obtain accurate results?

a. dilute the specimen and recount
b. warm the specimen and recount
c. check the tube for clots
d. clean the aperture tubes and recount

Hematology Answer Key

1.	B	48.	C	95.	B	142.	B
2.	A	49.	A	96.	D	143.	A
3.	A	50.	A	97.	B	144.	D
4.	B	51.	D	98.	D	145.	C
5.	C	52.	A	99.	B	146.	D
6.	D	53.	A	100.	D	147.	D
7.	A	54.	A	101.	B	148.	C
8.	B	55.	D	102.	B	149.	A
9.	B	56.	D	103.	D	150.	C
10.	C	57.	C	104.	A	151.	B
11.	D	58.	C	105.	D	152.	C
12.	C	59.	B	106.	B	153.	A
13.	C	60.	C	107.	C	154.	B
14.	D	61.	C	108.	C	155.	A
15.	B	62.	A	109.	B	156.	D
16.	D	63.	C	110.	D	157.	B
17.	D	64.	A	111.	C	158.	A
18.	D	65.	C	112.	D	159.	D
19.	D	66.	D	113.	D	160.	D
20.	A	67.	B	114.	D	161.	C
21.	B	68.	C	115.	B	162.	C
22.	C	69.	A	116.	B	163.	D
23.	D	70.	A	117.	D	164.	C
24.	D	71.	A	118.	C	165.	A
25.	B	72.	B	119.	C	166.	B
26.	A	73.	C	120.	A	167.	A
27.	A	74.	C	121.	A	168.	D
28.	D	75.	B	122.	D	169.	C
29.	C	76.	A	123.	B	170.	A
30.	B	77.	B	124.	B	171.	D
31.	B	78.	C	125.	C	172.	B
32.	C	79.	D	126.	A	173.	D
33.	A	80.	C	127.	B	174.	A
34.	B	81.	B	128.	A	175.	C
35.	B	82.	A	129.	A	176.	A
36.	A	83.	D	130.	A	177.	B
37.	A	84.	C	131.	A	178.	B
38.	C	85.	C	132.	D	179.	C
39.	D	86.	A	133.	B	180.	B
40.	D	87.	A	134.	A	181.	A
41.	B	88.	A	135.	A	182.	B
42.	C	89.	D	136.	A	183.	B
43.	C	90.	B	137.	A	184.	A
44.	C	91.	B	138.	D	185.	B
45.	A	92.	C	139.	A	186.	C
46.	D	93.	A	140.	D	187.	C
47.	B	94.	D	141.	D	188.	C

189.	D	221.	D	253.	C	285.	C
190.	B	222.	D	254.	B	286.	B
191.	D	223.	A	255.	D	287.	B
192.	C	224.	B	256.	A	288.	D
193.	B	225.	D	257.	D	289.	A
194.	D	226.	D	258.	B	290.	A
195.	C	227.	D	259.	A	291.	A
196.	B	228.	A	260.	B	292.	C
197.	B	229.	D	261.	D	293.	D
198.	C	230.	B	262.	B	294.	D
199.	C	231.	C	263.	D	295.	D
200.	D	232.	B	264.	D	296.	A
201.	A	233.	D	265.	D	297.	D
202.	D	234.	B	266.	C	298.	B
203.	D	235.	D	267.	C	299.	C
204.	B	236.	A	268.	C	300.	D
205.	A	237.	D	269.	C	301.	B
206.	C	238.	D	270.	B	302.	D
207.	A	239.	C	271.	A	303.	A
208.	D	240.	D	272.	B	304.	B
209.	A	241.	A	273.	C	305.	D
210.	C	242.	D	274.	C	306.	C
211.	A	243.	D	275.	D	307.	B
212.	C	244.	D	276.	C	308.	C
213.	D	245.	A	277.	C	309.	C
214.	B	246.	C	278.	C	310.	B
215.	B	247.	A	279.	D	311.	C
216.	D	248.	D	280.	C	312.	D
217.	B	249.	D	281.	C	313.	B
218.	B	250.	A	282.	C		
219.	D	251.	A	283.	C		
220.	A	252.	A	284.	A		

CHAPTER 15

Immunology

The following items have been identified as appropriate for both entry level medical technologists and medical laboratory technicians.

1. Antibodies are secreted by:

    a. killer cells
    b. marrow stem cells
    c. mast cells
    d. B cells

2. Antibody class and antibody subclass is determined by major physiochemical differences and antigenic variation found primarily in the:

    a. constant region of heavy chain
    b. constant region of light chain
    c. variable regions of heavy and light chains
    d. constant regions of heavy and light chains

3. The ratio of kappa to lambda light chains in serum is

    a. 1:1
    b. 2:1
    c. 3:1
    d. 4:1

4. With which of the following immunoglobulin classes is secretory component or transport piece associated?

    a. IgA
    b. IgD
    c. IgE
    d. IgG

5. The immunoglobulin class typically found to be present in saliva, tears and other secretions is:

    a. IgG
    b. IgA
    c. IgM
    d. IgD

6. Treatment of IgG with papain results in how many fragments?

   a. 2
   b. 3
   c. 4
   d. 5

7. The immunoglobulin class associated with hypersensitivity or allergenic reactions is:

   a. IgA
   b. IgM
   c. IgD
   d. IgE

8. Which of the following immunoglobulins is the most efficient agglutinator?

   a. IgG
   b. IgA
   c. IgM
   d. IgE

9. The rapid rise, elevated level, and prolonged production of antibody following a repeat exposure to antigen is called:

   a. hypersensitivity
   b. arthus reaction
   c. anamnestic response
   d. primary response

10. Which of the following is the "recognition unit" in the classical complement pathway?

    a. C1q
    b. C3a
    c. C4, C2, C3
    d. C5, C6, C7, C8, C9

11. Which of the following is the "C3 activation unit" in the classical complement pathway?

    a. C1q
    b. C3
    c. C4b, C2a
    d. C5, C6, C7, C8, C9

12. Which of the following is the "membrane attack unit" in the classical complement pathway?

    a. C1
    b. C3
    c. C4, C2, C3
    d. C5, C6, C7,

13. Which of the following releases histamine and other mediators from basophils?

    a. C3a
    b. properdin factor B
    c. C1q
    d. C4

14. The complement component C3:

    a. is increased (in plasma levels) when complement activation occurs
    b. can be measured by immunoprecipitin assays
    c. releases histamine from basophils or mast cells
    d. is NOT involved in the alternate complement pathway

15. The serum hemolytic complement level (CH_{50}):

    a. is a measure of total complement activity
    b. provides the same information as a serum factor B level
    c. is detectable when any component of the classical system is congenitally absent
    d. can be calculated from the serum concentrations of the individual components

16. Double precipitin rings on radial immunodiffusion (RID) plates for serum haptoglobin assays can be caused by:

    a. haptoglobin-hemoglobin complexes
    b. haptoglobin-hemopexin interactions
    c. refrigeration at 4°C of RID plates during immunodiffusion
    d. antigen excess

17. Which of the following is an important cellular mediator of immune complex tissue injury?

    a. monocyte
    b. neutrophil
    c. basophil
    d. eosinophil

18. Which of the following mediators is released during T-cell activation?

   a. immunoglobulins
   b. thymosin
   c. serotonin
   d. lymphokines

19. Polyclonal B cell activation:

   a. inhibits antibody production
   b. requires the participation of T-helper cells
   c. results from the activation of suppressor T-cells
   d. can induce autoantibody production

20. Substances which are antigenic only when coupled to a protein carrier are:

   a. opsonins
   b. haptens
   c. adjuvants
   d. allergens

21. A haptenic determinant will react with:

   a. both T-cells and antibody
   b. T-cells but not antibody
   c. neither T-cells nor antibody
   d. antibody but not T-cells

22. HLA antibodies are generally obtained from which of the following?

   a. multiparous women
   b. nonidentical siblings
   c. sheep
   d. rabbits

23. Which of the following terms describes a graft between genetically unidentical individuals?

   a. autograft
   b. isograft
   c. allograft
   d. xenograft

24. Incompatibility by which of the following procedures is an absolute contraindication to allotransplantation?

    a. mixed lymphocyte culture
    b. HLA typing
    c. Rh typing
    d. ABO typing

25. A bacterial protein used to bind human immunoglobulins is:

    a. HAV antibody, IgA type
    b. *Escherichia coli* protein C
    c. staphylococcal protein A
    d. HAV antibody, IgG type

26. What is the cluster of differentiation (CD) designation for the E-rosette receptor?

    a. CD 2
    b. CD 3
    c. CD 8
    d. CD 10
    e. CD 21

27. Select the appropriate sensitivity limits for radial immunodiffusion.

    a. 0.1 mg/dL
    b. 0.5 mg/dL
    c. < 1-2 mg/dL
    d. < 1 pg/dL

28. Select the appropriate sensitivity limits for nephelometry.

    a. 0.1 mg/dL
    b. 0.5 mg/dL
    c. 1-2 mg/dL
    d. < 1 pg/dL

29. Select the appropriate sensitivity limits for radioimmunoassay.

    a. 0.1 mg/dL
    b. 0.5 mg/dL
    c. 1-2 mg/dL
    d. < 1 pg/dL

30. The visible serologic reaction between soluble antigen and its specific antibody is:

    a. sensitization
    b. precipitation
    c. agglutination
    d. opsonization

For questions 31 through 35, refer to the following diagram and data:

The curve below was obtained by adding increasing amounts of a soluble antigen to fixed volumes of monospecific antiserum.

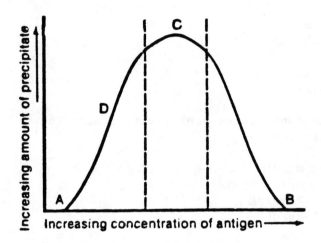

31. The area on the curve for equivalence precipitate is:

    a. A
    b. B
    c. C
    d. D

32. The area on the curve where no precipitate formed due to antigen excess is:

    a. A
    b. B
    c. C
    d. D

33. The area on the curve for prozone is:

    a. A
    b. B
    c. C
    d. D

34. The area on the curve where soluble antigen-antibody complexes have begun to form is:

    a. A
    b. B
    c. C
    d. D

35. The area in which the addition of more antibody would result in the formation of additional precipitate is:

    a. A
    b. B
    c. C
    d. D

---

36. Antiserum and a patient's serum specimen are added to opposing wells in an agar plate and an electrical current is then applied to this plate. This process is called:

    a. counterimmunoelectrophoresis
    b. radial immunodiffusion
    c. electroimmunodiffusion
    d. immunoelectrophoresis

37. Which of the following is the major difference between a fluorescent microscope with epi-illumination and a fluorescent microscope with transmitted light?

    a. The transmitted light microscope has a barrier filter.
    b. The transmitted light microscope has an exciter filter.
    c. The transmitted light microscope uses a halogen light source.
    d. The epi-illuminated microscope has a dichroic mirror.

For questions 38 through 41, refer to the following illustration.

Figure #1

Figure #2

Figure #3

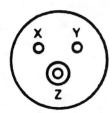
Figure #4

38. Which of the above figures demonstrates a reaction pattern of identity?

    a. Figure #1
    b. Figure #2
    c. Figure #3
    d. Figure #4

39. Which of the above figures demonstrates a reaction pattern of nonidentity?

    a. Figure #1
    b. Figure #2
    c. Figure #3
    d. Figure #4

40. Which of the above figures demonstrates a reaction pattern showing two different antigenic molecular species?

    a. Figure #1
    b. Figure #2
    c. Figure #3
    d. Figure #4

41. A nonspecific precipitin reaction is demonstrated in:

    a. Figure #1
    b. Figure #2
    c. Figure #3
    d. Figure #4

42. A substrate is first exposed to patient's serum, then exposed to a fluorescent antihuman immunoglobulin. The procedure described is:

    a. fluorescent quenching
    b. direct fluorescence
    c. indirect fluorescence
    d. fluorescence inhibition

43. A series of eight tubes are set-up with 0.79 mL of diluent in each. A serial dilution is performed by adding 10 µL of serum to the first tube and then transferring 10 µL through each remaining tube. What is the serum dilution of tube 7?

    a. 1:2.431 x 10^{11}
    b. 1:2.621 x 10^{11}
    c. 1:1.920 x 10^{13}
    d. 1:2.097 x 10^{13}

44. Detection of which of the following substances is most useful to monitor the course of a patient with testicular cancer?

    a. alpha-fetoprotein
    b. carcinoembryonic antigen
    c. prolactin
    d. testosterone
    e. 17-ketosteroids

45. Increased concentrations of alpha-fetoprotein (AFP) in adults are most characteristically associated with:

    a. hepatocellular carcinoma
    b. alcoholic cirrhosis
    c. chronic active hepatitis
    d. multiple myeloma

46. The standard HCG tube immunoassay is:

    a. a hemagglutination-inhibition test
    b. an indirect latex test
    c. a complement fixation test
    d. an enzyme immunoassay

47. The minimum human chorionic gonadotropin level needed for a positive rapid indirect latex slide immunoassay test is:

    a. < 0.5 IU/mL
    b. 0.5-1.0 IU/mL
    c. 0.75-1.5 IU/mL
    d. 1.5-2.5 IU/mL

48. A false-positive test using the standard HCG tube immunoassay
    can be the result of:

    a. cross-reactivity between HCG and luteinizing hormone (LH)
    b. the binding of HCG to urine protein
    c. extended incubation time
    d. an HCG level of 1.0 IU/mL

49. A rapid indirect latex slide pregnancy test result was negative
    on a woman who on physical examination was thought to be
    pregnant. A possible reason for the negative test result is:

    a. urine glucose was increased
    b. the lack of agglutination was interpreted as a negative test
    c. the specific gravity of the urine was greater than 1.015
    d. the urine protein content was greater than 100 mg/dL

50. The more specific radioimmunoassay (RIA) procedure for serum
    HCG utilizes antisera against which subunit of HCG?

    a. alpha
    b. gamma
    c. chorionic
    d. beta

51. Which of the following is accurate 23-32 days from the last
    normal menstrual period?

    a. radioreceptor assay
    b. standard HCG tube immunoassay
    c. rapid indirect latex slide immunoassay
    d. radioimmunoassay

52. A serologic test for syphilis that depends upon the
    detection of cardiolipin-lecithin-cholesterol antigen is:

    a. FTA-ABS
    b. RPR
    c. MHA-TP
    d. TPI

53. The most important use of a nontreponemal antibody (NTA) test
    alone is in:

    a. establishing the diagnosis of acute active syphilis
    b. establishing the diagnosis of chronic syphilis
    c. evaluating the success of therapy
    d. determining the prevalence of disease in the general
       population

54. The serologic test for syphilis recommended for detecting antibody in cerebrospinal fluid is:

    a. nontreponemal antibody
    b. CSF-VDRL
    c. FTA-ABS
    d. MHA-TP

55. In direct fluorescent antibody screening for the diagnosis of primary syphilis, which of the following labels is used:

    a. antibody for the presence of spirochetes in the chancre
    b. antibody for the presence of spirochetes in the skin rash
    c. antigen for the presence of circulating antibodies
    d. antigen for the presence of antibodies in situ

56. In the FTA-ABS test, the presence of a beaded pattern of fluorescence along the treponeme indicates:

    a. positive identification of *Treponema pallidum*
    b. presumptive diagnosis of active syphilis
    c. presence of nontreponemal antibody (NTA)
    d. false-positive reaction

57. The FTA-ABS test for the serologic diagnosis of syphilis is:

    a. less sensitive and specific than the VDRL if properly performed
    b. likely to remain positive after adequate antibiotic therapy
    c. currently recommended for testing cerebrospinal fluid
    d. preferred over darkfield microscopy for diagnosing primary syphilis

58. In serologic tests for rubella using latex agglutination testing, rheumatoid factor has been shown to interfere giving erroneous results. To prevent this interference, the technician should remove:

    a. IgG by heating the serum
    b. IgM by heating the serum
    c. IgG by protein A adsorption
    d. IgM by gel filtration

59. The initial immune response following fetal infection with rubella is the production of:

    a. IgG antibody
    b. IgA antibody
    c. IgM antibody
    d. both IgG and IgA antibody

60. Within one week after exposure to rash illness, a maternal serum hemagglutination inhibition rubella titer that is equal to or greater than 1:8 indicates:

    a. immunity to rubella
    b. evidence of acute rubella infection
    c. susceptibility to rubella infection
    d. absence of acute rubella

61. A single and reliable screening test for detecting neonatal infection in the absence of clinical signs is:

    a. serum immunoelectrophoresis
    b. differential leukocyte count
    c. nitroblue tetrazolium (NBT) test
    d. quantitative serum IgM determination

62. Other hepatitis-causing viruses, such as cytomegalovirus and varicella-zoster virus, can be differentiated from HAV and HBV by:

    a. incubation period
    b. complement fixation
    c. immune electron microscopy
    d. tissue culture isolation

63. A 26-year-old nurse developed fatigue, a low-grade fever, polyarthralgias and urticaria. Two months earlier she had cared for a patient with hepatitis. Which of the following findings are likely to be observed in this nurse?

    a. a negative hepatitis B surface antigen test
    b. elevated AST and ALT activities
    c. a positive rheumatoid factor
    d. a positive Monospot™ test

64. The classic antibody response pattern following infection with hepatitis A is:

    a. increase in IgM antibody; decrease in IgM antibody; increase in IgG antibody
    b. detectable presence of IgG antibody only
    c. detectable presence of IgM antibody only
    d. decrease in IgM antibody; increase in IgG antibody of the IgG3 subtype

For questions 65 through 68, refer to the following illustration:

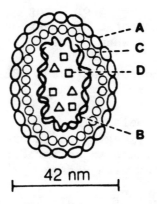

42 nm

65. Select the corresponding lettered component indicated on the diagram for surface antigen.

    a. A
    b. B
    c. C
    d. D

66. Select the corresponding lettered component indicated on the diagram for e antigen.

    a. A
    b. B
    c. C
    d. D

67. Select the corresponding lettered component indicated on the diagram for core antigen.

    a. A
    b. B
    c. C
    d. D

68. Select the corresponding lettered component indicated on the diagram for viral DNA.

    a. A
    b. B
    c. C
    d. D

69. The 20-nm spheres and filamentous structures of the HBV are:

   a. infectious
   b. circulating aggregates of HBcAg
   c. circulating aggregates of HBsAg
   d. highly infectious when present in great abundance

70. The enzyme-linked immunosorbent assay (ELISA) technique for the detection of HBsAg:

   a. requires radiolabeled Clq
   b. is quantitated by degree of fluorescence
   c. uses anti-HBs linked to horseradish peroxidase
   d. uses beads coated with HBsAg

71. Twelve weeks after onset of the disease, patients with uncomplicated acute hepatitis B usually will demonstrate which of the following in their serum?

   a. HBsAg
   b. HBe
   c. Anti-HBe
   d. Anti-HBs

72. The antigen marker most closely associated with transmissibility of HBV infection is:

   a. HBs
   b. HBe
   c. HBc
   d. HBV

73. Chronic carriers of HBV:

   a. have chronic symptoms of hepatitis
   b. continue to carry the HBV
   c. do not transmit infection
   d. carry the HBV but are not infectious

74. Patients who appear to be high risk for the development of chronic hepatitis are those who maintain high titers of antibody to the:

   a. core antigen
   b. surface antigen
   c. e antigen
   d. delta antigen

75. Hepatitis C (nonenteric form of non-A, non-B hepatitis) differs from hepatitis A and hepatitis B because it:

a. has a highly stable incubation period
b. is associated with a high incidence of icteric hepatitis
c. is associated with a high incidence of the chronic carrier state
d. is seldom implicated in cases of posttransfusion hepatitis

76. Which of the following causes 90% of posttransfusion hepatitis?

a. HAV
b. HBV
c. HCV
d. HDV

77. A benign monoclonal gammopathy:

a. usually is associated with a decrease in other immunoglobulins
b. occasionally is associated with radiographic bone lesions
c. occurs in approximately 10% of people over the age of 70
d. usually is of the IgM class

78. The enzyme control tube in an ASO hemolytic assay exhibits no cell lysis. What is the most likely explanation for this?

a. incorrect pH of buffer
b. low ionic strength buffer
c. oxidation of the enzyme
d. reduction of the enzyme

79. A false-negative cold agglutinin test may result if:

a. the specimen is centrifuged at room temperature
b. the cold agglutinin demonstrates anti-I specificity
c. the specimen is refrigerated prior to serum separation
d. adult human O red cells are used in the assay

80. Which is a recognized theory of the origin of autoimmunity?

a. sequestration of antigen
b. enhanced suppressor T cell function
c. diminished helper T cell activity
d. defects in the idiotype-anti-idiotype network
e. deficient B cell activation

81. In an autoimmune response, an individual makes:

    a. antigen to an autoantibody
    b. T cells to an autoantibody
    c. B cells to an autoantibody
    d. T cells to a self antigen

82. Rheumatoid factors are immunoglobulins with specificity for the:

    a. Fc fragment of IgG
    b. Fab fragment of IgG
    c. C3
    d. J chain of IgM
    e. secretory compound of IgA

83. Rheumatoid factor in a patient's serum may cause a false:

    a. positive test for the detection of IgM class antibodies
    b. negative test for the detection of IgM class antibodies
    c. positive test for the detection of IgG class antibodies
    d. negative test for the detection of IgG class antibodies

84. The Rose-Waaler test for rheumatoid factor utilizes:

    a. washed human erythrocytes
    b. sheep erythrocytes coated with human IgG
    c. latex particles coated with rabbit IgM
    d. sheep erythrocytes coated with rabbit IgG

85. The latex agglutination titer commonly considered as the lower limit of positivity for a diagnostic criterion of rheumatoid arthritis is:

    a. 1:2
    b. 1:40
    c. 1:160
    d. 1:640

86. Systemic lupus erythematosus patients often have which of the following test results?

    a. high titers of DNA antibody
    b. decreased serum immunoglobulin levels
    c. high titers of anti-smooth muscle antibodies
    d. high titers of anti-mitochondrial antibody

87. Active systemic lupus erythematosus patients often have which of the following test results?

    a. high titers of anti-microsomal antibodies
    b. high titers of anti-smooth muscle antibodies
    c. marked decrease in serum CH_{50}
    d. decreased serum immunoglobulin levels

88. Which of the following is <u>DECREASED</u> in serum during the active stages of systemic lupus erythematosus?

    a. antinuclear antibody
    b. immune complexes
    c. complement (C3)
    d. anti-DNA

89. A positive ANA with the pattern of anticentromere antibodies is most frequently seen in patients with:

    a. rheumatoid arthritis
    b. systemic lupus erythematosus
    c. CREST syndrome
    d. Felty's syndrome
    e. Sjögren's syndrome

90. Which of the following is an organ specific autoimmune disease?

    a. myasthenia gravis
    b. rheumatoid arthritis
    c. Addison's disease
    d. progressive systemic sclerosis

91. In chronic active hepatitis, titers greater than 1:100 of which of the following antibodies are seen?

    a. anti-mitochondrial
    b. anti-smooth muscle
    c. anti-DNA
    d. anti-parietal cell

92. In primary biliary cirrhosis, which of the following antibodies are seen in high titers?

    a. anti-mitochondrial
    b. anti-smooth muscle
    c. anti-DNA
    d. anti-parietal cell

93. High titers of anti-microsomal antibodies are most often found in:

   a. rheumatoid arthritis
   b. systemic lupus erythematosus
   c. chronic hepatitis
   d. thyroid disease

94. True statements about anti-thyroid antibodies include:

   a. They may be directed against thyroglobulin or microsomal antigens.
   b. Their titers are reliable in children with suspected thyroiditis.
   c. They are rarely present in patients with Grave's disease.
   d. They are rarely present in patients with parietal cell antibodies.

95. Anti-RNA antibodies are often present in individuals having an antinuclear antibody immunofluorescent pattern which is:

   a. speckled
   b. rim
   c. diffuse
   d. nucleolar

96. Anti-extractable nuclear antigens are most likely associated with which of the following antinuclear antibody immunofluorescent patterns?

   a. speckled
   b. rim
   c. diffuse
   d. nucleolar

97. In an antinuclear antibody indirect immunofluorescent test, a serum shows a positive, speckled pattern. Which would be the most appropriate additional test to perform?

   a. anti-mitochondrial antibody
   b. serum protein electrophoresis
   c. immunoglobulin quantitation
   d. screen for Sm and RNP antibodies
   e. anti-DNA antibody using *C.lucilliae*

98. In the indirect antinuclear antibody test, a homogenous pattern indicates the presence of antibody to:

    a. RNP
    b. Sm
    c. RNA
    d. DNA

99. In the indirect antinuclear antibody test, a speckled pattern indicates the presence of antibody to:

    a. histone
    b. Sm
    c. RNA
    d. DNA

100. In skin tests for allergy, a wheal and flare development is indicative of:

    a. immediate sensitivity
    b. delayed hypersensitivity
    c. anergy
    d. Arthus reaction

101. Which immunologic mechanism is usually involved in bronchial asthma?

    a. immediate hypersensitivity
    b. antibody mediated cytotoxicity
    c. immune complex
    d. delayed hypersensitivity

102. Antihistamines:

    a. stimulate IgE antibody production
    b. stimulate IgG blocking antibodies
    c. bind histamine
    d. block histamine receptors
    e. cause smooth muscle relaxation

103. When testing a patient for HIV antibody, which of the following is used to confirm a positive screening test?

    a. radioimmunoassay
    b. Western blot
    c. immunofluorescence
    d. ELISA

104. Which of the following forms of exposure places a technologist at the highest risk for infection with human immunodeficiency virus (HIV)?

    a. aerosol   (e.g., AIDS patient's sneeze)
    b. swallow   (e.g., mouth pipetting of positive serum)
    c. needlestick (e.g., from AIDS contaminated needle)
    d. splash   (e.g., infected serum spill onto intact skin)

105. The most prevalent job-related disease hazard in clinical laboratories is:

    a. tuberculosis
    b. hepatitis
    c. AIDS
    d. meningitis

The following items(*) have been identified as more appropriate for the entry level medical technologist.

*106. Which of the following statements about immunoglobulins is true?

    a. Immunoglobulins are produced by T lymphocytes.
    b. The IgA class is determined by the gamma heavy chain.
    c. The IgA class exists as serum and secretory molecules.
    d. There are two subclasses of IgG.

*107. Membrane bound immunoglobulin molecules:

    a. have an additional amino-terminal sequence of about 40 residues
    b. are not anchored in a transmembrane configuration
    c. are anchored by a hydrophobic sequence of about 26 residues
    d. form a membrane spanning double beta helix

*108. The key structural difference which distinguishes immuno-globulin subclasses is the:

    a. number of domains
    b. stereometry of the hypervariable region
    c. number and arrangement of interchain disulfide bridges
    d. covalent linkage of the light chains

*109. Bence Jones proteins are:

    a. immunoglobulin catabolic fragments in the urine
    b. monoclonal light chains synthesized *de novo*
    c. any light chains in the urine
    d. Fab fragments of a monoclonal protein

*110. The area of the immunoglobulin molecule referred to as the hinge region is located between which domains?

    a. VH and VL
    b. CH1 and CH2
    c. CH2 and CH3
    d. CH3 and VL

*111. Areas of the immunoglobulin molecule that are referred to as domains are:

    a. formed by intrachain disulfide bonds
    b. formed by interchain disulfide bonds
    c. used for classification of molecules
    d. insignificant

*112. Immunoglobulin idiotypic diversity is best explained by the
       theory of:

       a. somatic mutation
       b. germ line recombination
       c. antigen induction
       d. clonal selection

*113. Antibody idiotype is dictated by the:

       a. constant region of heavy chain
       b. constant region of light chain
       c. variable regions of heavy and light chains
       d. constant regions of heavy and light chains

*114. Antibody allotype is determined by:

       a. constant region of heavy chain
       b. constant region of light chain
       c. variable regions of heavy and light chains
       d. constant regions of heavy and light chains

*115. A patient's serum IgA as measured by radial immunodiffusion
       (RID) was 40 mg/dL. Another laboratory reported IgA absent.
       A possible explanation for this discrepancy is:

       a. rabbit antiserum was used in the RID plates
       b. the IgA has an Fc deletion
       c. the IgA antiserum has kappa specificity
       d. the serum has antibodies against a protein in the antiserum

*116. Which of the following are true statements about selective IgA
       deficiency?

       a. It is associated with a decreased incidence of allergic
          manifestations.
       b. There is a high concentration of secretory component in the
          saliva.
       c. It is associated with an increased incidence of autoimmune
          diseases
       d. It is found in approximately 1 out of every 50 persons.

*117. Monoclonal IgD proteins are unusual in that they are:

       a. mostly lambda type and associated with Bence Jones
          proteinuria
       b. mostly lambda type and rarely associated with Bence Jones
          proteinuria
       c. mostly kappa type and associated with Bence Jones
          proteinuria
       d. highly resistant to enzymatic fragmentation

*118. Goat anti-human IgG is a:

    a. monoclonal reagent that reacts with gamma heavy chains
    b. monoclonal reagent that reacts with light chains
    c. polyclonal reagent that reacts with gamma heavy chains
    d. polyclonal reagent that reacts with light chains

*119. Which IgG subclass is most efficient at crossing the placenta?

    a. IgG1
    b. IgG2
    c. IgG3
    d. Each is equally efficient

*120. The J-chain is associated with which of the following immunoglobulins?

    a. IgA
    b. IgG
    c. IgE
    d. IgD

*121. The serologic test that can be modified to selectively detect only specific IgM antibody in untreated serum is:

    a. complement fixation
    b. immunofluorescence/ELISA
    c. hemagglutination inhibition
    d. passive hemagglutination

*122. Which class of immunoglobulin is thought to function as an antigenic receptor site on the surface of immature B lymphocytes?

    a. IgD
    b. IgM
    c. IgA
    d. IgG

*123. The hyperviscosity syndrome is most likely to be seen in monoclonal disease involving which of the following immunoglobulin classes?

    a. IgA
    b. IgM
    c. IgG
    d. IgD

*124. The presence of immune complexes indicates:

    a. polyclonal hypergammaglobulinemia
    b. inflammatory tissue injury
    c. protection from complement-dependent neutrophil chemotaxis
    d. normal host response to antigenic exposure

*125. A procedure for the detection of circulating immune complexes in human sera uses Raji cells which are:

    a. thymic lymphocytes
    b. B cells from a patient with Burkitt's lymphoma
    c. peritoneal macrophages
    d. polymorphonuclear neutrophils

*126. The Raji cell line:

    a. has membrane receptors for C3b
    b. is used in an assay to measure insoluble immune complexes
    c. is a human T-type lymphoblastoid cell line
    d. has high affinity membrane receptors for IgG-Fc

*127. Initiation of the activation mechanism of the alternative complement pathway differs from that of the classical pathway in that:

    a. antigen-antibody complexes containing IgM or IgG are required
    b. endotoxin alone cannot initiate activation
    c. C1 component of complement is involved
    d. antigen-antibody complexes containing IgA or IgE may initiate activation

*128. Which of the following is cleaved as a result of activation of the classical complement pathway?

    a. properdin factor B
    b. C1q
    c. C4
    d. C3b

*129. The component associated only with the alternative pathway of complement activation is:

    a. C4
    b. C1q
    c. properdin factor B
    d. C3a

*130. Edema is most likely the result of the activation of which complement component?

    a. C1
    b. C1, 4
    c. "C2 kinin"
    d. C3a

*131. Which of the following complement components is a potent anaphylatoxin?

    a. C1
    b. C1, 4
    c. "C2 kinin"
    d. C3a

*132. Which of the following complement components is a viral neutralizer?

    a. C1
    b. C1, 4
    c. "C2 kinin"
    d. C3a

*133. Which of the following complement components is a weak chemotactic factor?

    a. C1
    b. C1, 4
    c. "C2 kinin"
    d. C3a

*134. The C3b component of complement:

    a. is undetectable in pathologic sera
    b. is a component of the C3 cleaving enzyme of the classical
       pathway
    c. is cleaved by C3 inactivator into C3c and C3d
    d. migrates farther toward the cathode than C3

*135. Which of the following is the major residual split portion of C3?

    a. C3a
    b. C3b
    c. C4
    d. Clq

*136. Which of the following activities is associated with C3b?

    a. opsonization
    b. weak anaphylatoxin
    c. vasoconstriction
    d. potent chemotactic factor

*137. Which of the following activities is associated with C3b?

    a. vasoconstriction
    b. lysis
    c. bone marrow neutrophil release
    d. macrophage migration inhibition factor

*138. Which of the following activities is associated with C5a?

    a. opsonization
    b. vasoconstriction
    c. potent chemotactic factor
    d. bone marrow neutrophil

*139. The biologic function of the C42 complex is:

    a. cytolysis
    b. to serve as a substrate of properdin factor B
    c. cleavage and activation of the C3 molecule
    d. formation and activation of the Cls molecule

*140. Components of the complement system most likely to coat a cell are:

   a. C1 and C2
   b. C3 and C4
   c. C6 and C7
   d. C8 and C9

*141. Hereditary angioedema is characterized by:

   a. decreased activity of C3
   b. decreased activity of C1 esterase inhibitor
   c. increased activity of C1 esterase inhibitor
   d. increased activity of C2

*142. Which of the following has been associated with patients who have homozygous C3 deficiency?

   a. undetectable hemolytic complement activity in the serum
   b. systemic lupus erythematosus
   c. no detectable disease
   d. a lifelong history of life-threatening infections

*143. Hereditary deficiency of early complement components C1, C4 and C2 is associated with:

   a. pneumococcal septicemia
   b. small bowel obstruction
   c. systemic lupus erythematosus
   d. gonococcemia

*144. Hereditary deficiency of late components of complements C5, C6, C7, or C8 can be associated with which of the following conditions?

   a. pneumococcal septicemia
   b. small bowel obstruction
   c. systemic lupus erythematosus
   d. gonococcemia

*145. In a complement fixation test, all reagent control tubes give the expected reactions. Both the unknown test and its serum control fail to hemolyze. What is the most likely explanation?

   a. old sheep red blood cells
   b. absence of antibody in the serum
   c. heat inactivated serum
   d. anticomplementary serum

*146. A transfusion reaction to erythrocyte antigens will activate which of the following immunopathologic mechanisms?

       a. reaginic sensitivity
       b. Arthus reaction
       c. delayed hypersensitivity
       d. complement-dependent antibody cytotoxicity

*147. For several months a 31-year-old woman has had migratory polyarthritis and a skin rash. Upon admission to the hospital, the following laboratory data were obtained:

	Patient	Normal
Leukocyte count	$4.7 \times 10^3/\mu L$	$5.0\text{-}10.0 \times 10^3/\mu L$
Differential	Normal	
Serum hemolytic complement	< 22 U	80-150 U
C3 (by RID)	117 U	96-148 U
C4 (by RID)	31 U	14-40 U

ANA: Positive in a homogenous pattern
Rheumatoid factor test: Negative
Urinalysis: Protein 1+, occasional RBC's

This patient's test results are consistent with:

       a. dermatomyositis
       b. C2 deficiency
       c. systemic lupus erythematosus
       d. mixed connective tissue disease

*148. A decreased ratio of synovial fluid complement to serum complement is most consistent with:

       a. pseudogout
       b. osteoarthritis
       c. rheumatoid arthritis
       d. lupus erythematosus

*149. The pathogenesis of common variable immunodeficiency is most likely due to:

       a. absence of B cells
       b. decreased helper activity
       c. increased suppressor cell activity
       d. inappropriate antigen presentation by macrophages

*150. Which of the following is the most common humoral immune deficiency disease?

   a. Bruton's agammaglobulinemia
   b. IgG deficiency
   c. selective IgA deficiency
   d. Wiskott-Aldrich syndrome

*151. Which of the following are true statements about Bruton's agammaglobulinemia?

   a. It is found only in females.
   b. There are normal numbers of circulating B cells.
   c. There are decreased to absent concentrations of immunoglobulins.
   d. The disease presents with pyogenic infections one week after birth.

*152. Infantile X-linked agammaglobulinemia is referred to as:

   a. Bruton's agammaglobulinemia
   b. DiGeorge's syndrome
   c. Swiss-type agammaglobulinemia
   d. ataxia telangiectasia

*153. Immunodeficiency with thrombocytopenia and eczema is often referred to as:

   a. DiGeorge's syndrome
   b. Bruton's agammaglobulinemia
   c. ataxia telangiectasia
   d. Wiskott-Aldrich syndrome

*154. Severe combined immunodeficiency disease is referred to as:

   a. Bruton's agammaglobulinemia
   b. Swiss-type agammaglobulinemia
   c. DiGeorge's syndrome
   d. Wiskott-Aldrich syndrome

*155. Combined immunodeficiency disease with loss of muscle coordination is referred to as:

   a. DiGeorge's syndrome
   b. Bruton's agammaglobulinemia
   c. ataxia telangiectasia
   d. Wiskott-Aldrich syndrome

*156. Patients suffering from Waldenström's macroglobulinemia demonstrate excessively increased concentrations of which of the following?

    a. IgG
    b. IgA
    c. IgM
    d. IgD

*157. Which of the following immunologic abnormalities is associated with a high incidence of amyloidosis?

    a. alpha chain disease
    b. gamma chain disease
    c. mu chain disease
    d. IgD myeloma

*158. Which of the following immunologic abnormalities is associated with malabsorption syndrome?

    a. alpha chain disease
    b. gamma chain disease
    c. IgD myeloma
    d. IgE myeloma

*159. Which of the following immunologic abnormalities is associated with lymphadenopathy and fever?

    a. mu chain disease
    b. gamma chain disease
    c. alpha chain disease
    d. IgE myeloma

*160. Which of the following immunologic abnormalities is most likely associated with chronic lymphocytic leukemia?

    a. IgE myeloma
    b. IgD myeloma
    c. mu chain disease
    d. gamma chain disease

For questions 161 and 162, refer to the following illustration:

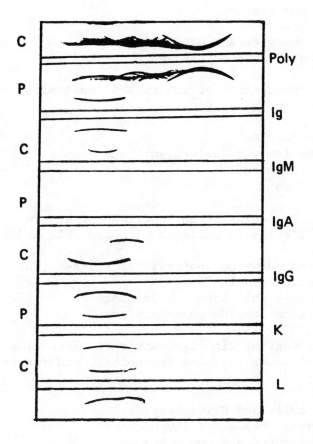

*161. The serum immunoelectrophoretic pattern shown above is most likely associated with which of the following?

        a. IgG lambda myeloma
        b. IgA kappa myeloma
        c. light chain myeloma, lambda type
        d. light chain myeloma, kappa type

*162. When the serum immunoelectrophoretic pattern has the findings depicted, appropriate studies should be performed to exclude:

        a. malignant lymphoma with monoclonal protein
        b. IgD and/or IgE myeloma
        c. heavy chain disease
        d. plasma cell leukemia

*163. C3 and Fc receptors are present on:

    a. B lymphocytes
    b. monocytes
    c. B lymphocytes and monocytes
    d. neither B lymphocytes and monocytes

*164. Immunologic enhancement of tumors and renal allografts is thought to be mediated by:

    a. T lymphocytes
    b. antibodies and antigen-antibody complexes
    c. B lymphocytes
    d. C3 and C5

*165. Which of the following is an important marker for the presence of immature T cells in patients with leukemia and lymphomas?

    a. terminal deoxynucleotidyl transferase (TdT)
    b. adenosine deaminase
    c. glucose-6-phosphate dehydrogenase
    d. purine nucleoside phosphorylase

*166. Cells from a patient with leukemic reticuloendotheliosis ("hairy cell" leukemia) have immunologic and functional features of:

    a. mast cells and B lymphocytes
    b. B lymphocytes and T lymphocytes
    c. granulocytes and monocytes
    d. B lymphocytes and monocytes

*167. T-cell lymphocytes that possess Fc receptors for aggregated IgM have been found to be specific for which of the following types of T cell functions?

    a. suppressor
    b. prosuppressor
    c. cytotoxic
    d. helper

*168. Which T-cell malignancy may retain "helper" activity with regard to immunoglobulin synthesis by B cells?

    a. Hodgkin's lymphoma
    b. acute lymphocytic leukemia (ALL)
    c. Sezary syndrome
    d. chronic lymphocytic leukemia (CLL)

*169. Failure of polymorphonuclear leukocytes to reduce nitroblue tetrazolium (NBT) following endotoxin stimulation is found in:

    a. rheumatoid arthritis
    b. *Staphylococcus aureus* septicemia
    c. DiGeorge's syndrome
    d. chronic granulomatous disease

*170. A patient demonstrating abnormal cerebriform lymphocytes which form rosettes with sheep red blood cells, and lacks C3 receptors or surface membrane markers most likely has:

    a. Hodgkin's disease
    b. acute lymphocytic leukemia
    c. chronic lymphocytic leukemia
    d. Sezary syndrome

*171. A patient's abnormal lymphocytes form rosettes with sheep red blood cells and lack C3 receptors and surface membrane immunoglobulin. This can be classified as a disorder of:

    a. T cells
    b. B cells
    c. monocytes
    d. null cells

*172. Immunologic surveillance of tumors is thought to be affected by:

    a. B lymphocytes and T lymphocytes
    b. B lymphocytes and macrophages
    c. T lymphocytes and macrophages
    d. macrophages and lymphokines

*173. What is the immunologic method utilized in the flow cytometer?

    a. latex agglutination
    b. enzyme linked immunoassay
    c. immunofluorescence
    d. radioimmunoassay

For questions 174 and 175, refer to the following data:

WBC $5.0 \times 10^3/\mu L$
Lymphs   15%
CD4   8%

*174. Calculate the absolute CD4 from the data given above.

    a. 40
    b. 60
    c. 400
    d. 750

*175. Which of the following is the correct interpretation of the above data?

    a. CD4% and absolute CD4 normal
    b. consistent with an intact immune system
    c. consistent with a viral infection such as HIV

---

*176. HLA typing of a family yields the following results:

	Locus A	Locus B
Father	(8, 12)	(17, 22)
Mother	(7, 12)	(13, 27)

On the basis of these genotypes, you would predict the possibility of ankylosing spondylitis in:

    a. 75% of their children
    b. 50% of their children
    c. 25% of their children
    d. female children only

*177. HLA-B8 antigen has been associated with which one of the following diseases?

    a. ankylosing spondylitis and myasthenia gravis
    b. celiac disease and ankylosing spondylitis
    c. myasthenia gravis and celiac disease
    d. Reiter's disease and multiple sclerosis

*178. The presence of HBsAg, anti-HBc and often HBeAg is characteristic of:

    a. early acute HBV hepatitis
    b. early convalescent phase HBV hepatitis
    c. recovery phase of acute HBV hepatitis
    d. carrier state of acute HBV hepatitis

*179. Refer to the following data:

	HB$_s$Ag	anti-HB$_c$ IgM	anti-HAV IgM
Patient #1	-	-	+
Patient #2	+	+	
Patient #3	-	+	

From the test results above, it can be concluded that Patient #3 has:

    a. recent acute hepatitis A
    b. acute hepatitis B
    c. acute hepatitis C (non-A/non-B hepatitis)
    d. chronic hepatitis B

*180. The disappearance of HBsAg and HBeAg, the persistence of anti-HBc, the appearance of anti-HBs and often of anti-HBe indicate:

    a. early acute HBV hepatitis
    b. early convalescent phase HBV hepatitis
    c. recovery phase of acute HBV hepatitis
    d. carrier state of acute HBV hepatitis

*181. True statements about the antibody response to infection with group A, beta-hemolytic streptococci include:

    a. 80% to 90% of patients with streptococcal pharyngitis who are treated will have significant rises (greater than two tubes) of antistreptolysin O (ASO) titers.
    b. The anti-DNase B titer is a less sensitive index of nephritogenic skin infection than the ASO titer.
    c. Rheumatic fever is more likely to be present in individuals who have strong antibody responses than in those who have weak responses.
    d. The anti-DNase B antibody titer is a more sensitive indicator than anti-group A specific carbohydrate titers for the detection of rheumatic fever.

*182. A 16-year-old boy with infectious mononucleosis has a cold agglutinin titer of 1:2000. An important consideration of this antibody's clinical relevance is the:

    a. thermal range
    b. titer at 4°C
    c. specificity
    d. light chain type

*183. Carcinoembryonic antigen (CEA) is most likely to be produced in a malignancy involving the:

    a. brain
    b. testes
    c. bone
    d. colon

*184. Which of the following infectious disease tests is important in evaluating AIDS patients?

    a. Group B streptococcal antigen latex agglutination
    b. *Cryptococcal* antigen latex agglutination
    c. *Cryptococcal* antibody ELISA
    d. *Borrelia burgdorferi* antibody ELISA

*185. What syphilis phenomenon has been observed in AIDS patients?

    a. rapid progression to tertiary syphilis
    b. treatment failure with penicillin
    c. high incidence of congenital syphilis

*186. Which of the following fungal agents is a frequent complication of AIDS?

    a. *Sporothrix* species
    b. *Blastomyces* species
    c. *Histoplasma* species
    d. *Trichophyton* species

*187. For a thorough evaluation of the possibility of *Toxoplasma* in the AIDS patient, which is the most appropriate specimen(s) for testing?

    a. CSF
    b. serum
    c. urine
    d. CSF and serum
    e. urine and serum

*188. Which of the following is a true statement about autoimmune diseases?

    a. They are associated with HLA-B and HLA-D antigens.
    b. They are B cell disorders.
    c. All autoimmune disorders are drug induced.
    d. Most autoimmune diseases are caused by viral infections.

*189. Which of the following lymphoproliferative disorders is often associated with autoimmune phenomenon and hypergamma-globulinemia?

   a. Burkitt's lymphoma
   b. immunoblastic lymphadenopathy
   c. acute lymphoblastic leukemia
   d. histiocytic lymphoma

*190. The rheumatoid factor in rheumatoid arthritis is which type of immunoglobulin?

   a. IgM
   b. IgA
   c. IgG
   d. IgE

*191. Tissue injury in systemic rheumatic disorders such as systemic lupus erythematosus is thought to be caused by:

   a. cytotoxic T cells
   b. IgE activity
   c. deposition of immune complexes
   d. cytolytic antibodies

*192. Anti-glomerular basement membrane antibody is most often associated with:

   a. systemic lupus erythematosus
   b. celiac disease
   c. chronic active hepatitis
   d. Goodpasture's disease

*193. A 25-year-old woman is seen by a physician because of Raynaud's phenomenon, myalgias, arthralgias and difficulty in swallowing. There is no evidence of renal disease. An ANA titer is 1:8,000 with a speckled pattern. Which of the following is also likely to be found in this patient?

   a. high level nDNA antibody and a low CH_{50} level
   b. high level Sm antibody
   c. high titer rheumatoid factor
   d. high level ribonucleoprotein (RNP) antibody

*194. In pernicious anemia, which of the following antibodies is detected?

   a. anti-mitochondrial
   b. anti-smooth muscle
   c. anti-DNA
   d. anti-parietal cell

*195.   Delayed hypersensitivity is related to:

        a. contact sensitivity to inorganic chemicals
        b. transfusion reaction
        c. anaphylactic reaction
        d. bacterial septicemia

*196.   Which of the following is used to detect allergen specific IgE?

        a. RIA
        b. IEP
        c. RAST
        d. CRP

*197.   A child has severe hay fever. A total IgE measurement was
        performed by the Ouchterlony immunodiffusion method. No lines
        of precipitation appeared on the immunodiffusion plate. The
        most likely explanation is:

        a. IgE antibodies are not produced in people who have hay fever
        b. antibody production is not adequately developed
        c. IgE is in too low a concentration to be detected by this
           method
        d. IgA is the antibody commonly produced in people with hay
           fever

Immunology Answer Key

1.	D	48.	A	95.	D	142.	D
2.	A	49.	B	96.	A	143.	C
3.	B	50.	D	97.	D	144.	D
4.	A	51.	D	98.	D	145.	D
5.	B	52.	B	99.	B	146.	D
6.	B	53.	C	100.	A	147.	B
7.	D	54.	B	101.	A	148.	C
8.	C	55.	A	102.	D	149.	C
9.	C	56.	D	103.	B	150.	C
10.	A	57.	B	104.	C	151.	C
11.	C	58.	D	105.	B	152.	A
12.	D	59.	C	106.	C	153.	D
13.	A	60.	A	107.	C	154.	B
14.	B	61.	D	108.	C	155.	C
15.	A	62.	D	109.	B	156.	C
16.	A	63.	B	110.	B	157.	D
17.	B	64.	A	111.	A	158.	A
18.	D	65.	A	112.	B	159.	B
19.	D	66.	D	113.	C	160.	C
20.	B	67.	C	114.	D	161.	C
21.	D	68.	B	115.	D	162.	B
22.	A	69.	B	116.	C	163.	C
23.	C	70.	C	117.	A	164.	B
24.	D	71.	D	118.	C	165.	A
25.	C	72.	B	119.	A	166.	D
26.	A	73.	B	120.	A	167.	D
27.	C	74.	D	121.	B	168.	C
28.	A	75.	C	122.	B	169.	D
29.	D	76.	C	123.	B	170.	D
30.	B	77.	C	124.	D	171.	A
31.	C	78.	C	125.	B	172.	C
32.	B	79.	C	126.	A	173.	C
33.	A	80.	D	127.	D	174.	B
34.	D	81.	D	128.	C	175.	C
35.	B	82.	A	129.	C	176.	C
36.	A	83.	A	130.	C	177.	C
37.	D	84.	D	131.	D	178.	A
38.	A	85.	C	132.	B	179.	B
39.	B	86.	A	133.	D	180.	C
40.	C	87.	C	134.	C	181.	C
41.	D	88.	C	135.	B	182.	A
42.	C	89.	C	136.	A	183.	D
43.	D	90.	C	137.	C	184.	B
44.	A	91.	B	138.	C	185.	A
45.	A	92.	A	139.	C	186.	C
46.	A	93.	D	140.	B	187.	D
47.	D	94.	A	141.	B	188.	A

Immunology Answer Key (continued)

189. B	192. D	194. D	196. C
190. A	193. D	195. A	197. C
191. C			

CHAPTER 16

Microbiology

The following items have been identified as appropriate for both entry level medical technologists and medical laboratory technicians.

1. Which of the following is the most appropriate method for collecting a urine specimen from a patient with an indwelling catheter?

    a. remove the catheter, cut the tip, and submit it for culture
    b. disconnect the catheter from the bag, and collect urine from the terminal end of the catheter
    c. collect urine directly from the bag
    d. aspirate urine aseptically from the catheter tubing

2. Which one of the following specimen requests is acceptable?

    a. feces submitted for anaerobic culture
    b. foley catheter tip submitted for aerobic culture
    c. rectal swab submitted for direct smear for gonococci
    d. urine for culture of acid-fast bacilli

3. Which of the following groups of specimens would be acceptable for anaerobic culture?

    a. vaginal, eye
    b. ear, nose
    c. pleural fluid, brain abscess
    d. urine, sputum

4. A liquid fecal specimen from a three-month-old infant is submitted for microbiologic examination. In addition to culture on routine media for *Salmonella* and *Shigella*, this specimen routinely should be:

    a. examined for the presence of *Entamoeba hartmanni*
    b. examined for the presence of *Campylobacter* sp.
    c. screened for the detection of enterotoxigenic *Escherichia coli*
    d. placed in thioglycollate broth to detect *Clostridium botulinum*

5. An aspirate of a deep wound was plated on blood agar plates aerobically and anaerobically. At 24 hours there was growth on the anaerobic plate only. The next step in the evaluation of this culture is to:

    a. reincubate for another 24 hours
    b. begin organism identification
    c. issue the final report
    d. set up a Bauer-Kirby sensitivity

6. A cerebrospinal fluid is submitted for Gram stain and culture. The physician also requests that an aliquot of spinal fluid be saved for possible direct antigen screen. The microbiology laboratory is closing in five minutes. The technologist should:

    a. inoculate culture, perform a Gram stain and refrigerate remaining specimen at 4°C
    b. inoculate culture, perform a Gram stain and incubate remaining specimen at 36°C
    c. incubate entire specimen at 36°C, perform culture and Gram stain the next day
    d. refrigerate entire specimen, perform culture and Gram stain the next day

7. Cerebrospinal fluid from a febrile 25-year-old man with possible meningitis is rushed to the laboratory for a stat Gram stain and culture. While performing the Gram stain, the technologist accidentally spills most of the specimen. The smear shows many neutrophils and no microorganisms. Since there is only enough specimen to inoculate one plate, the technologist should use a:

    a. blood agar plate
    b. chopped meat glucose
    c. chocolate agar plate
    d. Thayer-Martin plate

8. A cerebrospinal fluid has been inoculated onto sheep blood and chocolate agar plates and into a tube of trypticase soy broth. All media were incubated in an atmosphere of 5% CO_2. Which of the following organisms would usually be isolated by this procedure?

    a. *Francisella tularensis*
    b. *Haemophilus influenzae*
    c. *Bordetella pertussis*
    d. *Bacteroides fragilis*

9. A catheterized urine specimen from a 82-year-old woman with recurrent infections is submitted for culture. The Gram stain reveals:

> Many WBCs
> Many pleomorphic gram-negative rods
> Many gram-positive cocci in chains
> Few gram-positive rods

The physician requests that sensitivities be performed on all pathogens isolated. In addition to the sheep blood agar and EMB plates routinely used for urine cultures, the technologist should also inoculate a(n):

   a. CNA agar plate
   b. chocolate agar plate
   c. XLD agar plate
   d. chopped meat glucose

10. Which of the following is the most appropriate specimen source and primary media battery combination?

   a. endocervical - chocolate, Thayer-Martin
   b. sputum - sheep blood, Thayer-Martin, KV-laked blood
   c. CSF - Columbia CNA, MacConkey
   d. urine - sheep blood, chocolate, Columbia CNA

11. Which of the following is the most appropriate organism and media combination?

   a. *Legionella* species - Mueller Hinton
   b. *Clostridium difficile* - Phenylethyl alcohol (PEA)
   c. *Campylobacter* species - charcoal yeast extract
   d. *Yersinia enterocolitica* - cefsulodin-irgasan-novobiocin (CIN)

12. A Gram stain from a swab of a hand wound reveals:

> Moderate gram-positive cocci in chains
> Moderate large gram-negative bacilli

Select the appropriate media which will selectively isolate each organism.

   a. KV-laked agar, Thayer-Martin
   b. sheep blood, MacConkey
   c. Columbia CNA, chocolate
   d. Columbia CNA, MacConkey

13. The organism most commonly associated with neonatal purulent meningitis is:

    a. *Neisseria meningitidis*
    b. *Streptococcus pneumoniae*
    c. group B streptococci
    d. *Haemophilus influenzae*

14. An important cause of acute exudative pharyngitis is:

    a. *Staphylococcus aureus* (beta-hemolytic)
    b. *Streptococcus pneumoniae*
    c. *Streptococcus agalactiae*
    d. *Streptococcus pyogenes*

15. Which of the following would you LEAST expect to culture from a case of otitis media?

    a. *Moraxella (Branhamella) catarrhalis*
    b. *Neisseria meningitidis*
    c. *Haemophilus influenzae*
    d. *Streptococcus pneumoniae*

16. Of the following bacteria, the most frequent cause of prosthetic heart valve infections occurring within two to three months after surgery is:

    a. *Streptococcus pneumoniae*
    b. *Streptococcus pyogenes*
    c. *Staphylococcus aureus*
    d. *Staphylococcus epidermidis*

17. The bacterium most often responsible for acute epiglottitis is:

    a. *Bordetella pertussis*
    b. *Haemophilus influenzae*
    c. *Haemophilus aphrophilus*
    d. Group A beta-hemolytic streptococcus

18. Because ultraviolet light is used to decontaminate the work surface inside a biological safety cabinet, the lamp should be replaced when the intensity compared to the original output reading differs by:

    a. 10%
    b. 20%
    c. 30%
    d. 40%

19. Nonmetallic surfaces contaminated with blood should be disinfected with:

    a. a phenol solution
    b. 5% bleach (sodium hypochlorite)
    c. 70% isopropyl alcohol
    d. green soap

20. Which of the following substances can be used to inactivate HIV and HBV on equipment/instrument parts for which bleach is corrosive?

    a. phenol
    b. formaldehyde
    c. hydrogen peroxide
    d. iodine

21. Used needles from blood collection should be:

    a. recapped and placed in a biohazard bag
    b. placed in a biohazard bag and autoclaved
    c. placed in a biohazard bag with bleach
    d. placed in a puncture-proof container

22. Aerosol-associated laboratory infections:

    a. largely occur in untrained laboratory helpers
    b. usually cause clinical disease with an organism of low infectivity
    c. have been associated with improper laboratory air venting
    d. can occur from an accidental needle puncture wound

23. The prevention of aerosols:

    a. involves the use of spray disinfectant applied on work surfaces
    b. involves initial plating within a single-pass laminar airflow cabinet
    c. requires the use of plastic autoclavable bags
    d. can be minimized by the use of formaldehyde gas decontamination

24. Lab workers should always work under a biological safety hood when working with cultures of:

    a. *Streptococcus pyogenes*
    b. *Staphylococcus aureus*
    c. *Candida albicans*
    d. *Coccidioides immitis*

25. Upon review of a sputum Gram stain, the technician notes that the nuclei of all of the neutrophils present in the smear are staining dark blue. The best explanation for this finding is:

   a. the slide was inadequately decolorized with acetone/ alcohol
   b. the sputum smear was prepared too thin
   c. the cellular components have stained as expected
   d. the iodine was omitted from the staining procedure

26. The Gram stain procedure in the Policies and Procedures Manual calls for acetone-alcohol decolorization for 2 minutes. The best course of action for a newly employed technologist should be to:

   a. perform the stain according to the manual's directions
   b. perform the stain according to the manufacturer's directions
   c. ask the supervisor if this is indeed the timing to be followed
   d. change the timing in the manual and initial the change with the date

27. Which of the following results would you expect if motility agar was made with a 1% agar concentration?

   a. false-negative for *Acinetobacter lwoffii*
   b. false-positive for *Alcaligenes faecalis*
   c. false-positive for *Moraxella osloensis*
   d. false-negative for *Pseudomonas aeruginosa*

28. The Schick test allows for:

   a. detection of *Clostridium tetani* toxin
   b. identification of *Bacillus anthracis*
   c. detection of circulating antitoxin to *Corynebacterium diphtheriae*
   d. detection of immunity to *Streptococcus pyogenes*

29. The reverse CAMP test, lecithinase production, double zone hemolysis, and Gram stain morphology are all useful criteria in the identification of:

   a. *Clostridium perfringens*
   b. *Streptococcus agalactiae*
   c. *Streptococcus pyogenes*
   d. *Clostridium tetani*

30. Coagglutination is associated with:

    a. *Chlamydia trachomatis*
    b. *Neisseria gonorrhoeae*
    c. *Streptococcus pneumoniae*
    d. *Klebsiella pneumoniae*

31. When performing a Kovac's Indole Test, the substrate must contain:

    a. indole
    b. tryptophane
    c. ornithine
    d. paradimethylaminobenzaldehyde

32. The ONPG test allows organisms to be classified as a lactose fermenter by testing for which of the following:

    a. permease
    b. beta-galactosidase
    c. beta-lactamase
    d. phosphatase

33. Sodium bicarbonate + sodium citrate are a component of which of the following?

    a. JEMBEC system
    b. MTM agar
    c. NYC medium
    d. ML agar

34. Chocolate agar base containing vancomycin, colistin, nystatin, and trimethoprim is also known as:

    a. EMB agar
    b. modified Thayer-Martin agar
    c. Columbia CNA agar
    d. KV-laked agar

35. A medium which is used for primary isolation and enhances the growth of a particular organism is called:

    a. enrichment
    b. simple
    c. differential
    d. nutrient

36. SPS is used as an anticoagulant for blood cultures because it:

    a. inactivates penicillin and cephalosporins
    b. prevents clumping of red cells
    c. is anticomplementary and antiphagocytic
    d. facilitates growth of anaerobes

37. Thioglycollate broth is stored at room temperature and in the dark so that:

    a. ureases are not formed
    b. the cysteine is not decomposed
    c. sunlight does not hydrolyze the glucose in the medium
    d. there is a decreased absorption of oxygen by the medium

38. The stock cultures needed for quality control testing of motility are:

    a. *Salmonella typhimurium/Escherichia coli*
    b. *Escherichia coli/Pseudomonas aeruginosa*
    c. *Serratia marcescens/Escherichia coli*
    d. *Klebsiella pneumoniae/Escherichia coli*

39. The stock cultures needed for quality control testing of oxidase production are:

    a. *Escherichia coli/Klebsiella pneumoniae*
    b. *Salmonella typhimurium/Escherichia coli*
    c. *Escherichia coli/Pseudomonas aeruginosa*
    d. *Proteus mirabilis/Escherichia coli*

40. The stock cultures needed for quality control testing of deamination activity are:

    a. *Escherichia coli/Klebsiella pneumoniae*
    b. *Salmonella typhimurium/Escherichia coli*
    c. *Escherichia coli/Pseudomonas aeruginosa*
    d. *Proteus mirabilis/Escherichia coli*

41. The stock cultures needed for quality control testing deoxyribonuclease (DNase) production are:

    a. *Salmonella typhimurium/Escherichia coli*
    b. *Escherichia coli/Pseudomonas aeruginosa*
    c. *Proteus mirabilis/Escherichia coli*
    d. *Serratia marcescens/Escherichia coli*

42. Which one of the following combinations of organisms would be appropriate as controls to test the functions listed?

   a. beta-hemolysis---*Escherichia coli* and *Streptococcus pyogenes*
   b. catalase---*Staphylococcus aureus* and *Staphylococcus epidermidis*
   c. hydrogen sulfide production---*Proteus mirabilis* and *Salmonella typhi*
   d. indole---*Escherichia coli* and *Proteus mirabilis*

43. A characteristic helpful in separating *Pseudomonas aeruginosa* from other members of the *Pseudomonas* family is:

   a. a positive test for cytochrome oxidase
   b. oxidative metabolism in the O/F test
   c. production of fluorescein pigment
   d. production of pyocyanin pigment

44. Which of the following gram-negative bacilli ferments carbohydrates?

   a. *Alcaligenes faecalis*
   b. *Pseudomonas cepacia*
   c. *Acinetobacter lwoffii*
   d. *Yersinia enterocolitica*

45. Most of the automated microbiology equipment currently available has been designed to replace:

   a. manual susceptibility procedures
   b. manual methods that are infrequently performed but are time consuming
   c. repetitive manual methods that are performed daily on a large number of specimens
   d. all manual methods used in the clinical microbiology laboratory

46. When combined antimicrobial drugs are clearly less effective than the most active drug alone, the condition is described as:

   a. minimal inhibitory concentration
   b. synergism
   c. minimum bacteriocidal concentration
   d. antagonism

47. If the effect of combined antimicrobials is greater than the sum of the effects observed with the two drugs independently, the condition is described as:

   a. indifference of additive
   b. inhibition
   c. synergism
   d. antagonism

48. The smallest concentration of antimicrobial agent which prevents growth in subculture or results in a 99.9% decrease of the initial inoculum, is the definition of:

   a. minimum bacteriocidal concentration
   b. indifference of additive
   c. minimal inhibitory concentration
   d. synergism

49. The amount of test antimicrobial that will inhibit visible growth of a microbe, is the definition of:

   a. synergism
   b. minimal inhibitory concentration
   c. indifference of additive
   d. minimum bacteriocidal concentration

50. One advantage of the antimicrobial dilution tests is that:

   a. it is based on a predetermined breakpoint
   b. contamination can be detected easily
   c. it provides categorical reports
   d. it can detect varying degrees of organism sensitivity and resistance

51. Which of the following is the most likely cause of a sharp increase in the minimum inhibitory concentration (MIC) of a quality control organism to ampicillin?

   a. increase in the inoculum size from 10^5 to 10^6 organisms per mL
   b. mutation of the organism to a more resistant strain
   c. increased incubation time from 14 to 18 hours
   d. instability of the antibiotic during incubation

52. Which of the two different antimicrobial agents listed below are commonly used and may result in synergistic action in the treatment of endocarditis caused by *Enterococcus faecalis*?

   a. an aminoglycoside and a macrolide
   b. a penicillin derivative and an aminoglycoside
   c. a cell membrane active agent and nalidixic acid
   d. a macrolide and a penicillin derivative

53. In a disk diffusion susceptibility test, which of the following can result if disks are placed on the inoculated media and left at room temperature for an hour before incubation?

   a. the antibiotic would not diffuse into the medium, resulting in no zone
   b. zones of smaller diameter would result
   c. zones of larger diameter would result
   d. there would be no effect on the final zone diameter

54. Which of the following factors would make an organism appear to be more resistant on a disk diffusion susceptibility test?

   a. too little agar in the plate
   b. too many organisms in the inoculum
   c. the presence of 0.5% NaCl in the medium
   d. a medium with a pH of 7.4

55. First-generation cephalosporins can be adequately represented by:

   a. streptomycin
   b. chloramphenicol
   c. cephalothin
   d. colistin

56. Microorganisms resembling L-forms have been isolated from the blood of patients treated with antibiotics that:

   a. complex with flagellar protein
   b. interfere with cell membrane function
   c. inhibit protein synthesis
   d. interfere with cell wall synthesis

57. An antibiotic that inhibits cell wall synthesis is:

   a. chloramphenicol
   b. penicillin
   c. sulfonamide
   d. colistin

58. Clinical resistance to penicillin dosages appears to correlate with beta-lactamase production in:

    a. *Neisseria gonorrhoeae*
    b. *Neisseria meningitidis*
    c. *Streptococcus agalactiae*
    d. *Streptococcus pyogenes*

59. Which one of the following organisms does not require susceptibility testing when isolated from a clinically significant source?

    a. *Staphylococcus aureus*
    b. *Proteus mirabilis*
    c. Group A streptococcus
    d. *Escherichia coli*

60. Antibiotics which are tested for isolates of *Pseudomonas* species include:

    a. penicillin
    b. erythromycin
    c. clindamycin
    d. gentamicin

61. Which of the following is a true statement about collection of a stool specimen for suspected enteric disease?

    a. Rectal swabs are equally as good as freshly passed stools.
    b. Rectal swabs are very useful in surveying convalescent patients or screening for carriers.
    c. Stool specimens should be collected early in the course of the disease before antibiotics are administered.
    d. If the specimen cannot be cultured immediately, it should be placed in a suitable transport medium such as buffered glycerol-saline (pH 6.0).

62. Which of the following organisms must be incubated in a microaerophilic environment for optimal recovery of the organism?

    a. *Campylobacter fetus* subspecies *fetus*
    b. *Escherichia coli*
    c. *Pseudomonas aeruginosa*
    d. *Proteus mirabilis*

63. A culture from a CSF specimen grows gray, mucoid, stringy colonies on sheep blood. The isolate grows readily on MacConkey agar and forms mucoid, dark pink colonies. The colonies yield the following test results:

    ONPG: positive
    Indole: negative
    Glucose: positive
    Oxidase: negative
    Citrate: positive
    VP: positive

The organism is most likely:

    a. *Edwardsiella tarda*
    b. *Klebsiella pneumoniae*
    c. *Escherichia coli*
    d. *Proteus vulgaris*

64. An organism was inoculated into a TSI tube and gave the following reactions:

    alkaline slant/acid butt, H_2S, gas produced

This organism most likely is:

    a. *Klebsiella pneumoniae*
    b. *Shigella dysenteriae*
    c. *Salmonella typhimurium*
    d. *Escherichia coli*

65. An isolate from a stool culture gives the following growth characteristics and biochemical reactions:

    MacConkey agar: colorless colonies
    Hektoen agar: yellow-orange colonies
    TSI: acid slant/acid butt, no gas, no H_2S
    Urea: positive

These screening reactions are consistent with which of the following enteric pathogens?

    a. *Yersinia enterocolitica*
    b. *Shigella sonnei*
    c. *Vibrio parahaemolyticus*
    d. *Campylobacter jejuni*

66. An organism was inoculated into a TSI tube and gave the following reactions:

acid slant/acid butt, no H_2S, gas produced

This organism most likely is:

a. Klebsiella pneumoniae
b. Shigella dysenteriae
c. Salmonella typhimurium
d. Salmonella typhi

67. The epidemiologic investigation of a possible *Salmonella typhimurium* outbreak includes the documentation of single strain identity by:

a. bacteriocin typing
b. biotyping
c. phage typing
d. serologic typing

68. Diagnosis of typhoid fever during the first two days of illness can be confirmed best by:

a. stool culture
b. urine culture
c. blood culture
d. demonstration of antibodies against O antigen in the patient's serum

69. True statements about *Salmonella typhi* include:

a. It does not invade the bloodstream.
b. It can be recovered easily from stool during the early stages of typhoid fever.
c. It produces copious gas from glucose.
d. It can be recovered from bile.

70. *Vibrio parahaemolyticus* can be isolated best from feces on:

a. eosin methylene blue (EMB) agar
b. Hektoen enteric (HE) agar
c. Salmonella Shigella (SS) agar
d. thiosulfate citrate bile salts (TCBS) agar

71. Which of the following organisms can grow in the small bowel and cause diarrhea in children, traveler's diarrhea, or a severe cholera-like syndrome through the production of enterotoxins?

    a. *Yersinia enterocolitica*
    b. *Escherichia coli*
    c. *Salmonella typhi*
    d. *Shigella dysenteriae*

72. One of the enterotoxins produced by enterotoxigenic *Escherichia coli* in traveler's diarrhea is similar to a toxin produced by:

    a. *Clostridium perfringens*
    b. *Clostridium difficile*
    c. *Vibrio cholerae*
    d. *Yersinia enterocolitica*

73. Shigella species characteristically are:

    a. urease positive
    b. non-motile
    c. oxidase positive
    d. lactose fermenters

74. A gram-negative rod has been isolated from feces, and the confirmed biochemical reactions fit those of *Shigella*. The organism does not agglutinate in *Shigella antisera*. What should be done next?

    a. test the organism with a new lot of antisera
    b. test with Vi antigen
    c. repeat the biochemical tests
    d. boil the organism and retest with the antisera

75. Biochemical reactions of an organism are consistent with *Shigella*. A suspension is tested in polyvalent antiserum without resulting agglutination. However, after 15 minutes of boiling, agglutination occurs in polyvalent and group D antisera. This indicates that the:

    a. organism contains a blocking O antigen
    b. antiserum is of low potency
    c. organism possesses capsular antigens
    d. antiserum is of low specificity

76. A *Campylobacter* species isolated from a stool culture gives the following biochemical reactions:

   Nalidixic acid   - susceptible
   Cephalothin   - resistant
   Hippurate hydrolysis - positive
   Oxidase   - positive
   Catalase   - positive

   This biochemical profile is consistent with:

   a. *Campylobacter fetus* subspecies *fetus*
   b. *Campylobacter jejuni*
   c. *Campylobacter coli*
   d. *Campylobacter laridis*

77. Which one of the following results is typical of *Campylobacter jejuni*:

   a. optimal growth at 42°C
   b. oxidase negative
   c. catalase negative
   d. nonmotile

78. A *Campylobacter* species has been isolated from a blood culture. The organism is susceptible to nalidixic acid and resistant to cephalothin. Which of the following tests would aid in the differentiation between *Campylobacter jejuni* and *Campylobacter coli*?

   a. raffinose fermentation
   b. hippurate hydrolysis
   c. optochin susceptibility
   d. 5% NaCl tolerance

79. Optimum growth of *Campylobacter jejuni* is obtained on suitable media incubated at 42°C in an atmosphere containing:

   a. 6% O_2, 10-15% CO_2, 85-90% nitrogen
   b. 10% H_2, 5% CO_2, 85% nitrogen
   c. 10% H_2, 10% CO_2, 80% nitrogen
   d. 25% O_2, 5% CO_2, 70% nitrogen

80. Which of the following media is routinely used to culture *Campylobacter jejuni*?

   a. Skirrow's medium
   b. CIN agar
   c. anaerobic CNA agar
   d. bismuth sulfate

81. Greater than 100,000 col/mL of a gram-negative bacilli were isolated on MacConkey from a urine specimen. Biochemical results are as follows:

> Glucose: acid, gas produced
> Indole: negative
> Urea: positive
> TDA: positive
> H$_2$S: positive

The organism is most likely:

   a. *Morganella morganii*
   b. *Proteus mirabilis*
   c. *Proteus vulgaris*
   d. *Providencia stuartii*

82. A urine culture had the following culture results:

> Sheep blood: swarming
> Columbia CNA: no growth
> MacConkey: 1. >100,000 col/mL nonlactose-fermenter
> 2. >100,000 col/mL magenta, nonlactose-fermenter

The isolates from MacConkey agar had the following biochemical reactions:

	Isolate 1	Isolate 2
Glucose	positive	positive
Urea	positive	negative
TDA	positive	negative
H$_2$S	positive	negative

The organisms are most likely:

   a. *Proteus vulgaris* and *Enterobacter cloacae*
   b. *Proteus mirabilis* and *Serratia marcescens*
   c. *Morganella morganii* and *Klebsiella pneumoniae*
   d. *Providencia stuartii* and *Serratia liquefaciens*

83. A gram-negative bacillus was isolated on a chocolate agar plate but not on a sheep blood agar plate after overnight incubation. Which laboratory test result would be MOST useful in speciation of the organism?

   a. negative porphyrin
   b. positive oxidase
   c. positive ornithine
   d. negative indole

84. A positive porphyrin production test indicates that the organism:

    a. requires both X and V factors
    b. requires X factor
    c. does not require X factor
    d. requires V factor

85. The porphyrin test was devised to detect strains of *Haemophilus* capable of:

    a. ampicillin degradation
    b. capsule production
    c. synthesis of porphobilinogen
    d. chloramphenicol resistance

86. *Haemophilus influenzae* is most likely considered normal indigenous flora in the:

    a. oropharynx
    b. female genital tract
    c. large intestine
    d. small intestine

87. *Haemophilus influenzae* becomes resistant to ampicillin when the organism produces a(n):

    a. capsule of polysaccharide material
    b. affinity for the beta-lactam ring of the ampicillin
    c. requirement for hemin
    d. beta-lactamase

88. A small gram-negative rod isolated from an eye culture has the following test results:

X Factor requirement	Yes
V Factor requirement	Yes
Hemolysis on rabbit blood agar	No

    This organism is most probably *Haemophilus*:

    a. *influenzae*
    b. *parainfluenzae*
    c. *haemolyticus*
    d. *parahaemolyticus*

89. Tests for beta-lactamase production in *Haemophilus influenzae*:

   a. are not commercially available
   b. include tests that measure a change to an alkaline pH
   c. should be performed on all blood and CSF isolates
   d. are not valid for any other bacterial species

90. An isolate on chocolate agar from a patient with epiglottitis was suggestive of *Haemophilus* species. Additional testing showed that the isolate required NAD for growth and was nonhemolytic. The organism is most likely *Haemophilus*:

   a. *haemolyticus*
   b. *ducreyi*
   c. *influenzae*
   d. *parainfluenzae*

91. Media used to support growth of *Legionella pneumophila* should contain which of the following additives?

   a. X and V factors
   b. hemin and vitamin K
   c. charcoal and yeast extract
   d. dextrose and laked blood

92. The best medium for culture of *Bordetella pertussis* is:

   a. Bordet-Gengou
   b. cystine blood agar
   c. Thayer-Martin medium
   d. Loeffler's medium

93. The best medium for culture of *Francisella tularensis* is:

   a. Bordet-Gengou
   b. cystine blood agar
   c. Loeffler's medium
   d. Lowenstein-Jensen's

94. The most rapid and specific method for detection of *Francisella tularensis* is:

   a. serological slide agglutination utilizing specific antiserum
   b. dye stained clinical specimens
   c. fluorescent antibody staining techniques on clinical specimens
   d. biotyping

95. Relapsing fever in humans is caused by:

 a. *Borrelia recurrentis*
 b. *Brucella abortus*
 c. *Leptospira interrogans*
 d. *Spirillum minor*

96. When a *Brucella* species is suspected in a blood culture, the bottle should be held for a minimum of:

 a. 5 days
 b. 7 days
 c. 14 days
 d. 21 days

97. Patient specimens are being tested for *Brucella* antibody. Which course of action is most appropriate when the control serum displays a titer which is fourfold lower than expected?

 a. The results should be reported; this represents expected variability.
 b. The results should not be reported; the test should be repeated on the original and a new control.
 c. The results should be corrected by reporting titers fourfold higher than observed values.
 d. The results should be reported as: results questionable, please repeat.

98. Humans commonly acquire leptospirosis by:

 a. ingestion of contaminated milk
 b. ingestion of contaminated salads
 c. inhalation of aerosol droplets from another person
 d. penetration through skin abrasions

99. Cotton swabs submitted for culture of gonococci should be plated onto culture medium:

 a. immediately
 b. within 2 hours
 c. within 4 hours
 d. within 24 hours

100. All species of the genus *Neisseria* have the enzyme to oxidize:

 a. naphthylamine
 b. dimethylaminobenzaldehyde
 c. glucopyranoside
 d. tetramethyl-phenylenediamine

101. The diagnosis of *Neisseria gonorrhoeae* in females is best made from:

    a. a single cervical culture
    b. cervical and anal cultures
    c. a Gram stain of cervical secretions
    d. vaginal and cervical cultures

102. A vaginal smear is submitted for a Gram stain for *Neisseria gonorrhoeae*. The technologist finds the following results on the Gram stain:

    Many white blood cells
    Few epithelial cells
    Many gram-positive rods
    Few gram-negative diplococci
    Few gram-positive cocci in chains

    The technologist should:

    a. report out smear positive for gonorrhea
    b. report out smear negative for gonorrhea
    c. request a new specimen due to number of white blood cells
    d. report out smear as unacceptable for gonorrhea screen

103. Which of the following is the most reliable test to differentiate *Neisseria lactamica* from *Neisseria meningitidis*?

    a. acid from maltose
    b. growth on modified Thayer-Martin
    c. lactose degradation
    d. nitrite reduction to nitrogen gas

104. When using cystine-trypticase agar (CTA) for carbohydrate tests of *Neisseria* species, one should not:

    a. use a heavy inoculum
    b. use reagent grade carbohydrates
    c. work with pure subcultures
    d. store inoculated media in a CO_2 incubator

105. Definitive identification of *Neisseria gonorrhoeae* is made with the:

    a. Gram stain
    b. oxidase test
    c. degradation of amino acid
    d. hydrolysis of carbohydrates

106. A gram-negative diplococcus that grows on modified Thayer-Martin medium can be further confirmed as *Neisseria gonorrhoeae* if it is:

   a. oxidase positive, glucose positive, and maltose positive
   b. oxidase positive and glucose positive, maltose negative
   c. oxidase positive and maltose positive, glucose negative
   d. glucose positive, oxidase negative and maltose negative

107. An organism previously thought to be nonpathogenic, Moraxella (Branhamella) catarrhalis, is now known to be associated with infection and nosocomial transmission. Characteristic identification criteria include:

   a. oxidase negative
   b. carbohydrates negative
   c. beta-lactamase negative
   d. Gram stain: gram-negative bacilli

108. A catheterized urine is inoculated onto blood and MacConkey agar using a 0.01 mL loop. After 48 hours, 68 colonies of a small translucent non-hemolytic organism grew on blood agar but not MacConkey. Testing reveals small gram-positive, catalase-negative cocci. The preliminary report and follow-up testing would be:

   a. growth of 680 colonies/mL of gram-positive cocci, optochin and bacitracin susceptibility tests to follow
   b. growth of 6,800 colonies/mL of a *Staphylococcus* species, coagulase test to follow
   c. growth of 6,800 colonies/mL of a *Streptococcus* species, esculin hydrolysis and NaCl growth to follow
   d. growth of 6,800 colonies/mL of *Streptococcus* species, no further testing

109. When processing throat swabs for a strep screen, the medium of choice is:

   a. sheep blood agar plates
   b. rabbit blood agar plates
   c. human blood agar plates
   d. horse blood agar plates

110. Children who have infections with beta-hemolytic streptococci can develop:

   a. acute pyelonephritis
   b. acute glomerulonephritis
   c. chronic glomerulonephritis
   d. nephrosis

111. A gram-positive coccus isolated from a blood culture has the following characteristics:

Optochin susceptibility	negative
Bacitracin (0.04 U) susceptibility	negative
Bile	no growth
Esculin hydrolysis	negative
Hippurate hydrolysis	positive
Catalase	negative

This organism is most likely:

a. *Staphylococcus aureus*
b. *Streptococcus pneumoniae*
c. *Streptococcus pyogenes* (group A)
d. *Streptococcus agalactiae* (group B)

112. A review of the previous 12 month's culture reports reveals that group A beta-hemolytic streptococcus was recovered from approximately 5% of all throat cultures submitted. The best explanation for this finding is that the recovery rate is:

a. low; check current lot of blood agar for ability to support growth
b. normal; the majority of pharyngitis cases were probably viral
c. high; check blood agar plates for contamination with group A streptococcus

113. A beta-hemolytic streptococcus which is bacitracin sensitive and CAMP negative is:

a. group B
b. group A
c. beta-hemolytic, not Group A, B, or D
d. beta-hemolytic, Group D

114. A beta-hemolytic streptococcus which is bacitracin resistant and CAMP positive is:

a. group A or B
b. group A
c. group B
d. beta-hemolytic, Group D

115. Group B, beta-hemolytic streptococci may be distinguished from other hemolytic streptococci by which of the following procedures?

    a. coagglutination
    b. growth in 6.5% NaCl broth
    c. growth on bile esculin medium
    d. bacitracin susceptibility

116. It is important to identify individual members of the group D streptococci because:

    a. viridans streptococci are often confused with enterococci
    b. several enterococci cause severe puerperal sepsis
    c. nonenterococcal group D streptococci are avirulent
    d. enterococci often show more resistance to penicillin than other group D streptococci

117. *Streptococcus pneumoniae* can be differentiated best from the viridans group of streptococci by:

    a. Gram stain
    b. the type of hemolysis
    c. colonial morphology
    d. bile solubility

118. Characteristically, group D enterococci are:

    a. unable to grow in 6.5% NaCl
    b. relatively resistant to penicillin
    c. sodium hippurate positive
    d. bile esculin negative

119. The ability to detect methicillin-resistant *Staphylococcus aureus* may be enhanced by:

    a. shortening incubation of standard susceptibility plates
    b. incubating susceptibility plates at 39-41°C
    c. using Mueller-Hinton agar with 4% NaCl
    d. adjust inoculum to 0.1 McFarland before inoculating susceptibility plates

120. A beta-hemolytic, catalase positive, gram-positive coccus is coagulase-negative by the slide coagulase test. Which of the following is the most appropriate action in identification of this organism?

    a. report a coagulase-negative *Staphylococcus*
    b. report a coagulase-negative *Staphylococcus aureus*
    c. reconfirm the hemolytic reaction on a fresh 24 hour culture
    d. do a tube coagulase test to confirm the slide test

121. The most critical distinction between *Staphylococcus aureus* and other *Staphylococcus* is:

    a. phosphatase reaction
    b. DNA production
    c. coagulase production
    d. hemolysis

122. Which feature distinguishes *Erysipelothrix rhusiopathiae* from other clinically significant nonspore-forming, gram-positive, facultatively anaerobic bacilli?

    a. "tumbling" motility
    b. beta-hemolysis
    c. more pronounced motility at 25°C than 37°C
    d. H_2S production

123. *Listeria* can be confused with some streptococci because of its hemolysis and because it is:

    a. nonmotile
    b. catalase negative
    c. oxidase positive
    d. esculin positive

124. The optimal wound specimen for culture of anaerobic organisms would be:

    a. a swab of lesion obtained before administration of antibiotics
    b. a swab of lesion obtained after administration of antibiotics
    c. a syringe filled with pus, obtained before administration of antibiotics
    d. a syringe filled with pus, obtained after administration of antibiotics

125. Failure to obtain anaerobiosis in anaerobe jars is most often due to the:

    a. inactivation of the palladium-coated alumina catalyst pellets
    b. condensation of water on the inner surface of the jar
    c. instability of reactants in the disposable hydro-carbon dioxide generator envelope
    d. expiration of the methylene blue indicator strip that monitors oxidation

126. A control strain of *Clostridium* should be used in the GasPak™ anaerobe jar to assure:

    a. that plate media is working
    b. that anaerobic environment is achieved
    c. to fill the jar with a sufficient number of plates
    d. to check the indicator strip

127. Which of the following statements regarding methods for the isolation of anaerobic bacteria is the most accurate?

    a. When properly performed, the use of the GasPak™ system is comparable to the roll tube or anaerobic chamber methods.
    b. The use of prereduced anaerobically sterilized (PRAS) media in roll tubes is the best and most practical method.
    c. The use of liquid media such as thioglycollate is comparable to other methods.
    d. The use of the anaerobic chamber is a most effective method because the growth of facultative organisms is inhibited.

128. A throat swab is submitted for anaerobic culture. This specimen should be:

    a. set-up immediately
    b. rejected
    c. inoculated into thioglycollate broth
    d. sent to a reference laboratory

129. Anaerobic susceptibility tests are helpful in the management of patients with:

    a. synovial infections
    b. rectal abscesses
    c. streptococcal pharyngitis
    d. pilonidal sinuses

130. Which of the following anaerobes is inhibited by sodium polyanethol sulfonate (SPS)?

    a. *Peptostreptococcus magnus*
    b. *Peptostreptococcus prevotii*
    c. *Peptostreptococcus anaerobius*
    d. *Veillonella parvula*

131. Which of the following organisms may exhibit a brick red fluorescence?

    a. *Bacteroides melaninogenicus* and *Clostridium difficile*
    b. *Clostridium difficile* and *Fusobacterium sp.*
    c. *Veillonella parvula* and *Bacteroides melaninogenicus*
    d. *Fusobacterium* sp. and *Veillonella parvula*

132. Pseudomembranous colitis caused by *Clostridium difficile* toxin is confirmed by which of the following laboratory findings?

    a. isolation of the causative agent
    b. Gram-stain showing many gram-positive rods
    c. gas production in chopped meat glucose
    d. presence of toxin in stool

133. *Clostridium difficile* can best be recovered from feces on:

    a. enteric media and incubated aerobically
    b. blood agar incubated anaerobically
    c. CCFA incubated at 37°C under 5% CO_2
    d. CCFA incubated at 37°C anaerobically

134. At the present time *Clostridium difficile* toxin can be detected by:

    a. radioimmunoassays
    b. chromatographic procedures
    c. cytotoxicity
    d. high-pressure liquid chromatography

135. Staib's medium (Niger seed agar) is useful in the identification of which of the following?

    a. *Candida albicans*
    b. *Candida (Torulopsis) glabrata*
    c. *Saccharomyces cerevisiae*
    d. *Cryptococcus neoformans*

136. An antibiotic used to suppress or kill contaminating fungi in media is:

    a. penicillin
    b. cycloheximide
    c. streptomycin
    d. amphotericin B

137. Gram stain examination of a CSF specimen indicates the presence of yeast-like cells with gram-positive granular inclusions. Which of the following techniques should be used next to assist in the identification of this organism?

    a. 10% KOH
    b. lactophenol cotton blue
    c. India ink
    d. periodic acid-Schiff

138. Which of the following statements concerning the germ tube test is true?

    a. Using a heavy inoculum enhances the rapid production of germ tubes.
    b. Germ tubes should be read after 2 hours incubation at 25°C.
    c. *Candida albicans* and *Candida tropicalis* can be used as positive and negative controls, respectively.
    d. Serum will be stable for one year if stored at 4°C prior to use.

139. The one characteristic by which an unknown *Cryptococcus* species can be identified as Cryptococcus *neoformans* is:

    a. appearance of yellow colonies
    b. positive urease test
    c. presence of a capsule
    d. positive Niger seed agar test

140. A specimen of hair that fluoresced under a Wood's lamp was obtained from a child with low grade scaling lesions of the scalp. Cultures revealed a fungus with mycelium and very few macroconidia or microconidia. This fungus is most likely:

    a. *Microsporum gypseum*
    b. *Microsporum audouinii*
    c. *Trichophyton tonsurans*
    d. *Epidermophyton floccosum*

141. Many fungal infections are transmitted to man via inhalation of infectious structures. Which of the following is usually NOT contracted in this manner?

    a. histoplasmosis
    b. blastomycosis
    c. coccidioidomycosis
    d. sporotrichosis

142. Structures important in the microscopic identification of *Coccidioides immitis* are:

    a. irregular staining, barrel-shaped arthrospores
    b. tuberculate, thick-walled macroconidia
    c. thick-walled sporangia containing sporangiospores
    d. small pyriform microconidia

143. Which of the following is the most useful morphological feature in identifying the mycelial phase of *Histoplasma capsulatum*?

    a. arthrospores every other cell
    b. microspores 2-5 microns
    c. tuberculate macroconidia 8-14 microns
    d. nonseptate macroconidia of 5-7 cells

144. A mold grown at 25°C exhibited delicate septate hyaline hyphae and many conidiophores extending at right angles from the hyphae. Oval, 2-5 μm conidia were formed at the end of the conidiophores giving a flowerlike appearance. In some areas "sleeves" of spores could be found along the hyphae as well. A 37°C culture of this organism produced small, cigar-shaped yeast cells. This organism is most likely:

    a. *Histoplasma capsulatum*
    b. *Sporothrix schenckii*
    c. *Blastomyces dermatitidis*
    d. *Acremonium falciforme*

145. Which of the following is a dimorphic fungus?

    a. *Sporothrix schenckii*
    b. *Candida albicans*
    c. *Cryptococcus neoformans*
    d. *Aspergillus fumigatus*

146. The best medium for culture of *Mycobacterium tuberculosis* is:

   a. Bordet-Gengou
   b. Loeffler's medium
   c. Lowenstein-Jensen's medium
   d. cystine blood agar

147. Which of the following combinations of media provides an egg base, agar base, and a selective egg or agar base media?

   a. Lowenstein-Jensen, American Thoracic Society (ATS), Middlebrook 7H11
   b. Lowenstein-Jensen, Middlebrook 7H11, Lowenstein-Jensen (Gruft Modification)
   c. Middlebrook 7H10, Petragnani, Lowenstein-Jensen
   d. Middlebrook 7H10, Middlebrook 7H11, 7H11 (Mitchison's)

148. Which of the following reagents should be used as a mucolytic, alkaline reagent for digestion and decontamination of a sputum for mycobacterial culture?

   a. N-acetyl-L-cysteine and NaOH
   b. NaOH alone
   c. zephiran-trisodium phosphate
   d. oxalic acid

149. Recent evidence has shown that specimens to be inoculated for the recovery of acid-fast bacilli should be centrifuged at approximately:

   a. 2000 X g
   b. 2500 X g
   c. 3000 X g
   d. 3500 X g

150. Which group of mycobacteria require an isolation temperature of 20-32°C?

   a. *M. chelonei, M. ulcerans, M. kansasii*
   b. *M. chelonei, M. ulcerans, M. haemophilum*
   c. *M. marinum, M. chelonei, M. ulcerans*
   d. *M. marinum, M. ulcerans, M. haemophilum*

151. A positive niacin test is most characteristic of *Mycobacterium*:

   a. *chelonei*
   b. *marinum*
   c. *tuberculosis*
   d. *xenopi*

152. The nitrate test for mycobacteria can be performed with a reagent impregnated paper strip or by the use of standard reagents. In order to quality control the test properly, which of the following should be used for a positive control?

    a. *Mycobacterium bovis*
    b. *Mycobacterium gordonae*
    c. *Mycobacterium tuberculosis*
    d. *Mycobacterium intracellulare*

153. Characteristics necessary for the definitive identification of *Mycobacterium tuberculosis* are:

    a. buff color, slow growth at 37°C, niacin production-positive, nitrate reduction-negative
    b. rough colony, slow growth at 37°C, nonpigmented
    c. rough, nonpigmented colony, cording positive, niacin production-negative, catalase-negative at pH 7/68°C
    d. rough, nonpigmented colony, slow growth at 37°C, niacin production-positive, nitrate reduction-positive

154. A 27-year-old scuba diver has an abrasion on his left thigh. A culture of his wound grew an acid-fast organism at 30°C. This isolate most likely is:

    a. *Mycobacterium chelonei*
    b. *Mycobacterium marinum*
    c. *Mycobacterium tuberculosis*
    d. *Mycobacterium xenopi*

155. A nonphotochromogen which grows best at 42°C and is highly resistant to antibiotics is:

    a. *Mycobacterium chelonei*
    b. *Mycobacterium marinum*
    c. *Mycobacterium tuberculosis*
    d. *Mycobacterium xenopi*

156. A nonchromogen which grows unusually fast for the genus *Mycobacterium* is:

    a. *Mycobacterium bovis*
    b. *Mycobacterium kansasii*
    c. *Mycobacterium fortuitum*
    d. *Mycobacterium intracellulare*

157. Photochromogens produce pigment when

   a. kept in the dark at 22°C
   b. exposed to light for one hour
   c. grown in the presence of CO_2
   d. incubated with x-ray film

158. The main reason for the administration of two or more drugs for the treatment of pulmonary tuberculosis is to:

   a. obtain a greater therapeutic effect
   b. prevent the emergence of bacilli resistant to the action of either or both drugs
   c. reduce the toxicity of either drug if used alone
   d. reduce the deleterious effect of tuberculin hypersensitivity

---

For questions 159 and 160, refer to the following illustration:

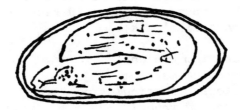

159. The egg depicted above is most likely to be found in children suffering from:

   a. diarrhea
   b. constipation
   c. perianal itching
   d. stomach pain

160. The specimen of choice for finding the above parasite is:

   a. stool
   b. duodenal washing
   c. rectal swab
   d. perianal skin impression

For questions 161 through 164, refer to the following illustration:

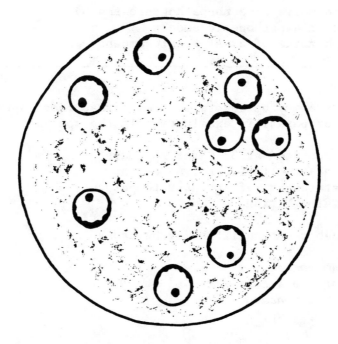

161. Trophozoites of the organism depicted above are likely to:

    a. contain red blood cells
    b. have clear, pointed pseudopodia
    c. contain few if any vacuoles
    d. have slow, undefined motility

162. Upon finding the above in a fecal concentrate, the technologist should:

    a. report this pathogen to the physician
    b. review the fecal concentration carefully for the presence of other microorganisms which may be pathogenic
    c. look for motile trophozoites
    d. request a new specimen because of the presence of excessive pollen grains

163. An inexperienced parasitology student may confuse the above organism with:

    a. *Entamoeba histolytica*
    b. *Dientamoeba fragilis*
    c. *Giardia lamblia*
    d. *Trichomonas vaginalis*

164. The structure depicted:

    a. cyst of a nonpathogenic amoeba
    b. trophozoite of a nonpathogenic amoeba
    c. cyst of a pathogenic amoeba
    d. trophozoite of a pathogenic amoeba

---

165. The cyst stage may be recovered from formed fecal specimens submitted for parasitic examination if the specimen:

    a. is incubated at 37°C for 24 hours
    b. is the result of a saline enema
    c. is stored at refrigerator temperature
    d. contains barium

166. Primary amoebic-encephalitis may be caused by:

    a. *Entamoeba coli*
    b. *Dientamoeba fragilis*
    c. *Endolimax nana*
    d. *Naegleria* sp.

167. The examination of human feces is no help in the detection of:

    a. *Strongyloides stercoralis*
    b. *Entamoeba histolytica*
    c. *Echinococcus granulosus*
    d. *Ancylostoma duodenale*

168. The causative agent of cysticercosis is:

    a. *Taenia solium*
    b. *Taenia saginata*
    c. *Ascaris lumbricoides*
    d. *Trichuris trichuria*

169. Organisms that can be easily identified to the species level from the ova in fecal specimens include:

    a. *Metagonimus yokogawai, Heterophyes heterophyes*
    b. *Taenia solium, Taenia saginata*
    c. *Necator americanus, Ancylostoma duodenale*
    d. *Paragonimus westermani, Hymenolepsis nana*

170. The scolex of *Taenia saginata* has:

    a. 4 suckers
    b. no suckers and 14 hooklets
    c. 24 hooklets
    d. 26 to 28 sucking discs

For questions 171 and 172, refer to the following illustration:

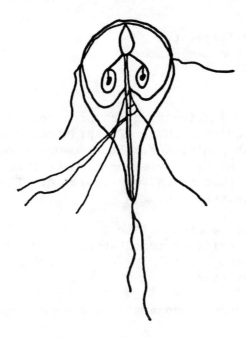

171. The organism depicted is a(n):

    a. amoeba
    b. flagellate
    c. trypanosoma
    d. sporozoan

172. A 24-year-old woman who just returned from vacationing in Russia, became ill with steatorrheal diarrhea. The above organism was found in her stool. The patient most likely is suffering from:

    a. giardiasis
    b. amebiasis
    c. ascariasis
    d. balantidiasis

173. When stool examination is negative, the preferred specimen for the diagnosis of paragonimiasis is:

    a. bile drainage
    b. duodenal aspirate
    c. sputum
    d. rectal biopsy

174. Prior to inoculation, clinical material collected for viral culture should be:

    a. stored in the refrigerator
    b. maintained at room temperature
    c. frozen at -20°C
    d. frozen at 0°C

175. The virology laboratory institutes a new protocol for the isolation of cytomegalovirus (CMV). The protocol requires inoculating throat swabs on tissue culture monolayers within 24 hours after being frozen. In reviewing results from 500 throat swabs, it was observed that no CMV was isolated. The most likely reason for no recovery is:

    a. incorrect culture medium
    b. prolonged delay prior to inoculation
    c. incorrect specimen
    d. specimens were frozen

176. Occasionally Reye's syndrome appears as a severe complication of:

    a. poliomyelitis
    b. coxsackie B
    c. mumps encephalitis
    d. influenza

177. Adenovirus infections primarily involve the:

    a. respiratory tract
    b. gastrointestinal tract
    c. genital tract
    d. urinary tract

178. The most rapid means of detecting herpes virus in clinical specimens is:

    a. serologic testing
    b. Gram stain
    c. cell culture
    d. direct immunofluorescence

179. Encephalitis is most commonly associated with which of the following viruses?

    a. Epstein-Barr
    b. herpes simplex
    c. coxsackie B
    d. varicella zoster

180. Colds and other acute respiratory diseases, are most often associated with:

    a. Epstein-Barr virus
    b. adenovirus
    c. coxsackie B
    d. reovirus

181. Psittacosis is transmissible to man via contact with:

    a. insects
    b. birds
    c. cattle
    d. dogs

182. Chlamydial infections have been implicated in:

    a. urethritis and conjunctivitis
    b. gastroenteritis and urethritis
    c. neonatal pneumonia and gastroenteritis
    d. neonatal meningitis and conjunctivitis

183. Mycoplasmas differ from bacteria in that they:

    a. do not cause disease in humans
    b. cannot grow in artificial inanimate media
    c. lack cell walls
    d. are not serologically antigenic

The following items(*) have been identified as more appropriate for the entry level medical technologist.

*184. Production of beta-lactamase is inducible in which of the following:

    a. *Haemophilus influenzae*
    b. *Staphylococcus aureus*
    c. *Corynebacterium diphtheriae*
    d. *Streptococcus pyogenes*

*185. An autopsy performed on an 8-year-old child revealed Waterhouse Friderichsen syndrome. Blood and throat cultures taken just prior to death were positive for which organism?

    a. *Neisseria gonorrhoeae*
    b. *Neisseria meningitidis*
    c. *Haemophilus influenzae*
    d. *Klebsiella pneumoniae*

*186. Fluid from a cutaneous black lesion was submitted for routine bacteriological culture. After 18 hours of incubation at 35°C there was no growth on MacConkey agar, but 3+ growth on sheep blood agar. The colonies were nonhemolytic, 4 to 5 mm in diameter and off-white with a ground glass appearance. Each colony had an irregular edge with comma-shaped outgrowths that stood up like "beaten egg whites" when gently lifted with an inoculating needle. A Gram stained smear of a typical colony showed large, gram-positive rectangular rods. The organism is most likely:

    a. *Clostridium perfringens*
    b. *Aeromonas hydrophila*
    c. *Bacillus anthracis*
    d. *Mycobacterium marinum*

*187. Which of the following is a synergistic bacterial infection?

    a. scarlet fever
    b. Strep throat
    c. erythrasma
    d. Vincent's angina

*188. The usefulness of counterimmunoelectrophoresis (CIE) in the diagnosis of meningitis is limited because:

   a. commercial antisera are not available for the detection of the organisms that commonly cause meningitis
   b. cross-reactions commonly occur between *Streptococcus pneumoniae*, *Haemophilus influenzae* and *Neisseria menigitidis*
   c. antigens are detected in less than 50% of bacteriologically proven cases of meningitis
   d. a concentration with 10^5 colony-forming units per milliliter is required before sufficient antigen can be detected

*189. The sensitivity of the DNA probe is dependent on:

   a. guanine-cytosine binding
   b. biotin-avidin binding
   c. nucleic acid
   d. polypeptide sequence

*190. A test that aids in differentiating between upper (kidney) and lower (bladder) urinary tract infection is:

   a. luciferase assay of adenosine triphosphate
   b. creatinine clearance
   c. triphenyl tetrazolium chloride (TTC) test
   d. demonstration of antibody-coated bacteria in the urine

*191. A Gram stained sputum smear revealed 25-50 squamous epithelial cells and 10-25 polymorphonuclear leukocytes per 100x field, as well as many lancet-shaped, gram-positive cocci; many gram-negative rods and many gram-positive cocci in pairs, clumps and long chains. The technologist's best course of action would be to:

   a. inoculate appropriate media and incubate aerobically
   b. inoculate appropriate media and incubate anaerobically
   c. call the physician and notify him of this "life-threatening" situation
   d. call the nursing station and request a new specimen

*192. "Clue cells" are best seen in a:

   a. Gram stain of vaginal discharge
   b. saline wet preparation of a colony of *Gardnerella vaginalis*
   c. saline wet preparation of vaginal discharge material
   d. Gram stain of a typical colony of *Gardnerella vaginalis*

*193. A technologist is reading a Gram stain from a CSF and observes small structures suggestive of gram-negative coccobacilli. Chemistry and hematology CSF results which would indicate bacterial meningitis include:

	WBC	Glucose	Protein
a.	increased	increased	increased
b.	decreased	decreased	decreased
c.	increased	decreased	increased
d.	decreased	increased	decreased

*194. It has been recommended that cephalexin be incorporated into Bordet-Gengou agar instead of penicillin because:

a. cephalexin is more stable at incubation temperature
b. cephalexin inhibits organisms indigenous to the nasopharynx
c. cephalexin may inactivate some inhibitory fatty acids and peroxides
d. penicillin may inhibit some strains of *Bordetella pertussis*

*195. Routine quality control tests revealed that a batch of chocolate agar was able to support the growth of *Haemophilus influenzae* only as satellite colonies around *Staphylococcus aureus*. The most likely source of difficulty is:

a. excess heating in preparation of the medium
b. dehydration during storage of the medium
c. attenuation of the quality control organism
d. use of improperly-cleaned glassware

*196. When testing for oxidase activity, for which of the following organisms is it recommended that a 5% aqueous solution of tetramethyl-phenylenediamine dihydrochloride be used, rather than commercially available strips?

a. *Eikenella corrodens*
b. *Haemophilus aphrophilus*
c. *Flavobacterium meningosepticum*
d. *Pasteurella multocida*

*197. Filters generally used in biological safety cabinets to protect the laboratory worker from particulates and aerosols generated by microbiology manipulations are:

a. fiberglass
b. HEPA
c. APTA
d. charcoal

*198. All of the following are advantages of automated susceptibility testing EXCEPT:

    a. endpoint objectivity
    b. greater sensitivity of readings
    c. cost reduction with small volumes
    d. reduction of experimental error

---

*199. Refer to the following illustration:

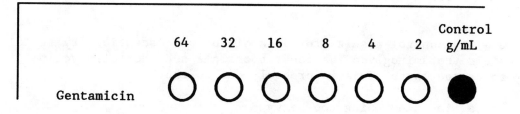

Examine the minimum inhibitory concentration (MIC) tray shown above and determine the MIC for gentamicin.

    a. ≥64 g/mL
    b. 32 g/mL
    c. 16 g/mL
    d. ≤ 2 g/mL

---

*200. When combination antibiotic therapy is used:

    a. antagonistic effects should exist between the antibiotics
    b. the combination effect of the drugs should be less than the sum of the independent effects of the two drugs
    c. the synergistic effects of the drugs should be assessed
    d. the killing power of the combination must be at least fourfold greater than the antimicrobic used alone

*201. Which of the following tests is used to monitor bactericidal activity during antimicrobic therapy in cases of endocarditis?

    a. Elek
    b. tolerance
    c. Sherris synergism
    d. Schlicter

*202. The macro-broth dilution method for determining antibiotic susceptibility of the *Enterobacteriaceae* cannot be used effectively for the sulfonamides or trimethoprim because:

    a. misleading results can occur due to inadequate concentrations of Mg++ and Ca++
    b. organisms are resistant at 35°C; at 37°C endpoints are less clear unless incubated for 48 hours
    c. definite endpoints have not yet been established
    d. endpoints are difficult to determine as susceptible organisms can go through several generations before being inhibited

*203. Quality control results for disk diffusion susceptibility tests yield the aminoglycoside zones too small and the tetracycline zones too large. This is probably due to the:

    a. inoculum being too heavy
    b. inoculum being too light
    c. pH of Mueller-Hinton agar being too low
    d. calcium and magnesium concentration in the agar being too high

*204. When using control strains of *Staphylococcus aureus* and *Streptococcus agalactiae* the technologist notices that the zones around the methicillin disk are too small. This is probably due to the use of:

    a. too heavy an inoculum
    b. too light an inoculum
    c. Mueller-Hinton agar which is too acidic
    d. outdated antibiotic disks

*205. In the disk diffusion method of determining antibiotic susceptibility, the size of the inhibition zone used to indicate susceptibility has been determined by:

    a. testing thirty strains of one genus of bacteria
    b. correlating the zone size with minimum inhibitory concentrations
    c. correlating the zone size with minimum bactericidal concentrations
    d. correlating the zone size with the antibiotic content of the disk

*206. All of the following are in vitro methods of determining synergism EXCEPT:

    a. kill-curve method
    b. kill-curve using an MIC endpoint
    c. checkerboard using an MIC endpoint
    d. checkerboard using an MBC endpoint

*207. A urine culture plated on MacConkey and blood agar appears to be growing greater than 100,000 colonies/cc of two gram-negative rods. One of the organisms is swarming across the surface of the agar preventing isolation of the second organism. The best course of action would be to:

    a. report as greater than 100,000 colonies/cc of mixed gram-negative rods
    b. subculture using media with an increased agar concentration or increased selectivity
    c. discard the current lot of MacConkey; organisms should not swarm on this medium
    d. subculture to CNA agar to inhibit swarming

*208. A presumptive identification of *Campylobacter jejuni* can be made using a combination of the following:

    a. Gram stain, catalase and oxidase test reactions, phase-contrast microscopy
    b. Gram stain, catalase and oxidase test reactions, motility media
    c. catalase and oxidase test reactions, phase-contrast microscopy, motility media
    d. H & E stain, catalase and oxidase test, motility media

*209. Which one of the following results is typical of *Campylobacter fetus* subspecies *fetus*?

    a. optimal growth at 42°C
    b. oxidase negative
    c. growth at 37°C
    d. catalase negative

*210. An 8-year-old girl was admitted to the hospital with a three-day history of fever, abdominal pain, diarrhea, and vomiting. Stool culture grew many lactose-negative colonies that yielded the following test results:

Oxidase	negative
TSI	acid slant/acid butt
Indole	negative
Urease	positive
Ornithine decarboxylase	positive
Sucrose	positive
H_2S	negative
Motility at 22°C	positive

The most probable identification of this organism is:

a. *Providencia alcalifaciens*
b. *Providencia stuartii*
c. *Yersinia enterocolitica*
d. *Providencia rettgeri*

*211. A suspension of organism suspected to be *Shigella* based on biochemical reactions did not agglutinate with *Shigella antisera* subgroups A, B, C, and D. You would conclude that:

a. this particular *Shigella* possesses a capsular antigen that blocks agglutination in O antiserum and must first be destroyed by heating
b. this organism is not a *Shigella*
c. the bacterial suspension was not dense enough, resulting in a false-negative reaction
d. a rough colony was used for the serotyping procedure

*212. Which of the following sets of tests best differentiates *Salmonella* and *Citrobacter* species?

a. KCN, malonate, beta-galactosidase, lysine decarboxylase
b. dulcitol, citrate, indole, H_2S production
c. lactose, adonitol, KCN, motility
d. lysine decarboxylase, lactose, sucrose, malonate, indole

*213. An organism was inoculated into a TSI tube and gave the following reactions:

Acid slant/Acid butt, no H_2S, no gas

This organism most likely is:

a. *Yersinia enterocolitica*
b. *Salmonella typhi*
c. *Salmonella typhimurium*
d. *Shigella dysenteriae*

*214. A false statement regarding surveillance of chronic nosocomial infection with *Klebsiella pneumoniae* include:

a. As the incidence of infection increases, the organism may become resistant to gentamicin, tobramycin, and other aminoglycosides if these drugs are used extensively.
b. Antibiotic susceptibility patterns (antibiograms) can be useful as epidemiological markers for documenting cross infections.
c. If only Bauer-Kirby disk diffusion testing is done, it is difficult to determine whether more than one strain is responsible.
d. Commercially available identification panels (API-20E™ Micro-ID™, Enterotube™) provide reproducible differentiation of species into biotypes and can be routinely used in infection control.

*215. A fecal specimen, inoculated to xylose lysine deoxycholate (XLD) and hektoen enteric (HE) agars produced colonies with black centers. Additional testing results are as follows:

Biochemical Screen		Serological Testing	
Glucose:	positive	Polyvalent:	no agglutination
H_2S:	positive	Group A:	no agglutination
Lysine			
decarboxylase:	positive	Group B_1:	no agglutination
Urea:	negative	Group C:	no agglutination
ONPG:	negative	Group D:	no agglutination
Indole:	positive	Group Vi:	no agglutination

The most probable identification is:

a. *Salmonella choleraesuis*
b. *Edwardsiella tarda*
c. *Salmonella typhi*
d. *Shigella sonnei*

*216. A request is received in the laboratory for assistance in selecting the appropriate test(s) for detecting Lyme disease. Which of the following would be suggested?

    a. Stool culture should be done to isolate the causative organism.
    b. The organism is difficult to isolate, and antibody titers will provide the most help.
    c. *Borrelia burgdorferi* is easily isolated from routine blood cultures.
    d. This is an immunologic syndrome, and cultures are not indicated.

*217. A jaundiced 7-year-old boy, with a history of playing in a pond in a rat-infested area, has a urine specimen submitted for a direct darkfield examination. Several spiral organisms are seen. Which of the following organisms would most likely be responsible for the patient's condition?

    a. *Spirillum minor*
    b. *Streptobacillus moniliformis*
    c. *Listeria monocytogenes*
    d. *Leptospira interrogans*

*218. Multiple blood cultures from a patient with endocarditis grew a facultatively anaerobic, pleomorphic gram-negative bacillus with the following characteristics:

Hemolysis	negative
MacConkey agar	no growth
Catalase	negative
Oxidase	negative
Nitrate	positive, reduced to nitrites
Bile solubility	insoluble
Indole	negative
Glucose	acid & gas produced

Enhanced growth on blood & chocolate agar in 5% CO_2
Required X factor under 5-10% CO_2 atmosphere

The most likely identification is:

    a. *Brucella abortus*
    b. *Actinobacillus actinomycetemcomitans*
    c. *Haemophilus aphrophilus*
    d. *Cardiobacterium hominis*

*219. Which of the following is a growth requirement for the
       isolation of *Leptospira*?

       a. an atmosphere of 10% CO_2
       b. an incubation temperature of 4°C
       c. four to five day incubation
       d. medium containing 10% serum plus fatty acids

*220. Blood cultures from a case of suspected leptospiremia should be
       drawn:

       a. between 10 p.m. and 2 a.m.
       b. in the first 7-10 days of infection
       c. during febrile periods, late in the course of the
           disease
       d. after the first 10 days of illness

*221. A gram-negative rod was isolated from a wound infection caused
       by a bite from a pet cat. The following characteristic
       reactions were seen:

Oxidase	positive
Glucose OF	fermentative
Catalase	positive
Motility	negative
MacConkey agar	no growth

       Which of the following is the most likely organism?

       a. *Pseudomonas aeruginosa*
       b. *Pasteurella multocida*
       c. *Aeromonas hydrophila*
       d. *Vibrio cholerae*

*222. *Eikenella corrodens* characteristically is:

       a. identical to the organism known as *Bacteroides
           corrodens*
       b. dependent on factor X for initial aerobic growth
       c. arginine dihydrolase and lysine decarboxylase
           positive
       d. an obligate anaerobe

*223. A culture from an infected dog bite on a small boy's finger
yielded a small, gram-negative coccobacillus that was smooth,
raised and beta-hemolytic on blood agar. The isolate was found
to grow readily on MacConkey agar forming colorless colonies.
The organism was motile with peritrichous flagella, catalase
positive, oxidase positive, reduced nitrate, utilized citrate,
and was urease positive within 4 hours. No carbohydrates were
fermented. The most likely identification of this isolate is:

    a. *Brucella canis*
    b. *Yersinia pestis*
    c. *Francisella tularensis*
    d. *Bordetella bronchiseptica*

*224. While swimming in a lake near his home, a young boy cut his
foot as he stepped on a piece of glass from a broken bottle.
An infection developed and the site was cultured. A
nonfastidious gram-negative, oxidase positive, beta-hemolytic,
motile bacillus was recovered. The organism produced
deoxyribonuclease and was most probably identified as:

    a. *Enterobacter cloacae*
    b. *Serratia marcescens*
    c. *Aeromonas hydrophila*
    d. *Escherichia coli*

*225. A 25-year-old man who had recently worked as a steward on a
transoceanic grain ship presented to the emergency room with
high fever, diarrhea and prostration. Axillary lymph nodes
were hemorrhagic and enlarged. A Gram stained smear was
prepared from a lymph node aspirate and many gram-negative
bacilli were noted. The bacilli demonstrated a marked bipolar
staining reaction described as a "safety-pin appearance" with
Wayson's stain. The most likely identification of this
organism is:

    a. *Brucella melitensis*
    b. *Streptobacillus moniliformis*
    c. *Spirillum minor*
    d. *Yersinia pestis*

*226. An aerobic, gram-negative coccobacillus was isolated on blood agar from a nasopharyngeal swab 48 hours after culture from a 6-month-old infant with suspected pertussis. The organism exhibited the following characteristics:

Urea   negative at 4 hours, positive at 18 hours
Oxidase   negative
Catalase   positive
Citrate   positive

Small zones of beta-hemolysis
Slight brownish coloration of the medium

The most probable identification of this isolate is:

a. *Pasteurella multocida*
b. *Pasteurella ureae*
c. *Bordetella pertussis*
d. *Bordetella parapertussis*

*227. Which of the following characteristics best differentiates *Bordetella bronchiseptica* from *Alcaligenes* species?

a. flagellar pattern
b. growth at 24°C
c. oxidase activity
d. rapid hydrolysis of urea

*228. Serum samples collected from a patient with pneumonia demonstrate a rising antibody titer to *Legionella*. A bronchoalveolar lavage (BAL) specimen from this patient had a positive antigen test for *Legionella* but no organisms were recovered from this specimen on buffered charcoal yeast extract (BCYE) medium after 2 days of incubation. The best explanation is that the:

a. antibody titer represents an earlier infection
b. positive antigen test is a false positive
c. specimen was cultured on the wrong media
d. culture was not incubated long enough

*229. Which characteristic best differentiates between *Acinetobacter* species and *Moraxella* species?

a. production of indophenol oxidase
b. growth on MacConkey agar
c. motility
d. susceptibility to penicillin

*230. An organism has been identified as a member of the fluorescent group of *Pseudomonas*. Which of the following sets of tests should be used to determine the species of the organism?

    a. growth at 42°C, pyocyanin production, gelatinase production
    b. pyocyanin production, gelatinase production, OF glucose
    c. growth at 37°C, pyocyanin production, OF glucose
    d. gelatinase production, growth at 52°C, H₂S

*231. Two different size colonies are often observed on a chocolate agar plate subculture of *Neisseria gonorrhoeae* due to the:

    a. appearance of penicillin-resistant variants
    b. appearance of spontaneous lipopolysaccharide mutants
    c. presence of spontaneous auxotrophic mutants
    d. presence of both piliate (small) and nonpiliated (large) colonies

*232. Organisms that may be mistaken for *Neisseria gonorrhoeae* in Gram stained smears of uterine cervix exudates include:

    a. *Lactobacilli* species
    b. *Streptococcus agalactiae*
    c. *Pseudomonas aeruginosa*
    d. *Moraxella osloensis*

*233. An aspirated specimen of purulent material was obtained from a brain abscess. After 24 hours incubation, pinpoint colonies grew on sheep blood and small, yellowish colonies grew on chocolate. Gram stain of the organism showed gram-negative cocci. Results of carbohydrate degradation studies were as follows:

    Dextrose: acid
    Maltose: acid
    Sucrose: acid
    Lactose: acid

Additional testing revealed that the organism was oxidase positive and beta-galactosidase negative. The organism is most likely *Neisseria*:

    a. *meningitidis*
    b. *sicca*
    c. *lactamica*
    d. *gonorrhoeae*

*234. A 73-year-old man diagnosed as having pneumococcal meningitis is not responding to his penicillin therapy. Which of the following tests should be performed on the isolate to best determine this organism's susceptibility to penicillin agents?

   a. beta-lactamase
   b. oxacillin disk diffusion
   c. penicillin disk diffusion
   d. Schlichter test

*235. A beta-hemolytic gram-positive coccus was isolated from the cerebrospinal fluid of a 2-day-old infant with signs of meningitis. The isolate grew on sheep blood agar under aerobic conditions and was resistant to a bacitracin disk. Which of the following should be performed for the presumptive identification of the organism?

   a. oxidase production
   b. catalase formation
   c. CAMP test
   d. esculin hydrolysis

*236. How many hours after eating contaminated food do initial symptoms of staphylococcal food poisoning typically occur?

   a. 5 to 7 hours
   b. 12 to 18 hours
   c. 24 to 48 hours
   d. 72 hours to a week

*237. During the past month, *Staphylococcus epidermidis* has been isolated from blood cultures at two to three times the rate from the previous year. The most logical explanation for the increase in these isolates is that:

   a. the blood culture media are contaminated with this organism
   b. the hospital ventilation system is contaminated with *Staphylococcus epidermidis*
   c. there has been a break in proper skin preparation before blood drawing
   d. a relatively virulent isolate is being spread from patient to patient

*238. Items to consider when using the staphyloccocal CoA procedure include:

    a. Hyperproteinemia may cause autoagglutination and thus false-positive test results.
    b. Direct testing of group A, beta-hemolytic streptococci isolates from agar plates results in pseudoagglutination.
    c. Gonococcal isolates must be cold-treated to avoid pseudoagglutination.
    d. Cerebrospinal fluid must be heated to 56°C for five minutes before testing.

*239. An outbreak of *Staphylococcus aureus* has occurred in a hospital nursery. In order to establish the epidemiological source of the outbreak, it is helpful to do:

    a. phage typing
    b. serological typing
    c. coagulase testing
    d. catalase testing

*240. A branching gram-positive, partially acid-fast organism is isolated from a bronchial washing on a 63-year-old woman receiving chemotherapy. The organism does NOT hydrolyze casein, tyrosine or xanthine. The most likely identification is:

    a. *Actinomadura madurae*
    b. *Nocardia caviae*
    c. *Streptomyces somaliensis*
    d. *Nocardia asteroides*

*241. An 18-year-old man from Mexico has had chronic infected lesions on his feet. Culture of the lesions reveals an organism which is a branching gram-positive rod that hydrolyzes casein and tyrosine and is urease positive. The most likely identification is:

    a. *Nocardia caviae*
    b. *Nocardia asteroides*
    c. *Nocardia brasiliensis*
    d. *Actinomadura madurae*

*242. Anaerobic infections differ from aerobic infections in which of the following?

    a. They usually respond favorably with aminoglycoside therapy.
    b. They usually arise from exogenous sources.
    c. They are usually polymicrobic.
    d. Gram stained smears of the specimens are less helpful in diagnosis.

*243. An anaerobic gram-positive bacilli with subterminal spores was isolated from a peritoneal abscess. The most likely identification of this organism is:

    a. *Bacillus cereus*
    b. *Clostridium septicum*
    c. *Eubacterium lentum*
    d. *Bifidobacterium dentium*

*244. An isolate of an anaerobic organism from a vaginal specimen was found to be a gram-positive bacillus with the following characteristics: catalase negative, glucose positive and trehalose fermentation. The gas liquid chromatography (GLC) pattern revealed large lactic, acetic and formic acid peaks. The most likely identification is:

    a. *Eubacterium limosum*
    b. *Propionibacterium acnes*
    c. *Bifidobacterium dentium*
    d. *Arachnia propionica*

*245. The most meaningful laboratory procedure in confirming the diagnosis of clinical botulism is:

    a. demonstration of toxin in the patient's serum
    b. recovery of *Clostridium botulinum* from suspected food
    c. recovery of *Clostridium botulinum* from the patient's stool
    d. Gram stain of suspected food for gram-positive, sporulating bacilli

*246. Which one of the following organisms could be used as the positive quality control test for lecithinase on egg yolk agar?

    a. *Bacteroides fragilis*
    b. *Fusobacterium necrophorum*
    c. *Clostridium perfringens*
    d. *Clostridium sporogenes*

*247. An anaerobic gram-negative bacillus isolated from a blood
culture following bowel surgery grew, smooth, white
nonhemolytic colonies. A Gram stained smear showed a pale,
bipolarly-stained rod with rounded ends. Bile stimulated
growth of the organism and catalase was produced.   The isolate
was not inhibited by colistin, kanamycin or vancomycin; indole
was not produced. The most likely identification of this
isolate is:

    a. *Bacteroides fragilis*
    b. *Bacteroides melaninogenicus*
    c. *Fusobacterium nucleatum*
    d. *Fusobacterium varium*

*248. A 1-2 mm translucent, nonpigmented colony, isolated from an
anaerobic culture of a lung abscess after 72 hours, was found
to fluoresce brick-red under ultraviolet light. A Gram stained
smear of the organism revealed a coccobacillus that had the
following characteristics:

Growth in bile	inhibited
Vancomycin	resistant
Catalase	negative
Esculin hydrolysis	negative
Indole	negative
Nitrate	negative
Glucose, lactose, and sucrose	acid produced

The most likely identification of this isolate is:

    a. *Bacteroides ovatus*
    b. *Bacteroides oralis*
    c. *Bacteroides melaninogenicus*
    d. *Bacteroides asaccharolyticus*

*249. A thin anaerobic gram-negative bacillus with tapered ends
isolated from an empyema was found to be indole positive,
lipase negative and inhibited by 20% bile. Colonies were
described as "speckled" or resembling "ground glass" and
fluoresced weakly when exposed to ultraviolet light. The
most probable identification of this isolate would be:

    a. *Bacteroides ureolyticus*
    b. *Bacteroides melaninogenicus*
    c. *Fusobacterium nucleatum*
    d. *Fusobacterium mortiferum*

*250. Which of the following anaerobes would be positive for indole?

    a. *Bacteroides thetaiotaomicron*
    b. *Bacteroides fragilis*
    c. *Bacteroides distasonis*
    d. *Bacteroides ureolyticus*

*251. The presence of 20% bile in blood agar would probably enhance the growth of:

    a. *Fusobacterium nucleatum*
    b. *Bacteroides ovatus*
    c. *Bacteroides melaninogenicus*
    d. *Bacteroides disiens*

*252. The diagnosis of antibiotic-associated pseudomembranous colitis is best made by:

    a. isolation of *Clostridium difficile* from stool specimens
    b. demonstration of *Clostridium difficile* anti-toxin in the serum
    c. prevention of cytopathogenic effect (CPE) on a fibroblast monolayer by *Clostridium sordellii* antitoxin
    d. demonstration of cytopathogenic effect (CPE) on a fibroblast monolayer

*253. The tissue culture assay for *Clostridium difficile* toxin:

    a. is usually interpreted at 6-12 hours post-inoculation
    b. may show changes within four hours of inoculation
    c. shows a good correlation between the toxin titer and the severity of the disease
    d. is interpreted as positive when cytotoxicity affects at least 5% of the cell monolayer

*254. The drug of choice for treating *Clostridium difficile* is:

    a. chloramphenicol
    b. colistin
    c. penicillin
    d. vancomycin

*255. *Clostridium difficile*:

    a. is associated with all cases of pseudomembranous colitis
    b. is a likely pathogen in antibiotic-associated diarrhea
    c. defines the colonic lesions
    d. is the causative pathogen for many gastrointestinal diseases

*256. While reading the quality control smear for the periodic acid-Schiff (PAS) stain, you note that the background and fungal elements appear pink. Which of the following is most likely?

    a. The periodic acid has deteriorated and is no longer able to oxidize the hydroxyl groups.
    b. The sodium meta-bisulfite solution is no longer stable and has lost its bleaching properties.
    c. The basic fuchsin solution is unstable and has deteriorated.
    d. The procedure is in control and all solutions are stable.

*257. A major limitation of flucytosine (5-fluorocytosine) in the treatment of yeast infections is that:

    a. absorption from the gastrointestinal tract is erratic and unpredictable
    b. there is an antagonistic reaction when it is combined with amphotericin B
    c. *Candida* and *Cryptococcus* develop resistance during therapy
    d. penetration into cerebrospinal fluid is negligible in cryptococcal meningitis

*258. A yeast isolate from a CSF specimen produced the following results:

    India ink: no encapsulated yeast cells
    Cryptococcal antigen: negative
    Urea: negative
    Germ tube: negative

What should the technologist do next to identify this organism?

    a. inoculate Niger seed agar
    b. ascospore stain
    c. cycloheximide susceptibility
    d. carbohydrate assimilation

*259. Which of the following organisms produce a positive nitrate assimilation test?

    a. *Cryptococcus neoformans*
    b. *Candida albicans*
    c. *Candida tropicalis*
    d. *Cryptococcus albidus*

*260. The typical tissue inflammatory response to invasion with *Cryptococcus* is:

   a. polymorphonuclear
   b. lymphocytic
   c. monocytic
   d. minimal or absent

*261. The recovery of some *Cryptococcus* species may be compromised if the isolation media contains:

   a. cycloheximide
   b. gentamicin
   c. chloramphenicol
   d. penicillin

*262. False-positive reactions to the immunodiffusion test for histoplasmosis have been seen after:

   a. amphotericin B therapy
   b. skin testing with histoplasmin
   c. cultures have reverted to negative
   d. complement-fixing antibodies have disappeared

*263. A fungal isolate from the sputum of a patient with a pulmonary infection is suspected to be *Histoplasma capsulatum*. Tuberculate macroconidia were seen on the hyphae of the mold phase which was isolated at room temperature on Sabouraud's dextrose agar, containing chloramphenicol and cycloheximide (SDA-CC). A parallel set of cultures incubated at 35°C showed bacterial growth on SDA but no growth on SDA-CC. Which of the following is the appropriate course of action?

   a. Repeat subculture of the mold phase to tubes of moist SDA-CC, incubated at 35°C.
   b. Subculture the mold phase to tubes of moist BHI-blood media incubated at 25°C.
   c. Subculture the mold phase to moist BHI-blood media incubated at 35°C.
   d. Perform animal inoculation studies.

*264. The serologic test most helpful in determining the prognosis of coccidioidomycosis is the:

   a. precipitin test
   b. complement fixation test
   c. latex particle agglutination test
   d. hemagglutination inhibition test

*265. Skin scrapings obtained from the edge of a crusty wrist lesion were found to contain thick-walled, spherical yeast cells (8-15 μm in diameter) that had single buds with a wide base of attachment. Microscopic examination of the room temperature isolate from this specimen would probably reveal the presence of:

    a. "rosette-like" clusters of pear-shaped conidia at the tips of delicate conidiophores
    b. thick-walled, round to pear-shaped tuberculate macroconidia
    c. numerous conidia along the length of hyphae in a "sleevelike" arrangement
    d. septate hyphae bearing round or pear-shaped small conidia attached to conidiophores of irregular lengths

*266. *Trichophyton rubrum* characteristically:

    a. gives a positive hair penetration test
    b. has granular colonies
    c. has a green reverse
    d. has numerous small spherical to clavate microconidia

*267. Which of the following is the best aid in the identification of *Epidermophyton floccosum* macroconidia?

    a. parallel side walls with at least ten cells
    b. spindle-shaped spore with thin walls
    c. spindle-shaped spore, thick walls and distinct terminal knob with echinulations
    d. smooth walls, club-shaped

*268. Culture of a strand of hair, that fluoresced yellow-green when examined with a Wood's lamp, produced a slow-growing, flat gray colony with a salmon-pink reverse. Microscopic examination demonstrated racquet hyphae, pectinate bodies, chlamydospores, and a few abortive or bizarre-shaped macroconidia. The most probable identification of this isolate is:

    a. *Microsporum gypseum*
    b. *Microsporum canis*
    c. *Microsporum audouinii*
    d. *Trichophyton rubrum*

*269. A fungus superficially resembles *Penicillium* species but may be differentiated because its sterigmata are long and tapering and bend away from the central axis. The sterigmata also arise singly from the hyphae. The most probable identification is:

    a. *Exophiala* sp.
    b. *Acremonium* sp.
    c. *Cladosporium* sp.
    d. *Paecilomyces* sp.

*270. Crust from a cauliflower-like lesion on the hand exhibited brown spherical bodies 6-12 µm in diameter when examined microscopically. After 3 weeks of incubation at room temperature, a slow-growing black mold grew on Sabouraud's dextrose agar. Microscopic examination revealed cladosporium, phialophora and acrotheca types of sporulation. The probable identification of this organism is:

    a. *Fonsecaea pedrosoi*
    b. *Pseudallescheria boydii*
    c. *Phialophora verrucosa*
    d. *Cladosporium carrionii*

*271. Pus from a draining fistula on a foot was submitted for culture. Gross examination of the specimen revealed the presence of a small (0.8 mm in diameter), yellowish, oval granule. Direct microscopic examination of the crushed granule showed hyphae 3-4 µm in diameter and the presence of chlamydospores at the periphery. After two days a cottony, white mold was seen that turned gray with a gray to black reverse after a few days. When viewed microscopically, moderately large hyaline septate hyphae with long or short conidiophores, each single pear-shaped aleuriospore, 5-7 x 8-10 µm, were seen. The most likely identification is:

    a. *Exophiala jeanselmei*
    b. *Fonsecaea pedrosoi*
    c. *Pseudallescheria boydii*
    d. *Cladosporium carrionii*

*272. An isolate from a cornea infection had the following culture results:

-Sabouraud dextrose: white & cottony at 2 days, rose color at 6 days
-Slide culture: slender sickle shape micro- and macroconidia

The most likely organism is :

   a. *Acremonium* sp.
   b. *Pseudallescheria* sp.
   c. *Fusarium* sp.
   d. *Geotrichum* sp.

*273. Differential skin testing for mycobacteriosis has diagnostic value in young children because:

   a. immaturity of the immune system allows useful reactions
   b. infections develop more slowly, yielding more definitive immune response
   c. they have not yet become sensitized to many mycobacteria
   d. they develop hypersensitivity at an early age

*274. When staining acid-fast bacilli with Truant's auramine-rhodamine stain, potassium permanganate is used as a:

   a. decolorizing agent
   b. quenching agent
   c. mordant
   d. dye

*275. Middlebrook 7H10 and 7H11 media must be refrigerated in the dark and incubated in the dark as well. If these conditions are not met, the media may prove toxic for *Mycobacteria* because:

   a. carbon dioxide will be released, retarding growth
   b. growth factors will be broken down
   c. sunlight destroys the ammonium sulfate necessary in the mycobacterial metabolism
   d. formaldehyde may be produced

*276. Which of the following reagents is used only for decontamination of urine for mycobacterial culture?

   a. NaOH alone
   b. N-acetyl-L-cysteine and NaOH
   c. sulfuric acid
   d. zephiran-trisodium phosphate

*277. The most important constituent of the tubercle bacillus for the activity of the various tuberculoins is the:

    a. phospholipid
    b. protein
    c. wax D
    d. polysaccharide

*278. A two-week-old culture of a urine specimen produced a few colonies of acid-fast bacilli which were rough and nonpigmented. The niacin test was weakly positive and the nitrate test was positive. Which of the following is the most appropriate action when a presumptive identification has been requested as soon as possible?

    a. Report the organism as presumptive *Mycobacterium tuberculosis*.
    b. Wait a few days and repeat the niacin test; report presumptive *Mycobacterium tuberculosis* if the test is more strongly positive.
    c. Subculture the organism and set up the routine battery of biochemicals; notify the physician that results will not be available for three weeks.
    d. Set up a thiophene-2-carboxylic acid hydrazide (TCH); if the organism is sensitive, report *Mycobacterium bovis*.

*279. An acid-fast bacillus recovered from an induced sputum had the following characteristics:

Pigmentation: yellow in the dark, turning a deeper yellow-orange after two weeks of light exposure
Nitrate reduction: negative
Tween hydrolysis: positive at 5-10 days
Urease: negative

Based on this information, the organism is most likely *Mycobacterium*:

    a. *scrofulaceum*
    b. *gordonae*
    c. *szulgai*
    d. *flavescens*

*280. Which of the following characteristics best distinguishes *Mycobacterium scrofulaceum* from *Mycobacterium gordonae*?

    a. iron uptake
    b. Tween hydrolysis
    c. good growth at 25°C
    d. niacin production

*281. A nonpigmented acid-fast organism was cultured in five days from a cutaneous infection aspirate. No branching filamentous extensions were noted on the Middlebrook 7H11 plate. The biochemical results were as follows:

Nitrate: negative
Arylsulfatase
　3 day: positive
　2 week: positive
Iron-uptake: negative
Tween hydrolysis: negative

The organism most likely is:

a. Mycobacterium fortuitum
b. Mycobacterium smegmatis
c. Mycobacterium phlei
d. Mycobacterium chelonei

*282. Which of the following is a true statement about pigment production by Mycobacterium kansasii?

a. It is a result of beta carotene formation and accumulation.
b. It can be an indication of virulence.
c. It can be inhibited by inclusion of albumin in growth medium.
d. It is increased at 30°C incubation.

*283. Differentiation of Mycobacterium avium from Mycobacterium intracellulare can be accomplished by:

a. nitrate reduction test
b. Tween hydrolysis test
c. resistance to 10 μg thiophene-2-carboxylic acid hydrazide (TCH)
d. DNA probe

*284. Which one of the following species of Mycobacterium does NOT usually fluoresce on fluorochrome stain?

a. Mycobacterium fortuitum
b. Mycobacterium tuberculosis
c. Mycobacterium ulcerans
d. Mycobacterium bovis

*285. *Mycobacterium szulgai* characteristically:

    a. produces niacin
    b. is a low catalase producer (45 mm) and is nitrate
       reduction positive
    c. loses catalase after heating at 68°C, and has a negative
       Tween hydrolysis test at five days
    d. is scotochromogenic at 37°C and photochromogenic at 25°C

*286. The rapid growing mycobacteria can produce disease in humans.
Therapy for this group of organisms should include:

    a. isoniazid, ethambutol and paraminosalicylic acid
    b. rifampin, amikacin and SXT/TMP
    c. ampicillin, isoniazid and rifampin
    d. streptomycin, rifampin and cycloserine

*287. A FALSE statement about drug susceptibility testing of
mycobacteria is:

    a. It is difficult to standardize because of the variation
       in stability of drugs under different sterilization
       and storage methods.
    b. It may be performed directly on a digested, concentrated
       specimen if acid-fast bacilli are seen on a prepared
       film.
    c. Resistance is defined as 1% or more of the organisms
       that grow on the control quadrant also grow on a drug
       quadrant.
    d. It requires the use of *Mycobacterium tuberculosis*
       H37Rv and known resistant strains as controls run on
       egg-base media.

*288. The disease-producing capacity of *Mycobacterium tuberculosis*
depends primarily upon:

    a. production of exotoxin
    b. production of endotoxin
    c. capacity to withstand intracellular digestion by
       macrophages
    d. lack of susceptibility to the myeloperoxidase system

*289. Assuming that the host has no known immunologic defect, which
of the following is most likely to be associated with
resistance to standard drug therapy?

    a. *Mycobacterium tuberculosis*
    b. BCG *(Mycobacterium bovis)*
    c. *Mycobacterium intracellulare-avium*
    d. *Mycobacterium scrofulaceum*

*290. *Mycobacterium tuberculosis* can usually be distinguished from *Mycobacterium bovis* by positive tests for niacin accumulation and nitrate reductase. Occasional strains of *Mycobacterium bovis* may produce small amounts of both niacin and nitroreductase. In these strains, differentiation between the two species can best be accomplished by:

   a. Tween 80 hydrolysis within 10 days
   b. demonstration of heat stable catalase
   c. a positive arylsulfatase test within three days
   d. growth inhibition by thiophene-2-carboxylic acid hydrazide (TCH)

*291. Which species of *Mycobacteria* includes a BCG strain used for vaccination against tuberculosis?

   a. *tuberculosis*
   b. *bovis*
   c. *kansasii*
   d. *fortuitum/chelonei* complex

*292. Which of the following organisms grows slowest?

   a. *Mycobacterium tuberculosis*
   b. *Mycobacterium bovis*
   c. *Mycobacterium kansasii*
   d. *Mycobacterium intracellulare*

*293. A skin abscess is submitted for mycobacterial culture on a patient who scraped his hand while cleaning his fish aquarium. The technologist should:

   a. inoculate one tube of media at 30°C
   b. set up an anaerobic culture in addition to the acid-fast culture
   c. process the specimen immediately upon receipt
   d. keep inoculated media under a constant light source

*294. A formed stool is received in the laboratory at 3:00 a.m. for ova and parasite exam. The night shift technologist is certain that the workload will prevent examination of the specimen until 6 a.m. when the next shift arrives. The technologist should:

   a. request that a new specimen be collected after 6 a.m.
   b. perform a zinc sulfate flotation procedure for eggs and hold the remaining specimen at room temperature
   c. examine a direct prep for trophozoites and freeze the remaining specimen
   d. refrigerate the specimen until the next shift arrives

*295. A batch of trichrome-stained slides for ova and parasite examination contains numerous minute crystals which totally obscure the microscopic field. Which of the following measures is the most appropriate remedial action?

    a. Change the Schaudinn's fixative, remove coverslips and restain.
    b. Change the acid alcohol and restain.
    c. Remove coverslips and remount using fresh Permount or similar medium.
    d. Change the iodine alcohol solution to obtain a strong tea-colored solution, restain.

*296. Protozoan cysts are found in a wet mount of sediment from ethyl-acetate concentrated material. The cysts are without peripheral chromatin on the nuclear membrane. Each cyst has four nuclei and each nuclei has a large karyosome which appears as a refractive dot. These oval-shaped cysts are most likely:

    a. *Endolimax nana*
    b. *Chilomastix mesnili*
    c. *Entamoeba histolytica*
    d. *Entamoeba hartmanni*

*297. Which of the following organisms may be mistaken for the cyst of *Iodamoeba butschlii* due to the presence of an apparent large vacuole?

    a. the pre-cyst of *Entamoeba histolytica*
    b. vacuolated cyst of *Entamoeba coli*
    c. *Endolimax nana*
    d. *Blastocystis hominis*

*298. A stool specimen for ova and parasite examination contained numerous rhabditiform larvae. Which factor does NOT aid in the identification of larvae?

    a. length of the buccal cavity
    b. age of the specimen
    c. appearance of the genital primordium
    d. endemic area traveled

*299. The term "internal autoinfection" is generally used in referring to infections with:

    a. *Ascaris lumbricoides*
    b. *Necator americanus*
    c. *Trichuris trichuria*
    d. *Strongyloides stercoralis*

*300. A 44-year-old man was admitted to the hospital following a two-week history of low grade fever, malaise and anorexia. Examination of a Giemsa stained blood film revealed many intraerythrocytic parasites. Further history revealed frequent camping trips near Martha's Vineyard and Nantucket Island, but no travel outside the continental United States. This parasite could easily be confused with:

    a. *Trypanosoma cruzi*
    b. *Trypanosoma rhodesiense/gambiense*
    c. *Plasmodium falciparum*
    d. *Leishmania donovani*

*301. What material should be used to prepare slides for direct smear examination for virus detection by special stains or FA technique?

    a. vesicular fluid
    b. leukocytes from the edge of the lesion
    c. the top portion of the vesicle
    d. epithelial cells from the base of the lesion

*302. The most commonly used cell line in the clinical virology laboratory for viral propagation is the:

    a. KB cell
    b. Hep-2
    c. FL
    d. HeLa

*303. If gentamicin is incorporated into 2SP transport medium, there may be a compromise in the recovery of:

    a. *Ureaplasma urealyticum*
    b. *Chlamydia trachomatis*
    c. *Chlamydia psittaci*
    d. both *Chlamydia trachomatis* and *Chlamydia psittaci*

*304. An example of a live attenuated vaccine used for human immunization is:

    a. rabies
    b. tetanus
    c. influenza
    d. measles (Edmonston)

*305. A whooping cough syndrome such as the one seen with infections caused by *Bordetella pertussis* can be seen in the infections due to:

    a. rhinovirus
    b. adenovirus
    c. coxsackie virus
    d. respiratory syncytial virus

*306. Which of the following viruses may only be detected by use of an electron microscope or ELISA methods?

    a. respiratory syncytial virus
    b. influenza A
    c. rotavirus
    d. herpes simplex 1

*307. Throat swabs may be inoculated directly into a special HeLa cell line when which of the following viruses is suspected?

    a. respiratory syncytial virus
    b. influenza A
    c. rotavirus
    d. herpes simplex 1

*308. Holding medium recommended for use in transporting urine or throat specimens for the recovery of cytomegalovirus contains:

    a. buffered tryptose phosphate broth
    b. sorbitol
    c. Hank's balanced salt solution
    d. 10% fetal albumin

*309. The preferred specimen for laboratory diagnosis of acquired cytomegalovirus infection is:

    a. blood
    b. urine
    c. stool
    d. cutaneous vesicular fluid

*310. The Epstein-Barr virus is associated with which of the following?

    a. chicken pox
    b. Hodgkin's lymphoma
    c. Burkitt's lymphoma
    d. smallpox

*311. Which of the following statements is true regarding the diagnosis of herpes simplex encephalitis caused by *Herpesvirus hominis*?

   a. The virus can usually be recovered from spinal fluid during the first week of illness.
   b. The virus can usually be recovered from feces during the first week of illness.
   c. The virus is rarely recoverable from either spinal fluid or feces during herpes encephalitis.
   d. Cytopathic effects are slow to develop in cell cultures compared to those induced by mumps virus.

*312. A twenty-nine-year old man is seen for recurrence of a purulent urethral discharge ten days after the successful treatment of culture proven gonorrhea. The most likely etiology of his urethritis is:

   a. *Mycoplasma hominis*
   b. *Chlamydia trachomatis*
   c. *Trichomonas vaginalis*
   d. *Neisseria gonorrhoeae*

*313. *Ureaplasma urealyticum* are difficult to grow in the laboratory on routine media because of their requirement for:

   a. sterols
   b. horse blood
   c. ferric pyrophosphate
   d. surfactant such as Tween 80

*314. Which of the following is the single most important difference between viruses and chlamydia?

   a. obligate intracellular parasitism
   b. complex life cycle
   c. possession of mitochondria
   d. possession of a single type of nucleic acid

*315. The serological test that is most sensitive for detecting all chlamydial infections is:

   a. complement fixation (CF)
   b. microimmunofluorescence (MIF)
   c. single antigen immunofluorescence
   d. indirect fluorescent antibody

*316. A cell culture line commonly used for the recovery of
Chlamydia trachomatis from clinical specimens is:

    a. HeLa 229
    b. Hep-2
    c. BHK-21
    d. McCoy's

*317. Which of the following is characteristic of rickettsial disease
testing?

    a. The Weil-Felix test is one of the most specific.
    b. Rickettsiae can be seen in infected tissue with
       immunofluorescent techniques.
    c. The complement fixation test is one of the least
       specific.
    d. Antibody to the Q fever agent will cross-react with the
       Rocky Mountain Spotted Fever agent.

*318. Rickettsiae infecting man multiply preferentially within which
of the following cells?

    a. reticuloendothelial
    b. hepatic
    c. renal tubule
    d. endothelial

*319. The most reliable serologic test for the diagnosis of Q fever
is the:

    a. cold agglutinin test
    b. heterophile antibody test
    c. complement fixation test
    d. Weil-Felix test

Microbiology Answer Key

1.	D	48.	A	95.	A	142.	A
2.	D	49.	B	96.	D	143.	C
3.	C	50.	D	97.	B	144.	B
4.	B	51.	D	98.	D	145.	A
5.	B	52.	B	99.	A	146.	C
6.	B	53.	C	100.	D	147.	B
7.	C	54.	B	101.	B	148.	A
8.	B	55.	C	102.	D	149.	D
9.	A	56.	D	103.	C	150.	D
10.	A	57.	B	104.	D	151.	C
11.	D	58.	A	105.	D	152.	C
12.	D	59.	C	106.	B	153.	D
13.	C	60.	D	107.	B	154.	B
14.	D	61.	C	108.	C	155.	D
15.	B	62.	A	109.	A	156.	C
16.	D	63.	B	110.	B	157.	B
17.	B	64.	C	111.	D	158.	B
18.	C	65.	A	112.	A	159.	C
19.	B	66.	A	113.	B	160.	D
20.	C	67.	D	114.	C	161.	D
21.	D	68.	C	115.	A	162.	B
22.	C	69.	D	116.	D	163.	A
23.	B	70.	D	117.	D	164.	A
24.	D	71.	B	118.	B	165.	C
25.	A	72.	C	119.	C	166.	D
26.	C	73.	B	120.	D	167.	C
27.	D	74.	D	121.	C	168.	A
28.	C	75.	C	122.	D	169.	D
29.	A	76.	B	123.	D	170.	A
30.	B	77.	A	124.	C	171.	B
31.	B	78.	B	125.	A	172.	A
32.	B	79.	A	126.	B	173.	C
33.	A	80.	A	127.	A	174.	A
34.	B	81.	B	128.	B	175.	D
35.	A	82.	B	129.	A	176.	D
36.	C	83.	A	130.	C	177.	A
37.	D	84.	C	131.	C	178.	D
38.	D	85.	C	132.	D	179.	B
39.	C	86.	A	133.	D	180.	B
40.	D	87.	D	134.	C	181.	B
41.	D	88.	A	135.	D	182.	A
42.	D	89.	C	136.	B	183.	C
43.	D	90.	D	137.	C	184.	B
44.	D	91.	C	138.	C	185.	B
45.	C	92.	A	139.	D	186.	C
46.	D	93.	B	140.	B	187.	D
47.	C	94.	C	141.	D	188.	D

189.	B	222.	B	255.	B	288.	C
190.	D	223.	D	256.	A	289.	C
191.	D	224.	C	257.	C	290.	D
192.	C	225.	D	258.	D	291.	B
193.	C	226.	D	259.	D	292.	B
194.	D	227.	D	260.	A	293.	A
195.	A	228.	D	261.	A	294.	D
196.	D	229.	A	262.	B	295.	D
197.	B	230.	A	263.	C	296.	A
198.	C	231.	D	264.	B	297.	D
199.	D	232.	D	265.	D	298.	D
200.	C	233.	B	266.	D	299.	D
201.	D	234.	B	267.	D	300.	C
202.	D	235.	C	268.	C	301.	D
203.	C	236.	A	269.	D	302.	D
204.	D	237.	C	270.	A	303.	A
205.	B	238.	A	271.	C	304.	D
206.	B	239.	A	272.	C	305.	B
207.	B	240.	D	273.	C	306.	C
208.	A	241.	C	274.	B	307.	A
209.	C	242.	C	275.	D	308.	B
210.	C	243.	B	276.	C	309.	B
211.	B	244.	C	277.	B	310.	C
212.	A	245.	A	278.	B	311.	C
213.	A	246.	C	279.	B	312.	B
214.	D	247.	A	280.	B	313.	A
215.	B	248.	C	281.	D	314.	D
216.	B	249.	C	282.	A	315.	B
217.	D	250.	A	283.	D	316.	D
218.	C	251.	B	284.	A	317.	B
219.	D	252.	C	285.	D	318.	D
220.	B	253.	B	286.	B	319.	C
221.	B	254.	D	287.	D		

CHAPTER 17

Laboratory Management

The following items (*) have been identified as more appropriate for the entry level medical technologist.

* 1. Good performance by a manager could best be defined as:

  a. being a care taker
  b. the ability to get ideas implemented
  c. the ability to respond to crises
  d. being a good organizer

* 2. According to most organizational theorists, managerial functions include:

  a. planning and organizing
  b. clerical work and proofreading
  c. specimen processing and benchwork
  d. buying and selling

* 3. The ability to make good decisions often depends on the use of a logical sequence of steps which includes, but is not limited to which of the following?

  a. define problem, consider options, implement
     decision
  b. obtain facts, consider alternatives, review results
  c. define problem, obtain facts, consider options
  d. obtain facts, define problem, implement decision

* 4. In the context of the planning process, the term "goal" has been defined as a:

  a. plan for reaching certain objectives
  b. set of specific tasks
  c. set of short and long-term plans
  d. major purpose or final desired result

* 5. Delegation is a process in which:

  a. interpersonal influence is redefined
  b. authority of manager is surrendered
  c. power is given to subordinates
  d. responsibility for specific tasks is given to
     subordinates

* 6. Refer to the following illustration:

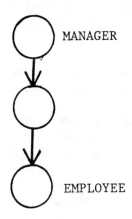

MANAGER

EMPLOYEE

Which statement best describes the communication style
illustrated above?

    a. is most commonly used by "democratic" leaders
    b. promotes high morale among employees
    c. is best suited for emergency situations
    d. is best suited for group problem-solving

* 7. What action should be taken when dealing with a long-term
problem?

    a. ignore the problem
    b. seek more information
    c. base decision on available information
    d. refer the problem to another level of management

* 8. A major laboratory policy change is going to take place that
will affect a significant portion of the laboratory employees.
In order to minimize the resistance to change the supervisor
should:

    a. announce the change one day after it goes into
       effect
    b. discuss the change in detail with all concerned,
       well in advance
    c. announce only the positive aspects in advance
    d. discuss only the positive aspects with those
       concerned

* 9. Which of the following actions will facilitate group interactions
      at staff meetings?

      a. adhering strictly to an agenda
      b. treating every problem consistently
      c. encouraging input from all staff
      d. announcing the assignments for upcoming projects

* 10. As information is reported upward through an organization, the
       amount of detail communicated will generally:

      a. decrease to facilitate the flow of information
      b. increase to allow consideration of all options
      c. remain the same to ensure consistency in reporting
      d. remain the same to ensure goal accomplishment

* 11. A good way to monitor precision is by:

      a. running duplicate assays
      b. repeated serial testing
      c. processing unknown specimens
      d. running normal and abnormal controls

* 12. The reliability of a test to be positive in the presence of the
       disease it was designed to detect is known as:

      a. accuracy
      b. sensitivity
      c. precision
      d. specificity

* 13. Which of the following parameters of a diagnostic test will
       vary with the prevalence of a given disease in a population?

      a. predictive value
      b. sensitivity
      c. accuracy
      d. specificity

* 14. The major workload in most hospital laboratories is generated
       in:

      a. Hematology
      b. Chemistry
      c. Microbiology
      d. Immunohematology

* 15. A new laboratory is being designed to include a STAT lab with a method of specimen transport from critical care areas. What laboratory services should be provided in the STAT lab?

        a. Microbiology and Hematology
        b. Chemistry and Serology
        c. Hematology and Chemistry
        d. Chemistry and Microbiology

* 16. Employees are guaranteed the right to engage in self-organization and collective bargaining through representatives of their choice, or to refrain from these activities by which of the following?

        a. Civil Rights Act
        b. Freedom of Information Act
        c. Clinical Laboratory Improvements Act (CLIA)
        d. National Labor Relations Act

* 17. The purpose of the Clinical Laboratory Improvement Act of 1967 (CLIA) was to:

        a. license laboratories that accepted fewer than 100 specimens per year
        b. license laboratories that engaged in interstate commerce
        c. exempt laboratories that were operated by private physicians
        d. dictate standards for laboratory personnel

* 18. Which of the following is an anticipated change in laboratory operations of the 1990's?

        a. elimination of education/training standards for personnel
        b. permitting patients direct access to ordering certain lab tests and obtaining results
        c. federal government licensure of medical laboratory technologists and technicians
        d. decreasing test volumes attributable to cost containment efforts of the federal government

* 19. Which of the following organizations was formed to encourage the voluntary attainment of uniformly high standards in institutional medical care?

  a. Centers for Disease Control (CDC)
  b. Health Care Finance Administration (HCFA)
  c. Joint Commission on Accreditation of Health Care Organizations (JCAHO)
  d. Federal Drug Administration (FDA)

* 20. The process by which an agency or organization evaluates and recognizes that a program of study in an institution has predetermined standards is:

  a. regulation
  b. licensure
  c. accreditation
  d. credentialing

* 21. A general term for the formal recognition of professional or technical competence is

  a. regulation
  b. licensure
  c. accreditation
  d. credentialing

* 22. Package inserts may be used:

  a. in lieu of the typed procedure
  b. as a reference in a complete procedure
  c. at the bench but not in the procedure manual
  d. if initialed and dated by the laboratory director

* 23. Which of the following is considered to be a variable cost in a clinical laboratory?

  a. overtime pay
  b. health insurance premiums
  c. FICA
  d. pension contributions

* 24. Direct, indirect and overhead costs incurred during the production of tests per unit time are classified as:

  a. total costs
  b. actual costs
  c. standard costs
  d. controllable costs

* 25. An advantage of reagent lease/rental agreements is:

    a. less time spent by the laboratory manager justifying new instrumentation
    b. more flexibility to adjust to changes in work load, test menu methods, etc.
    c. flexibility in reagent usage from one manufacturer to another
    d. less expenditures over life expectancy of instrument

* 26. A new clinic in the area is sending a very large number of additional chemistry tests to the laboratory. The existing chemistry instrument is only 2 years old and works well, however, there is a need to acquire a new high throughput instrument. Which one of the following is the appropriate "Justification Category"?

    a. replacement
    b. volume increase
    c. reduction of FTEs
    d. new service

* 27. The number of hours used to calculate the annual salary of a full-time employee is:

    a. 1920
    b. 1950
    c. 2080
    d. 2800

* 28. The overtime budget for the laboratory is $38,773, but $50,419 has already been spent. What percent over budget does this ' represent?

    a. 30%
    b. 70%
    c. 77%
    d. 100%

* 29. Matching the content and requirements of the task with the skills, abilities and needs of the worker is a function of:

    a. leadership
    b. job design
    c. recruitment
    d. reward systems

* 30. When coping with a "difficult" employee, the manager should initially:

    a. intricate appropriate disciplinary intervention
    b. determine if this is an acute or chronic trait
    c. ascertain whether the goals of the group or individual are being served
    d. diffuse the situation by changing the employee's shift

* 31. Evaluating the performance of employees should be done:

    a. annually
    b. semiannually
    c. as needed in the judgment of management
    d. in the form of immediate feedback and at regular intervals

* 32. Which one of the following is NOT a reason for doing a performance evaluation?

    a. to give employee performance feedback
    b. to determine training needs
    c. to help the employee improve performance
    d. to criticize a problem employee

* 33. The most important part of any effective behavior modification system is:

    a. feedback to employees
    b. salary structure
    c. job enrichment
    d. tactful discipline
    e. delegation of authority

* 34. Disciplinary policy is generally developed as a series of steps, each one being more punitive. Normally, the first step in the process is to:

    a. send the employee a warning letter
    b. send the employee a counseling memo
    c. counsel the employee verbally
    d. dismiss less serious infractions

* 35. A supervisor notices that one of her technologists continues to mouth-pipet liquids when making reagents. The supervisor's best course of action is to:

       a. allow the technologist to continue this practice as long as it is not done when dealing with specimens
       b. discuss this problem with the employee immediately
       c. order a mechanical device (bulb-pipet) for employee to use
       d. compliment the employee on his rapid pipetting technique

* 36. A technologist on the night shift has been observed sleeping on repeated occasions by the day shift supervisor. Which of the following is the most appropriate INITIAL course of action for the day supervisor?

       a. Ignore the repeated incidents.
       b. Discuss the facts with the technologist's immediate supervisor.
       c. Notify the personnel department of policy violations.
       d. Advise the laboratory director in writing of the apparent misconduct.

* 37. A workload reporting system is an important part of laboratory management because it:

       a. tells exactly how much should be charged per test
       b. keeps personnel busy in their free time
       c. counts only tests done and specimens received in the laboratory without inflating these figures by adding in quality control and standardization efforts
       d. helps in planning, developing, and maintaining efficient laboratory services with administrative and budget controls

* 38. If twelve technologists were paid for a total of 2076 hours, of which 212 were vacation, sick and paid professional leave, what would be the productivity per hour worked if the workload units were 58,000?

       a. 18 units
       b. 28 units
       c. 31 units
       d. 52 units

* 39. Which one of the following questions can be legally asked on an employment application?

    a. Are you a U. S. citizen?
    b. What is your date of birth?
    c. Is your wife/husband employed full-time?
    d. Do you have any dependents?

* 40. Which of the following topic areas should NOT be discussed with a prospective employee during a job interview?

    a. location of clinical education program
    b. number of dependents
    c. previous employment that the applicant disliked
    d. specific details in the job description

* 41. An effective program of continuing education for medical laboratory personnel should first:

    a. find a good speaker
    b. motivate employees to attend
    c. determine an adequate budget
    d. identify the needs

Laboratory Management Answer Key

1.	B	12.	B	23.	A	34.	C
2.	A	13.	C	24.	B	35.	B
3.	C	14.	B	25.	B	36.	B
4.	D	15.	C	26.	B	37.	D
5.	D	16.	D	27.	C	38.	C
6.	C	17.	B	28.	A	39.	A
7.	B	18.	B	29.	B	40.	B
8.	B	19.	C	30.	C	41.	D
9.	C	20.	C	31.	D		
10.	A	21.	D	32.	D		
11.	A	22.	B	33.	A		

APPENDIX A

ITEM DESCRIPTORS FOR
1990 MEDICAL LABORATORY TECHNICIAN EXAMINATIONS

GLOSSARY OF TERMS USED IN ITEM DESCRIPTORS
MEDICAL LABORATORY TECHNICIAN EXAMINATION - FEBRUARY 1990

SUBTEST

BBNK	BLOOD BANK
BF	BODY FLUID
CHEM	CHEMISTRY
HEMA	HEMATOLOGY
IMMU	IMMUNOLOGY
MICR	MICROBIOLOGY

TASK

AKFC	APPLIES KNOWLEDGE OF FUNDAMENTAL BIOLOGICAL CHARACTERISTICS		EDMI	EVALUATES LABORATORY DATA TO MAKE IDENTIFICATIONS
AKOP	APPLIES KNOWLEDGE OF STANDARD OPERATING PROCEDURES		EDVR	EVALUATES LABORATORY DATA TO VERIFY TEST RESULTS
AKSE	APPLIES KNOWLEDGE TO IDENTIFY SOURCES OF ERROR		ESOE	EVALUATES SOURCES OF ERROR
APBP	APPLIES PRINCIPLES OF BASIC LABORATORY PROCEDURES		PCAT	PREPARES CONTROLS FOR APPROPRIATE TEST PROCEDURES
CALC	CALCULATES		PIPT	PREPARES INSTRUMENTS TO PERFORM TESTS
CCLD	CORRELATES CLINICAL AND LABORATORY DATA		PRM	PREPARES REAGENTS/MEDIA/BLOOD
CDAR	CORRELATES LABORATORY DATA WITH OTHER LABORATORY DATA TO ASSESS TEST RESULTS		SCOA	SELECTS COURSE OF ACTION
			SIPT	SELECTS INSTRUMENT TO PERFORM APPROPRIATE TESTS
EDHD	EVALUATES LABORATORY DATA TO ASSESS HEALTH AND DISEASE STATES		SMRM	SELECTS METHODS/REAGENTS/MEDIA
			SPVR	SELECTS ROUTINE LABORATORY PROCEDURES TO VERIFY TEST RESULTS
EDIR	EVALUATES LABORATORY DATA TO DETERMINE POSSIBLE INCONSISTENT RESULTS		SSLP	SELECTS SPECIAL LABORATORY PROCEDURES

CONTENT SPECIFICS

A&P	ANATOMY AND PHYSIOLOGY		HCG	HUMAN CHORIONIC GONADOTROPIN
AB	ANTIBODY		HLA	HUMAN LEUKOCYTE ANTIGEN
ABE	ACID BASE ELECTROLYTES		ID	IDENTIFICATION
AG	ANTIGEN		INST	INSTRUMENTS, INSTRUMENTATION
AGG	AGGLUTINATION, AGGLUTININ		LDL	LOW DENSITY LIPOPROTEIN
AIDS	ACQUIRED IMMUNODEFICIENCY SYNDROME		MACRO	MACROCYTIC, MACROSCOPIC
AIHA	AUTOIMMUNE HEMOLYTIC ANEMIA		MICRO	MICROCYTIC, MICROSCOPIC
ASO	ANTISTREPTOLYSIN O		MORPH	MORPHOLOGY
BIOCHEM	BIOCHEMICAL		P&E	PROTEINS AND ENZYMES
BTP	BIOLOGICAL THEORY AND PRINCIPLE		PTT	PARTIAL THROMBOPLASTIN TIME
CALC	CALCULATE		QC	QUALITY CONTROL
CBC	COMPLETE BLOOD COUNT		RA	RHEUMATOID ARTHRITIS
CLL	CHRONIC LYMPHOCYTIC LEUKEMIA		RBC	RED BLOOD CELLS
COAG	COAGULATION		RHIG	RH IMMUNE GLOBULIN
CSF	CEREBROSPINAL FLUID		RID	RADIAL IMMUNODIFFISION
CV	COEFFICIENT OF VARIATION		RXN	REACTION
FE	IRON		SCH	SPECIMEN COLLECTION AND HANDLING
FFP	FRESH FROZEN PLASMA		SG	SPECIFIC GRAVITY
FSP	FIBRIN SPLIT PRODUCTS		SLE	SYSTEMIC LUPUS ERYTHEMATOSUS
GNB	GRAM NEGATIVE BACILLI		TSI	TRIPLE SUGAR IRON
GNC	GRAM NEGATIVE COCCI		WBC	WHITE BLOOD CELL
GPC	GRAM POSITIVE COCCI		X-MATCH	CROSSMATCH
GTP	GENETIC THEORY AND PRINCIPLE			
GTT	GLUCOSE TOLERANCE TEST			

1. MICR/AKFC/BASIC TESTS/TSI/1
2. MICR/AKFC/MICROSCOPY/SPIROCHETE/1
3. MICR/CDAR/BLOOD CULTURE/CONTAMINANT/2
4. MICR/SMRM/GNC/URETHRAL DISCHARGE/1
5. MICR/PCAT/QC/BETA HEMOLYSIS/3
6. MICR/AKFC/BASIC TESTS/GPC/1
7. MICR/AKFC/BIOCHEM TESTS/ENTEROBACTERIACEAE/1
8. MICR/APBP/SCH/MYCOBACTERIUM/1
9. MICR/SMRM/SCH/PROTOZOA/1
10. MICR/EDMI/BIOCHEM TEST/GNB/2
11. MICR/SCOA/MICRO MORPH/SCH/3
12. MICR/EDMI/MICRO MORPH/STREPTOCOCCUS/3
13. MICR/SCOA/SCH/GNC/3
14. MICR/CCLD/BASIC TESTS/STREPTOCOCCUS/2
15. MICR/PRM/MEDIA/X FACTOR/2
16. MICR/EDHD/BACTERIA/GRAM STAIN/2
17. MICR/SMRM/SCH/CAMPYLOBACTER/2
18. MICR/EDMI/MICRO-MACRO MORPH/GNC-BIOCHEM ID/3
19. MICR/CALC/BACTERIA/COLONY COUNT/2
20. MICR/APBP/MICRO MORPH/FUNGI/1
21. MICR/AKFC/NEMATODE/TRANSMISSION/1
22. MICR/EDVR/MICRO MORPH/ANAEROBE/2
23. MICR/CDAR/GNB/BIOCHEM TESTS/2
24. MICR/APBP/VIRAL TITER/1
25. MICR/AKFC/DIMORPHIC FUNGI/1
26. MICR/EDMI/FLAGELLATE/3
27. MICR/EDMI/AMOEBA/2
28. MICR/AKFC/MEDIA/1
29. MICR/EDMI/GNB/VAGINAL FLORA/2
30. MICR/SCOA/SCH/CSF/1
31. MICR/ESOE/BASIC TESTS/SUSCEPTIBILITY/2
32. MICR/AKFC/GPC/BIOCHEM TEST/1
33. MICR/AKFC/BIOCHEM ID/PROTEUS/1
34. MICR/APBP/GNB/NONFERMENTATIVE/1
35. MICR/APBP/GPC/BIOCHEM TEST/1
36. MICR/EDVR/BIOCHEM ID/ENTEROBACTERIACEAE/2
37. MICR/AKFC/GNB/GROWTH CHARACTERISTIC/1
38. MICR/AKFC/GNB/MACRO MORPH/1
39. MICR/AKFC/MACRO MORPH/PROTEUS/1
40. BF/AKOP/URINE SEDIMENT/CASTS/1
41. BF/SMRM/SCH/24-HOUR URINE/1
42. BF/EDVR/URINALYSIS/REAGENT STRIP/2
43. BF/SCOA/SCH/CELL COUNT CSF/1
44. BF/CDAR/MICRO MORPH/URINE SEDIMENT/2
45. BF/EDVR/URINE REAGENT STRIP/2
46. BF/CDAR/COMPOSITION/PLEURAL FLUID/2
47. BF/AKFC/COMPOSITION/URINE/1
48. BF/AKFC/COMPOSITION/URINE/1
49. BF/APBP/URINE/REAGENT STRIP/1
50. BF/SPVR/URINALYSIS/QC/2
51. BF/ESOE/URINE/PROTEIN/3
52. BF/SCOA/SCH/CREATININE CLEARANCE/2
53. BF/EDHD/URINE CHEMISTRY/REDUCING SUBSTANCE/3
54. BF/SCOA/SCH/URINE PROTEIN/1
55. BF/AKFC/SPECIMEN APPEARANCE/CSF/1
56. BF/ESOE/SCH/URINE/2
57. BF/PRM/URINE PROTEIN/2
58. BF/AKFC/URINE CHEM/REAGENT STRIP/1
59. IMMU/AKFC/PHYSIOLOGY/IMMUNOGLOBULIN/1
60. IMMU/AKFC/COLD AGG/1

61. IMMU/ESOE/QC/RA TEST/3
62. IMMU/CCLD/AIDS/1
63. IMMU/AKFC/HUMORAL/IMMUNITY/1
64. IMMU/EDMI/AG AB COMPLEX/1
65. IMMU/AKFC/A&P/AB SECRETION/1
66. IMMU/AKSE/IMMUNOASSAY/HCG/2
67. IMMU/SMRM/SYPHILIS TESTING/1
68. IMMU/AKFC/AUTOIMMUNITY/IMMUNOFLUORESCENCE/1
69. IMMU/AKOP/SPECIMEN COLLECTION/COLD AGG/1
70. IMMU/APBP/RA/PRINCIPLE/1
71. IMMU/EDHD/ALLERGIC RXN/1
72. IMMU/SCOA/RID/3
73. IMMU/ESOE/BASIC TESTS/ASO TITER/2
74. IMMU/SPVR/SLE/1
75. IMMU/SMRM/QC/SCREENING PROCEDURE/1
76. IMMU/CDAR/BASIC TESTS/C-REACTIVE PROTEIN/1
77. BBNK/AKFC/GTP/AB RESPONSE/1
78. BBNK/AKFC/ELUTION/1
79. BBNK/AKFC/RBC/EXPIRATION/1
80. BBNK/AKFC/AGG RXN/1
81. BBNK/AKFC/SCH/COMPATIBILITY TEST/1
82. BBNK/AKOP/ABO SUBGROUPS/1
83. BBNK/AKFC/NATURAL AB/1
84. BBNK/SCOA/TRANSFUSION RXN/2
85. BBNK/ESOE/RBC/CELL SUSPENSION/3
86. BBNK/AKFC/QC/STORAGE/1
87. BBNK/SCOA/RHIG/TREATMENT/3
88. BBNK/AKFC/RBC/ANTICOAGULANT/1
89. BBNK/AKOP/CLINICAL APPLICATIONS/AUTOLOGOUS/1
90. BBNK/SCOA/FREEZER QC/2
91. BBNK/SMRM/HEMOTHERAPY/FACTOR DEFICIENCY/3
92. BBNK/AKFC/HLA TYPING/1
93. BBNK/AKFC/HEMOTHERAPY/ADVERSE RXN/1
94. BBNK/SMRM/COMPONENT/PLATELET POOLING/2
95. BBNK/CDAR/RBC/ADVERSE RXN/2
96. BBNK/AKFC/SCH/PLATELETS/1
97. BBNK/EDAT/RBC/FETOMATERNAL HEMORRHAGE/2
98. BBNK/EDAT/RBC/ANTIGLOBULIN TEST/2
99. BBNK/AKOP/RBC/REAGENT QC/1
100. BBNK/AKFC/BLOOD COMPONENT/CLOTTING FACTORS/1
101. BBNK/AKFC/RBC/ANTIGLOBULIN TEST/2
102. BBNK/EDMI/HEMOTHERAPY/BLOOD COMPONENT/3
103. BBNK/SMRM/HEMOTHERAPY/BLOOD COMPONENT/3
104. BBNK/EDMI/AB ID/3
105. BBNK/ESOE/RBC/COMPATIBILITY/2
106. BBNK/EDMI/X-MATCH/AUTOCONTROL/3
107. BBNK/CCLD/HEMOTHERAPY/ADVERSE RXN/2
108. BBNK/CDAR/HEMOLYTIC TRANSFUSION/2
109. BBNK/AKFC/SCH AB SCREEN/X-MATCH/1
110. BBNK/AKOP/TRANSFUSION TRANSMITTANCE DISEASE/1
111. BBNK/EDVR/ABO TYPING/2
112. BBNK/SMRM/ABO AB/2
113. BBNK/ESOE/ABO TESTING/3
114. BBNK/CCLD/RBC/AIHA/1
115. CHEM/AKFC/INST/QC/1
116. CHEM/ESOE/INST/FLAME PHOTOMETRY/3
117. CHEM/AKFC/PROTEIN/FETOPROTEIN/1
118. CHEM/CALC/SAMPLE DILUTION/2
119. CHEM/EDHD/LIPIDS/LDL/3
120. CHEM/EDVR/P&E/GLOBULIN/3

121. CHEM/AKFC/PROTEIN/COPPER/1	155. HEMA/EDHD/MICRO MORPH/ANEMIA/2
122. CHEM/AKFC/CARBOHYDRATES/GLUCOSE/1	156. HEMA/AKFC/RBC/DILUENT/1
123. CHEM/PCAT/SPECIMEN/QC/1	157. HEMA/SPVR/HEMOSTASIS/INTRINSIC/1
124. CHEM/ESOE/SCH/ELECTROLYTES/2	158. HEMA/CALC/WBC/DILUTION/2
125. CHEM/SMRM/INST/KINETIC ASSAY/2	159. HEMA/CALC/RBC/CHAMBER COUNT/2
126. CHEM/AKFC/BTP/ELECTROLYTES/1	160. HEMA/CALC/QC/CONTROL LIMITS/2
127. CHEM/CALC/QC/CV/2	161. HEMA/ESOE/RBC/AUTOMATED COUNT/2
128. CHEM/EDHD/ABE/KETOACIDOSIS/2	162. HEMA/EDMI/SOURCE OF ERROR/SLIDE PREPARATION/2
129. CHEM/CALC/MOLECULAR WEIGHT/2	163. HEMA/EDMI/BASIC TESTS/WBC DIFFERENTIAL/2
130. CHEM/AKFC/INST/OSMOMETER/1	164. HEMA/EDMI/WBC INCLUSION/2
131. CHEM/SMRM/SCH/ACID-BASE/1	165. HEMA/SCOA/MICRO MORPH/MEGALOBLASTIC ANEMIA/3
132. CHEM/CCLD/P&E/AMYLASE/1	166. HEMA/CALC/WBC DILUTION/2
133. CHEM/SCOA/SCH/POTASSIUM/3	167. HEMA/AKFC/WBC MATURATION/1
134. CHEM/AKFC/ABE/OSMOLARITY/1	168. HEMA/AKFC/WBC MATURATION/1
135. CHEM/CDAR/ELECTROLYTES/CALCIUM/1	169. HEMA/CDAR/FE/1
136. CHEM/AKFC/DRUG MONITOR/DIGOXIN/1	170. HEMA/AKFC/PHYSIOLOGY/HEMATOPOIESIS/1
137. CHEM/AKFC/QC/STATISTICS/1	171. HEMA/AKFC/RBC MATURATION/1
138. CHEM/APBP/SPECIAL TESTS/T-3 UPTAKE/1	172. HEMA/CDAR/WBC/MONONUCLEAR MORPH/2
139. CHEM/EDIR/QC/GLUCOSE/2	173. HEMA/CCLD/HEMOSTASIS/FACTOR DEFICIENCY/3
140. CHEM/ESOE/SCH/P&E/3	174. HEMA/SMRM/HEMOGLOBIN S/2
141. CHEM/CALC/STANDARD SOLUTION/2	175. HEMA/APBP/PLATELET COUNT/1
142. CHEM/SIPT/INST/DOWNTIME/2	176. HEMA/CCLD/FSP/FIBRINOLYSIS/2
143. CHEM/SCOA/SCH/ACID PHOSPHATASE/1	177. HEMA/EDMI/LEUKOCYTE/1
144. CHEM/SSLP/SCH/GTT/2	178. HEMA/CDAR/MICRO MORPH/CLL/1
145. CHEM/AKFC/CARDIAC ENZYMES/2	179. HEMA/CDAR/HEMATOCRIT/2
146. CHEM/AKFC/SPECIAL TESTS/ELECTROPHORESIS/1	180. HEMA/ESOE/COAG/PTT/2
147. CHEM/APBP/SPECIAL CHEM/AMMONIA/1	181. HEMA/PRM/DILUTING FLUID/2
148. CHEM/ESOE/SCH/BILIRUBIN/3	182. HEMA/AKFC/HEMOGLOBIN/QC/1
149. CHEM/AKFC/BTP/LIPIDS/1	183. HEMA/AKFC/PLATELETS/THROMBASTHENIA/1
150. CHEM/AKSE/ACID PHOSPHATASE/1	184. HEMA/AKFC/HEMOGLOBINOPATHY/THALASSEMIA/1
151. CHEM/CCLD/ENZYMES/MYOCARDIAL INFARCT/2	185. HEMA/AKFC/RBC INCLUSIONS/1
152. CHEM/APBP/ISOENZYMES/1	186. HEMA/APBP/BASIC TESTS/PROTHROMBIN TIME/1
153. HEMA/AKFC/A&P/PLATELETS/1	187. HEMA/SCOA/RBC INDICES/MANUAL METHODS/3
154. HEMA/CALC/WBC/CORRECTED COUNT/2	188. HEMA/PRM/DILUTION/2

TAXONOMIC LEVELS

TAX 1 - <u>Recall</u>:   Ability to recall or recognize previously learned (memorized) knowledge ranging from specific facts to complete theories.

TAX 2 - <u>Interpretive Skills</u>: Ability to utilize recalled knowledge to interpret or apply verbal, numeric or visual data.

TAX 3 - <u>Problem Solving</u>:   Ability to utilize recalled knowledge and the interpretation/application of distinct criteria to resolve a problem or situation and/or make an appropriate decision.

GLOSSARY OF TERMS USED IN ITEM DESCRIPTORS
MEDICAL LABORATORY TECHNICIAN EXAMINATION - AUGUST 1990

SUBTEST

BBNK	BLOOD BANK
BF	BODY FLUID
CHEM	CHEMISTRY
HEMA	HEMATOLOGY
IMMU	IMMUNOLOGY
MICR	MICROBIOLOGY

TASK

AKFC	APPLIES KNOWLEDGE OF FUNDAMENTAL BIOLOGICAL CHARACTERISTICS	EDIR	EVALUATES LABORATORY DATA TO DETERMINE POSSIBLE INCONSISTENT RESULTS
AKLO	APPLIES KNOWLEDGE OF LABORATORY OPERATIONS	EDMI	EVALUATES LABORATORY DATA TO MAKE IDENTIFICATIONS
AKOP	APPLIES KNOWLEDGE OF STANDARD OPERATING PROCEDURES	EDPP	EVALUATES DATA TO RECOGNIZE COMMON PROCEDURAL/TECHNICAL PROBLEMS
AKSE	APPLIES KNOWLEDGE TO IDENTIFY SOURCES OF ERROR	EDVR	EVALUATES LABORATORY DATA TO VERIFY TEST RESULTS
APBP	APPLIES PRINCIPLES OF BASIC LABORATORY PROCEDURES	ESOE	EVALUATES SOURCES OF ERROR
CALC	CALCULATES	PCAT	PREPARES CONTROLS FOR APPROPRIATE TEST PROCEDURES
CCLD	CORRELATES CLINICAL AND LABORATORY DATA		
CDAR	CORRELATES LABORATORY DATA WITH OTHER LABORATORY DATA TO ASSESS TEST RESULTS	PIPT	PREPARES INSTRUMENTS TO PERFORM TESTS
		PRM	PREPARES REAGENTS/MEDIA
EDAI	EVALUATES DATA TO DETERMINE APPROPRIATE INSTRUMENT ADJUSTMENTS	SCOA	SELECTS COURSE OF ACTION
		SMRM	SELECTS METHODS/REAGENTS/MEDIA
EDAV	EVALUATES DATA TO ASSESS VALIDITY/ACCURACY OF PROCEDURES FOR A GIVEN TEST	SPVR	SELECTS ROUTINE LABORATORY PROCEDURES TO VERIFY TEST RESULTS
EDCA	EVALUATES DATA TO TAKE CORRECTIVE ACTION ACCORDING TO PREDETERMINED CRITERIA		
EDHD	EVALUATES LABORATORY DATA TO ASSESS HEALTH AND DISEASE STATES		

CONTENT SPECIFICS

A&P	ANATOMY AND PHYSIOLOGY	HDN	HEMOLYTIC DISEASE OF THE NEWBORN
AB	ANTIBODY	HGB	HEMOGLOBIN
ABE	ACID BASE ELECTROLYTES	HLA	HUMAN LEUKOCYTE ANTIGEN
AFP	ALPHA FETOPROTEIN	ID	IDENTIFICATION
AGG	AGGLUTINATION, AGGLUTININ	IG	IMMUNOGLOBULIN
AIDS	ACQUIRED IMMUNODEFICIENCY SYNDROME	INST	INSTRUMENTS, INSTRUMENTATION
AIHA	AUTOIMMUNE HEMOLYTIC ANEMIA	LAP	LEUKOCYTE ALKALINE PHOSPHATASE
ANA	ANTINUCLEAR ANTIBODY	MACRO	MACROCYTIC, MACROSCOPIC
AS	ADENINE-SALINE	MEGALO	MEGALOBLASTIC
BIOCHEM	BIOCHEMICAL	MICRO	MICROCYTIC, MICROSCOPIC
BTP	BIOLOGICAL THEORY AND PRINCIPLE	MORPH	MORPHOLOGY
CHARACT	CHARACTERISTIC	P&E	PROTEINS & ENZYMES
CML	CHRONIC MYELOCYTIC LEUKEMIA	PBS	PERIPHERAL BLOOD SMEAR
COAG	COAGULATION	PNH	PAROXYSMAL NOCTURNAL HEMOGLOBINURIA
COMPAT	COMPATIBILITY	PREP	PREPARE, PREPARATION
CSF	CEREBROSPINAL FLUID	QC	QUALITY CONTROL
DAT	DIRECT ANTIGLOBULIN TEST	RA	RHEUMATOID ARTHRITIS
ELECT	ELECTROPHORESIS	RBC	RED BLOOD CELLS
ENTEROBACT	ENTEROBACTERIACEAE	RHIG	RH IMMUNE GLOBULIN
ESR	ERYTHROCYTE SEDIMENTATION RATE	RSV	RESPIRATORY SYNCYTIAL VIRUS
FFP	FRESH FROZEN PLASMA	RXN	REACTION(S)
FSP	FIBRIN SPLIT PRODUCTS	SCH	SPECIMEN COLLECTION & HANDLING
GPC	GRAM POSITIVE COCCI	SPEC	SPECTROPHOTOMETER/SPECTRUM
GNB	GRAM NEGATIVE BACILLI	UTI	URINARY TRACT INFECTION
GNC	GRAM NEGATIVE COCCI	WBC	WHITE BLOOD CELLS
GTP	GENETIC THEORY AND PRINCIPLE	X-MATCH	CROSSMATCH
HA	HEMOLYTIC ANEMIA		

ITEM DESCRIPTOR LIST
MEDICAL LABORATORY TECHNICIAN EXAMINATION - AUGUST 1990

1. BF/AKFC/URINE/RENAL THRESHOLD/1
2. BF/AKFC/URINE/CAST FORMATION/1
3. BF/AKOP/LAB STATISTICS/1
4. BF/ESOE/SCH/URINE/2
5. BF/AKFC/URINE/CAST/2
6. BF/CDAR/MICRO MORPH/URINE SEDIMENT/2
7. BF/EDVR/URINE/REAGENT STRIP/2
8. BF/SCOA/MICRO MORPH/URINE SEDIMENT/2
9. BF/AKFC/URINE SEDIMENT/CRYSTALS/1
10. BF/AKFC/CSF/BACT MENINGITIS/1
11. BF/SMRM/SCH/24-HOUR URINE/1
12. BF/SCOA/SCH/CREATININE CLEARANCE/2
13. BF/SCOA/SCH/CELL COUNT CSF/1
14. BF/CALC/URINE/DILUTION/2
15. BF/SMRM/URINE/OSMOLALITY/1
16. BF/AKFC/URINE CHEMISTRY/REAGENT STRIP/1
17. BF/ESOE/URINE/CRYSTALS/3
18. BF/CCLD/REAGENT STRIP/UTI/2
19. IMMU/EDHD/ALLERGIC RXN/NASAL SMEAR/1
20. IMMU/ESOE/RA TEST/INTERFERENCE/3
21. IMMU/AKFC/SERODIAGNOSIS/INFECTIOUS DISEASE/1
22. IMMU/AKLO/LAB OPERATIONS/SAFETY/1
23. IMMU/EDHD/SYPHILIS TEST/INTERFERENCE/2
24. IMMU/SMRM/QC/SCREENING PROCEDURE/1
25. IMMU/EDAV/BASIC TESTS/COLD AGG/2
26. IMMU/CCLD/AIDS/1
27. IMMU/CDAR/ANA/2
28. IMMU/AKFC/IMMUNE RESPONSE/2
29. IMMU/AKFC/B-LYMPHOCYTES/1
30. IMMU/AKFC/AB/AIHA/1
31. IMMU/AKFC/PHYSIOLOGY/IMMUNOGLOBULIN/1
32. IMMU/CCLD/C-REACTIVE PROTEIN/2
33. IMMU/AKFC/HUMORAL/IMMUNOGLOBULIN/1
34. IMMU/AKFC/RA TEST/1
35. IMMU/AKFC/HUMORAL/IMMUNOGLOBULIN/1
36. BBNK/PRM/RBC/EXPIRATION/2
37. BBNK/EDMI/ANTIBODY ID/PANEL/3
38. BBNK/SMRM/HEMOTHERAPY/FEBRILE RXN/1
39. BBNK/EDPP/RBC/K PHENOTYPING/2
40. BBNK/SMRM/HEMOTHERAPY/FACTOR DEFICIENCY/3
41. BBNK/ESOE/RBC/CELL SUSPENSION/3
42. BBNK/SCOA/RBC/ABO TESTING/1
43. BBNK/AKFC/HLA TYPING/1
44. BBNK/EDIR/RBC/ABO DISCREPANCY/3
45. BBNK/CCLD/GTP/RH/2
46. BBNK/AKOP/RBC/DIRECTED DONATIONS/1
47. BBNK/AKFC/SCH/PLATELETS/1
48. BBNK/AKFC/HEMOTHERAPY/PACKED CELLS/1
49. BBNK/CCLD/HEMOTHERAPY/ADVERSE RXN/2
50. BBNK/PCAT/RBC/REAGENT CONTROL/1
51. BBNK/CCLD/HEMOTHERAPY/ADVERSE RXN/2
52. BBNK/EDMI/OTHER COMPONENT/RHIG DOSE/2
53. BBNK/AKFC/OTHER/IG CLASS/1
54. BBNK/AKFC/HDN/ABO SYSTEM/1
55. BBNK/APBP/ABO GROUPING/2
56. BBNK/AKFC/RBC BASIC TEST/DAT/1
57. BBNK/AKOP/RBC/DONOR ACCEPTIBILITY/2
58. BBNK/SMRM/DU TESTING/CONDITIONS/1
59. BBNK/PRM/OTHER COMPONENT/FFP HANDLING/1
60. BBNK/AKFC/STORAGE/BLOOD PRODUCTS/1
61. BBNK/SMRM/FACTOR VIII/TREATMENT/1
62. BBNK/EDMI/X-MATCH/AUTOCONTROL/3
63. BBNK/SMRM/PLATELET POOLING/ABO COMPATIBILITY/2
64. BBNK/SMRM/RBC/ABO COMPATIBILITY/1
65. BBNK/AKFC/HEMOTHERAPY/ANTENATAL RHIG/1
66. BBNK/EDMI/RBC/MNS CHARACTERISTICS/2
67. BBNK/AKLO/LAB OPERATION/BIOSAFETY/1
68. BBNK/SMRM/RBC/DAT SAMPLE/2
69. BBNK/EDMI/HEMOTHERAPY/HDN/3
70. BBNK/CALC/RBC/REAGENT DILUTION/2
71. CHEM/AKFC/ABE KETOACIDOSIS/2
72. CHEM/CDAR/ELECTROLYTES/CALCIUM/1
73. CHEM/SMRM/SCH/ARTERIAL BLOOD GAS/1
74. CHEM/PRM/ELECTROLYTES/SWEAT CHLORIDE/1
75. CHEM/AKFC/BTP/ALBUMIN/1
76. CHEM/PIPT/INSTRUMENTATION/ABSORBANCE SPECTRUM/2
77. CHEM/EDVR/P&E/GLOBULIN/3
78. CHEM/PIPT/INSTRUMENTATION/INST MAINTENANCE/1
79. CHEM/CCLD/ENZYMES/MYOCARDIAL INFARCT/2
80. CHEM/AKFC/QC/STATISTICS/1
81. CHEM/SMRM/PROTEIN/AFP/1
82. CHEM/EDVR/ELECTROPHORESIS/CSF/2
83. CHEM/AKFC/BTP/IRON/1
84. CHEM/EDHD/LIPIDS/PROFILE/3
85. CHEM/APBP/SPECIAL CHEMISTRY/AMMONIA/1
86. CHEM/CALC/MILLIEQUIVALENT/2
87. CHEM/SMRM/PROTEIN/REAGENT/1
88. CHEM/AKFC/INST/NEPHELOMETRY/1
89. CHEM/SMRM/P&E/BUFFER/1
90. CHEM/AKFC/INST/OSMOLALITY/1
91. CHEM/PCAT/INSTRUMENTATION/QC/1
92. CHEM/AKFC/ENZYME RXN/1
93. CHEM/SCOA/ACID-BASE/SAMPLE/2
94. CHEM/AKFC/P&E/ALBUMIN/1
95. CHEM/PRM/PROTEIN/TOTAL PROTEIN/1
96. CHEM/EDHD/HEME DERIVATIVE/UROBILINOGEN/1
97. CHEM/PRM/STANDARD SOLUTION/1
98. CHEM/AKFC/STEROIDS/TARGET ORGAN/1
99. CHEM/AKFC/STANDARD SOLUTION/1
100. CHEM/EDAI/ELECTROLYTES/CALCIUM/3
101. CHEM/SCOA/INST/ELECT/2
102. CHEM/AKFC/BTP/BILIRUBIN/2
103. CHEM/AKFC/BTP/LIPIDS/1
104. CHEM/SMRM/SCH/GLUCOSE/1
105. CHEM/ESOE/INST/SPEC/3
106. CHEM/ESOE/ELECTROLYTES/pH/2
107. CHEM/ESOE/SCH/P&E/3
108. CHEM/APBP/CARBOHYDRATE/GLUCOSE OXIDASE/1
109. CHEM/EDHD/CARBOHYDRATE/MALABSORPTION/2
110. CHEM/AKFC/PROTEIN/COPPER/1
111. CHEM/CCLD/HEME DERIVATIVE/HAPTOGLOBIN/1
112. HEMA/AKFC/WBC MATURATION/1
113. HEMA/PRM/SLIDE PREP/ANGLE/1
114. HEMA/AKSE/ERYTHROCYTES/ESR/1
115. HEMA/AKFC/ANTICOAGULANT/1
116. HEMA/SMRM/SCH/PLATELET FUNCTION TEST/1
117. HEMA/AKFC/SPECIAL STAIN/RBC INCLUSIONS/1
118. HEMA/AKFC/PBS/MULTIPLE MYELOMA/1
119. HEMA/CALC/WBC/CORRECTED COUNT/2
120. HEMA/SCOA/BASIC TESTS/HYPOCHROMIC ANEMIA/2

121. HEMA/CALC/RBC/INDICES/2
122. HEMA/ESOE/AUTOMATED COUNT/HGB/2
123. HEMA/SCOA/RBC INDICES/MANUAL METHODS/3
124. HEMA/EDIR/PBS/RETICULOCYTE COUNT/3
125. HEMA/AKOP/TEMPLATE BLEEDING TIME/1
126. HEMA/CDAR/RBC MICRO MORPH/2
127. HEMA/CDAR/MICRO MORPH/OSMOTIC FRAGILITY/2
128. HEMA/CDAR/MICRO MORPH/INFECTIOUS DISEASE/2
129. HEMA/ESOE/MICRO MORPH/RBC/3
130. HEMA/EDMI/MICRO MORPH/WBC INCLUSION/2
131. HEMA/EDMI/MICRO MORPH/WBC/2
132. HEMA/SCOA/MICRO MORPH/MEGALOBLASTIC ANEMIA/3
133. HEMA/EDHD/HEMOSTASIS/THROMBOCYTOPENIA/3
134. HEMA/AKFC/LEUKOCYTES/PELGER-HUET/1
135. HEMA/APBP/ANALYTIC TEST/PROTHROMBIN TIME/1
136. HEMA/AKFC/LAP/CML/1
137. HEMA/AKFC/WBC DEGENERATION/1
138. HEMA/CDAR/CML/GENETICS/1
139. HEMA/AKFC/LEUKOCYTE COUNT/1
140. HEMA/PRM/DILUTING FLUID/2
141. HEMA/CCLD/FSP/FIBRINOLYSIS/2
142. HEMA/AKOP/SCH/PATIENT ID/1
143. HEMA/AKFC/BLEEDING TIME/1
144. HEMA/EDMI/RBC/ROULEAUX/2
145. HEMA/EDMI/RBC/ERYTHROPOIESIS/2
146. HEMA/CCLD/PLATELETS/ACUTE LEUKEMIA/1
147. HEMA/CCLD/PLATELET TESTS/ASPIRIN/2
148. HEMA/AKLO/SCH/PHLEBOTOMY/1
149. HEMA/AKFC/MACROCYTOSIS/ANEMIA/1
150. HEMA/PRM/COAGULATION/SPECIAL HANDLING/1
151. HEMA/AKFC/HEMOGLOBINOPATHY/HA/1
152. MICR/APBP/BASIC TESTS/IMVIC/1
153. MICR/AKFC/BIOCHEM ID/PROTEUS/1

154. MICR/AKFC/BASIC TESTS/GPC/1
155. MICR/AKFC/GROWTH CHARACT/STREPTOCOCCUS/2
156. MICR/SCOA/WOUND CULTURE/ANAEROBES/3
157. MICR/AKFC/BACTERIA/LYME DISEASE/1
158. MICR/SCOA/SCH/CSF/1
159. MICR/SCOA/GRAM STAIN/WOUND/3
160. MICR/CDAR/BLOOD CULTURE/CONTAMINANT/2
161. MICR/CDAR/GNC/GENITAL CULTURE/2
162. MICR/EDMI/GPC/GROWTH CHARACT/1
163. MICR/EDMI/MICRO MORPH/STREPTOCOCCUS/3
164. MICR/EDHD/GPC/TOXIC SHOCK/2
165. MICR/AKFC/GNB/GROWTH REQUIREMENTS/2
166. MICR/CALC/COLONY COUNT/URINE CULTURE/2
167. MICR/EDMI/GPC/STREPTOCOCCUS/2
168. MICR/EDMI/BIOCHEM ID/GPC/2
169. MICR/EDMI/GNB/BIOCHEM ID/3
170. MICR/AKFC/BIOCHEM TESTS/ENTEROBACTERIACEAE/1
171. MICR/AKFC/GNB/MACRO MORPH/1
172. MICR/AKFC/URINE COUNT/NORMAL/1
173. MICR/CDAR/AMOEBA/1
174. MICR/AKFC/MEDIA/DIFFERENTIAL/1
175. MICR/ESOE/BASIC TESTS/SUSCEPTIBILITY/2
176. MICR/EDMI/BASIC TESTS/MYCOBACTERIA/1
177. MICR/AKFC/LIFE CYCLE/NEMATODE/1
178. MICR/ESOE/BASIC TEST/GNB/2
179. MICR/AKFC/DIMORPHIC FUNGI/1
180. MICR/AKFC/SCH/OVA & PARASITE/1
181. MICR/PRM/PARASITE/MALARIA/1
182. MICR/SMRM/SAFETY-DISINFECTION/VIROLOGY/1
183. MICR/EDMI/GNB/GARDNERELLA/1
184. MICR/SCOA/GPC/BIOCHEM TEST/2
185. MICR/CDAR/GNB/BIOCHEM TESTS/2 1

TAXONOMIC LEVELS

TAX 1 - Recall:

Ability to recall or recognize previously learned (memorized) knowledge ranging from specific facts to complete theories.

TAX 2 - Interpretive Skills:

Ability to utilize recalled knowledge to interpret or apply verbal, numeric or visual data.

TAX 3 - Problem Solving:

Ability to utilize recalled knowledge and the interpretation/application of distinct criteria to resolve a problem or situation and/or make an appropriate decision.

APPENDIX B

ITEM DESCRIPTORS FOR
1990 MEDICAL TECHNOLOGIST EXAMINATIONS

SUBTEST

BBNK	BLOOD BANK	HEMA	HEMATOLOGY
BF	BODY FLUIDS	IMMU	IMMUNOLOGY
CHEM	CHEMISTRY	MICR	MICROBIOLOGY

TASK

AKFC APPLIES KNOWLEDGE OF FUNDAMENTAL BIOLOGICAL CHARACTERISTICS

AKLO APPLIES KNOWLEDGE OF LABORATORY OPERATIONS

AKOP APPLIES KNOWLEDGE OF STANDARD OPERATING PROCEDURES

AKSE APPLIES KNOWLEDGE TO IDENTIFY SOURCES OF ERROR

APBP APPLIES PRINCIPLES OF BASIC LABORATORY PROCEDURES

APSP APPLIES PRINCIPLES OF SPECIAL PROCEDURES

CALC CALCULATES

CCLD CORRELATES CLINICAL AND LABORATORY DATA

CDAR CORRELATES LABORATORY DATA WITH OTHER LABORATORY DATA TO ASSESS TEST RESULTS

CDPP CORRELATES LABORATORY DATA WITH PHYSIOLOGICAL PROCESSES

EDAT EVALUATES LABORATORY DATA TO RECOGNIZE AND REPORT THE NEED FOR ADDITIONAL TESTING

EDAV EVALUATES LABORATORY DATA TO ASSESS VALIDITY OF PROCEDURE

EDHD EVALUATES LABORATORY DATA TO RECOGNIZE HEALTH AND DISEASE STATES

EDIR EVALUATES LABORATORY DATA TO DETERMINE POSSIBLE INCONSISTENT RESULTS

EDMI EVALUATES LABORATORY DATA TO MAKE IDENTIFICATIONS

EDRP EVALUATES LABORATORY DATA TO RECOGNIZE PROBLEMS

EDVR EVALUATES LABORATORY DATA TO VERIFY TEST RESULTS

ELOP EVALUATES LABORATORY OPERATIONAL PROCEDURES

ESOE EVALUATES SOURCES OF ERROR

PCAT PREPARES CONTROLS APPROPRIATE FOR TESTING

PRM PREPARES REAGENTS/MEDIA/BLOOD

SACT SELECTS APPROPRIATE CONTROLS FOR TEST PERFORMED

SCOA SELECTS COURSE OF ACTION

SMRM SELECTS METHODS/REAGENTS/MEDIA

CONTENT SPECIFICS

AB	ANTIBODY
AFB	ACID FAST BACILLI
AG	ANTIGEN
AGG	AGGLUTININ,AGGLUTINATION
AHG	ANTI-HUMAN GLOBULIN
AIDS	ACQUIRED IMMUNODEFICIENCY SYNDROME
AIHA	AUTOIMMUNE HEMOLYTIC ANEMIA
ATYP	ATYPICAL
AUTO	AUTOLOGOUS
BIOCHEM	BIOCHEMICAL
BTP	BIOLOGICAL THEORY AND PRINCIPLE
CBC	COMPLETE BLOOD COUNT
CLL	CHRONIC LYMPHOCYTIC LEUKEMIA
CMV	CYTOMEGALOVIRUS
COAG	COAGULATION
CONC	CONCENTRATION, CONCENTRATE
CRYO	CRYOPRECIPITATE/CRYPRECIPITATED AHF
CSF	CEREBROSPINAL FLUID
CYTO	CYTOMETRY
DNA	DEOXYRIBONUCLEIC ACID
ER	EMERGENCY ROOM
FFP	FRESH FROZEN PLASMA
FRAG	FRAGILITY
GLC	GAS LIQUID CHROMATOGRAPHY
GNB	GRAM NEGATIVE BACILLI
GNC	GRAM NEGATIVE COCCI
GNR	GRAM NEGATIVE ROD
GPB	GRAM POSITIVE BACILLI
GPC	GRAM POSITIVE COCCI
GTP	GENETIC THEORY AND PRINCIPLE
GTT	GLUCOSE TOLERANCE TEST
HBS-AG	HEPATITIS B SURFACE ANTIGEN
HDN	HEMOLYTIC DISEASE OF THE NEWBORN
HGB	HEMOGLOBIN
HI	HEMAGGLUTINATION INHIBITION
HIV	HUMAN IMMUNODEFICIENCY VIRUS

ID	IDENTIFICATION
IEF	IMMUNOELECTROFIXATION
INST	INSTRUMENTATION
LAP	LEUKOCYTE ALKALINE PHOSPHATASE
LD	LACTATE DEHYDROGENASE
LO	LABORATORY OPERATIONS
LYMPH	LYMPHOCYTE
MACRO	MACROSCOPIC
ME	MYELOID:ERYTHROID
MIC-MAC	MICRO MACRO
MICRO	MICROSCOPIC
MORPH	MORPHOLOGY
MYCO	MYCOBACTERIA
%	PERCENT
P&E	PROTEINS AND ENZYMES
PAS	PERIODIC ACID-SCHIFF
PLT	PLATELET
PMN	POLYMORPHONUCLEAR
PNH	PAROXYSMAL NOCTURNAL HEMOGLOBINURIA
QA	QUALITY ASSURANCE
QC	QUALITY CONTROL
REQUIRE	REQUIREMENT
RBC	RED BLOOD CELLS
RCD	RELATED CONDITIONS AND DISORDERS
RID	RADIAL IMMUNODIFFUSION
RPR	RAPID PROTEIN REAGIN
RXN	REACTION
RBC	RED BLOOD CELL
SCH	SPECIMEN COLLECTION AND HANDLING
SERO	SEROLOGICAL
SPE	SERUM PROTEIN ELECTROPHORESIS
SPH	SPECIMEN PROCESSING AND HANDLING
TXN	TRANSFUSION
WBC	WHITE BLOOD CELL
X-MATCH	CROSSMATCH

1. MICR/AKOP/CAMPYLOBACTER/ISOLATION/1
2. MICR/SCOA/HAEMOPHILUS/CSF/3
3. MICR/EDHD/GPC/BASIC TESTS/2
4. MICR/EDHD/OPPORTUNISTIC INFECTION/3
5. MICR/EDMI/PROTEUS/BASIC TESTS/2
6. MICR/EDMI/GNC/BIOCHEM RXN/2
7. MICR/ESOE/SCH/FUNGAL MEDIA/3
8. MICR/CDAR/DIMORPHIC FUNGI/2
9. MICR/CCLD/MICRO MORPH/TREMATODES/2
10. MICR/SMRM/SCH/NEMATODE/2
11. MICR/AKFC/MACRO MORPH/MYCOBACTERIA/1
12. MICR/EDMI/AMOEBA/3
13. MICR/CCLD/GPB/ACTINOMYCETES/2
14. MICR/AKFC/SPECIAL TESTS/STAPHYLOCOCCUS/2
15. MICR/EDHD/SPUTUM/SMEAR/2
16. MICR/EDMI/GNB-BASIC TESTS/STOOL CULTURE/3
17. MICR/SMRM/BASIC TESTS/AFB/1
18. MICR/AKFC/INFECTIOUS PATHOLOGY/RICKETTSIA/1
19. MICR/SMRM/SCH/AFB/1
20. MICR/SCOA/SEROLOGIC TEST/HIV/1
21. MICR/EDMI/MICRO-MACRO MORPH/DIMORPHIC/2
22. MICR/SCOA/FILAMENTOUS MOLD/ID TECHNIQUE/3
23. MICR/CCLD/GPC/CULTURE CHARACTERISTIC/2
24. MICR/CCLD/MICRO-MACRO MORPH/LISTERIA/2
25. MICR/AKSE/SPECIMEN STORAGE/HELMINTH/2
26. MICR/EDVR/GNB/QC BIOCHEM TEST/3
27. MICR/AKFC/STREPTOCOCCUS/ANTIBIOTIC TREATMENT/1
28. MICR/EDMI/MICRO-MACRO MORPH/NOCARDIA/2
29. MICR/EDMI/GPC/BLOOD CULTURE/3
30. MICR/AKFC/V FACTOR/2
31. MICR/CCLD/MICRO-MACRO MORPH/HAEMOPHILUS/2
32. MICR/EDMI/BIOCHEM ID/GNB-ENTERIC/3
33. MICR/EDMI/GNB/BIOCHEM RXN/2
34. MICR/EDMI/GNB/BIOCHEM ID/3
35. MICR/SMRM/SCH/VIRUSES/1
36. BF/APBP/REAGENT STRIP/PROTEIN/1
37. BF/ESOE/URINE/GLUCOSE/3
38. BF/EDMI/PLEURAL FLUID/2
39. BF/AKFC/TRANSUDATES/DESCRIPTION/1
40. BF/CCLD/MICRO MORPH/URINE CRYSTALS/2
41. BF/CDPP/URINE SEDIMENT/CHEMICAL TEST/3
42. BF/SMRM/SEMEN ANALYSIS/1
43. BF/AKFC/PHOSPHOLIPIDS/AMNIOTIC FLUID/1
44. BF/CCLD/RCD/URINE SEDIMENT/2
45. BF/SMRM/URINE/SEDIMENT STAIN/2
46. BF/EDRP/MICRO MORPH/REAGENT STRIP/2
47. BF/AKFC/PHYSIOLOGY/CREATININE CLEARANCE/1
48. BF/SCOA/URINE/REDUCING SUBSTANCE/3
49. BF/ESOE/SCH/URINALYSIS/2
50. BF/SCOA/LO/ORGANIZING STRUCTURE/2
51. BF/APSP/ALPHA FETOPROTEIN/1
52. BF/AKFC/URINE/AMINOACIDURIA/1
53. BF/AKLO/QC/ACCURACY & PRECISION/1
54. IMMU/CALC/SERIAL DILUTION/2
55. IMMU/AKFC/QC/STATISTICS/1
56. IMMU/CALC/DILUTION/2
57. IMMU/APBP/RID/1
58. IMMU/SMRM/HBS-AG/1
59. IMMU/AKLO/SCH/AIDS/1
60. IMMU/AKFC/ACTIVE IMMUNITY/1

61. IMMU/EDHD/IEF/3
62. IMMU/SMRM/IGE QUANTITATION/1
63. IMMU/CCLD/CELL/FLOW CYTOMETRY/2
64. IMMU/EDVR/T-CELL/PHENOTYPING/3
65. IMMU/CCLD/SERO TITER/FEBRILE/3
66. IMMU/ESOE/SCH/COLD AGG/3
67. IMMU/CCLD/COLD AGG/POLYCLONAL/2
68. IMMU/APSP/AUTOIMMUNITY/DNA/2
69. IMMU/EDVR/PREGNANCY TEST/2
70. IMMU/EDVR/HI TEST/2
71. IMMU/APBP/DISEASE STATE/SYPHILIS/1
72. BBNK/CCLD/HEMOTHERAPY/COMPONENT/3
73. BBNK/PRM/COOMBS/CONTROL/1
74. BBNK/SCOA/ER TXN/3
75. BBNK/ESOE/ABO DISCREPANCY/3
76. BBNK/EDMI/HEMOTHERAPY/FACTOR DEFICIENCY/3
77. BBNK/CCLD/HEMOTHERAPY/BLOOD COMPONENTS/3
78. BBNK/SMRM/HEMOTHERAPY/RBC/1
79. BBNK/EDVR/GENOTYPE/PATERNITY TESTING/2
80. BBNK/AKFC/SAFETY/HEPATITIS/1
81. BBNK/AKFC/METABOLISM/IRON/1
82. BBNK/CALC/HEMOTHERAPY/2
83. BBNK/SMRM/PROCESSING/CMV TESTING/2
84. BBNK/EDVR/AB ID/3
85. BBNK/EDIR/HEMOTHERAPY/ADVERSE RXN/2
86. BBNK/AKFC/BLOOD COMPONENT/1
87. BBNK/ESOE/STORAGE/BLOOD/2
88. BBNK/EDRP/ABO DISCREPANCY/3
89. BBNK/EDRP/X-MATCH/INCOMPATIBLE/2
90. BBNK/AKFC/REAGENTS/AHG/1
91. BBNK/CCLD/DONOR REQUIREMENT/PLASMAPHERESIS/2
92. BBNK/SCOA/DU TEST/1
93. BBNK/SCOA/SCH/AB ID/2
94. BBNK/SCOA/PROBLEM AB/3
95. BBNK/AKLO/EDUCATION/PROGRAM DEVELOPMENT/1
96. BBNK/EDIR/RBC/AB ID/3
97. BBNK/EDHD/RBC/PNH/3
98. BBNK/EDRP/ABO DISCREPANCY/3
99. BBNK/AKFC/RBC/ANTICOAGULANT/1
100. BBNK/EDVR/GTP/RBC/2
101. BBNK/AKFC/LECTIN/1
102. BBNK/AKFC/RBC/AB ID/1
103. BBNK/AKOP/PLT STORAGE/1
104. BBNK/AKOP/HEMOTHERAPY/AUTO TRANSFUSION/1
105. BBNK/CALC/RBC SUSPENSION/2
106. BBNK/CALC/PLT/1
107. BBNK/ESOE/RH TYPING/HDN/2
108. CHEM/AKLO/BILIRUBIN/BEERS LAW/2
109. CHEM/ELOP/QC/PRECISION/3
110. CHEM/CDAR/CARBOHYDRATES/GTT/2
111. CHEM/AKFC/BTP/ALBUMIN/1
112. CHEM/CCLD/LIPIDS/LIPOPROTEINS/1
113. CHEM/SCOA/CARBOHYDRATE/FECES/2
114. CHEM/CCLD/P&E/ACID PHOSPHATASE/3
115. CHEM/EDHD/LD ISOENZYMES/2
116. CHEM/SMRM/HYPOTHYROIDISM/2
117. CHEM/CCLD/ABNORMAL STATES/OSMOLALITY/2
118. CHEM/EDAV/QA/LEVY-JENNINGS/3
119. CHEM/AKFC/ENDOCRINOLOGY/CATECHOLAMINE/1
120. CHEM/ESOE/ENZYME ASSAY/1

121. CHEM/AKFC/B12/1
122. CHEM/APSP/INST/GLC/1
123. CHEM/ESOE/INST/ANALYTICAL BALANCE/2
124. CHEM/CALC/QC/STANDARD DEVIATION/2
125. CHEM/EDVR/ACID-BASE/SPECIMEN HANDLING/1
126. CHEM/EDAV/TOXICOLOGY/SPECIMEN COLLECTION/1
127. CHEM/AKFC/TOXICITY/EPIDEMIOLOGY/1
128. CHEM/EDVR/P&E/ISOENZYME RESULTS/2
129. CHEM/ESOE/SERUM/OSMOLALITY/3
130. CHEM/APBP/PROTEIN/ELECTROPHORESIS/1
131. CHEM/AKLO/INST/BEERS LAW/2
132. CHEM/APBP/FLUOROMETER/1
133. CHEM/SMRM/BTP/BLOOD GAS/1
134. CHEM/APBP/PERFORMANCE STANDARDS/QA/2
135. CHEM/CALC/SOLUTE CONCENTRATION/2
136. CHEM/ESOE/INST/FLAME PHOTOMETRY/2
137. CHEM/SCOA/P&E/QA/3
138. CHEM/CCLD/SPECIAL CHEMISTRY/ADRENAL CORTEX/2
139. CHEM/CALC/% TRANSMISSION/2
140. CHEM/AKFC/CHLORIDE SHIFT/1
141. CHEM/SMRM/ACID BASE/ANTACID/2
142. CHEM/APSP/INST/NEPHELOMETRY/1
143. CHEM/SMRM/P&E/SPE/3
144. CHEM/CALC/METRIC UNITS/2
145. CHEM/ESOE/INST/SPECTROPHOTOMETER/3
146. CHEM/APBP/OSMOLALITY/1
147. HEMA/CCLD/GRANULOCYTES/INFECTION/2
148. HEMA/SMRM/MACROCYTIC ANEMIA/2
149. HEMA/AKFC/SUDAN BLACK/WBC/1
150. HEMA/EDHD/CBC/ACUTE LEUKEMIA/3
151. HEMA/SMRM/HEMOSTASIS/THROMBIN TIME/1
152. HEMA/EDIR/RBC/SCH/2

153. HEMA/CDAR/OSMOTIC FRAGILITY/3
154. HEMA/EDAT/ATYP LYMPH/2
155. HEMA/CCLD/CLL/3
156. HEMA/CDAR/MICRO MORPH/HEMOGLOBINOPATHY/2
157. HEMA/SMRM/RBC INCLUSION/2
158. HEMA/SMRM/PLT COUNT/MANUAL/2
159. HEMA/EDMI/MICRO MORPH/WBC INCLUSIONS/2
160. HEMA/ESOE/AUTOMATED COUNT/PLT/3
161. HEMA/CCLD/HEMOSTASIS/VON WILLEBRANDS/2
162. HEMA/EDVR/HEMOSTASIS/SUBSTITUTION STUDIES/3
163. HEMA/AKFC/ANTICOAGULANT/1
164. HEMA/ESOE/WBC/HISTOGRAM/3
165. HEMA/EDRP/COAG/HEPARIN NEUTRALIZATION/3
166. HEMA/AKFC/PAS/1
167. HEMA/EDHD/LAP SCORE/3
168. HEMA/AKFC/ERYTHROCYTOSIS/RELATIVE/1
169. HEMA/CCLD/BONE MARROW/ME RATIO/2
170. HEMA/AKFC/FUNCTION/BONE DESTRUCTION/1
171. HEMA/AKFC/INTRINSIC PATHWAY/ACTIVATION/1
172. HEMA/AKFC/PLATELET/PHYSIOLOGY/1
173. HEMA/AKSE/WBC/PHYSIOLOGY/2
174. HEMA/AKFC/INCLUSION/WBC/1
175. HEMA/AKFC/RBC/MEGALOBLASTIC ANEMIA/1
176. HEMA/AKFC/FACTOR DEFICIENCY/HEREDITARY/1
177. HEMA/EDVR/HEMOSTASIS/FACTOR DEFICIENCY/2
178. HEMA/SCOA/SYNOVIAL FLUID/CRYSTAL/2
179. HEMA/EDHD/SPECIAL TEST/HGB F/2
180. HEMA/AKSE/HGB/ANALYSIS/1
181. HEMA/AKFC/FIBRINOLYTIC SYSTEM/1
182. HEMA/CCLD/AIHA/2
183. HEMA/AKLO/QC/DELTA CHECK/1
184. HEMA/AKFC/LEUKOPENIA/LYMPHOCYTE/1

TAXONOMIC LEVELS

TAX 1 - <u>Recall:</u>   Ability to recall or recognize previously learned (memorized) knowledge ranging from specific facts to complete theories.

TAX 2 - <u>Interpretive Skills:</u>   Ability to utilize recalled knowledge to interpret or apply verbal, numeric or visual data.

TAX 3 - <u>Problem Solving:</u>   Ability to utilize recalled knowledge and the interpretation/application of distinct criteria to resolve a problem or situation and/or make an appropriate decision.

TASKS

AKFC	APPLIES KNOWLEDGE OF FUNDAMENTAL BIOLOGICAL CHARACTERISTICS
AKLO	APPLIES KNOWLEDGE OF LABORATORY OPERATIONS
AKOP	APPLIES KNOWLEDGE OF STANDARD OPERATING PROCEDURES
AKSE	APPLIES KNOWLEDGE TO IDENTIFY SOURCES OF ERROR
APBP	APPLIES PRINCIPLES OF BASIC LABORATORY PROCEDURES
APSP	APPLIES PRINCIPLES OF SPECIAL PROCEDURES
CALC	CALCULATES
CCLD	CORRELATES CLINICAL AND LABORATORY DATA
CDAR	CORRELATES LABOATORY DATA WITH OTHER LABORATORY DATA TO ASSESS TEST RESULTS
ECAT	EVALUATES LABORATORY AND CLINICAL DATA TO SPECIFY ADDITIONAL TESTS
EDAM	EVALUATES LABORATORY DATA TO DETERMINE ALTERNATE METHODS FOR A GIVEN TEST
EDAV	EVALUATES LABORATORY DATA TO ASSESS VALIDITY OF PROCEDURE
EDCA	EVALUATES LABORATORY DATA TO TAKE CORRECTIVE ACTION ACCORDING TO PREDETERMINED CRITERIA
EDHD	EVALUATES LABORATORY DATA TO RECOGNIZE HEALTH AND DISEASE STATES
EDIR	EVALUATES LABOATORY DATA TO DETERMINE POSSIBLE INCONSISTENT RESULTS
EDMI	EVALUATES LABOATORY DATA TO MAKE IDENTIFICATIONS
EDPS	EVALUATES LABORATORY AND CLINICAL DATA TO ASSESS PERSONNEL SAFETY
EDRP	EVALUATES LABORATORY DATA TO RECOGNIZE PROBLEMS
EDPS	EVALUATES LABORATORY AND CLINICAL DATA TO ASSURE PERSONNEL SAFETY
EDVR	EVALUATES LABORATORY DATA TO VERIFY TEST RESULTS
ELOP	EVALUATES LABORATORY OPERATIONAL PROCEDURES
ESOE	EVALUATES SOURCES OF ERROR
PCAT	PREPARES CONTROLS APPROPRIATE FOR TESTING
PIPT	PREPARES INSTRUMENTS TO PERFORM TESTS
PRM	PREPARES REAGENTS/MEDIA/BLOOD
SACT	SELECTS APPROPRIATE CONTROLS FOR TEST PERFORMED
SCOA	SELECTS COURSE OF ACTION
SMRM	SELECTS METHODS/REAGENTS/MEDIA
SPVR	SELECTS ROUTINE LABORATORY PROCEDURES TO VERIFY TEST RESULTS ACCORDING TO ESTABLISHED PROTOCOL

CONTENT SPECIFICS

AB	ANTIBODY
AG	ANTIGEN
AGG	AGGLUTININ, AGGLUTINATION, AGGREGATION
AIDS	ACQUIRED IMMUNODEFICIENCY SYNDROME
AIHA	AUTOIMMUNE HEMOLYTIC ANEMIA
ANA	ANTINUCLEAR ANTIBODY
AS	ADENINE-SALINE
AUTO	AUTOMATED
BIOCHEM	BIOCHEMICAL
BMD	BIOCHEMICAL MANIFESTATION OF DISEASE
BRONCH	BRONCHIAL
BTP	BIOLOGICAL THEORY AND PRINCIPLE
CBC	COMPLETE BLOOD COUNT
CHARAC	CHARACTERISTIC
CML	CHRONIC MYELOCYTIC LEUKEMIA
CMV	CYTOMEGALOVIRUS
COAG	COAGULATION
CSF	CEREBROSPINAL FLUID
CV	COEFFICIENT OF VARIATION
DAT	DIRECT ANTIGLOBULIN TEST
DEF	DEFICIENCY
DIFF	DIFFENTIAL
DNA	DEOXYRIBONUCLEIC ACID
ELISA	ENZYME-LINKED IMMUNOSORBENT ASSAY
ESR	ERYTHROCYTE SEDIMENTATION RATE
FFP	FRESH FROZEN PLASMA
FMH	FETAL-MATERNAL HEMORRHAGE
GC	GAS CHROMATOGRAPHY
GNB	GRAM NEGATIVE BACILLI
GNC	GRAM NEGATIVE COCCI
GPB	GRAM POSITIVE BACILLI
GPC	GRAM POSITIVE COCCI
GTP	GENETIC THEORY AND PRINCIPLE
GTT	GLUCOSE TOLERANCE TEST
HBS-AG	HEPATITIS B SURFACE ANTIGEN
HGB	HEMOGLOBIN
HIV	HUMAN IMMUNODEFICIENCY VIRUS
ID	IDENTIFICATION
IFA	IMMUNOFLUORESCENT ANTIBODY
IMD	IMMUNOLOGIC MANIFESTATION OF DISEASE
INST	INSTRUMENTATION
LAP	LEUKOCYTE ALKALINE PHOSPHATASE
LDL	LOW DENSITY LIPOPROTEIN
L-S	LECITHIN-SPHINGOMYELIN
MIC-MAC	MICRO-MACRO
MICRO	MICROSCOPIC
MORPH	MORPHOLOGY
NRBC	NUCLEATED RED BLOOD CELLS
OPPORT	OPPORTUNISTIC
%	PERCENT
P&E	PROTEINS AND ENZYMES
PNH	PAROXYSMAL NOCTURNAL HEMOGLOBINURIA
PREP	PREPARATION
PROCESS	PROCESSING
QC	QUALITY CONTROL
RAST	RADIOALLERGOSORBENT TEST
RBC	RED BLOOD CELL
REQUIRE	REQUIREMENT
RHIG	RH-IMMUNE GLOBULIN
RSV	RESPIRATORY SYNCYTIAL VIRUS
RXN	REACTION
SCH	SPECIMEN COLLECTION AND HANDLING
SPE	SERUM PROTEIN ELECTROPHORESIS
TSH	THYROID STIMULATING HORMONE
TRANS	TRANSFUSION
WBC	WHITE BLOOD CELL
X-MATCH	CROSSMATCH

1. BF/CALC/URINE/SPECIFIC GRAVITY/2
2. BF/ESOE/SCH/URINALYSIS/2
3. BF/APBP/SCH/CSF/1
4. BF/CCLD/L-S RATIO/2
5. BF/AKFC/URINE/PHYSIOLOGY/1
6. BF/EDVR/PERITONEAL FLUID/HEART FAILURE/3
7. BF/AKFC/PHYSIOLOGY/CREATININE CLEARANCE/1
8. BF/APBP/REAGENT STRIP/PROTEIN/1
9. BF/EDAV/SPECIFIC GRAVITY/METHODOLOGY/3
10. BF/EDHD/URINE/BILIRUBIN/3
11. BF/ESOE/URINE/GLUCOSE/3
12. BF/EDHD/MICRO MORPH/NEPHROTIC SYNDROME/3
13. BF/SMRM/URINE/SEDIMENT STAIN/2
14. BF/EDMI/MICRO MORPH/DEGENERATIVE CASTS/2
15. BF/SPVR/MICRO MORPH/BIOCHEM TESTS/3
16. BF/SMRM/SPECIAL STAIN/URINE SEDIMENT/2
17. BF/APSP/MICROSCOPY/POLARIZATION/2
18. BF/SCOA/URINE/REDUCING SUBSTANCE/3
19. BF/CCLD/CONFIRMATORY TESTS/PROTEINURIA/2
20. IMMU/APBP/BASIC TESTS/RHEUMATOID FACTOR/1
21. IMMU/APSP/AUTOIMMUNITY/DNA/2
22. IMMU/AKFC/IMD/AIDS/1
23. IMMU/AKFC/QC/SENSITIVITY/1
24. IMMU/AKFC/ALLERGY/AB PRODUCTION/1
25. IMMU/SMRM/ALLERGY/RAST/1
26. IMMU/ESOE/SCH/COLD AGGLUTININ/3
27. IMMU/EDAV/AUTOIMMUNITY/IFA ANA/2
28. IMMU/EDRP/BASIC TESTS/SYPHILIS/2
29. IMMU/SMRM/HBS-AG/METHOD/1
30. IMMU/CALC/SERIAL DILUTION/2
31. IMMU/CCLD/RUBELLA/TITER/2
32. IMMU/SMRM/HUMORAL/ELISA/1
33. IMMU/CCLD/SEROLOGIC RESPONSE/HEPATITIS/2
34. IMMU/CCLD/AB RESPONSE/HEPATITIS/2
35. IMMU/CALC/CELLULAR IMMUNITY/B CELLS/2
36. IMMU/AKFC/AUTOIMMUNITY/ANTI-TSH RECEPTORS/1
37. IMMU/ESOE/CELLULAR IMMUNITY/T LYMPHOCYTE/3
38. IMMU/SPVR/AUTOIMMUNITY/ANA/3
39. BBNK/SCOA/HEMOTHERAPY/MULTIPLE AB/2
40. BBNK/APBP/DAT/PRINCIPLE/1
41. BBNK/EDIR/HEMOTHERAPY/ADVERSE RXN/2
42. BBNK/SELC/HEMOTHERAPY/FFP/3
43. BBNK/EDHD/HEMOTHERAPY/FEBRILE RXN/3
44. BBNK/CALC/HEMOTHERAPY/DONOR SELECTION/3
45. BBNK/SCOA/OTHER COMPONENT/STORAGE/3
46. BBNK/SCOA/HEMOTHERAPY/TRANS RXN/2
47. BBNK/CALC/RBC SUSPENSION/2
48. BBNK/PRM/RBC/ALBUMIN CONTROL/2
49. BBNK/EDHD/RBC/ABO DISCREPANCY/2
50. BBNK/EDMI/OTHER COMPONENT/RHIG DOSE/2
51. BBNK/AKLO/EDUCATION/PROGRAM DEVELOPMENT/1
52. BBNK/SCOA/RBC/HEMOTHERAPY/3
53. BBNK/EDHD/RBC/FMH FETAL SCREEN/3
54. BBNK/AKOP/HEMOTHERAPY/ADVERSE RXN/2
55. BBNK/CDAR/X-MATCH/INCOMPATIBLE/2
56. BBNK/EDRP/RBC/ABO DISCREPANCY/3
57. BBNK/EDMI/SALIVA NEUTRALIZATION/3
58. BBNK/EDVR/ABO GROUPING/CORD BLOOD/3
59. BBNK/SACT/RBC/ANTISERA QC/1
60. BBNK/CDAR/RBC/RH CONTROL/2

61. BBNK/APBP/PLATELETS/DONOR REQUIRE/1
62. BBNK/SCOA/RBC/RH PHENOTYPE/2
63. BBNK/SCOA/DONOR PROCESS/UNACCEPTABLE UNIT/3
64. BBNK/AKOP/DONOR PROCESS/LOOK-BACK/1
65. BBNK/AKFC/RBC/AB ID/1
66. BBNK/AKFC/RBC/GTP/2
67. BBNK/EDRP/ABO DISCREPANCY/3
68. BBNK/SMRM/AB ID/COMPATIBILITY/3
69. BBNK/SMRM/HEMOTHERAPY/NEONATES CMV/1
70. BBNK/EDMI/COMPONENT SELECTION/FACTOR DEF/3
71. BBNK/AKFC/AG-AB/GTP/1
72. BBNK/CCLD/HEMOTHERAPY/BLOOD COMPONENTS/3
73. BBNK/AKFC/AB DOSAGE/1
74. CHEM/CDAR/SCH/CARBOHYDRATES/2
75. CHEM/CDAR/CARBOHYDRATES/GTT/2
76. CHEM/PRM/SCH/TRIGLYCERIDE/1
77. CHEM/CALC/% TRANSMISSION/2
78. CHEM/ESOE/INST/OSMOMETRY/2
79. CHEM/EDCA/ELECTROLYTES/ANION GAP/3
80. CHEM/EDVR/P&E/ISOENZYME RESULTS/2
81. CHEM/AKLO/BILIRUBIN/BEERS LAW/2
82. CHEM/ELF/PROTEIN/ELECTROPHORESIS/2
83. CHEM/CCLD/P&E/ALKALINE PHOSPHATASE/2
84. CHEM/APBP/P&E/IRON/1
85. CHEM/APBP/INST/FLUOROMETER/1
86. CHEM/SMRM/P&E/SPE/3
87. CHEM/ESOE/SCH/BLOOD GAS/2
88. CHEM/SMRM/BTP/BLOOD GAS/1
89. CHEM/ESOE/SPECTRAL CURVE/3
90. CHEM/CCLD/TOXICOLOGY/INSECTICIDES/2
91. CHEM/AKSE/ELECTROLYTES/CHLORIDE/1
92. CHEM/CCLD/BMD/ISOENZYMES/2
93. CHEM/AKFC/ELECTROLYTES/MAGNESIUM/1
94. CHEM/EDRR/CALCIUM/LINEARITY/3
95. CHEM/APBP/INST/PHOTOMETER/1
96. CHEM/AKLO/STATISTICS/CV/2
97. CHEM/CCLD/ELECTROLYTES/HYPOPARATHYROIDISM/2
98. CHEM/EDHD/BMD/METABOLIC ACIDOSIS/2
99. CHEM/ELOP/QC/PRECISION/3
100. CHEM/AKFC/ENZYMES/LIPASE/2
101. CHEM/AKFC/BTP/ALBUMIN/1
102. CHEM/APBP/CARBOHYDRATES/D-XYLOSE/1
103. CHEM/AKLO/INST/BEERS LAW/2
104. CHEM/SMRM/CARBOHYDRATE/MONITORING/2
105. CHEM/PIPT/DEIONIZER/INST/1
106. CHEM/AKFC/CHLORIDE SHIFT/1
107. CHEM/CALC/LIPIDS/LDL/2
108. HEMA/AKFC/CYTOGENETICS/CML/1
109. HEMA/AKFC/MATURATION/CELLS/1
110. HEMA/SMRM/HEMOSTASIS/THROMBIN TIME/1
111. HEMA/AKFC/PLATELET/PHYSIOLOGY/1
112. HEMA/EDHD/HEMATASIS/FACTOR DEFICIENCY/2
113. HEMA/AKOP/FLOW CYTOMETRY/BASIC PRINCIPLE/1
114. HEMA/CCLD/MICRO MORPH/WBC/3
115. HEMA/AKFC/RBC PHYSIOLOGY/2
116. HEMA/CCLD/MICRO MORPH/HEMOGLOBINOPATHY/2
117. HEMA/SMRM/RBC INCLUSION/2
118. HEMA/EDMI/MICRO MORPH/WBC INCLUSIONS/2
119. HEMA/CDAR/HEMOSTASIS/HEMOPHILIA/2
120. HEMA/SMRM/ERYTHROCYTES/PNH/1

121. HEMA/CALC/LEUKOCYTES/DIFF NRBC/2
122. HEMA/EDVR/COAGULATION TES/SUBSTITUTION STUDY/3
123. HEMA/APSP/PLATELET AGG STUDIES/2
124. HEMA/CCLD/MICRO MORPH/RBC/3
125. HEMA/EDHD/CBC/ACUTE LEUKEMIA/3
126. HEMA/CCLD/AIHA/SMEAR/2
127. HEMA/AKFC/RBC MICRO-MORPH/OSMOTIC FRAGILITY/1
128. HEMA/SPVR/THROMBOCYTES COUNT/2
129. HEMA/CALC/QC/HGB/2
130. HEMA/CCLD/COAG/FACTOR DEFICIENCY/3
131. HEMA/CCLD/GRANULOCYTES/INFECTION/2
132. HEMA/AKFC/WBC/SPECIAL STAIN/2
133. HEMA/EDHD/WBC/SPECIAL STAIN/3
134. HEMA/ESOE/ERYTHROCYTES/MORPHOLOGY/3
135. HEMA/EDHD/ERYTHROCYTES/MORPHOLOGY/3
136. HEMA/EDMI/THROMBOCYTES/MORPHOLOGY ORIGIN/2
137. HEMA/CCLD/LAP SCORE/3
138. HEMA/AKFC/INCLUSION/WBC/1
139. HEMA/EDHD/SPECIAL TEST/HGB F/2
140. HEMA/ESOE/AUTO CELL COUNT/HGB/3
141. HEMA/CCLD/HEMOSTASIS/2
142. HEMA/ESOE/SCH/WBC DIFFERENTIAL/2
143. MICR/AKFC/ANAEROBE/RECOVERY/1
144. MICR/CDAR/MIC-MAC MORPH/ANEROBIC-GNB/2
145. MICR/EDMI/NOCARDIA/BASIC TEST/2
146. MICR/ESOE/QC/GRAM STAIN/3
147. MICR/EDMI/ACTINOMYCES/2
148. MICR/SCOA/GPC/SPUTUM SPECIMEN/3
149. MICR/EDHD/GNB-URINE CULTURE/COLONY COUNT/3

150. MICR/EDMI/MICRO MORPH/DIMORPHIC FUNGI/2
151. MICR/AKFC/MICRO MORPH/DIMORPHIC FUNGUS/2
152. MICR/ECAT/GNB/X&V FACTOR/2
153. MICR/SMRM/SCH/ACID-FAST BACILLI/1
154. MICR/PCAT/BACTERIA GNB/QC/2
155. MICR/CCLD/BLOOD CULTURE/YEAST/2
156. MICR/ESOE/MYCOBACTERIA/SMEAR EVALUATION/3
157. MICR/SCOA/SCH/PARASITE/2
158. MICR/CDAR/BIOCHEM RXN/GNC/2
159. MICR/SCOA/BLOOD CULTURE/PROTOCOL/3
160. MICR/AKFC/GNB/BIOCHEM REACTION/2
161. MICR/EDHD/BRONCH LAVAGE/OPPORT INFECTION/3
162. MICR/EDPS/VIRUS/PERSONAL SAFETY/2
163. MICR/EDMI/MICRO MORPH/AMOEBA/2
164. MICR/AKFC/PROTOZOA/GIARDIA/2
165. MICR/CDAR/GPB/BASIC TESTS/2
166. MICR/SMRM/BACTERIA/GNB/1
167. MICR/CCLD/MYCOBACTERIUM/NON-CHROMAGEN/2
168. MICR/ECAT/BACTERIA/CHLAMYDIA/3
169. MICR/EDRP/SCH/BLOOD CULTURE/3
170. MICR/AKFC/GNB-BASIC TEST/STOOL CULTURE/3
171. MICR/AKFC/SPECIAL TESTS/STAPHYLOCOCCUS/2
172. MICR/EDMI/GNB/BIOCHEMICAL ID/2
173. MICR/SCOA/QC/MEDIA/3
174. MICR/AKFC/VIRUS/RSV/1
175. MICR/SMRM/FUNGI/EXOANTIGEN TECHNIQUE/2
176. MICR/EDMI/BIOCHEM TEST/GPC/2
177. MICR/ESOE/ANTIBIOTIC SUSCEPT/DISK DIFFUSION/3

TAXONOMIC LEVELS

TAX 1 - <u>Recall</u>:   Ability to recall or recognize previously learned (memorized) knowledge ranging from specific facts to complete theories.

TAX 2 - <u>Interpretive Skills</u>: Ability to utilize recalled knowledge to interpret or apply verbal, numeric or visual data.

TAX 3 - <u>Problem Solving</u>:   Ability to utilize recalled knowledge and the interpretation/application of distinct criteria to resolve a problem or situation and/or make an appropriate decision.

GLOSSARY OF TERMS USED IN ITEM DESCRIPTORS
MEDICAL TECHNOLOGIST EXAMINATION - AUGUST 1990

<u>SUBTEST</u>

BBNK	BLOOD BANK
BF	BODY FLUIDS
CHEM	CHEMISTRY
HEMA	HEMATOLOGY
IMMU	IMMUNOLOGY
MICR	MICROBIOLOGY

CONTINUED ON NEXT PAGE

Reading Lists

This list is intended only as a partial reference source. Its distribution does not indicate endorsement by the Board of Registry, American Society of Clinical Pathologists nor does the Society wish to imply that the content of the examination will be drawn solely from these publications:

General, Education, and Laboratory Operations

Bauer JD. *Clinical Laboratory Methods*. 9th ed. St. Louis, Mo: CV Mosby; 1982.

Becan-McBride K, ed. *Textbook of Clinical Laboratory Supervision*. New York, NY: Appleton-Lange; 1982.

Cembrowski GS, Carey RN. *Laboratory Quality Management: QC & QA*. Chicago, Ill: American Society of Clinical Pathologists; 1989.

Glass GV. Standards and Criteria. *J Educ Meas*. 1978;15:277-290.

Henry JB, ed. *Todd-Sanford-Davidsohn: Clinical Diagnosis and Management by Laboratory Methods*. 18th ed. 2 vol. Philadelphia, Pa: WB Saunders; 1990.

Howanitz PJ, Howanitz JH. *Laboratory Quality Assurance*. New York, NY: McGraw-Hill; 1987.

Karni KR, Viskochil K, eds. *Clinical Laboratory Management: A Guide for Clinical Laboratory Scientists*. Boston, Mass: Little, Brown & Company; 1982.

Lee LW, Schmidt LM. *Elementary Principles of Laboratory Instruments*. 5th ed. St. Louis, Mo: CV Mosby; 1983.

McNeely MD. *Microcomputer Applications in the Clinical Laboratory*. Chicago, Ill: American Society of Clinical Pathologists; 1987.

Miller BM. *Laboratory Safety: Principles and Practices*. Washington DC: American Society for Microbiology; 1986.

Narayanan S. *Principles and Applications of Laboratory Instrumentation*. Chicago, Ill: American Society of Clinical Pathologists; 1989.

Raphael SS. *Lynch's Medical Laboratory Technology*. 4th ed. Philadelphia, Pa: WB Saunders; 1983.

Snyder JR, Senhauser DA, eds. *Administration and Supervision in Laboratory Medicine*. 2nd ed. Philadelphia, Pa: JB Lippincott; 1989.

Thorndike RL, ed. *Educational Measurement*. 2nd ed. Washington DC: American Council on Education; 1971.

Weisbrot IM. *Statistics for the Clinical Laboratory*. Philadelphia, Pa: JB Lippincott; 1985.

Westgard JO, Barry PL, eds. *Cost-effective Quality Control: Managing the Quality & Productivity of Analytical Processes*. Washington DC: American Association of Clinical Chemistry; 1986.

Wright BD, Stone MH. *Best Test Design*. Chicago, Ill: Mesa Press; 1979.

Blood Bank

American Association of Blood Banks. *Standards for Blood Banks and Transfusion Services*. 13th ed. Arlington, Va: American Association of Blood Banks; 1990.

American Association of Blood Banks. *Technical Manual*. 10th ed. Arlington, Va: American Association of Blood Banks; 1990.

Harmening-Pittiglio D. *Modern Blood Banking and Transfusion Practices*. 2nd ed. Philadelphia, Pa: FA Davis; 1989.

Issit PD, Issit CH. *Applied Blood Group Serology*. 3rd ed. Rutherford, NJ: Becton, Dickinson and Co; 1985.

Miller WV, Rodey G. *HLA Without Tears*. Chicago, Ill: American Society of Clinical Pathologists; 1981.

Mollison PL. *Blood Transfusion in Clinical Medicine*. 8th ed. Oxford, UK: Blackwell Scientific; 1988.

Petz LD, Swisher SN, eds. *Clinical Practice of Blood Transfusion*. 2nd ed. New York, NY: Churchill Livingstone; 1989.

Race RR, Sanger R. *Blood Groups in Man*. 6th ed. Oxford, UK: Blackwell Scientific; 1975.

Stroup M, Treacey M. *Blood Group Antigens and Antibodies*. Raritan, NJ: Ortho Diagnostics Systems; 1982.

Body Fluids

Ames Division, Miles Laboratories. *Modern Urine Chemistry*. Elkhart IN: Ames Division, Miles Laboratory; 1990.

Haber MH. *Urinary Sediment: A Textbook Atlas*. Chicago, Ill: American Society of Clinical Pathologists; 1981.

Kjeldsberg CR, Knight JA. *Body Fluids: Laboratory Examination of Amniotic, Cerebrospinal, Seminal, Serous, & Synovial Fluids: A Textbook Atlas*. 2nd ed. Chicago, Ill: American Society of Clinical Pathologists; 1986.

Strasinger SK. *Urinalysis and Body Fluids*. 2nd ed. Philadelphia, Pa: FA Davis; 1989.

Chemistry

Bishop ML, Duben-VonLaufen J, Fody EP, eds. *Clinical Chemistry: Principles, Procedures, Correlations*. Philadelphia, Pa: JB Lippincott; 1985.

Campbell JM, Campbell JB. *Laboratory Mathematics: Medical & Biological Applications*. 4th ed. St Louis, Mo: CV Mosby; 1990.

Henry RJ, Cannon DC, Winkelman JW, eds. *Clinical Chemistry: Principles and Technics*. 2nd ed. New York, NY: Harper & Row; 1974.

Kaplan LA, Pesce AJ, eds. *Clinical Chemistry: Theory, Analysis and Correlation*. 2nd ed. St Louis, Mo: CV Mosby; 1989.

Kaplan LA, Szabo LL. *Clinical Chemistry: Interpretations and Techniques*. 3rd ed. Philadelphia, Pa: Lea and Febiger; 1988.

Lehninger AL. *Principles of Biochemistry*. 2nd ed. New York, NY: Worth Publishers; 1982.

Tietz NW, ed. *Textbook of Clinical Chemistry*. 3rd ed. Philadelphia, Pa: WB Saunders; 1987.

Hematology

Brown B. *Hematology: Principles and Procedures*. 5th ed. Philadelphia, Pa: Lea & Febiger; 1988.

Harmening-Pittiglio D. *Clinical Hematology and Fundamentals of Hemostasis*. Philadelphia, Pa: FA Davis; 1987.

Kapff CT, Jandl JH. *Blood: Atlas & Sourcebook of Hematology*. Boston, Mass: Little, Brown & Company; 1981.

McKenzie, SB. *Textbook of Hematology*. Philadelphia, Pa: Lea & Febiger; 1988.

Miale JB. *Laboratory Medicine: Hematology*. 6th ed. St. Louis, Mo: CV Mosby; 1982.

National Committee on Clinical Laboratory Standards. *Collection Transport and Preparation of Blood Specimens for Coagulation Testing and Performance of Coagulation Assays: Approved Guideline*. Villanova, Pa: National Committee on Clinical Laboratory Standards; 1986.

Sirridge MS, Shannon R. *Laboratory Evaluation of Hemostasis and Thrombosis*. 3rd ed. Philadelphia, Pa: Lea & Febiger; 1983.

Triplett DA, ed. *Laboratory Evaluation of Coagulation*. Chicago, Ill: American Society of Clinical Pathologists; 1982.

Williams WJ, Beutler E, Erslev AJ, et al, eds. *Hematology*. 3rd ed. New York, NY: McGraw-Hill; 1983.

Wintrobe MM. *Clinical Hematology*. 8th ed. Philadelphia, Pa: Lea & Febiger; 1981.

Immunology

Roitt I. *Essential Immunology*. 6th ed. Oxford, UK: Blackwell Scientific; 1988.

Rose NR, Friedman H, Fahey JL, eds. *Manual of Clinical Laboratory Immunology*. 3rd ed. Washington DC: American Society for Microbiology; 1986.

Sheehan C. *Clinical Immunology, Principles and Laboratory Diagnosis*. Philadelphia, Pa: JB Lippincott; 1990.

Stites DP, Stobo JD, and Wells JV. *Basic and Clinical Immunology*. 6th ed. Norwalk, CT: Appleton & Lange; 1987.

Microbiology

Ash L, Orihel T. *Atlas of Human Parasitology*. 3rd ed. Chicago, Ill: American Society of Clinical Pathologists; 1990.

Baron EJ, Finegold SM. *Bailey and Scott's Diagnostic Microbiology*. 8th ed. St Louis, Mo: CV Mosby; 1990.

Brown HW, Neva FA. *Basic Clinical Parasitology*. 5th ed. New York, NY: Appleton & Lange; 1983.

Howard BJ, Klaas J, Rubin SJ, Weissfeld AS, Tilton R. *Clinical and Pathogenic Microbiology*. St. Louis, Mo: CV Mosby; 1987.

Koneman EW, Allen SD, Dowell VR, et al. *Color Atlas and Textbook of Diagnostic Microbiology*. 3rd ed. Philadelphia, Pa: JB Lippincott; 1988.

Lennette EH, Balows A, Hausler WJ Jr, et al, eds. *Manual of Clinical Microbiology*. 4th ed. Washington DC: American Society for Microbiology; 1985.

McGinnis MR. *Laboratory Handbook of Medical Mycology*. New York, NY: Academic Press; 1980.

Rippon JW. *Medical Mycology*. 3rd ed. Philadelphia, Pa: WB Saunders; 1988.

Washington JA Jr, ed. *Laboratory Procedures in Clinical Microbiology*. 2nd ed. New York, NY: Springer-Verlag Inc; 1985.